POINTS & COUNTERPOINTS

Controversial Relationship

and

Family Issues

in the

21st Century

An Anthology

Marilyn Coleman
Lawrence Ganong
University of Missouri

Roxbury Publishing Company
Los Angeles, California

Library of Congress Cataloging-in-Publication Data

Points and counterpoints: controversial relationship and family issues in
the 21st century: an anthology / [edited by] Marilyn Coleman, Lawrence
Ganong.
     p. cm.
   Includes bibliographical references and index.
   ISBN 1-891487-90-6 (acid-free paper)
1. Family. 2. Marriage. 3. Man-woman relationships. 4. Couples. I.
Coleman, Marilyn. II. Ganong, Lawrence H.

HQ519 .P65 2003
306.85—dc21

                                                                    2002067903

**Points and Counterpoints: Controversial Relationship and Family Issues in the 21st
Century: An Anthology**

Publisher: Claude Teweles
Managing Editor: Dawn VanDercreek
Production Editor: Jim Ballinger
Copyeditor: Jackie Estrada
Proofreader: Stephanie Villavicencio
Typography: Abe Hendin
Cover Design: Marnie Kenney

Printed on acid-free paper in the United States of America. This book meets the standards for
recycling of the Environmental Protection Agency.

ISBN 1-891487-90-6

Roxbury Publishing Company
P.O. Box 491044
Los Angeles, California 90049-9044
Voice: (310) 473-3312 • Fax: (310) 473-4490
Email: roxbury@roxbury.net
Website: www.roxbury.net

Contents

About the Editors xi

About the Contributors xii

Introduction xv

PART ONE ✦ **CONTROVERSIAL RELATIONSHIP ISSUES** 1

Issue 1 ✦ **Does the Internet Help People Form Romantic Relationships? Is the Internet a Love Machine?** 3

1a ✦ Romance in Cyberspace: Understanding Online Attraction 4
Alvin Cooper and Leda Sportolari
Cooper and Sportolari summarize how the Internet facilitates interpersonal relations.

1b ✦ Love on the Internet? 10
B. Cornwell and D. C. Lundgren
In opposition to Cooper and Sportolari, Cornwell and Lundgren report that cyberspace relationships are less serious and participants are more likely to misrepresent themselves.

Issue 1 ✦ Questions to Consider 15

Issue 2 ✦ **Are Men and Women Really From Different Planets?** 16

2a ✦ Mars and Venus 17
Toni Schindler Zimmerman, Shelley A. Haddock, and Christine R. McGeorge
Zimmerman et al. provide a summary of John Gray's *Men Are From Mars and Women Are From Venus* philosophy.

2b ✦ Beyond Mars and Venus: Men and Women in the Real World . . . 25
Donna L. Sollie
Sollie points out the fallacies of the Mars and Venus point of view.

Issue 2 ✦ Questions to Consider 30

Issue 3 ✦ Can Men and Women Be 'Just' Friends? 31

   3a ✦ 'Just Friends'? Frequency of Sexual Activity in
       Cross-Sex Friendships 32
       Walid Afifi and Sandra L. Faulkner

       Aafifi and Faulkner report that many cross-sex friends act on
       their mutual attraction.

   3b ✦ 'I Like You . . . as a Friend': Attraction in Cross-Sex Friendship . . 37
       Heidi M. Reeder

       Reeder reports that men and women are attracted to their cross-
       sex friends in several, not necessarily mutual ways.

  Issue 3 ✦ Questions to Consider 42

**Issue 4 ✦ Living Together: Preparation for Marriage or Playing
       at Commitment?** 43

   4a ✦ Living Together Is Just Playing at a Committed Relationship . . . 45
       Esther Crain

       Crain is as opposed to cohabiting prior to marriage as Brown is
       accepting.

   4b ✦ Living Together Is Good Preparation for Marriage and for Life . . 47
       Robyn Brown

       Cohabiting prior to marriage is highly recommended by Brown.

  Issue 4 ✦ Questions to Consider 49

**Issue 5 ✦ Does Distance Make the Heart Grow Fonder or Go Wander?
       Can Long-Distance Romance Work?** 50

   5a ✦ Staying Close When Apart: Intimacy and Meaning in
       Long-Distance Dating Relationships 51
       Joyce A. Arditti and Melissa Kauffman

       The ways that college students maintain long distance romantic
       relationships as well as keys to success of these relationships are
       explored by Arditti and Kauffman.

  Issue 5 ✦ Questions to Consider 56

Issue 6 ✦ 'Goin' to the Chapel and . . .': Does Marriage Matter? 57

   6a ✦ Flying Solo 58
       *Tamala M. Edwards with Tammerlin Drummond and Elizabeth
       Kauhnan, Anne Mofiet, Jacqueline Savaiano, and Maggie Stager*

       Edwards and colleagues report on why women are increasingly
       avoiding marriage.

6b ✦ Why Marriage Matters 64
　　　Linda J. Waite

　　　Waite promotes the importance of marriage to both men and
　　　women as a form of social insurance.

Issue 6 ✦ Questions to Consider 70

PART TWO ✦ CONTROVERSIAL MARRIAGE ISSUES 71

Issue 7 ✦ When Should Women Marry? 73

　7a ✦ Women Who Marry When They Are Young Will Be Happier 74
　　　Danielle Crittenden

　　　According to Crittenden, women should marry young—evidence
　　　does not support waiting until one is older.

　7b ✦ Women Should Marry When, and If, They Are Ready—
　　　Fools Rush In 77
　　　Jennifer Pozner

　　　Pozner posits that early marriage limits women's potential in a
　　　variety of ways.

Issue 7 ✦ Questions to Consider 80

**Issue 8 ✦ 'I Now Pronounce You Husband and . . . Husband?'
　　　　　Legal Marriage and Same-Sex Couples** 81

　8a ✦ A Man and a Woman Are Needed for the 'Honorable Estate' 82
　　　William J. Bennett

　　　William Bennett believes that allowing same sex couples to marry
　　　will increase the fragility of marriage for all and perhaps destroy
　　　it.

　8b ✦ State Has No Compelling Reason to Bar Same-Sex Unions 84
　　　Scott Miller

　　　Same-sex marriage is an "equal rights" issue and is about com-
　　　mitment, not sex, according to Scott Miller.

Issue 8 ✦ Questions to Consider 86

Issue 9 ✦ Love and Marriage Go Together Like . . . ? 87

　9a ✦ Thinking About Romantic/Erotic Love 88
　　　Henry Grunebaum

　　　Grunebaum believes that love is a basis for marriage and that
　　　couples must meld everyday love with romantic/erotic love to be
　　　successful.

9b ✦ Fallacies About Love and Marriage 91
Joseph S. Silverman

Silverman examines fallacies regarding the connection between love and marriage.

Issue 9 ✦ Questions to Consider 94

Issue 10 ✦ Why Do Men Batter Women? Two Perspectives 95

10a ✦ Feminist Perspectives on Male Violence Against Women 97
Amy Marin and Nancy Felipe Russo

Feminist perspectives on male violence against women are examined by Russo.

10b ✦ Family Systems Perspectives on Battering: The Importance of Context 106
Stephen Anderson and Margaret Schlossberg

A family systems perspective examining male violence against women is offered by Anderson and Schlossberg.

Issue 10 ✦ Questions to Consider 115

PART THREE ✦ CONTROVERSIAL ISSUES REGARDING PARENTING 117

Issue 11 ✦ Should Parenting Require a License? 119

11a ✦ Licensing Parents—A Controversial Cure for Crime 121
David T. Lykken

Lykken makes a strong case for parental licensure as a means of reducing rates of social pathology.

11b ✦ Toward Voluntary Parenthood 131
Sandra Scarr

Scarr opposes the restrictions to personal freedom that parental licensure would impose and proposes positive procreation—the encouragement of voluntary parenthood.

11c ✦ The Outcome of Parenting: What Do We Really Know? 136
Judith Rich Harris

Harris believes that parenthood is over emphasized and social environment and genetics are both stronger influences on children than parent's behavior.

Issue 11 ✦ Questions to Consider 142

Issue 12 ✦ Parenting by the Book—But *Whose* Book? Race, Ethnicity, and Parenting Styles 143

12a ✦ Race, Ethnicity, and Parenting Styles 144
   Linda Halgunseth, Catherine Cushinberry, and Tashel Bordere

   Halgunseth, Cushinberry, and Bordere believe that to understand parenting behaviors you must understand the social and cultural environment of the parents. Latino and African-American families provide examples.

Issue 12 ✦ Questions to Consider 152

Issue 13 ✦ 'Mama, He Says . . .': Children as Language Brokers for Their Parents 153

13a ✦ Language Brokering: Positive Developmental Outcomes 154
   Linda Halgunseth

   Child Language Brokering as a means of enhancing children's feelings of importance and usefulness and their self-esteem is the position presented by Halgunseth.

13b ✦ Language Brokering as a Stressor for Immigrant Children and Their Families 157
   Adriana J. Umaña-Taylor

   Umaña-Taylor presents the flip side of Halgunseth's argument, discusses how Child Language Brokering can create problems for the child, and proposes that providing translators in institutional settings be more common.

13c ✦ Language Brokering: A Personal Experience 160
   Susan Santiago

   Santiago presents her mixed experiences as a Child Language Broker.

Issue 13 ✦ Questions to Consider 162

Issue 14 ✦ Are Companies Becoming Friendlier to Working Moms and Dads? 163

14a ✦ Being There for the Children 165
   Carol Lippert Gray

   Gray recounts the struggles of young parents who are trying to balance work and family and promotes the importance of flexibility in the workplace.

14b ✦ Friendly for Whose Family? 167
   Betty Holcomb

   Holcomb conveys the plight of lower-level workers in companies widely recognized for being "family friendly" places.

14c ✦ Watch Out for 'Family Friendly' Policies 170
   Barbara Bergmann

   Bergmann cautions us to carefully scrutinize the across the board effects of family friendly policies.

Issue 14 ✦ Questions to Consider 173

Issue 15 ✦ Does Day Care Make Children Mean? The New Debate Over Working Mothers 174

15a ✦ Denying Reality Can't Change Day Care Facts 176
Mona Charen

Charen's take on a National Institute of Health report is that the glass is half-empty—that day care has a significantly negative effect on the behavior of kindergartners and moms should therefore stay home with their children.

15b ✦ Want Better Child Care? Hire Better Caregivers 178
Jack Shonkoff and Deborah Phillips

Shonkoff and Phillips see the glass as half-full—88 percent of children did not express negative behaviors and our goal should be improving day care quality rather than encouraging mothers to leave the work force.

Issue 15 ✦ Questions to Consider 180

Issue 16 ✦ Do Fathers Matter? 181

16a ✦ Yes, Fathers Really Matter! 182
Ross Parke and Armin Brott

Parke and Brott argue that fathers are important to children's development and cite research to support their argument.

16b ✦ Are Fathers Essential? Maybe Not 187
Louise B. Silverstein and Carl F. Auerbach

Silverstein and Auerbach believe those promoting the importance of fatherhood are primarily attempting to reassert traditional male dominance and they provide research to support their view.

Issue 16 ✦ Questions to Consider 192

Issue 17 ✦ Do These Genes Look OK? The Human Genome Project and Our Future 193

17a ✦ Blessings From the Book of Life 194
David Stipp

The view that HGP will increase the life span and cure now fatal illnesses is promoted by Stipp.

17b ✦ Designer Genes for All? 198
Garland E. Allen

Allen worries that our scientific technology is more advanced than our abilities to think through the ethical, legal, and moral problems created by HGP.

Issue 17 ✦ Questions to Consider 201

PART FOUR ✦ CONTROVERSIAL ISSUES RELATED TO
FAMILY DIVERSITY 203

Issue 18 ✦ Is Love (Color) Blind? 205

18a ✦ My Life in Black and White 206
Susan Fales-Hill

Fales-Hill talks about her mostly positive middle-class experiences as the child of a black mother and a white father.

18b ✦ Getting Under My Skin 210
Don Terry

Terry, the son of a white mother and a black father, shares a less
positive view than Fales-Hill of his childhood experiences.

Issue 18 ✦ Questions to Consider 215

Issue 19 ✦ Nuclear Family Wars: The Status of American Families . . . 216

19a ✦ Can the Nuclear Family Be Revived? 218
David Popenoe

Popenoe believes American society is in decay because the two-
natural parent family is in decline.

19b ✦ The American Family Today Is Not Worse Off Than in the Past . . 222
Stephanie Coontz

Coontz is more sanguine than Popenoe and points out that American families overall are in far better shape than was true at the
beginning of the last century.

Issue 19 ✦ Questions to Consider 226

Issue 20 ✦ How Harmful Is Divorce to Children? 227

20a ✦ Staying Together for the Sake of the Children 228
Walter Kirn

Walter Kirn promotes Judith Wallerstein's view that children
whose parents divorce are seriously harmed for life and couples
should stay together for the sake of the children.

20b ✦ Divorcing Reality 232
Stephanie Coontz

Stephanie Coontz reviews Wallerstein's work with a more critical
eye and raises concerns about the current move to make divorce
more difficult to obtain.

Issue 20 ✦ Questions to Consider 236

Issue 21 ✦ **Should Divorce Laws Be Reformed?** 237

    21a ✦ A Solution to America's Divorce Problem 238
        Steven L. Nock, James D. Wright, and Laura Sanchez

        Taking a "wait and see" approach, Nock and colleagues analyze
        "covenant marriage" and raise questions about what differences
        these marriages will or will not make in terms of marital stability,
        happiness, and the adjustment of children.

    21b ✦ Divorce Reform Won't Lower the Divorce Rate 242
        Ashton Applewhite

        Applewhite takes a much harsher view than Nock and colleagues
        and states that covenant marriage is morally problematic.

  Issue 21 ✦ Questions to Consider 245

Issue 22 ✦ **Are Stepparents 'Bad' for Children?** 246

    22a ✦ The Truth About Cinderella 247
        Martin Daly and Margo Wilson

        Daly and Wilson claim that stepparents are more inclined than
        biological parents to abuse stepchildren and use evolutional psy-
        chology and police data to support their position.

    22b ✦ Was Cinderella Right? The New Social Darwinism
        Targets Stepparents 255
        Mary Ann Mason

        According to Mason, the evolutionary discourse on stepparent
        abuse is motivated by politics and values, not science.

  Issue 22 ✦ Questions to Consider 263

Issue 23 ✦ **Cultural Values and Caregiving** 264

    23a ✦ Cultural Values and Caregiving 265
        M. Elise Radina

        Radina reviews research on how values and attitudes of Euro-
        pean-American, African-American, Asian-American, and Latinos
        may affect the caregiving of older kin.

  Issue 23 ✦ Questions to Consider 272

About the Editors

Dr. **Marilyn Coleman** is a Professor of Human Development and Family Studies at the University of Missouri. **Dr. Lawrence Ganong** is a Professor of Nursing and Human Development and Family Studies at the University of Missouri. They have co-authored over 150 articles and book chapters as well as three books, including *Changing Families, Changing Responsibilities: Family Obligations Following Divorce and Remarriage* (1999), *Remarried Family Relationships* (1994), and *Bibliotherapy With Stepchildren* (1988). They have conducted remarriage and stepfamily research for over 20 years and they also have studied family structure and family stereotyping, marital expectations, and divorce. Recent work has focused on family responsibilities following divorce and remarriage and the development of stepparent roles.

Dr. Coleman was editor of the *Journal of Marriage and the Family* from 1992 to 1995, Associate Editor of the *Home Economics Research Journal* from 1987 to 1990, and serves or has served on the editorial boards of *Family Relations, Journal of Family Issues, Lifestyles: Family & Economic Issues,* and *Journal of Divorce and Remarriage.* Dr. Ganong is Associate Editor of the *Journal of Social and Personal Relationships.* He serves or has served on the editorial boards of *Journal of Marriage and Family, Family Relations, Journal of Family Issues, Lifestyles: Family & Economic Issues, Journal of Family Nursing,* and *Journal of Divorce and Remarriage.* They teach courses on family dynamics, divorce, and remarriage and stepfamilies. ◆

About the Contributors

Walid Afifi is an assistant professor of communication studies at Pennsylvania State University.

Garland E. Allen is a professor of biology at Washington University in St. Louis.

Stephen Anderson is a professor of family studies and family therapy at the University of Connecticut.

Ashton Applewhite is the author of *Cutting Loose: Why Women Who End Their Marriages Do So Well*, and writes frequently on issues of marriage and divorce.

Joyce A. Arditti is a professor of human development at Virginia Tech University.

Carl F. Auerbach is a professor of psychology at Yeshiva University.

William J. Bennett is codirector of Empower America, a conservative think tank in Washington, DC.

Barbara Bergmann's recent books include *In Defense of Affirmative Action* and *Saving Our Children from Poverty: What the United States Can Learn from France.*

Tashel Bordere is a doctoral student in human development and family studies at the University of Missouri.

Armin Brott is an expert on fathers, an author of several books on fathers, and has his own radio show.

Robyn Brown is a writer.

Mona Charen is a nationally syndicated columnist for Creators Syndicate.

Stephanie Coontz is a family historian at Evergreen State College in Olympia, Washington. Her most recent book is *The Way We Really Are: Coming to Terms With America's Changing Families.*

Alvin Cooper is a therapist at the San Jose Marital and Sexuality Centre, Santa Clara, CA.

B. Cornwell is a professor of sociology at Ohio State University.

Esther Crain is a writer.

Danielle Crittenden is the author of *What Our Mothers Didn't Tell Us: Why Happiness Eludes the Modern Woman* and is founding editor of the *Women's Quarterly.*

Catherine Cushinberry is a doctoral student in human development and family studies at the University of Missouri.

Martin Daly is a professor of psychology at McMasters University in Hamilton, Ontario, Canada.

Tamala M. Edwards is a journalist.

Susan Fales-Hill is a director and producer of television series and programs.

Sandra L. Faulkner is an assistant professor of communication studies at East Carolina State University.

Carol Lippert Gray was the founding editor of *DAD—The Magazine for Today's Involved Father.*

Henry Grunebaum, M.D., is Clinical Professor of Psychiatry at the Harvard Medical School and Director of the Family Division of the Cambridge Hospital, Cambridge, MA.

Shelley A. Haddock, M.S., is a lecturer and clinical supervisor in human development and family studies at Colorado State University and a doctoral candidate in education at Colorado State.

Linda Halgunseth is a doctoral student in human development and family studies at the University of Missouri.

Judith Rich Harris is the author of *The Nurture Assumption.*

Betty Holcomb is the author of *"Not Guilty!": The Good News About Working Mothers* (Touchstone, 1998).

Melissa Kauffman, M.S., is a graduate of human development at Virginia Tech University.

Walter Kirn is a journalist.

D. C. Lundgren is a professor of sociology at the University of Cincinnati.

David T. Lykken is Professor Emeritus of Psychology at the University of Minnesota.

Amy Marin is a psychology professor at Phoenix College.

Mary Ann Mason is Dean of the Graduate School and a professor of social welfare at the University of California at Berkeley.

Christine R. McGeorge, M.S., is a doctoral student in marriage and family therapy at the University of Minnesota.

Scott Miller is an author, composer, and theatre director in St. Louis.

Steven L. Nock is professor of sociology at the University of Virginia. His most recent book is *Marriage in Men's Lives.*

Ross Parke is a professor of psychology at the University of California at Riverside.

Deborah Phillips is a professor of psychology at Georgetown University.

David Popenoe is a professor of sociology at Rutgers University.

Jennifer Pozner is a media analyst for *Sojourner: The Women's Forum* and a commentator for the Fox News Channel.

M. Elise Radina recently completed her Ph.D. in human development and family studies at the University of Missouri.

Heidi M. Reeder is an assistant professor of communication studies at the University of North Carolina at Greensboro.

Nancy Felipe Russo is the Regent's Professor of Psychology and Women's Studies at Arizona State University.

Laura Sanchez is an assistant professor of sociology at Tulane University.

Susan Santiago is a former doctoral student in human development and family studies at the University of Missouri.

Sandra Scarr is Professor of Psychology Emeritus at the University of Virginia.

Margaret Schlossberg is affiliated with the Johns Hopkins University School of Medicine.

Jack Shonkoff is Dean of the Heller School at Brandeis University.

Joseph S. Silverman is a therapist in private practice in Altoona, Pennsylvania.

Louise B. Silverstein is a professor of psychology at Yeshiva University.

Donna L. Sollie is Alumni Professor of Human Development and Family Studies at Auburn University.

Leda Sportolari is a therapist at the San Jose Marital and Sexuality Centre, Santa Clara, CA.

David Stipp is a journalist.

Don Terry is a journalist and author.

Adriana J. Umaña-Taylor is an assistant professor of human and community development at the University of Illinois in Champaign-Urbana.

Linda J. Waite is a professor of sociology at the University of Chicago.

Margo I. Wilson is a professor of psychology at McMasters University in Hamilton, Ontario, Canada.

James D. Wright is the Favrot Professor of Human Relations in Sociology at Tulane University.

Toni Schindler Zimmerman is a family therapist and faculty member in human development and family studies at Colorado State University. ✦

Introduction

Encouraging Critical Thinking

This book is designed to facilitate students' critical thinking skills and to encourage dialogue and discussion about important controversial issues related to marriage, families, and close relationships. For each topic, multiple perspectives are presented that should encourage students to think carefully about their own value systems as well as "ways of knowing." Often, when students read compelling arguments presenting different views on the same issue, they become confused and do not know what to believe. All sides presented sound reasonable to them, even if they realize you cannot rationally and logically hold two competing perspectives at the same time. These students are not yet critical thinkers.

Students who are used to merely trusting their instincts or who believe everything they have been taught also are not critical thinkers, and they will struggle in their attempts to determine a "right" answer. To think critically, students must realize that articles, essays, newspaper items, and other forms of written communication have a purpose, and that this written work is presented from a particular point of view. This point of view may or may not be supported by evidence and logic. Before drawing a conclusion about the veracity of the work, a critical thinker will (a) question the purpose of the writing, (b) examine the purpose of assumptions made by the writer, (c) determine the bias of the author, (d) examine the evidence presented, and (e) decide whether or not the assertions made are logical.

According to Beyer (1997),

> critical thinking means applying the criteria of accuracy (truth) and soundness (proof) to evaluate information, assertions, reasoning, and evidence in order to make judgments of acceptability and worth. (p. 86)

Kurfiss (1988) defines critical thinking as an investigation for the purpose of exploring a situation, phenomenon, question, or problem to arrive at a hypothesis or conclusion about it that integrates all available information and that can therefore be convincingly justified. Scriven and Paul (www.criticalthinking.org) define critical thinking as the intellectually disciplined process of actively and skillfully conceptualizing, applying, analyzing, synthesizing, and/or evaluating information gathered from, or generated by, observation, experience, reflection, reasoning, or communication as a guide to belief and action.

Beyer (1997: 219) posed nine questions that cue students to think critically:

1. What verifiable facts vs. reasoned opinions vs. value claims are presented in this source of information?

2. What claims, reasons, or statements did you find in this material that were relevant and irrelevant to the main topic of your inquiry?

3. What, if any, bias did you detect in this information? How did you arrive at this evaluation?

4. What unstated assumptions are there in this material?

5. What, if any, ambiguous or equivocal claims are made in this material? What are your reasons for your response?

6. How credible is the source of this material? What criteria did you use to determine credibility?

7. What is the point of view presented in this material? How do you know?

8. How strong is the argument made in this material? What did you do to arrive at this judgment?

9. How accurate is the information in this material? What did you do to determine accuracy?

According to Paul (1992), uncritical thinkers are "often unclear, imprecise, vague, illogical, unreflective, superficial, inconsistent, inaccurate, or trivial" (p. 11).

Because information about relationships and families is highly value laden and politically volatile, it is extremely important that students learn to think critically about relationship- and family-related issues. The points of view presented in this book are designed to expand students' abilities to relate new information to information in their textbooks or to prior knowledge that they have about relationships and families, to make use of logic in comparing and contrasting the various perspectives presented on each issue, to learn to distinguish between trivial and critical information presented as arguments, to be persistent in searching for solutions (this means paying careful attention to the introductory material and the questions posed at the end of the readings, and to carefully read and think about each selection), to be open-minded enough to tolerate ambiguity, and to consider possibilities that they have either previously not explored or disbelieved (McCarthy-Tucker, 2001).

Another reason for promoting critical thinking in this set of readings is that the subject matter is relevant to the personal experience of each student. It is important that students learn that their history is not the only or best way to experience family life, nor is it appropriate to generalize to all families from their own family. It also is important that students be able to recognize multiple truths and ways of knowing, including understanding the standpoints or views of those who are different from them in racial and ethnic backgrounds, ages, social classes, etc.

For this book we selected important issues on which there are sharply divergent viewpoints. We included cutting-edge topics that are not covered in other books, such as on-line dating, a proposal to license parents, and the impact of the Human Genome Project on families. The content comes from a wide variety of fields and a wide variety of sources (e.g., magazines, professional journals, popular and professional books). Among the authors are psychologists, attorneys, sociologists, marriage and family therapists, family scholars, communication scholars, political scientists, and journalists. In addition, there are first-person accounts by people from all walks of life. Some of the papers were commissioned for this book, and others, although not written for this book, were previously unpublished.

In addition to "standard" hot-button issues (e.g., divorce, gay marriage), we added topics such as licensing parents and covenant marriage laws. Most papers take a distinct position; we think this fosters livelier class discussions and challenges students to think more critically. With a few exceptions, the papers are presented in point-counterpoint fashion around a specific issue. Sometimes we present two ways a phenomenon has been explained (e.g., why men batter women), sometimes we explore a controversial subject with one selection (e.g., long-distance relationships) and sometimes with three (e.g., family-friendly work environments). Students will be introduced to a variety of theories, research methods, and value stances regarding interpretations of social science data on relationships and families.

Each issue is preceded by a brief introduction that provides background and raises questions for students to ponder as they read the papers. In addition, after each set of readings we include questions that could be used for classroom discussions or for homework assignments. These questions are designed to facilitate the development of critical thinking about controversial issues related to close relationships.

This book is designed to supplement introductory marriage, family, and close relationship texts in departments of sociology, human development and family studies, communications, social work, and psychology. In planning which issues to include, we surveyed 10 instructors of introductory marriage and family/close relationship courses and asked them what topics were missing from current texts that they would like to see covered. The 27 topics they identified provided a beginning point. We also examined the content of best-selling introductory marriage and family/close relationship textbooks. This led us to add a few more issues. Our reviewers suggested additional topics, particularly issues related to ethnicity and race. Ultimately, we had more ideas for controversial topics than we could include. The 23 issues included in the book are more than instructors will likely have time to cover in one term, but enough to provide flexibility for teachers in different types of courses on relationships.

Some papers present multiple and complex issues, and certain themes reoccur throughout the book (e.g., the importance of fathers, superiority of first marriage families). This makes it possible for teachers to assign multiple readings around broader themes than the 23 individual issues we are presenting. We assist in doing this by connecting the readings to broader themes, including other issues in this book, in the introductory comments that precede each issue. In this way, students may be helped to make associations between issues, and instructors may be helped in leading students to consider these and other issues more complexly. For example, *gender issues in relationships between men and women* are dealt with in Issues 1, 2, 3, 6, 7, 8, and 10. Although gender dynamics are not explicitly mentioned, gender in adult relationships is also part of Issues 4, 5, 9, 14, and 18. *Gender issues in parenting* are included, explicitly and implicitly, in several Issues: 11, 12, 14,

15, 16, 17, 20, and 22. *Public policy* is discussed as part of several Issues: 8, 10, 11, 13, 14, 15, 16, 17, 20, and 21. Issues 6, 8, 11, 16, 19, 20, 21, 22, and 23 deal with *family structure*. *Race and ethnicity* are explicitly dealt with in Issues 11, 12, 13, 17, 18, and 23. *Divorce* is covered in Issues 4, 16, 19, 20, 21, and 22. *Lifestyle diversity* is handled in Issues 4, 5, 6, 7, 8, 18, and 19. The *evolutionary basis for human behavior* is discussed as part of Issues 3, 7, 10, 11, 16, 17, and 22. There are many ways in which these readings could be assigned—these are only a few of them.

Acknowledgements

We thank Pei Feng and Sue Serota for their assistance with this book. We also wish to thank the following reviewers for their insights and comments: Kristin Bates (California State University, San Marcos), J. Kenneth Davidson, Sr. (University of Wisconsin, Eau Claire), Lynda Dickson (University of Colorado at Colorado Springs), Mark Fine (University of Missouri—Columbia), Norval D. Glenn (University of Texas, Austin), Bron Ingoldsby (Brigham Young University), Meg Wilkes Karraker (University of St. Thomas), David M. Klein (University of Notre Dame), Patrick McKenry (Ohio State University), Sharon Price (University of Georgia), Scott Sernau (Indiana University, South Bend), and Glenna Van Metre (Wichita State University).

References

Beyer, B. K. (1997). *Improving student thinking: A comprehensive approach.* Boston: Allyn & Bacon.

Kurfiss, J. G. (1988). *Critical thinking: Theory, research, practice, and possibilities.* Higher Education Report No. 2, Washington, D.C.: Association for the study of Higher Education—ERIC.

McCarthy-Tucker, S. (2001). Developing student critical thinking skills through teaching psychology: An interview with Claudio S. Hutz. *Teaching of Psychology,* 28(1), 72–76.

Paul, R. (1992). Critical thinking: What, why, and how. In C. A. Barnes (ed.), *Critical*

Thinking: Educational Imperative. New Di-
rections for Community Colleges, 77, Vol. XX
(1). Los Angeles: ERIC Clearinghouse for Junior Colleges. ✦

Part One

Controversial Relationship Issues

Issue 1: Introduction

Does the Internet Help People Form Romantic Relationships? Is the Internet a Love Machine?

Almost every aspect of twenty-first century life has been affected in some way by the Internet—business, education, medicine, shopping, and entertainment have all been profoundly changed by its widespread use. It is not surprising, therefore, that in recent years the Internet has increasingly been used by men and women of all ages to meet other people with the goal of possibly developing romantic relationships.

Social scientists have become interested in how the Internet affects close relationships. Some of them are concerned that the Internet isolates people and cuts off genuine social relationships, whereas others think that the Internet will improve social relationships because its users are not limited to meeting and communicating only with individuals whom they encounter in person. People can have Internet conversations with people on the other side of the world, and they can have them at the convenience of the message sender, since Internet "meetings" can be held for days at a time. For example, you can send an e-mail message to a friend who opens it two days later and then replies the next afternoon. You open the reply as soon as you get it, but you don't respond for six hours because you are working on a paper. This clearly would not be possible in a face-to-face relationship.

Internet advocates argue that rather than being smitten by a potential partner's appearance, you get to know them on a less superficial basis first on the Internet. This is true as long as they are being honest about who they are, a caution offered by Internet critics.

In the selections that follow, two pairs of authors write about the Internet's potential to help people create and develop romantic relationships. In the first selection, Cooper and Sportolari summarize the ways in which "online relating facilitates positive, warm interpersonal connections." Although they recognize the possible downsides of Internet relating, they "consider how sexual intensity may develop in positive ways within these relationships."

In the second selection, Cornwell and Lundgren report the results of a study in which they found that people in what they called "cyberspace" relationships were more prone to misrepresent themselves "because they regarded their relationships as less serious and felt less commitment" toward their partners, which does not seem to be a positive predictor for successful romantic relationships.

As you read these two papers about the Internet and romantic relationships, think about other close relationships (e.g., between a parent and child). How have the Internet and computer technology in general affected these relationships? How might these relationships be affected in the future? The Internet is here to stay, and its use will increase as it becomes more convenient and readily available. It is important that we think about the effects of Internet use on individuals and relationships. ✦

Romance in Cyberspace: Understanding Online Attraction

Alvin Cooper and Leda Sportolari

This article presents and discusses ways in which the structure and process of online relating facilitates positive, warm interpersonal connections, including the healthy development of romantic relationships, which may indeed carry over into "real life." While recognizing that the Net can be used in sexually compulsive or deviant ways, we consider how sexual intensity may develop in positive ways within these relationships. By applying psychosocial theories of relationship formation as well as describing qualities of the interpersonal space that's created online, we account for the richness and depth relationships may take on via this seemingly impersonal medium.

A priori assumptions about Internet relating tend to be that it is less involving, less rich, and less personal than face-to-face (FTF) communication due to the lack of facial and body language cues, the lack of the "felt presence" of the other, the lack of a "shared social context" between the communicators, and the "lean" bandwidth of the medium (i.e., written text alone without visual, auditory, olfactory, and other non-verbal impressions of the other available) (Walther, 1994).

While some experimental research seemed to substantiate the notion that computer mediated communication (CMC) was less personally engaging and more task oriented than FTF communication, field research showed contrary results. CMC relationships were found to take longer to develop than FTF relationships because of the slowness of the communication exchange and the limited bandwidth (it takes longer to form impressions of the other), but over time they did become as personal as FTF relationships, along dimensions such as affection, immediacy, receptivity, trust, and depth (Walther and Burgoon, 1992). Asynchronous CMC was even found to allow for more personal relating than FTF when groups were involved in task completion, because the sender did not have to worry about slowing the whole group down by interjecting personal comments or asking personal questions, since receivers could individually read the comments addressed to the group at their own leisure (Walther and Burgoon, 1992). Indeed, some experienced computer users rated e-mail and computer conferencing as "rich" or "richer" than FTF and telephone conversations (Jaffe, Lee, Huang, and Oshagan, 1995).

Online Relationship Development

To make sense of these research findings as well as the many popular press reports of online love affairs, both of which point to the personally involving, even captivating, nature of electronic relating—we turn to theories of interpersonal attraction and early relationship formation, which were conceptualized with FTF relating in mind, and apply them to this new high-tech forum. Many "real world" relationships begin with attraction based on external attributes, such as physical appearance. If the relationship progresses, the attraction then evolves into an attachment based on similarity of values and beliefs. The development of rapport, mutual self-disclosure, and the empathic understanding of the other (Brehm, 1992, p. 156) are involved in a deepening of the connection, which moves the relationship to a more intimate stage. The relationship may become sexualized at any point, either initially as a spark from physical attraction or later based on a sense of being intimately connected emotionally. Certainly, each relationship online as well as offline is unique and its evolution defies simple categorizing.

Physical Attractiveness

Clearly, as the technology stands now, CMR [computer mediated relating] does not start off or develop due to attraction based on physical attributes. In a culture that emphasizes physical appearance, the Internet affords a different way of developing initial attraction. This may change if video cameras become standard equipment; for many people video imaging will likely be experienced as a loss of the freedom to not care about how they look when communicating. However, even with a videocam image, the physical press of the interaction will not be as powerful as it is in FTF interaction; it will be less salient, relegated to one aspect of the overall online presentation, rather than the overwhelmingly dominant one.

Initial impressions online are based on how someone describes and expresses him/herself. Online, one's physical presence—attractiveness, age, race, ethnicity, gender, and mannerisms—is not evident except through what is conveyed by a name unless users choose to describe these aspects of themselves. People can present themselves and be "seen" free from some of the conscious and unconscious stereotypic notions that affect FTF relating from the outset. Self-presentation is more under one's con-

trol online; people can make decisions about when and how to disclose negative information about themselves. Sometimes it is better (in terms of advancing the relationship) to reveal such information about oneself early on; under other conditions, it may be best to wait (Hendrick and Hendrick, 1983).

In FTF interaction, people make quick judgments based on physical attributes, and good-looking individuals have a distinct social advantage. People over-generalize from appearance, assuming that those who are attractive on the outside are also nicer on the inside and have better future prospects; this well known phenomenon has been termed the "what-is-beautiful-is-good stereotype" (Brehm, 1992, p. 65). People who may in FTF encounters unwittingly keep themselves from intimate relationships by being overly focused upon or critical of their or others' physical appearance are freed up online to develop connections. Electronic relating offers a different basis for interaction than that of the "meat market" of the singles scene: "Concepts of physical beauty on the Net don't apply. We are all just bits and bytes blowing in the phosphorous stream" (Deuel, 1996, p. 143).

On the Net, the vast array of people to whom we are not physically drawn, yet with whom we might connect quite well if given the opportunity, become available to us. As one online participant commented, "You meet everyone you pass on the street without speaking to . . . you learn to look at people differently" (Turkle, 1995, p. 224). The compelling but often risky appeal of chemistry or "love at first sight" is reduced. The experience of being swept away upon first contact often involves a combination of raw physical attraction and tangled up projections, and for many people would better serve as a red flag than a basis for jumping right in (Hendrix, 1988).

Rheingold reflects,

The way you meet people in cyberspace puts a different spin on affiliation: In traditional kinds of communities, we are accustomed to meeting people, then getting to know them; in virtual communities we get to know someone and then choose to meet them. (Rheingold, 1993, pp. 26–27)

By the time people meet each other in person, an intimate bond can already be formed. The felt intensity and meaning of any unappealing physical traits are then more likely to be mitigated by the overall attraction that exists. Certainly, the subjective experience of knowing and liking someone can profoundly influence how attractive s/he *seems:* Perceived beauty correlates more strongly than objective beauty to interest in dating (Brehm, 1992).

Attraction is also known to be fostered through proximity and familiarity. There is some evidence that mere frequency of exposure can create a degree of attraction between people (Hendrick and Hendrick, 1983). Electronic communication

creates a feeling of greater propinquity [spatial proximity] with others, regardless of their actual geographic dispersion. This 'electronic propinquity' might be expected to foster friendships, as actual propinquity is known to do. (Walther, 1992)

Rapport can develop easily and casually online. Frequent contact with others is possible with little inconvenience or cost, from the comfort and safety of one's own home or workplace. One can access synchronous groups anytime for immediate interaction and can e-mail others whenever desired without being concerned about intruding, since they can retrieve messages at their convenience.

Similarity

Studies point to attraction being highest when the partner is perceived as being both physically attractive and attitudinally similar to oneself (Brehm, 1992). The Net increases one's chances of connecting with like-minded people due to the computer's ability to rapidly sort along many dimensions simultaneously.

People who have difficulty connecting with others in FTF interactions have a better chance of meeting a compatible person online. For instance, an obese woman who feels insecure approaching new people in FTF interactions because of her weight may interact online with a variety of people who share her interests. She may then

put [her weight] out to 40 different potential partners and eventually one of them will say 'Your weight doesn't bother me.' Emotionally speaking, it's much harder to say that to 40 different people in person. But on the Internet, it feels a lot less painful. (Williams, 1996, p. 11)

Self-Disclosure

Mutual self-disclosure is a key ingredient in developing intimacy between two people. Partners who self-disclose more to each other report greater emotional involvement in dating relationships and greater satisfaction in marriage (Brehm, 1992). A person who discloses intimate information about him/herself is generally better liked than one who is superficial. New acquaintances tend to match each other's level of self-disclosure, each disclosing more if the other person does so and holding back if the other person withdraws (Hendrick and Hendrick, 1983).

CMR provides sufficient distance to make it safer for people who may be restrained in FTF encounters to reveal more than they normally would. A woman who married a man she met online states,

Had we met each other in person, I think we would have talked, but I don't think we would have given each other the opportunity to know each other. . . . It's pretty easy to talk about feelings and hopes and hurts when you don't see the person and think you're never going to meet. (Puzzanghera, 1996, p. 1A)

People who are shy have an opportunity to relate online, developing social skills and increasing their confidence as they go. A shy so-called computer "nerd" may connect better online because he is more confident: ". . . being able to type fast and write well is equivalent to having great legs or a tight butt in the real world" (Branwyn, 1993, p. 784). He may be able to carry the confidence and the social skills acquired online with him into FTF encounters; if not, with the ease of meeting people online he may meet a compatible person who will accept him with all his social awkwardness off as well as online.

> Some people, many people, don't do well in spontaneous spoken interaction, but turn out to have valuable contributions to make in a conversation in which they might have time to think about what they say. These people, who might constitute a significant proportion of the population, can find written communication more authentic than the FTF kind. (Rheingold, 1993, p. 23)

For people who may normally stay clear of intimate relationships due to concerns about feeling trapped or burdened or losing themselves in some way, online relating makes it easier to feel in control and therefore to get involved. Net relating tends toward frequent small, casual interactions, as compared to a long talk that can induce a sense of pressure and so be avoided or put off. People are freer to engage and disengage when they want to, to modulate the intensity of their interactions.

> The computer is sort of practice to get into closer relationships with people in real life. If something is bothering me, you don't have to let the person know or you can let the person know (Turkle, 1995, p. 203)

or you can log off.

Because of its informality, online written text resembles oral communication more than most other forms of writing. At the same time, certain qualities distinctive to writing and unavailable in spoken interactions can heighten the experience of being intimately understood: Writing offers time for reflection and revision, so that what is communicated may be complete and intentional, with the author neither forgetting important points nor saying too much. Due to the diminished interpersonal press, the weakened link between sender and receiver in CMR, the receiver is able to offer focused attention while staying centered within him/herself. S/he can access the message when s/he has the time and inclination to fully attend to it. Because words can be saved, they can be reread by the receiver, their importance not lost in a quickly spoken phrase, their meaning not denied in an anxious moment. There's a quality of putting oneself on the line in writing, of being more vulnerable and exposed to the other, a confessional quality: "As high tech as it is, there's something very old-fashioned about it. The writing and the feelings . . . [sic]" (Puzzanghera, 1996).

Erotic Connection

All psychological intimacy has the potential to provoke an eroticization of the person with whom it is shared (Levine, 1992), a desire to physically express the intimate connection. Online relating has some features that may promote and heighten such an erotic connection in positive ways. By minimizing an initial attraction based on physical attributes and facilitating intimate, less inhibited sharing, the Net allows erotic interests to develop out of emotional involvement rather than lustful attraction. "Psychological intimacy . . . is an intangible, subtle, powerful motivator of our sexual expression" (Levine, cited in Lobitz and Lobitz, 1996, p. 71). Desire is strongest and most enduring when both partners value sexuality as a means of expressing intimacy.

Communication is a key to maintaining robust erotic connections. Failing to communicate intimately can spill over and impair sexual relationships (Chesney, Blackeney, Cole, and Chen, 1981). Online, partners have to verbally communicate, they can't fall back on unstated romantic scripts and nonverbal cues: "It's not like you can go to the movie together and not say anything" (Anning, 1996, p. 1A). Turn taking is built in so both people need to put themselves forward and cannot interrupt each other or speak at the same time.

All too often, psychological intimacy and sexuality are disconnected rather than integrated, with gender strongly influencing how people hold these two dimensions of relating. The interpersonal space the Net provides, reducing the emotional and physical press of FTF dating, may facilitate men and women's freedom to deviate from constricting gender roles related to sexuality that are often automatically activated in FTF encounters.

Internet relating can be conducive to the way many females in our culture experience sexuality, linking sexual desire to the overall relationship context and the degree of emotional intimacy. Online relating also frees women from the concern that if they or their partner reveal too much too soon, the relationship will get too intimate, too sexual too quickly: Women don't have to be primarily concerned about saying "no" online. In the anonymity and safety of Net-space, women may feel free to be more directly and explicitly sexual, to take charge of their desire, without fear of potential real life consequences (e.g., pregnancy, forced sex, or STD's) or the need to deal with the male's more powerful physical presence.

A woman who feels inhibited about presenting herself as sexual yet desires to be sexually attractive to men can experiment with being more flirtatious. She may find a way to describe herself online as attractive and sexually appealing, affording her the chance to incorporate this view into her self-image, off as well as online. Physical attractiveness is not merely a question of endowment; how one comes across has much to do with projecting confidence, knowing how to accent one's strengths and minimize one's flaws, appreciating and presenting oneself as uniquely beautiful even when one's looks don't fit society's standard images of attractiveness.

Conversely, men, who often feel pressure to move a developing relationship along by being appropriately assertive and "getting somewhere," may feel less responsible for setting the pace of the relationship, including pushing for its sexual development; men can relax and let relationships develop in a more organic way, with sexuality springing from an emotional connection rather than vice versa.

Summary

While many people think that electronic relating promotes emotionally disconnected or superficially erotic contacts, the structure and process of online relating can facilitate positive interpersonal connections, including the healthy development of romantic relationships. Computer mediated relating (CMR) reduces the role that physical attributes play in the development of attraction, and enhances other factors such as propinquity, rapport, similarity, and mutual self-disclosure, thus promoting erotic connections that stem from emotional intimacy rather than lustful attraction. The Net is a model of intimate, yet separate, relating. It allows adult (and teen) men and women more freedom to deviate from typically constraining gender roles that are often automatically activated in face-to-face interactions.

References

Anning, V. (1996). Doctors analyze effect of Internet on relationships. *Stanford Daily*, October 15.

Branwyn, G. (1993). Compu-sex: Erotica for cybernauts. *South Atlantic Quarterly, 92*(4), 779–791.

Brehm, S. (1992). *Intimate relationships*. New York: McGraw-Hill.

Chesney, A. P., Blackeney, P. E., Cole, C. M., and Chen, F. (1981). A comparison of couples who have sought sex therapy with couples who have not. *Journal of Sex and Marital Therapy, 7*, 131–140.

Deuel, N. (1996). Our passionate response to virtual reality. In S. Herring (Ed.), *Computer-mediated communication: Linguistic, social and cross-cultural perspectives*. Philadelphia: John Benjamin.

Hendrick, C., and Hendrick, S. (1983). *Liking, loving and relating*. Monterey: Brooks/Cole.

Hendrix, H. (1988). *Getting the love you want: A guide for couples*. New York: Henry Holt.

Jaffe, J. M., Lee, Y., Huang, L., and Oshagan, H. (1995). *Gender, pseudonyms and CMC: Masking identities and baring souls*. [Online]. Available: <http://www.iworld.net/~yesunny/gendereps.html>

Levine, S. B. (1992). *Sexual life: A clinician's guide*. New York: Plenum Press.

Lobitz, W. C., and Lobitz, G. K. (1996). Resolving the sexual intimacy paradoxes: A developmental model for the treatment of sexual desire disorder. *Journal of Sex and Marital Therapy, 22*(2), 71–84.

Puzzanghera, J. (1996). Double click on love. *San Jose Mercury News,* April 27, 1A.

Rheingold, H. (1993). *The virtual community: Homesteading on the electronic frontier.* Reading: Addison-Wesley.

Turkle, S. (1995). *Life on the screen.* New York: Simon and Schuster.

Walther, J. B. (1992). Interpersonal effects in computer-mediated interaction: A relational perspective. *Human Communication Research, 20*(4), 473–501.

——. (1994). Anticipated ongoing interaction versus channel effects on relational communication in computer mediated interaction. *Human Communication Research, 20*(4), 473–501.

Walther, J. B., and Burgoon, J. K. (1992). Relational communication in computer mediated interaction. *Human Communication Research, 19,* 50–88.

Williams, M. (1996). Intimacy and the Internet. *Contemporary Sexuality, 30*(9), 1–11. ✦

Adapted with permission from: Cooper, A., and Sportolari. L. (1997) "Romance in Cyberspace: Understanding online attraction." *Journal of Sex Education and Therapy,* 22, 7–14. Copyright © by the American Association of Sex Educators, Counselors, and Therapists.

1b

Love on the Internet?

B. Cornwell and D. C. Lundgren

With the creation and expansion of the Internet, computer-mediated communication (CMC) has become increasingly popular. CMC is used by individuals, groups, and organizations for many different functions, and an extensive social world has formed in what is often referred to as "cyberspace."

Cyberspace can be viewed as a microcosm of the vast, expansive physical and social world that preceded and exists apart from it ("realspace" as termed here). While numerous comparisons are possible, the most important difference for present purposes is that interaction in realspace is characterized by direct face-to-face communication and contact in immediate physical settings, whereas such events cannot occur in cyberspace. It is chat room interaction and the formation of romantic relationships in chat rooms with which this study is primarily concerned.

Chat rooms are electronic venues on the Internet where people can communicate with other Internet users. Instead of the oral communication that typically characterizes interaction in realspace, the typewritten word serves as the primary form of communication among people in chat rooms. Chat room users are provided with a field at the bottom of their computer screen in which they can enter any message that they wish. Upon clicking a button on the screen with their cursor, users can post a message to be displayed to all other users logged into that particular chat room. In addition, users have the option of sending private messages to particular individuals in the chat room. Upon reading another user's message, chat room users can post their own responses. Many people enjoy using chat rooms because they allow for anonymity. Thus, chat room users can say almost anything they like without others knowing who they are.

Rice (1993) and Weinberg (1996) observe that realspace communication is characterized by greater social presence among participants (i.e., opportunities for awareness of the other through a variety of communication channels, including nonverbal displays), while, in cyberspace, "all but the written modes of communication are removed" (Weinberg, 1996, p. 53).

From a series of recent studies using different methods McKenna (1999) concludes that friendships and romantic relationships developed on the Internet form more easily and develop more rapidly than do traditional relationships. The present research directly compares romantic relationships formed by chat room users in cyberspace vs. in realspace. Specifically, we examine differences in participants' levels of involvement and in their tendencies to misrepresent themselves to their partners in these respective types of relationships.

We hypothesize that participants in realspace romantic relationships will tend to report higher levels of involvement than those in romantic relationships formed and operating primarily in cyberspace. The richer opportunities for visual, aural, and physical stimulation offered in realspace relationships are likely to facilitate greater involvement, as are the vastly greater range of possibilities for social and physical activities and attendant rewarding outcomes. In this research we compare differences between cyberspace and realspace romantic relationships on four dimensions: participants' degrees of commitment, seriousness toward their relationships, perceived potential for emotional growth, and felt satisfaction.

A second potential difference between cyberspace and realspace relationships is the greater possibility for misrepresentation of features of one's identity offered by the former. Chat room interaction provides ideal circumstances under which people can mask various aspects of appearance, age, gender, personal attributes, or background characteristics. Noonan (1998) points out that the anonymity of cyberspace interaction opens up the possibility that details of individuals' physical and social characteristics "will be omitted, exaggerated, or falsified" (p. 64). In effect, chat rooms make it easy for one to pretend to be someone he or she isn't. Thus, Kendall (1998, p. 130) notes that

> accounts in both the academic and popular press . . . frequently emphasize the potential for portraying identities online that differ from offline identities.

Reid (1998), analyzing the freedom which CMC offers in obscuring or re-creating aspects of the self, notes that both liberating and potentially destructive consequences can occur as a result.

We suggest that cyberspace offers greater opportunities for exaggeration or outright deception in self-presentation. Potential romantic partners in cyberspace have less access to visual and verbal cues, direct observation of behaviors in everyday settings, and opportunities for consultation with mutual acquaintances or third parties than do parties to realspace relationships. Consequently there is less available information from which to check or confirm the actual identity of a potential romantic partner. Consistent with this argument, McKenna (1999, Study 4) found in a recent experimental study that individuals presented more idealized versions of self through CMC than in face-to-face interaction.

In addition to ease of opportunities for misrepresentation, research by Tice, Butler, Muraven, and Stillwell (1995) has found that individuals show more favorable self-enhancement in their self-presentation to strangers, but that modesty is more characteristic of self-presentation with friends. Because the people one meets in a chat room are usually total strangers at the outset, chat room users may present themselves more positively than they would with potential romantic partners with whom they had some history of acquaintance in realspace.

Our second hypothesis, then, is that misrepresentation of self with respect to interests, age, background, physical attractiveness, and other attributes will be greater in cyberspace than in realspace romantic relationships.

In addition to the comparison between cyberspace and realspace relationships, we are also interested in the link between involvement and misrepresentation. Levinger (1980) suggests that heightened involvement is associated with increases in positive social-emotional behavior, responsiveness, and concern for one's partner's outcomes. Presuming that these tendencies include greater adherence to norms of trustworthiness and authenticity, we hypothesize that involvement will be negatively associated with misrepresentation.

Methods

Thirty-six male and 44 female chat room users above the age of 17 participated in this study. Data were gathered via a series of private messages between the researcher (the first author) and users in chat rooms on weekday and weekend evenings over a period of two and a half weeks. Half of the participants were asked questions about cyberspace romantic relationships they had developed, and half were asked about realspace romantic relationships.

To recruit participants, the researcher logged on to various "random" or "general" chat room servers, including Lycos, Excite, and Yahoo, each of which placed him into a chat room with available space and a typical occupancy of 24–40 users. Approximately 25 percent of contacted chat room users agreed to participate in the research. After six interviews were completed in a given chat room, the researcher entered a different general chat room, again determined randomly by the server.

A "romantic relationship" was defined for participants as

> one that exists by virtue of an ongoing emotional involvement, in which you care for and possibly love your partner, and in which there exists a mutual expression of affection between yourself and your partner.

Respondents reporting realspace but not cyberspace romantic relationships were administered the realspace interview questions. Those who reported only cyberspace romantic relationships were administered questions about their cyberspace relationships, Those who reported experience with both types of relationships were administered either the realspace or cyberspace interview on an alternating basis until both versions of the interview had been completed by 40 respondents.

Twenty-one women and 19 men completed the cyberspace interview, and 23 women and 17 men completed the realspace questions. Ages ranged from 18 to 55, with a mean of 26.31. Thirty-four participants were high school students or graduates, 34 reported some college experience, and 12 were college graduates or had postgraduate degrees. Cyberspace respondents reported an average of 1.90 cyberspace romantic relationships in the past 2 years, and realspace respondents reported an average of 2.00 realspace romantic relationships during the same time period.

Cyberspace and realspace respondents were asked a parallel set of 17 questions. Phrasing was identical, except that cyberspace respondents were asked exclusively about "your Internet-based romantic relationships" and realspace respondents were asked about romantic relationships they had formed in the past 2 years, but "not including relationships that formed over the Internet."

We then asked four questions related to participants' degrees of involvement in their cyberspace or realspace relationships during the past 2 years. Specific items concerned the individual's seriousness regarding their recent romantic relationships (in cyberspace for one set of respondents; in realspace for the other), the perceived potential for emotional growth of these relationships, how satisfied they felt in their relationships, and their degree of commitment to their relationships. Ratings were made on 10-point scales from low (1) to high (10).

Five questions were asked regarding misrepresentation of self by individuals in their cyberspace or realspace relationships. Respondents were asked whether, in order to increase someone's interest in them, they had ever misrepresented: (1) their interests (e.g. "hobbies, religious orientation, musical preferences"); (2) their age ("somewhat older or younger than you really are"); (3) their background (e.g. "a different occupation, living arrangement, or level of education"); (4) any physical characteristics or aspect of appearance (e.g. "hair color, weight, state of health"); or (5) misrepresentation of "yourself in any other way."

Results

Respondents were asked how often they initiated communication with their partners. Fifty-five percent of cyberspace respondents and 75 percent of realspace respondents reported daily communication with their partners. While daily communication was common for both categories, frequency of communication did tend to be higher for realspace than for cyberspace respondents.

In the current sample, 50 percent of cyberspace respondents reported that they had met their partners face-to-face. A follow-up question revealed that cyberspace respondents reported face-to-face contact either never (50 percent), once (22.5 percent), a few times a year (12.5 percent), or a few times a month (15 percent), and none reported contact as often as a few times a week. In contrast, realspace respondents reported face-to-face contact daily (37.5 percent), a few times a week (60 percent), or a few times a month (2.5 percent).

Involvement

Realspace respondents reported that they were typically more committed to their realspace relationships and that they took these relationships more seriously than did chat room users describing romantic relationships formed over the Internet. Realspace and cyberspace respondents did not differ significantly on the perceived potential for emotional growth or the degree of satisfaction that they experienced in these respective romantic relationships. In sum, both groups perceived their relationships as satisfying and as offering opportunity for growth, but realspace respondents considered their relationships as more serious and they expressed greater commitment to them. Interestingly, seriousness and commitment were the highest two scores for realspace respondents, but the lowest two for cyberspace respondents.

Misrepresentation

Misrepresentation was not high in general, though some misrepresentation occurred on all of the dimensions. Where significant differences occurred, cyberspace respondents were always more likely to misrepresent themselves than were respondents in realspace romantic relationships. Specifically, cyberspace respondents were more likely to misrepresent their age, their physical attractiveness or other physical features, and to engage in misrepresentation in other areas, though the latter trend only approached significance. Fifty percent of cyberspace respondents and 35 percent of realspace respondents reported misrepresenting themselves.

Discussion

The study's two hypotheses received at least partial support from the results. That is, chat room users describing cyberspace romantic relationships reported less total involvement and tended to report greater total misrepresentation than did those describing realspace romantic relationships. In addition, involvement was negatively associated with misrepresentation, and the trend toward greater misrepresentation by cyberspace vs. realspace respondents appears to have been mediated by differing levels of involvement.

While fairly strong differences in total involvement were evident, it is interesting to note that cyberspace and realspace respondents differed significantly with respect to the seriousness with which they approached their relationships and their degree of commitment to these relationships, but that no significant differences were apparent for perceived potential for emotional growth or satisfaction. There were several instances during the interview process when individual respondents indicated that cyberspace relationships are "just for fun" or "unrealistic" and therefore should not be taken seriously, though many cyberspace respondents did indicate that they took their relationships quite seriously. We interpret these results as indicating that, insofar as romantic relationships are confined to cyberspace, there are substantial obstacles to the levels of intimacy and rewards obtainable, and thus serious and long-term commitment to these relationships tends to be limited.

Levels of satisfaction and potential for growth, however, were high and essentially equivalent in the two types of relationships. We speculate that cyberspace respondents were saying, in effect, that their relationships were fun, stimulating, gratifying in their own right, and, despite a lesser sense of seriousness or long-term commitment, these more transient relationships were experienced as offering opportunities for further development.

The findings also offer partial support for the hypothesis that participants in cyberspace romantic relationships are likely to be more prone to misrepresent themselves than those in realspace relationships. Significant differences were obtained for misrepresentation of age and physical characteristics. Total misrepresentation scores tended to be higher for cyberspace than realspace respondents.

Probably the most ready interpretation of these varying patterns has to do with the likely risk of detection by the partner. Exaggerations of age can be made readily in cyberspace, and misrepresentations of physical attributes are difficult to disconfirm on a computer screen. False claims regarding interests, occupation, education, or other background characteristics may be more difficult to sustain as these become the topics for conversation, questioning, and further exploration. In direct contrast, face-to-face interactants may find visible attributes like age or physical appearance far more difficult to alter than less immediately detectable features like interests or social background. As noted earlier, we found that our set of misrepresentation items held together less closely than did the involvement scale, and our results clearly suggest that tendencies toward misrepresentation in both cyberspace and realspace relationships vary depending upon the particular content domain. This is one interesting issue calling for further investigation.

While cyberspace and realspace respondents tended to differ in their amounts of misrepresentation, involvement was a critical mediating factor. Participants in cyberspace and realspace relationships experienced differing levels of involvement which, in turn, influenced their tendencies toward misrepresentation. It appears, then, that cyberspace participants were more prone to misrepresent personal characteristics specifically because they regarded their relationships as less serious and felt less commitment toward them, rather than simply that the communication channel offered greater opportunities for deception.

References

Kendall, L. (1998). Meaning and identity in "cyberspace": The performance of gender, class, and race online. *Symbolic Interaction, 11*, 129–153.

Levinger, G. (1980). Toward the analysis of close relationships. *Journal of Experimental Social Psychology, 16*, 510–544.

McKenna, K. Y. A. (1999). The computers that bind: Relationship formation on the Internet (Doctoral dissertation, Ohio University, 1998). *Dissertation Abstracts International, 59*, 2236.

Noonan, R. J. (1998). The psychology of sex: A mirror from the Internet. In J. Gackenbach, (Ed.), *Psychology and the Internet: Intrapersonal, interpersonal, and transpersonal implications* (pp. 143–168). San Diego: Academic Press.

Reid, E. (1998). The self and the Internet: Variations on the illusion of one's self. In J. Gackenbach, (Ed.), *Psychology and the Internet: Intrapersonal, interpersonal, and transpersonal implications* (pp. 29–42). San Diego: Academic Press.

Rice, R. E. (1993). Media appropriateness: Using social presence theory to compare traditional and new organization media. *Human Communication Research, 19*, 451–484.

Tice, D. M., Butler, J. L., Muraven, M. B., & Stillwell, A. M. (1995). When modesty prevails: Differential favorability of self-presentation to friends and strangers. *Journal of Personality and Social Psychology, 69*, 1120–1138.

Weinberg, N. (1996). Compassion by computer: Contrasting the supportiveness of computer-mediated and face-to-face interactions. *Computers in Human Services, 13*, 51–63. ✦

Issue 1: Questions to Consider

1. What are the potential pitfalls for anyone attempting to use the Internet to meet romantic partners?

2. What advantages do you see to using the Internet to find potential partners?

3. Is the use of the Internet to meet new people any different than putting an ad in the Personals column of a magazine or newspaper? Why do you think so?

4. Cooper and Sportolari identify some people who think that their computer-mediated relationships (CMR) are closer than they would have been if they had met initially face-to-face. Why do they believe this? Does their argument make sense to you? Why or why not?

5. Your best friend tells you he or she is going to go online to find someone to go out with. Based on these two articles, what would you tell him or her? What advice would you give to him or her?

6. Infidelity has usually been defined as a sexual relationship outside of marriage. However, the emergence of computer-mediated relationships and virtual sex has raised new questions about the boundaries of intimacy. Is it cheating if a married person has an emotionally intimate relationship on the Internet with someone other than his or her spouse? Can people have extramarital affairs with people that they never meet face-to-face? ✦

Issue 2: Introduction

Are Men and Women Really From Different Planets?

Ever wonder why the divorce rate is so high? Ever wonder if men and women can be friends with each other? Ever wonder why men and women are avoiding or delaying marriage? Ever wonder why romantic relationships are so fragile? The answers to all of these questions are simple, at least according to relationships guru John Gray—men and women are from different parts of the solar system, speaking different languages and having different needs and expectations for their relationships. The biggest question might be how these Martians and Venusians get together at all, given the inherent dissimilarities between them.

Gray's metaphor of "men are from Mars, women are from Venus" has struck a nerve with relationship-hungry men and women who are eager to figure out how to achieve compatibility with their spouses, lovers, and sweethearts. The Mars and Venus metaphor for relationships between the sexes has become the basis for an entire self-help cottage industry that includes books, television shows, websites, franchised counseling centers, workshops, and seminars. Despite questionable credentials and his own checkered relationship history, Gray has become a widely listened-to expert on men's and women's relationships. His views have attracted a following not only among the general public, but among counselors, educators, journalists, and even a few social scientists.

The counterpoint view, although perhaps lacking the popularity of Gray's work, is nonetheless widely supported by many. Bolstered by the findings of research on how men and women communicate and relate to each other, the counterpoint to Mars and Venus suggests that men and women are more alike than they are different. Critics of Gray's philosophy argue that the Mars and Venus theory consists of thinly disguised stereotypes of men and women that fail to accurately describe what most women and men actually do in their close relationships.

In the first selection that follows, Zimmerman, Haddock, and McGeorge briefly summarize the Mars and Venus philosophy (note that this selection is an excerpt from a larger article in which these authors critique this philosophy for family therapists). These authors succinctly capture the essence of the Mars and Venus point of view. In contrast, Sollie points out the fallacies of this philosophy as well as evidence on the compatibility of the genders. As you read these selections, think about your observations regarding the relationships between men and women. Think also about what you have read about men and women interacting in this and other classes you have taken—what evidence have you read that supports the Mars and Venus philosophy? That refutes it? ✦

2a

Mars and Venus

*Toni Schindler Zimmerman, Shelley A. Haddock, and
Christine R. McGeorge*

Men *Are From Mars, Women Are From Venus* (Gray, 1992) is not just any self-help book. With more than 7 million copies sold in 40 languages and an unprecedented 339 weeks on the *New York Times* bestseller list, it has become the self-help book of our times. The ideas of this book have swept the nation to the extent that when we hear the words "Mars" and "Venus," many of us no longer first think of planets but, instead, immediately think of men and women. Many therapists also embrace this book and advertise themselves as "certified Mars and Venus counselors."

In simple terms, Gray's thesis is that men and women are extremely different, that these differences are instinctual and natural, and that (heterosexual) couples must accept these differences in order to maintain a successful relationship. Although Gray never overtly discusses power, when taken together, his recommendations endorse and encourage power differentials between women and men. Gray's basic argument [is] that men and women are innately different "in all areas of their lives"—including how they "communicate, . . . think, feel, perceive, react, respond, love, need, and appreciate."

How can its popularity be explained? First, given the ubiquitousness of gender socialization, Gray's descriptions of women and men may "ring true" for many people. Relayed with humor and dressed up in a metaphorical package, the "kernels of truth" within these descriptions may give credibility to Gray's recommendations. A second explanation is that people tend to readily accept theories based on gender differences because these ideas support a social system founded on gender-based power differentials. The mass media often emphasize differences [because] points of similarity between women and men do not make news.

Finally, because many of Gray's messages are consistent with gender-based stereotypes that are portrayed in other popular press materials, such as certain magazines and television programs, readers may lack the necessary information to analyze his overall message and recommendations critically. In fact, it is likely that readers grant even more credibility to self-help books than to other popular press reports, relying on the author's claims of expertise and assuming that the recommendations in the books are based on research or established clinical principles.

In this article, we will present particularly salient themes in Gray's (1992) book and videotape, [and] provide illustrative quotes for each theme. Thematic analysis revealed three themes (assumptions) that are particularly salient in the book and videotape: (1) gender differences in communication, (2) gender differences in stress response, and (3) gender differences in desire for intimacy. For each of these presumed differences, Gray provided information such as the types of differences between men and women, the typical problems that result when men and women misunderstand these differences, and suggestions for managing these differences more effectively. This information is summarized below for each theme.

Theme 1: Differences in Communication

Purpose of Talking

In general, Gray (1992, 1994) paints a picture in which women have high needs (even desperation) to communicate with male partners who would prefer to talk very little or not at all. Women are depicted as needing to talk to achieve emotional intimacy, to reduce personal stress, and to gain clarity about their own identity and experiences. Men are portrayed as valuing conversation only as a way to achieve a goal or result. Therefore, men communicate with coworkers and women they are dating because these conversations are goal driven. On the subject of dating, Gray (1994) explained:

> One of the reasons men listen in the beginning is that they are gathering information. Once they understand you they figure they don't need to gather information. 'Now I know you. Why do we have to keep talking?'. . . We all listen until we get the information; then what else do you listen to?

Gray (1994) stated that, unlike their interest in communication with women they are dating, men often experience communicating to their wives as frustrating, painful, depressing, and a waste of time. "My wife can talk sometimes, and I go, 'Not more details! Not more details!' It's painful sometimes to listen to that stuff."

Style of Talking

According to Gray men are direct and get to the point when they talk, whereas women's style is described as "circling" or talking in detail about many subjects at the same time with no apparent point to their male partners. Gray gives the example of a woman in the role of dispatcher who receives a call that a house is on fire and children are dying. Instead of quickly and efficiently gathering pertinent information and sending help, the dispatcher asks such questions as, "Well, how do you feel about that? What are your hopes? What are your dreams? Let's share. I also felt that way once."

According to Gray, women cope with problems by talking but often do not know what their problems are when they begin talking. They just talk about one problem after another in great detail and with no logical sequence. As Gray described in the video,

> Women talk sometimes to discover what the problem is. Now this is an amazing phenomena, a woman will talk about 15 things which may be problems, but she's not sure yet, so she just flies them out.

Although Gray states that women, like men, can talk to make points, to gather or convey information, and to solve problems, he only provided descriptions of women talking "for other reasons," such as to feel better, to change their attitude, or to feel close. Gray described "the most frustrating lunch he ever had." He was listening in on a conversation between women at a restaurant. He described it this way:

> What they did was to take polite turns and talk about random things that were upsetting them. This bugs them, this bothers them. And then the next person would talk, this bugs her, this bothers her. And somebody over here . . . it wasn't always circular like that. Another one pops up over here, 'Oh yeah! And my husband did that the other day! And da da da da da da da duh.' And somebody else says, 'And I went to Disneyland as well!' A whole other subject, it was just like run on, fluid flow, you know. No logical, structured, linear progression towards a goal. No point they were making, just sharing and lots of details. . . . They are just sharing. I wasn't even married to these women and I was frustrated and hated them. None of them stopped and asked, 'What are you going to do about that?' There was no sense of 'I made this mistake. I will handle it this way,' or 'This is what you ought to do.'

Listening

With regard to listening, women are described as good listeners and men as incompetent and insensitive listeners. Gray explained that men are only able to listen for about 2 minutes and only make eye contact at work. While their female partners are talking, they tend to interrupt, go blank or tune out, reach for and read magazines, and look around.

Given men's difficulty and dislike of listening, Gray provided many suggestions for women to ease this process for their partners (see Table 2a-1). However, although Gray repeatedly recommended to men that they listen—even stating that lack of listening was the most common reason for women to seek divorce—it is noteworthy that he does not provide specific suggestions for men on how to listen in his book. Gray did provide a few examples for men on how to listen. Unfortunately, he framed these as a way for men to ensure that they can get sex and be happy, saying:

> So, basically, when a woman doesn't want to, there are reasons why she doesn't want to talk that need to be attended to. And now if my wife doesn't want to talk, I go, 'Uh-oh, I want sex, let's get her talking. I want to be happy. Let's get her talking.' (Gray, 1994).

He then recommended that men basically fake listening, suggesting that men remind themselves:

> OK, I am going to be a good listener; I am going to listen to her. This could be 15 minutes. . . . Buckle in; hang in there for a while. Make yourself comfortable. Look in her direction. Zip it up; don't say anything. Nod your head. Make Venusian noises . . . 'Uh huh . . . uh huh . . . Oh! Really! Then what? What did you say? Oh! That's terrible! That's awful! You paid that much?! Really! Oh!'

Offering Solutions or Advice

Gray states that couples experience difficulties when men offer solutions to women instead of listening and when women offer men unsolicited advice. The consequences of women offering unsolicited advice are

---

Table 2a-1

How to Talk to a Man
According to Gray (1992, 1994)

If you want to talk to a man, you should:

- Only speak for 2 minutes (1994).
- Only speak about one topic at a time (1994).
- Tell him the outcome of the story first, then fill in details (1994).
- Ideally, provide few, if any details (1994).
- Be clear and direct about your point and/or desired result (1994).
- Expect no eye contact and several interruptions (1994).
- Remove all magazines that are in arm's reach (1994).
- Clearly state that you just want him to listen (but be sure to ask for this support correctly so that he doesn't feel unaccepted for just who he is [1992]).
- Initiate the conversation when he wants sex to motivate him to listen (1994).
- Be sure to appreciate him for listening (1992).
- Be aware that sharing of emotions may cause him to "instinctively" and "immediately" pull away (1992, p. 98).
- Wait until he is out of the cave to avoid being burned (but be careful not to chase him back in by breaking any of the above rules [1992]).

---

extreme. For example, her partner feels "controlled," "offended," "incompetent," "weak," "unloved," "insulted," "humiliated," "broken," and "hurt." Men also feel "turned off," "smothered," and may "have a strong reaction." The consequences of men offering solutions are less serious; he "makes things worse" for her, or "displeases" or "frustrates" his partner. Gray states that men can offer solutions at times—just not when their partner is upset—but women should never offer unsolicited advice, especially over "small things" or "when it comes to fixing mechanical things, getting places, or solving problems." The following is an example that Gray provides for how women can "unknowingly and unintentionally hurt and offend the man she loves most":

> Tom and Mary were going to a party. Tom was driving. After about 10 minutes and going around the same block a few times, it was clear to Mary that Tom was lost. She finally suggested that he call for help. Tom became very silent. They eventually arrived at the party, but the tension from that moment persisted the whole evening. Mary had no idea of why he was so upset.

In future situations, Gray states that

> Mary learned how to support Tom at such difficult times. The next time he was lost, instead of offering help she restrained herself from offering any advice, took a deep relaxing breath, and appreciated in her heart what Tom was trying to do for her.

Requesting and Offering Support

Gray maintains that women find it "much more frustrating and disappointing to ask for support than men do." Women "instinctively feel the needs of others and give whatever they can [and] they mistakenly expect men to do the same." Men, however, are "not instinctively motivated to offer more support; they need to be asked." This "can be very confusing because if you ask a man for support in the wrong way he gets turned off, and if you don't ask at all you'll get little or none." Therefore, Gray argues that women need to learn how to properly ask men for support; to help women with this complex process, he devotes an entire chapter on the topic intended just for female readers. In this chapter, women learn that it is important to ask for support in a specific way because, "When a man feels a woman wanting more, he receives the message that she feels he is broken; naturally he doesn't feel loved just the way he is."

Gray provides a complex, three-step process for women to ask a man for support. In step 1, a woman should

become aware of what [her] partner is already doing for [her], especially the little things, like carrying boxes, fixing things, cleaning up, making calls, and other little chores.

Then, she learns that "the important part of this stage is to begin asking him to do the things he already does and not to take him for granted" and "make sure he feels appreciated for what he is already giving." Women are to practice for "at least 3 months correcting the way [she] asks for things before moving on to step 2." This is necessary to "recondition" him to respond positively to requests because "he may be conditioned by [her] (or his mother) immediately to say no to requests."

Gray suggests that women practice using "five secrets of how to correctly ask a Martian for support" because "if they are not observed, he may be easily turned off." These secrets are to use "appropriate timing," to use a "non-demanding attitude," to "be brief," to "be direct," and to "use correct wording." With regard to the last secret, Gray explained,

> On Mars it would be an insult to ask a man, 'Can you empty the trash?' Of course he can empty the trash! The question is not can he empty the trash but will he empty the trash. After he has been insulted, he may say no just because you have irritated him.

Before moving on to step two, Gray cautions women to "make sure he feels appreciated for what he is already giving," so that they can "risk asking for more without giving him the message that he is not good enough." With this step, women are guided to ask for more while "making it safe for him to refuse." Gray provides several examples of "when to ask" and "what to say" in certain situations. For illustration, the first three of these examples of the following situations are: "He is working on something and you want him to pick up the kids," "He normally comes home and expects you to make dinner," "He normally watches TV after dinner while you wash the dishes." Gray then suggests that "as you gently continue to ask for more, occasionally your partner will be able to stretch his comfort zone and say yes."

Women are then instructed to move on to step three—practicing assertive asking. Gray explains that "the art of assertive asking is to remain silent after you have made a request." After the woman has made her request, Gray says to "expect him to moan, groan, scowl, growl, mumble, and grumble" but to take this as "a good sign—he is trying to consider your request versus his needs." At this point, women are guided to "be careful not to disapprove of his grumbles" but to remain silent and listen, letting "him grumble and say things." Gray claims that "he won't hold it against you as long as you don't insist or argue with him." "If he continues to resist then practice step 2—accept his rejection. This is not the time to share how disappointed you are. Be assured that if you can let go at this time, he will remember how loving you were and be more willing to support you next time."

Theme 2: Differences in Stress Responses

Men and the Cave

According to Gray men become more focused, withdrawn, forgetful, unresponsive, and preoccupied when stressed, whereas women become overwhelmed and emotionally involved. Just as women are unable to "calm down and make complete sense," men are "powerless" to release their mind from their problems. When a man is stressed, he needs to withdraw from relationships and go to his "cave":

> When he comes home, he wants to relax and unwind by quietly reading about the news. He never talks about what is bothering him. Instead he becomes very quiet and goes to his private cave to think about his problem. When he has found a solution, he feels much better and comes out of his cave. If he can't find a solution then he does something to forget his problems, like reading the news or playing games. If his stress is really great it takes getting involved with something even more challenging, like

racing his car, competing in a contest, or climbing a mountain.

Although he never explicitly states how long men need to spend in the cave, he does say that it depends on the level of stress. In one example that he mentions, it took several hours; in another, it took one day; in still another, it took two days. Going to the cave appears to be a common need for men, given the emphasis that he places on this need in the book and videotape.

Gray explains that men are quite uncomfortable with their own and others' feelings and use the cave to "escape" feelings by thinking about something or by "cutting off" from their feelings:

> We [men] can just cut off from our feelings in an instant. Boom, gone. And it is so relaxing, women. That's what we do. We are like that blank slate, we just cut off from those feelings. Oh! Freedom from feelings! Not upset about anything, so long as we don't talk.

When a man tries to retire to his cave, his partner begins to worry that he does not love her or that something is wrong, so she follows him by asking questions. "At this point, he loses control and begins saying things that he will regret later." Gray depicts men as becoming angry (or irritated, repulsed, and insulted) quite easily, typically when women are initiating intimate connections or asking for support (e.g., knocking on the cave, asking questions, trying to resolve an argument, and talking to their partner about their day). Women are warned not to enter a man's cave so that they are not "burned by the dragon" and are advised to treat an angry man "like a tornado" and "lie low" (p. 203). Gray describes the way in which his wife, Bonnie, effectively handles him coming out of the cave:

> When I begin showing signs of interest in her, she recognizes that I am coming out of the cave, and it is then a time to talk. Sometime she will casually say, 'When you feel like talking, I would like to spend some time together. Would you let me know when?' In this way she can test the waters without being pushy or demanding.

Gray suggests ways in which women can support men in withdrawing to the cave. He also provides strategies for men to facilitate their own withdrawal, such as giving his partner reassurance that he will be back, not judging her for needing this reassurance, and listening to her when he comes out of the cave. Although a man's partner typically feels unloved and ignored during this time, for a man,

a moment happens that is very precious: We [men] forget the problems at work and we remember what is most important to us. Which is why we are even going to work. Which is our family, our wife.

Women and the Well

During stressful times, women find themselves not in a cave, but instead, in a "well," where they "suddenly experience a host of unexplained emotions and vague feelings" that "may have to do with the relationship, but usually are heavily charged from her past relationships and childhood." Gray explains that

a woman's ability to give and receive love in her relationships is generally a reflection of how she is feeling about herself. When she is not feeling as good about herself, she is unable to be as accepting and appreciative of her partner. At her down times, she tends to be overwhelmed or more emotionally reactive.

Regarding the well, Gray cautions women against suppressing their negative emotions or pretending that everything is fine. Instead, he suggests they should allow themselves to experience this natural cycle.

A Woman Is Like a Wave

When she feels loved her self-esteem rises and falls in a wave motion. When she is feeling really good, she will reach a peak, but then suddenly her mood may change and her wave crashes down. This crash is temporary. After she reaches bottom suddenly her mood will shift and she will again feel good about herself. Automatically her wave begins to rise back up.

Gray provides men with a list of 13 "warning signs" for what their partner might say (and the corresponding feeling) that may indicate that her wave is crashing (e.g., "There is too much to do"—she is overwhelmed; "I need more"—she is insecure; "I do everything"—she is resentful; "Well, did you . . . ?"—she is controlling). Gray notes that she may also feel worried, confused, exhausted, hopeless, passive, demanding, withholding, mistrustful, and/or disapproving. Unlike men, women do not cope with stress by pursuing personal time and autonomy but, instead, by talking about their problems in the aforementioned circular fashion.

Although Gray provides specific instructions to women on how to support a man in his cave, he only offers two short paragraphs on "How a man can support a woman in the well." These paragraphs provide the general suggestion that "weather[ing] a few emotional storms or droughts" is worth the "reward." Gray indicates that they should not try to fix or rescue their partner; instead, they should "release judgments and demands" and recognize that this is the time that she needs him the most. Gray also recommends that men should view their partner's tendency to go into the well as "an opportunity to support her with unconditional love."

However, Gray provides two pages of specific suggestions for when he is unable to support his partner while she's in the well because: "When a man needs to pull away and a woman needs to talk, his trying to listen only makes matters worse." After a short time he either will be judging her and possibly explode with anger or he will become incredibly tired or distracted, and she will become more upset.

Theme 3: Differences in Desire for Intimacy

According to Gray, another difference between women and men is that men have an "instinctual urge" to alternate between needing intimacy and autonomy. Although women tend only to pull away when they are upset with their partner, Gray explains that men are like rubber bands; if they get too close, they lose themselves, and their "desire, power and passion." Therefore, men need to pull away more frequently. This instinctive need can happen at any time, but is often triggered during "the most intimate moments."

When a woman opens up and shares deeper and more intimate feelings it may actually trigger a man's need to pull away. A man can only handle so much intimacy before his alarm bells go off, saying it is time to find balance by pulling away. At the most intimate moments a man may suddenly automatically switch to feeling his need for autonomy and pull away. Women typically respond by "panicking" and then either "chasing" or "punishing" her partner. Gray strongly cautions women against chasing or punishing as it "obstructs her male partner's natural intimacy circle," which causes him to "easily assume that he no longer loves" her (p. 96). He then offers suggestions to men: They should reassure their partner that they will be back before pulling away, listen to her when they are not withdrawn, and initiate a conversation before pulling back. For women, he offers detailed instructions on trying to get her needs for closeness fulfilled under the following subheadings, "When to talk with a man," "How to get a man to talk," "How to initiate a conversation with a man," "When a man won't talk," and "When a man doesn't pull away" (p. 104). These suggestions are summarized in Table 2a-2.

In summary, Gray describes men and women as different in all areas, providing information about primarily three types of differences—those related to communication, stress responses, and intimacy. He provides suggestions for dealing with the common problems that arise from these differences.

Clinical Implications

The popularity of *Men Are From Mars, Women Are From Venus* suggests that Gray's (1992) theories appear to be mirroring—with some degree of accuracy—the difficul-

---

Table 2a-2

How to Get a Man to Talk to You, According to Gray (1992)

To get a man to talk, you should:

- Act as though you are not trying to get him to talk. (Gray cautions that "the more a woman tries to get a man to talk the more he will resist.")
- Do not ask him questions so that you do not "unknowingly turn him off by interrogating him." To gradually get him to open up, you need to: Be the first to begin sharing (using the methods stated above). Appreciate him for listening.
- Do not make him feel pressured to talk; in fact, discourage him from talking at first.
- Do not make him feel blamed for not talking or for anything else.
- Do not want him to talk more than he already is. Do not resent him for pulling away.
- Accept him just the way he is.

---

ties that many couples experience. The book seems to normalize many couples' conflicts and suggest a seemingly and relatively easy path for resolving them—that is, "don't try to change things, just accept them the way they are."

Although it is beyond the scope of this article to review particular approaches that may be effective in helping clients to "rethink" gender assumptions, we have a few recommendations (based on our clinical experiences) for discussing Gray's books with clients who have accepted his messages. We have found that it is often helpful to validate that Gray's materials may be descriptive of some of the couple's experiences and to inquire about the specific aspects of the book that resonated with clients' experiences of or desires for their relationship. These inquiries may lead to or enhance the process of relationship goal setting.

The subsequent discussion can serve as an opportunity for psychoeducation about research on marriage and can support ther-

apeutic efforts for understanding and resolving the couple's particular difficulties
within a societal context. A few recent resources that offer practical guidance for
therapists on integrating gender and power
in the practice of couple's therapy include
Gottman (1999) and Rabin (1996). Therapists may also recommend alternative self-
help books to clients that are consistent
with research, such as *Seven Principles for
Successful Relationships* (Gottman and Silver, 1999) and *Love Between Equals: How
Peer Marriage Really Works* (Schwartz,
1994).

References

Gottman, J. M., and Silver. N. (1999). *Seven
principles for making marriage work*. New
York: Crown.

Gray, J. (1992). *Men are from Mars, women are
from Venus: A practical guide for improving
communication and getting what you want in
your relationships*. New York: HarperCollins.

——. (1994). *Men are from Mars, women are
from Venus: Secrets of successful relationships* [video]. Genesis Intermedia. Rolling
Start Films.

Rabin, C. (1996). *Equal partners, good friends:
Empowering couples through therapy*. New
York: Routledge.

Schwartz, P. (1994). *Love between equals: How
peer marriage really works*. New York: Free
Press. ✦

2b

Beyond Mars and Venus: Men and Women in the Real World

Donna L. Sollie

For the last decade, American culture has been brimming with images of men and women who do not understand each other and who just cannot get along. The popularity of self-help books such as John Gray's *Men Are From Mars, Women Are From Venus* and Fein and Schneider's *The Rules* reflects pervasive cultural stereotypes that depict men and women as inhabiting different relational worlds. Perhaps the popularity of these books, and the beliefs they advocate, should not be all that surprising. The changes that occurred in gender roles during the last half of the twentieth century have resulted in uncertainty about what it means to be a man or a woman, a husband or a wife.

This uncertainty is often coupled with deeply ingrained personal views about masculinity and femininity that seem to contradict current expectations about gender roles. Men and women grasp at the easy answers and simple solutions presented in the popular media, including self-help books and talk television. The generalizations presented in these popular forums, especially in Gray's proliferating cottage industry, often do seem to fit people's experiences, though only superficially. People can usually find descriptions of themselves that have the ring of truth, just as they do in horoscopes, which frequently seem to provide an accurate portrayal. However, the problem is that these depictions are so general that they are not particularly useful.

How accurate are these perspectives? And does this depiction of men and women as inhabiting different worlds help husbands and wives to understand each other and resolve relationship difficulties, or does it create a gulf between them and hinder their ability to recognize the complexity of people and their intimate relationships?

Even though the perspective that men and women inhabit "different cultures" is a major theme on best-seller lists, recent research presents a more complicated scenario. This scenario challenges the oversimplified Mars/Venus perspective that magnifies and reifies relatively small sex differences and overlooks more common similarities. Popular culture fails to note that gender is a complex phenomenon, and we must go beyond simply comparing men and women if we are to unlock the myriad ways that gender influences relationships.

The Emotional Domain of Marriage

At least since the Industrial Revolution, gender roles have been in a state of transition. As a result, cultural scripts about marriage have undergone change. One of the more obvious changes has occurred in the roles that women play. Women have moved into the world of work and have become adept at meeting expectations in that arena, while maintaining their family roles of nurturing and creating a home that is a haven for all family members. Even though many women experience strain from trying to "do it all," they often enjoy the increased rewards that can result from playing multiple roles. As women's roles have changed, changing expectations about men's roles have become more apparent. Many men are relinquishing their major responsibility as the family provider. Probably the most significant change in men's roles, however, is in the emotional domain of family life. Men are increasingly expected to meet the emotional needs of their families, especially their wives.

In fact, expectations about the emotional domain of marriage have become more significant for marriage in general. Research on how marriage has changed over recent decades points to the increasing importance of the emotional side of the relationship, and the importance of sharing in the "emotion work" necessary to nourish marriages and other family relationships. Men and women want to experience marriages that are interdependent, where both partners nurture each other, attend and respond to each other, and encourage and promote each other. Pepper Schwartz's research has identified an emerging type of marriage: Peer marriage. Peer marriages are characterized by sharing between husbands and wives in all aspects of their lives, with an emphasis on the primacy of the emotional relationship between the husband and wife. We are thus seeing marriages where men's and women's roles are becoming increasingly more similar.

In both the popular and scientific literature, though, women are portrayed as the emotional specialists in marriages, while men are depicted as distant and emotionally withdrawn. Women are also portrayed as being more invested in marriage, more dissatisfied with their husbands, and more demanding, expecting more than their partners are able or willing to give them. As John Gray describes it, men retreat into their caves because they need solitude in order to focus on the stresses in their lives and to identify solutions to these stresses. Talking about problems only adds to their stress. In contrast, women need to talk in great detail about the nuances of their problems, whether these problems are specific to their marital relationship or originate from another source. Men are impatient with this neediness and eager to quickly find a solution to the problem and move on to other things. These characterizations mirror the images of men and women as inhabiting different worlds, struggling to meet the needs of a partner that conflict with their own needs and nature, but failing to succeed.

Certainly, men and women enter marriage with expectations about what it means to be a husband or a wife and what they expect from their partner. However, these expectations are also more likely to be similar than different. Although it is true that wives are typically more dissatisfied than husbands with their marriages, what predicts happiness for both men and women is the emotional quality of their relationships. So, men and women actually want the same things from their marriages. They both value emotional closeness and desire openness and affection from their partners. However, men are more likely than women to have these expressive needs met.

Why are men generally less emotionally expressive than women? Socialization experiences that emphasize that men should avoid showing weakness or expressing intimate feelings undoubtedly contribute to men's inability to meet their wives' emotional needs. Masculinity is prized in men, and exhibiting anything that might be viewed as feminine is generally disparaged. The gender-role messages that permeate our culture inhibit men's emotional expressivity and undoubtedly lead many men to doubt their ability to function effectively in the emotional realms of life. Ronald Levant, who specializes in treating men's individual and relationship disorders, reiterates that we must recognize the negative effects of such gender-role socialization experiences. Men frequently learn to channel their vulnerable feelings into aggressive behaviors or sexuality. Too often, men may feel that sexual interaction is the only appropriate way to express affection and love. A typical result of these life-long messages is that when men become involved with a partner, they frequently experience difficulty in communicating their intimate feelings and in experiencing emotional closeness. More traditional male behaviors, including emotional stoicism, difficulty in showing vulnerability, and withdrawal from their partners in response to conflict, lead women to feel that their male partners do not care about them. As a result, then, women are typically less satisfied in their intimate relationships than are men.

Examining Messages About Gender

It is important to examine more closely the ways that messages about gender affect relationship behaviors. We must tease out the nuances in gender-related perceptions that women and men bring to their intimate relationships. In recent work on expressive behaviors in marital relationships, Geoff Steurer and I were able to do just that. We were interested in daily patterns between husbands and wives, particularly in the emotional realm. That is, we wanted to better understand gender-related factors that influenced how openly partners talked with each other, how frequently they confronted relationship conflict with an understanding and cooperative problem-solving stance, and how supportive they were of each other.

Three different gender-related dimensions were assessed. Attitudes about societal roles for men and women included such dimensions as work roles, educational opportunities, and family responsibilities for provider, housework, and child-care roles. Stereotyped gender beliefs, on the other hand, reflected cliched views of men's and women's psychological make-up and emotional capacities and needs. For example, a person who held such typecast beliefs would believe that men and women have different emotional needs, want different things from their intimate relationships, and can never really understand each other.

Finally, male gender-role conflict focuses on the internal turmoil that men experience as they deal with conflicting expectations about their work and family roles and their feelings about emotional expressiveness. For example, a husband might have difficulty expressing tender feelings for his wife, or admitting his own emotional needs to his wife.

Our findings indicate that when we scrutinize gender-related factors more closely, we begin to understand more fully both the complexity and importance of teasing out the nuances of how gender influences what men and women actually do in their relationships. Attitudes about societal roles, in general, had little effect on what happens between husbands and wives. Whether husbands were more traditional or egalitarian in their views about societal gender roles was not significantly related to their own expressive behaviors, nor to wives' perceptions of their husbands' expressive behaviors. In addition, men's gender-role attitudes were not significantly correlated with men's or women's relationship satisfaction. A similar pattern was found for wives. For both husbands and wives, then, attitudes about men's and women's societal roles were not strong predictors of marital behavioral patterns.

However, men's gender-role conflict and stereotyped beliefs had significant negative effects on marriage for both husbands and wives. For men, being conflicted about what it means to be a man, to "do gender" with their wives, had a pervasive dampening influence on their openness and affectionate behaviors with their spouses. They were less likely to openly express their love or to listen and understand their wives. In turn, wives of men who were more conflicted about their gender roles described their husbands as less expressive across a number of dimensions. So, husbands who experience more conflict in their beliefs about how to play out the male role are less disclosing, affectionate, and supportive of their wives.

Husband's stereotyped beliefs about the sexes were also significantly and negatively correlated with their expressive behaviors.

And the wives of men who hold stereotyped beliefs described their husbands as less open, affectionate, and reassuring. Husbands who believe that men and women have different emotional needs, psychological makeups, and relationship needs, then, are less likely to engage in emotionally expressive relationship behaviors with their spouses. Husbands' stereotyped beliefs about men and women were also negatively related to marital satisfaction for both husbands and wives. Such beliefs can result in greater distance between men and women, encouraging them to retreat to opposite corners and resort to gender blinders. These blinders hinder their ability to understand each other and to recognize that while there may indeed be differences in the relationship styles they each bring to a marriage, these differences result from many complex factors, not just gender.

Two points are especially interesting. First, the couples that we studied were generally happy with their marriages. Even so, the gender-related views that they brought to their marriage clearly affected the patterns of interaction that they developed. It was also intriguing that wives perceived their husbands to be more expressive than the husbands perceived themselves to be. What could be happening here? Perhaps husbands are harder on themselves than they need to be, and perhaps the cultural images that depict men as less expressive result in men not being able to accurately assess just how expressive they truly are.

Several scholars have documented that men who withdraw emotionally from their own families put their relationships at risk. Based on his extensive research on conflict patterns in marriage, John Gottman concluded that husbands who accept their wives' influence in the marriage and who are able to remain emotionally connected with their wives have happier and more stable marriages. Clinging to dysfunctional beliefs about men and women very likely impedes men's openness to their wives, thus leading to negative relationship patterns. And clinging to such beliefs may prevent women from recognizing or encouraging men's expressive behaviors.

Some Conclusions

These findings for gender attitudes and stereotyped beliefs clarify the ways that our perceptions of gender influence relationships. Massive strides toward equality have been made over the last few decades. As we continue to untangle the myriad ways that gender influences intimate relationships, we are beginning to understand that whether people have traditional or more egalitarian beliefs about men's and women's societal roles may not be as relevant for expressive behaviors as other gender-related perceptions. Rather, feeling conflicted about what it means to be a man and grasping at the stereotyped beliefs that permeate popular culture significantly influence men's marital styles. It is these conflicting expectations and stereotyped beliefs that lead men to be more restricted in their emotional behaviors, and therefore dampens not only their wives' satisfaction, but their own as well. This last point is an important one—men who are more emotionally skilled and expressive are themselves happier.

Stereotyped beliefs also had an impact on women's marital happiness. Wives who adhere to stereotyped views about men's and women's nature might tend to take more responsibility for the "emotion work" in marriage and experience difficulty in recognizing or encouraging their husbands to be emotionally open. These wives might also be less likely to recognize other ways that their husbands express caring. Francesca Cancian notes that our society has "feminized" love, which means that we do not always recognize diverse expressions of caring and closeness. For a man, working 12-hour days or keeping quiet about his own personal problems or being more involved in the practical side of life, such as making child-care arrangements—may be some ways that he strives to demonstrate caring and concern.

"Doing gender" has become a catchphrase in the social science lexicon, capturing the ongoing changes in the ways that men and women interact with each other in their close relationships. If we truly want to enhance marital satisfaction, and thus improve marital stability, we should educate men and women to recognize and embrace their similarities and to understand that for their relationships to flourish, they must both become actively engaged in "doing gender" and move away from putting each other into gender boxes that restrict the range of behaviors that is acceptable. Where gender-related attitudes seem to matter the most is in terms of how dysfunctional beliefs can negatively affect men's and women's daily interactions with each other and their relationship satisfaction. These stereotyped views, epitomized in the Mars/Venus dichotomy, might actually dampen the emotional climate of marriages by contributing to distancing behaviors that result in decreased satisfaction for both husbands and wives.

Too often, the popular culture portrays male-female relationships as a battle between opposites. Will there be an end to the gender wars? Yes—when we encourage both men and women to appreciate the unique strengths that both bring to their relationship, as individuals, and when we recognize the importance of nourishing emotional expressivity on the part of both partners, and when we value the diverse ways that we show our love for each other. Only then can we move beyond the Mars/Venus dichotomy that alienates men and women from each other. ✦

Issue 2: Questions to Consider

1. Zimmerman and her colleagues present several of Gray's ideas for women on how to talk to men and how to get men to talk to them. Pretend you are a Mars and Venus counselor and write a set of guidelines for men on how to talk to women and how to get women to talk to them. How do your guidelines compare to the ones in the Zimmerman et al. article?

2. Are men and women inherently different or are gender differences mostly created by social stereotypes? Where do you stand on this issue? Why is this your stance? What have been the major influences on your beliefs about gender?

3. Does the Mars and Venus depiction of men and women as inhabiting different worlds help husbands and wives to understand each other and resolve relationship difficulties, or does it create a gulf between them and hinder their ability to recognize the complexity of people and their intimate relationships? Justify your answer with evidence from these articles.

4. What does Sollie mean by "doing gender"?

5. What are the main reasons why Sollie discounts the Mars and Venus perspective?

6. Considering the lack of research to support Gray's notion of male/female relationship differences, why do you think this approach is so popular? ✦

Issue 3: Introduction

Can Men and Women Be 'Just' Friends?

Many people who view men and women as species from different planets (see issue 2) think that real friendship between men and women is unlikely, if not impossible, because their ways of thinking, feeling, and behaving are so different. From this perspective, men cannot see women as anything other than sexual objects. The only reason men are friendly to women, or the reason why men might fake friendship with women, is because they want to have sex with them. Similar views are expressed about women, although women are often seen as wanting men more for their status and money than for sex. Some people concede that men and women might be able to be friends, but only with individuals they do not find attractive. For example, a gay man and a straight woman could be friends. Otherwise, friendship is not a possibility.

In contrast, some argue that romantic love and long-term relationships between men and women (such as marriage) are more satisfying and stable when the partners are first friends with each other.

In the two studies of college students that follow, researchers examine slightly different questions surrounding the issue of whether or not cross-sex friendships are possible. Afifi and Faulkner studied sexual activity among cross-sex friends. They found that many college students act on the attraction they feel toward friends of the other sex. Reeder studied attraction between men and women who are friends. She reports that men and women are attracted to their friends in several ways, although the attraction is not always mutual. As you read these studies, make notes about the findings. What do these findings suggest about the question, Can men and women really be "just" friends? ◆

3a

'Just Friends'? Frequency of Sexual Activity in Cross-Sex Friendships

Walid Afifi and Sandra L. Faulkner

Research on cross-sex friendships has noted the presence of sexual tension in many of these relationships. Indeed, the available evidence suggests that at least one member of many cross-sex friendships experiences sexual attraction for his/her friend. Yet, cultural norms seem to discourage enactment of sexual interests in a friendship. Werking (1997), for example, argued that the occurrence of sexual activity in a friendship "signals the end of the 'friendship' and the beginning of a 'love relationship' since romance and sexuality are so closely aligned in romantic ideology" (p. 30). Recent evidence (e.g., O'Sullivan & Gaines, 1998) suggests that sexual activity may be a more common occurrence in friendships than Werking's claim suggests.

Characteristics of Cross-Sex Friendships

Cross-sex friendships seem to occupy an unusual place in the landscape of heterosexual relationships. They simultaneously occupy two roles: the role of friendship, where exclusivity and sexual contact are replaced by a more purist "attraction of the spirit" (Werking, 1997: 30), and the role of potentially romantic relationship, where feelings of sexual attraction may smolder. Given these competing cultural scripts for cross-sex friendships, it seems reasonable that some of these relationships experience

sexuality as "a backdrop that frames virtually all adult cross-sex friendships" (p. 106).

While it is clear that individuals may maintain cross-sex friendships without experiencing sexual tension, especially in later life, many of these relationships are characterized by some degree of sexual attraction by at least one member of the friendship. For example, 58 percent of Kaplan and Keys' (1997) participants reported at least slight levels of sexual attraction to their cross-sex friends, and 62 percent of Sapadin's (1988) sample indicated experiencing sexual tension in their cross-sex friendships. However, the general assumptions are that individuals experiencing sexual desire for a friend stop short of engaging in sexual activity in the friendship and that those who choose to engage in such activity do so only after the relational definition has shifted from a friendship to a romantic relationship (Werking, 1997).

Recent data challenge these assumptions. For example, 14 percent of Fuiman et al.'s (1997) participants reported engaging in sexual activity (e.g., petting, oral sex, or intercourse) with an opposite-sex friend, 11 percent of Monsour's (1992) sample noted sexual contact as a means of expressing intimacy in their cross-sex friendships, and 15 percent of Bleske and Buss's (2000) respondents reported having had sex *sometimes or often* with their close opposite sex friend. Given these results the following research questions are posed:

RQ1: What percent of individuals have engaged in sexual activity with an otherwise platonic friend of the opposite sex?

RQ2: What percentage of individuals have engaged in sexual activity with an otherwise platonic friend of the opposite sex without the relationship ever becoming romantic?

Effect of Sexual Contact on the Quality of Cross-Sex Friendships

Engaging in sexual activity in these relationships may have important implications for relationship development. For example, over half of the men possessing traditional values and attitudes believed that sexual involvement with a female friend would "destroy the relationship" (Bell, 1981: 414), and 79 percent of Sapadin's (1988) respondents agreed that "having a sexual relationship complicates friendships in a way [they] dislike" (p. 396). Messman, Canary, and Hause (2000) found that safeguarding the relationship was the individuals' primary motivation for keeping their cross-sex friendships platonic (i.e., not engaging in sexual activity).

In contrast, there is nothing inherent about sexual activity that should lead to a friendship's deterioration. Sexual encounters may be helpful for some friendships because "once the tensions of unexplored sex are behind them . . . they are freed from the strains that so often inhibit friendship between men and women" (Rubin, 1985, p. 150).

Methods

Sample

A sample size of 315 participants (male n = 159, female n = 150, and 6 did not indicate their sex) were recruited in communication and business courses at a large northeastern university and volunteered (without credit) to take part in the study. Ages ranged from 18 to 40 (average = 20.3). The sample was predominantly Caucasian (89 percent), followed by African American (4 percent), Asian (3 percent) and individuals from other ethnic origins (4 percent). In addition, 98.5 percent reported a heterosexual orientation. The 1.5 percent who reported a sexual orientation other than heterosexual (n = 5) were eliminated from the analyses because of potential cultural confounds.

Procedure

The researchers recruited participants by introducing the study at the beginning of small classes and asking for volunteers to complete a 15-minute survey during class. Seating was such that privacy was ensured. However, students were reminded of the sensitive nature of some of the questions and were asked to cover their answers as they were completing the survey and not to look across tables at other students' surveys.

We informed participants that we were "interested in studying sexual behavior in otherwise platonic male-female or same-sex friendships" and defined platonic as "people who you were not dating and had no intentions of dating." In [a] second wave of data collection, we added a broad definition of friendship to the instructions, asking participants to define friendships as "individuals who are more than acquaintances but not dating partners," in addition to the definition of platonic. We included a statement recognizing that not all participants were sexually active or had engaged in sexual activities with a friend. We applied a broad definition of friendship because we suspected that sexual activity might occur across a wide range of closeness levels.

Following these definitions, participants were asked to indicate which one of three categories of sexual involvement best matched their life experiences. The three categories were: (1) individuals who had "sex" with only one friend during their lifetime (we asked participants to define "sex" as they wished) (n = 81; 26 percent); (2) individuals who had sex with more than one friend in their lifetime (n = 79; 25 percent); and (3) individuals who had never had sex with a friend (n = 155; 49 percent).

All individuals who reported having had sex with a friend were asked to think of the first or only time they had sex with the specific friend. Those who indicated having had sex with more than one friend were asked to think of the friend with whom they had most recently had sex. Individuals in both of these sub-samples completed measures assessing the length of time since the occurrence of the event, the number of times they have had sex with this friend, the time elapsed since the last instance of sexual contact with this friend, the types of sexual activity in which they engaged, the dating status of both friendship members at the time of the sexual activity, whether a condom or dental dam was used during the sexual activity, the relational status history of the friendship, and the number of friends with whom they have had sex.

Results

Descriptive Information about Sex in Friendships

First, 51 percent of participants indicated membership in one of the first two categories (i.e., had engaged in sexual contact with at least one friend), but this percentage was affected by whether acquaintances were eliminated from the definition of friendship.

Fifty-six percent of the participants who claimed to have engaged in sexual activity with a friend (21 percent of the population

of participants) reported doing so with more than one friend. The mean number of friends with whom these individuals reported engaging in sexual activity was 3.32 (range = 2–15). Moreover, 54 percent of the participants who claimed to have engaged in sexual activity with a friend (20 percent of participants) reported engaging in "sex" more than once with the target friend. The mean number of times that these participants reported engaging in sexual activity in the target friendship was 6.81 (range = 2–30).

A small minority of participants (3 percent) reported stopping the sexual encounter at genital manipulation (i.e., sexual petting or mutual masturbation), followed by those who reported giving or receiving oral sex but not engaging in vaginal or anal penetration (15 percent), but the vast majority reported engaging in vaginal or anal penetration with the friend (82 percent). This distribution of types of sexual intimacy did not differ according to the friends' dating status (i.e., whether one of the friendship members was dating someone else at the time of the sexual activity), although a majority of the reported sexual encounters (68 percent) occurred in friendships where neither member was dating at the time.

Finally, of those who engaged in sexual contact and completed the survey during

Table 3a-1

Frequency Distribution of Sexual Activity in Cross-Sex Friendships

	Wave 1	Wave 2	Total
Incidence of sexual activity (N = 315)			
No sex with a friend	31 (30%)	124 (59%)	155 (49%)
Sex with 1 friend	33 (32%)	48 (23%)	81 (26%)
Sex with >1 friend	40 (38%)	39 (18%)	79 (25%)
Highest level of sexual activity (N = 157)			
Genital manipulation	1 (1%)	3 (4%)	4 (3%)
Oral sex	10 (14%)	14 (16%)	24 (15%)
Vaginal or anal intercourse	61 (85%)	68 (80%)	129 (82%)
Members' dating status at the time of sexual activity (n = 161)			
Both members single, not dating	46 (63%)	64 (73%)	110 (68%)
At least one member dating	27 (37%)	24 (27%)	51 (32%)

the second wave of data collection, most (59 percent) reported never having dated the friend exclusively, followed by those who were friends at the time of the reported sexual contact but had since become romantic partners (13 percent), those who were once romantic partners but had "broken up" prior to the reported sexual encounter (9 percent), those who became romantic partners following the described event but have since "broken up" (9 percent), and those represented by some other relational history (10 percent).

Discussion

Our findings suggest that many college students have engaged in sexual activity in an otherwise platonic friendship and that, for many, the experience produces a perceived strengthening in relational quality.

Sexual Activity in Cross-Sex Friendships

Fifty-one percent reported having "had sex" with an opposite sex friend with whom they had no intentions of dating at the time of the sexual activity. Moreover, 34 percent of participants reported engaging in sexual activity in a friendship on multiple occasions (either with more than one friend or on several occasions with the same friend). In other words, for one-third of individuals, having sex in cross-sex friendships was more than a one-time "experiment." Although the data regarding frequency are noteworthy, it is important to keep the findings in perspective. After all, half of those who had engaged in sexual contact with a friend did so with only one of their friends, and the other half did so with [an average] of three friends, most likely a relatively small fraction of all of their cross-sex friendships. Given that we did not limit our analyses to "close" cross-sex friendships and were interested in individuals' lifelong history of friendships, the size of the available relational pool would be expected to be much greater than three.

The results run counter to the majority of existing scientific and lay opinion that sexual contact in cross-sex friendships is inevitably detrimental to these relationships. In fact, 67 percent of those who reported engaging in sexual activity with a friend perceived that the sexual contact increased relational quality. Intriguingly, 56 percent of that sexually active sample also reported that the friendship did not develop into a romantic relationship following the sexual act. In other words, many of those individuals who engage in sexual contact in a cross-sex friendship seem to experience it as relationship-enhancing, but also recognize the activity as part of the friendship, rather than as a behavior that accompanies a change in relational definition (i.e., from friend to romantic partner).

Of course, this experience is not universally endorsed. Some participants reported considerable relational damage from the behavior. Sexual acts that are experienced as positive and lead to an increase in confidence about the friend's intentions and feelings may improve friendships, while sexual acts that are experienced as negative and lead to a decrease in confidence about the friend's intentions and feelings will likely damage the relationship.

One implication of these findings is that friends should extensively discuss the meaning of sexual activity within their relationship. Doing so will likely make the experience more pleasurable. Given the substantial evidence that sexual communication is tied to sexual satisfaction, it again appears wise for friends to discuss the decision to engage in sexual activity prior to its enactment.

There are several questions left unanswered. First, the reasons underlying the decision to have sex with a friend may play an important role in influencing the outcomes. Preliminary analyses lend credibility to this claim. Fifty-five percent of our sample reported that alcohol consumption played at least some role in the decision to engage in sexual activity in the friendship. This finding is consistent with evidence citing the large impact of alcohol on college campuses. Future investigations should more systematically examine the reasons underlying the decision to engage in sexual contact in a friendship.

Second, this investigation, like the majority of research on cross-sex friendships, is limited by a bias toward heterosexual college-age participants. Life-span research has shown that the frequency of contact with cross-sex friends decreases dramatically after college, due both to opportunity and changes in marital status (Monsour, 1996). In addition, the notion that cross-sex friendships are fertile grounds for developing romantic attachments does not hold true for homosexual individuals.

References

Bell, R. R. (1981). Friendships of men and women. *Psychology of Women Quarterly, 5,* 402–417.

Bleske, A. L., and Buss, D. M. (2000). Can men and women be just friends? An evolutionary perspective. *Personal Relationships, 7,* 131–151.

Fuiman, M., Yarab, P., and Sensibaugh, C. (1997, July). *Just friends? An examination of the sexual, physical, and romantic aspects of cross-sex friendships.* Paper presented at the biannual meeting of the International Network on Personal Relationships, Oxford, OH.

Kaplan, D. L., and Keys, C. B. (1997). Sex and relationship variables as predictors of sexual attraction in cross-sex platonic friendships between young heterosexual adults. *Journal of Social and Personal Relationships, 14,* 191–206.

Messman, S. J., Canary, D. J., and Hause, K. S. (2000). Motives, strategies, and equity in the maintenance of platonic opposite-sex friendships. *Journal of Social and Personal Relationships, 17,* 67–94.

Monsour, M. (1992). Meanings of intimacy in cross- and same-sex friendships. *Journal of Social and Personal Relationships, 9,* 277–295.

——. (1996). Communication and cross-sex friendships across the life cycle: A review of the literature. In B. Burleson (Ed.), *Communication Yearbook 20* (pp. 375–414). Thousand Oaks, CA: Sage.

O'Sullivan, L. F., and Gaines, M. E. (1998). Decision-making in college students' heterosexual dating relationships: Ambivalence about engaging in sexual activity. *Journal of Social and Personal Relationships, 15,* 347–363.

Rubin, L. B. (1985). *Just friends.* New York: Harper & Row.

Sapadin, L. A. (1988). Friendships and gender perspectives of professional men and women. *Journal of Social and Personal Relationships, 5,* 387–403.

Werking, K. J. (1997). *We're just good friends: Women and men in nonromantic relationships.* New York: Guilford Press. ✦

Adapted by permission of Sage Publications, Ltd. from Afifi, W. A. and Faulkner, S. T. (2000). "On Being 'Just Friends': The Frequency and Impact of Sexual Activity in Cross-Sex Friendships," *Journal of Social and Personal Relationships, 17,* 205–222. Copyright © 2000 by Sage Publications.

3b

'I Like You . . . as a Friend': Attraction in Cross-Sex Friendship

Heidi M. Reeder

The assumption that attraction is prevalent in cross-sex friendship is revealed in many sources. Two recent movies (*When Harry Met Sally*, 1989; *My Best Friend's Wedding*, 1997) have sent the message that sexual and romantic attraction is a strong possibility in male-female friendships and that such relationships cannot stay platonic for long. Similarly, several television shows (e.g., *Friends*, 1994) have indicated that romantic attraction underlies male-female interactions, even if the participants are friends or roommates. The media is not the only place, however, that suggests this view. Much of the research on cross-sex friendship tends to take the perspective that attraction is a potential part of the experience. For example, O'Meara (1989) defines male-female friendship as a:

> Nonromantic, nonfamilial, personal relationship between a man and a woman. . . . Nonromantic does not mean, however, that sexuality and passion are necessarily absent from the relationship. (p. 526)

What does it mean that attraction is a potential issue in cross-sex friendship? Does attraction in this context mean "sexuality and passion," as O'Meara suggests?

Men and Women in Friendship

When the established norms dictate that males and females are expected to relate to one another in a sexualized and romanticized manner, and when behaving otherwise is subtly discouraged, it may ultimately be difficult for men and women to see each other in the friendship role. Cross-sex friendships do become more common in young adulthood, perhaps not coincidentally about the time when men and women begin their search for a mate. Then, after people marry, they have fewer close cross-sex friends (Rubin, 1985), serving to further reinforce the assumption that men and women have primarily sexual and romantic bonds. Moving into late adulthood, men and women are likely to keep this established trend of sex-segregated friendships (Adams, 1985).

Attraction in Cross-Sex Friendships

Researchers who have investigated attraction in cross-sex friendship have focused almost exclusively on one type of attraction—sexual. Sapadin (1988) found that the statement, "Friends can become my sexual partners" was affirmed by 64 percent of the men and 44 percent of the women. Bell (1981) found that 40 percent of female respondents wanted a sexual dimension in at least some of their cross-sex friendships. However, 39 percent of the women and 20 percent of the men said they abstain from sex with friends because they fear it could ruin the friendship. In fact, Werking (1997) found that 24 percent of terminated cross-sex friendships were due to problems caused by one or both friends' desire for romance/sexuality. Rubin (1985) hypothesized that engaging in sex is problematic because it changes the nature of the friendship. Because cultural norms suggest that sexually active parties are supposed to become emotionally involved, possessive, and committed, sexual activity changes the relationship such that it no longer conforms to the definition of friendship.

Study I

The purpose of this study was to investigate attraction in cross-sex friendship from the perspective of both friends. A broad and exploratory research question was proposed: How is attraction experienced in heterosexual cross-sex friendships?

Members of close, heterosexual cross-sex friendships were recruited to participate in individual in-depth interviews. A call for respondents was announced in undergraduate communication courses at a large southwestern university. Respondents were asked if their cross-sex friend would also be willing to come in for an interview. Only relationships where both friends were interviewed were included.

Friends were interviewed individually rather than in pairs so that they would not influence one another's answers and would feel more free to share private or negative information about the relationship. Participants were guaranteed confidentiality and are referred to by pseudonyms to protect their identities. Interviews were audio-recorded and lasted 30–60 minutes.

Forty people (20 cross-sex pairs) participated. These friendships ranged in length from 4 months to 7 years, with [an average] of 2 years. The sample was primarily European American (36 of 40 participants), with middle or upper-middle class backgrounds (34 of 40 participants), and an age range of 19–36, with [an average] of 21 years. Almost half of the interviewees were single, almost half were in committed but non-marital relationships, and one was divorced.

Results

Types of attraction. Participants differentiated between types of attraction. These friends took pains to explain that their friendship had one kind of attraction, but not another.

It was discovered that there are four qualitatively different types of attraction: subjective physical/sexual attraction, objective physical/sexual attraction, romantic attraction, and friendship attraction. These forms of attraction could exist separately or together, in varying degrees, to create different experiences in friendship.

Subjective and objective physical/sexual attraction. The first two types of attraction occurred when one's friend was perceived to be good-looking or sexy. Subjective physical/sexual attraction occurred when one found oneself feeling physically or sexually attracted to one's friend. Rena said, "When I first saw Rob I was like, 'Wow, he's cute'." Sean claimed, "I wouldn't mind going to bed with Dorothy. I mean, she's a good-looking girl." In most cases, these feelings of physical/sexual attraction were strongest at the beginning of the friendship.

Objective physical/sexual attraction occurred when respondents thought their friend was physically attractive, but they did not feel attracted to him or her. For example, Greg said, "Marylin's really attractive and I see that and I can relate to that, but I just don't feel the attraction myself."

Other participants did not feel physically attracted to their friend, nor did they suggest that others may find them attractive. Kraig said, "Beattie's not the kind of girl that I look at in a bar or anything like that." Even when there was some form of physical attraction, however, a romantic relationship was not necessarily desired.

Romantic attraction. Romantic attraction occurred when a participant believed that his/her friend would make a good boyfriend, girlfriend, or spouse. Romantic attraction was rare. Robert said, "I was interested in her . . . I wanted more than just a friendship." Rob said, "I still think of her as really cool and so that would make her a good girlfriend."

What was more typical was the lack of romantic attraction. Participants often identified many things about their friend that made them fine for friendship, but unsuitable for romance. Michael said, "Molly's really wild . . . that's not what I'm looking for in a relationship." Molly's perspective was, "We could never date because Michael is too serious for me . . . I'd kill him." Carla explained,

> I am not attracted to Ray's personality. We get along real well as people and we relate on the same level . . . but he is kind of anal in different ways and there are just things about him that I am not attracted to.

In all of these cases, the participant described the reasons his/her friend was not attractive for a romantic relationship. This did not mean, however, that the friend was unattractive for friendship. In fact, participants often described their friendship attraction by differentiating it from romantic attraction.

Friendship attraction. Most of the friends in this sample had grown to like each other, and sometimes love each other, as friends. Millie said, "I adore the guy and I really value his friendship." Jeff said,

> There's definitely a connection there. A certain chemistry. I'd say [friendship] chemistry is where you can sit down with someone and talk.

Nina said, "We look like we're best friends, it's the cutest thing. I love Austin." Michael said about his friend, "I love her like a sister. . . . There's a lot of care involved."

Friendship attraction was the strongest form of attraction experienced in this sample. Even participants who felt subjective physical/sexual and/or romantic attraction explained that those feelings were not strong enough to warrant jeopardizing the friendship. For example, Michael:

> I'm not going to sit here and lie and say I've never thought about sleeping with her. . . But for the most part those are boundaries I'm not willing to overstep just because of the fact that I've got too much invested in [the friendship], she's

got too much invested in it, [and] it would just go out the window.

Molly felt similarly. She had put aside romantic intentions in favor of the friendship:

> All my girlfriends are like, 'You guys should date' you know, they'll say stuff like that of course. So, you know, I've thought about it, but then I just don't think it'll work. I think we would ruin the friendship. . . . I think that it is perfect as it is, and if we even attempted to kiss or anything I think the relationship would probably be doomed.

Summary. There were many different kinds of attraction. Finding one's friend "cute" or "handsome" did not mean that one was attracted to one's friend. Thinking that someone is attractive as a friend is not the same as feeling physically attracted to him or her. Being physically attracted to someone is not the same as wanting to be in a romantic relationship with that person. These different forms of attraction created qualitatively different experiences in cross-sex friendship.

Symmetrical attraction occurred when both friends experienced the same types of attraction. For example, both people felt friendship, and no other form of attraction. In other cases, both people experienced friendship plus subjective physical/sexual attraction. *Asymmetrical* feelings occurred when friends had different experiences of attraction. In some cases, one person had friendship attraction and subjective physical/sexual attraction, while the other had only friendship attraction. In other cases, one person felt romantic attraction, while the other experienced only friendship attraction.

Asymmetrical romantic attraction was the most detrimental condition for cross-sex friendships. The pressure of one person wanting to make the friendship romantic often caused these friendships to become strained and ultimately less close.

Asymmetrical subjective physical/sexual attraction was rarely detrimental to these cross-sex friendships because those with physical attraction did not typically feel a desire to change the friendship. There was little motivation to make the friendship into a sexual relationship because without the mutual attraction needed to create a "spark," the relationship often felt friendly rather than passionate. A second reason participants with subjective physical/sexual attraction were not motivated to alter their friendship is that they tended to value their friendship more than their feelings of physical attraction. They did not want a sexual encounter to jeopardize an important friendship. Vanessa explained,

> I guess maybe if we were really trashed out of our minds we might sleep together. But I would never want to because I really like the friendship that we have.

Changes in attraction. The experience of attraction in cross-sex friendship could remain constant, or it could vary. While a few participants reported that their romantic attraction had grown, the most common change was dissipating romantic attraction. It was also possible for the other forms of attraction to change. For example, Nina did not like Austin when they first met, but friendship developed over time, "I thought he was annoying at first. But later I realized he was caring and funny." For Suzanne, when physical and romantic interest went away there was not much left to the friendship,

> When we first started hanging out together we would go eat and talk and we would call each other on the phone all the time, and it seemed like there was a little bit of a spark there, but there wasn't. . . . Now we never talk just to talk.

Study II

Study II was conducted to discover the frequency of each type of attraction and the frequency with which participants experienced more than one type of attraction within a given cross-sex friendship.

Eight instructors in the communication department at a southeastern university agreed to administer a questionnaire during class time to volunteer undergraduates.

A total of 231 participants identified as heterosexual (103 males and 128 females) were included. Participants' ages ranged from 17 to 41 years, with [an average] of 21 years. The sample was 72 percent European American, 23 percent African American, and 5 percent other ethnicities. Friendship length ranged from 1 month to 21 years, with [an average] of 4 years.

Participants were instructed to "think of a friend of the opposite-sex who is not a member of your family, and who is not a past or present boyfriend/girlfriend." They were asked to evaluate the types of attraction, and perceived changes in attraction, they had experienced for that person by checking *true or false* for 10 statements.

Results

Validating Study I, current friendship attraction was the most common experience (96 percent). This was followed by increased friendship attraction over time (71 percent). The third most common form of attraction was objective physical/sexual attraction, which was reported by just over half of the participants. Less common [was] subjective physical/sexual attraction (28 percent). In terms of romantic attraction, decreased romantic attraction was the most common (39 percent). Current romantic attraction (14 percent) and increased romantic attraction (9 percent) occurred less often.

Of those who were currently romantically attracted to their friend, a significant number (90 percent) had current subjective physical/sexual attraction as well. However, of those who were currently subjectively physically/sexually attracted ($n = 65$), fewer than half were also currently romantically attracted (46 percent). Of those who reported more subjective physical/sexual attraction over time, a significant number (91 percent) also reported more friendship attraction over time.

Discussion

While most laypersons, researchers, and media focus on romantic or sexual bonds between men and women, this study reveals that other types of bonds can and do occur.

Indeed, the majority of participants in this research did not experience romantic or sexual attraction toward their friend (Study II), and even those who did tended to prioritize their friendship attraction and not attempt to alter the friendship (Study I). In addition, these studies reveal that attraction is much more complicated than past research has suggested.

There is a qualitative difference between being attracted to someone as a friend, as a dating partner, and as a sexual partner, and these distinctions are very important to many members of cross-sex friendships. Further, these forms of attraction can combine in various ways that create different outcomes in the experience of the friendship. For example, some friendships had only one form of attraction, while others had multiple forms. It is interesting that (in Study II), of those participants who were currently subjectively physically/sexually attracted to their friend, fewer than half were also currently romantically attracted, while nearly all of those who were currently romantically attracted also reported that they felt current subjective physical/sexual attraction. This indicates, perhaps, that physical/sexual attraction is a greater prerequisite for romantic attraction than romantic attraction is a prerequisite for physical attraction. For some people romantic and/or subjective physical/sexual attraction occurs along with friendship attraction, and when these former types of attraction decrease, the friendship attraction decreases as well.

There are several possible reasons why friendship attraction grows while romantic and physical/sexual attraction declines in most friendships. First, it may be that as friends get to know one another over time, they begin to see flaws (either physically and/or in terms of personality) that make the other less physically or romantically ideal. Second, it is potentially the case that, in order for friendships to be maintained, these attractions must decrease. It is possible that those relationships that sustained high levels of romantic attraction over time would not be included in this study because they would no longer be friendships.

Conclusion

The bonds between men and women may be changing. Male-female social relationships can be based on something other than romance and sex. Cross-sex friendships may be a place where men and women can see one another not only as mates and objects, but also as comrades and pals.

While cross-sex friends may be asked by mutual friends and researchers alike, "Are you two attracted to each other or not?," the results of this study suggest that there is not a yes or no answer to this question. Indeed, cross-sex friends would have to reply, "Which one of us, at what point in the friendship, and what kind of attraction?"

References

Adams, R. (1985). People would talk: Normative barriers to cross-sex friendship for elderly women. *The Gerontologist, 25,* 605–611.

Bell, R. (1981). *Worlds of friendship.* Beverly Hills, CA: Sage.

O'Meara, J. D. (1989). Cross-sex friendship: Four basic challenges of an ignored relationship. *Sex Roles, 21,* 525–543.

Rubin, L. (1985). *Just friends.* New York: Harper & Row.

Sapadin, L. (1988). Friendships and gender: Perspectives of professional men and women. *Journal of Social and Personal Relationships, 5,* 387–403.

Werking, K. (1997). *We're just good friends.* New York: Guilford Press. ✦

Adapted by permission of Sage Publications, Ltd. from Reeder, H. M. (2000). "I Like You . . . as a Friend: The Role of Attraction in Cross-sex Friendship," *Journal of Social and Personal Relationships, 17,* 329–348. Copyright © 2000 by Sage Publications.

Issue 3: Questions to Consider

1. Based on the findings of these two studies, what do you conclude—can men and women *really* be just friends?

2. Is the possibility of a sexual encounter always lurking in the background of friendships between men and women?

3. Are your friendships with the other sex the same as or different from the friendships you have with persons who are the same sex as you are? How do you explain this?

4. The results of both of these studies were based on samples of college students. Some researchers contend that this is not a valid age group (18–23) to study because adults older than 30 tend to have few friends of the other sex unless those friends are part of a couple. Do you think friendships between older men and women differ from friendships among men and women in college? Why or why not?

5. Were you surprised by the percentage of college students that were attracted to their cross-sex friends? Why or why not?

6. If these studies had been done at your school would the findings be similar or would they differ? Explain your answer. ✦

Issue 4: Introduction

Living Together: Preparation for Marriage or Playing at Commitment?

In a relatively short period of time, cohabitation has gone from being an unacceptable, socially stigmatized situation ("living in sin," "shacking up") to nearly the norm in the United States. The increase in cohabitation may be the most rapidly occurring demographic change in our history. In a period of less than 40 years, we have moved from cohabiting as grounds for expulsion from college to cohabiting as the residential choice of 30 to 40 percent of college students at any given time.

Cohabitation tends to be viewed in two ways—as an alternate to marriage or as a stage in courtship, sort of an advanced engagement period. Although we have not embraced cohabitation as an alternative to marriage to the extent that is true in some countries (e.g., about 30 percent of Swedish households consist of couples who cohabit compared to only 7 percent in the United States) (Rindfuss and VandenHeuvel, 1990), Seltzer (2001) concluded from her review of research in the '90s that cohabitation is becoming similar to legal marriage in that both are child-rearing institutions. Pamela J. Smock (2000), a sociologist at the University of Michigan Institute for Social Research, has reported that nearly half of previously married cohabiters and 35 percent of never-married cohabiters have children in the household.

Smock also reported that the percentage of marriages preceded by cohabitation increased from approximately 10 percent in 1965 to over half by 1994, and it is experienced by virtually all segments of society. According to Smock, about 40 percent of cohabiting couples end their relationship within five years, whereas another 55 percent eventually marry. Twenty percent of all first marriages have ended after five years so the five-year dissolution rate for cohabitation is approximately double that for marriage. Thus, cohabiting relationships are considerably less stable than legal marriages.

There has been considerable publicity in recent years implying that cohabitation increases the risk of later divorce. For example, the July 28, 2001, *USA Today* published an opinion piece by David Popenoe, a Rutgers sociologist, in which he warned about the dangers of cohabiting (e.g., increase in the risk of divorce, increase in domestic violence, lower levels of happiness and well-being), but he failed to note that the evidence he cited is correlational and *not causal*. That is, the fact that two events co-occur to some degree does not mean that one event causes the other. Many researchers refute Popenoe's claim. For example, Jay Teachman, also a sociologist, concluded from his research that the effect of cohabitation on marital stability could be attributed to the fact the cohabitants have spent more time in the relationship than noncohabitants (Teachman, Tedrow, and Crowder, 2000). When you consider the total length of time in the relationship, there is no difference in marital disruption between those who cohabited prior to marriage and those who didn't. Other researchers contend that the differences are due to *self-selection factors*. That is, people who cohabit tend to be less religious and conservative than those who don't. Because of their worldviews they are also more likely to divorce if they believe themselves to be in a bad marriage. Although couples who are more religious and conservative are less likely to cohabit or divorce because of their worldviews, this does not mean that they are happier or more satisfied in their marriages. There is no evidence to date that choosing to cohabit will *cause* you to divorce or *make* you happier in marriage. The *reasons* for your choice whether to cohabit or not are more salient than is your choice.

In spite of cohabitation becoming a more frequent alternative to legal marriage, the more common view of cohabitation continues to be that it is a stage in courtship or an advanced step in the engagement period. Some individuals, perhaps especially those who have experienced their parents' divorce, consider cohabitation as a way to screen partners and avoid a bad marriage and subsequent divorce. Similarly, some couples that cohabit are uncertain whether or not they want to marry, but they are considering it. Others plan to marry, but for financial constraints or other reasons must postpone marriage, at least for the near future. A final group cohabits, but at least one member of the couple is not considering marriage, at least to their current partner.

Demographers Ron Rindfuss and Audrey VandenHeuvel (1990) found that about two-thirds of the cohabiters in their study did not have immediate marriage plans, at least within the next 12 months. This finding would argue against the "cohabitation as advanced engagement stage" hypothesis. They concluded that cohabitation was more likely a convenient living arrangement for individuals not yet ready to make a long-term commitment. They concluded that cohabitation fell somewhere between marriage and being single, and that cohabiters were more similar to singles than to married couples. They raised questions about the reasons for the rise in cohabitation relative to the decline in marriage (at least early marriage). Is cohabitation another sign of individualism and a lack of commitment to institutions such as marriage and the family? Or is cohabitation a way to prepare for later marriage?

The two articles provided for your reading present two sides of cohabitation as "courtship stage." One highly recommends it; the other does not. Similar cases could probably be built for cohabitation as an alternative to legal marriage, but we assumed that students reading this book would more likely relate to cohabitation as courtship stage.

References

Rindfuss, R., and VandenHeuvel, A. (1990). Cohabitation: A precursor to marriage or an alternative to being single? *Population and Development Review, 16*, 703–726.

Seltzer, J. (2001). Families formed outside of marriage. *Journal of Marriage and the Family, 62*, 1247–1268.

Smock, P. J. (2000). Cohabitation in the United States: An appraisal of research themes, findings, and implications. *Annual Review of Sociology, 26*, 1–20.

Teachman, J., Tedrow, L., and Crowder, K. (2000). The changing demography of America's families. *Journal of Marriage and the Family, 62*, 1134–1246. ✦

4a

Living Together Is Just Playing at a Committed Relationship

Esther Crain

I lived through living together, and I'll never do it again. Sure, the first couple of months were ideal: We cooked elaborate dinners for friends and had super hot sex whenever we wanted. But after 3 months, the little things I once thought cute—his goofy morning milk mustache, his fascination with Bruce Lee flicks—began to irk me. Nor did he think my running up massive long-distance phone charges and expecting him to foot half the bill was so charming either. Our sex life slowed, grudges and irritations piled up. Before the lease was over, we admitted we had made a terrible mistake. And so a once-great relationship tanked completely—two people not ready for marriage crushed under all of marriage's burdens. So if you and your beau are contemplating cohabitation, unpack your bags and take this reality check.

You hear moving in together is like test driving a car? Well, if you're going to put love on the same level as a used Toyota, that's fine—but who says you need to cosign a lease to do it? If you pay attention, you can easily road test him while you're dating. Suss out his true character during long weekends at his apartment and on vacations. Then, if you can't work with his character flaws or quirks, you can break up—no real-estate agent required.

But even if you decide you can live with each other's little lunacies, there's another drawback to daily domesticity—boredom in the bedroom. "At first, we had sex all the time," recalls my friend Heather, who has lived with her man for a year.

Now we're down to cuddling in front of the 10 o'clock news. I hear lusty stories from single friends and think, That used to be us! We've become an old married couple and we're not even married yet!

Living together accelerates a relationship so much that if all it has going for it is lust, you'll find out fast when that lust dies. It's good to realize the relationship wasn't meant to be, but you'll save yourself trouble if you realize it before moving in.

Plenty of couples get tripped up by money, but at least in marriage, the guidelines are clearer: Most married couples pay the bills from a joint bank account, stash money away together for retirement, and when you buy things, they belong to you both. With living together, cash confusion soon crops up because you're handling finances the way any two platonic roommates do, yet you're not platonic roommates—you're a couple. Who will pay for the plumber when the drain is clogged . . . if your hair caused the clog? If he gets a raise, should his share of the rent rise too?

This is what came between my friend Dave and his live-in love, Melissa.

Once I got my new job and higher salary, Melissa thought she shouldn't have to pay half the rent anymore. That sounded fair until I realized I had new expenses that ate up my raise—better suits, dry-cleaning costs, and extra gas money. Melissa countered that she had hidden expenses too. We squabbled all the time. Whenever the rent check was due, we'd barely speak to each other.

Breaking off any relationship is hard, but breaking it off once you share a bathroom can be a real-estate nightmare. When my friend Audrey learned her live-in was sleeping with her best bud, she was horrified to find she couldn't leave because both their names were on the lease. "I crashed on friends' couches rather than go back to that apartment, though I was still paying rent."

Another couple forced to live out their lease pulled a Brady: They drew a line down the middle of the loft, just like Peter and Bobby did, and pledged to stay on their own sides with the help of a makeshift screen wall. Anthony explains: "I thought I was in a bad sitcom, but the way Jenna cried on the phone all the time to her friends proved to me it was real." And Jenna's side of the story?

> Of course I cried. I realized I had wasted my 20s with someone who didn't want to marry me. I had to start over, but I was still tied to this man because of a landlord. I felt trapped.

Jenna and Anthony's situation hits on another common cohabitation pitfall. Let's call it live-in limbo: One of you is content just to live together, while the other wants to take the next step—marriage. Living together can be a comfortable compromise, one that becomes harder and harder to move beyond. Your man may wonder why that little piece of paper should mean so much anyway. On the other hand, you've grown used to your comfy live-in status, and breaking up seems like more effort than it's worth. You're in live-in limbo: Unable to go forward, unwilling to go back.

This is what my friend Megan discovered after she and her boyfriend, Scott, grew so cozily cohabited that marriage became an institution he could do without.

> "Scott started thinking that since we already had health benefits through our jobs, and I wasn't planning to change my last name to his, what did we need marriage for?

Megan eventually got her man to the altar. But many couples trudge on, stuck living together—in live-in limbo indefinitely and unhappily.

Finally, the shakiest thing about living together is the term itself, which sounds casual and noncommittal. Any two people can do it—from college freshmen to prison inmates. It requires no emotional ties at all: no ceremony, no vows, and no promise to work things out when you hit those inevitable tough times, says my friend Matt, who is now married but lived with a previous girlfriend for 5 years.

"It's not enough to think you're as good as married just because both of your names are on the mailbox," Matt says.

> At my wedding, after we said our vows, it hit me—we were married. That little piece of paper I had made fun of for years actually means something. Without it, you're just playing house—a perfect way to ensure that a promising relationship will end painfully.

As for me, I'm dating someone who also has a cohabitation skeleton in his romantic closet. We're both leery of officially living in sin, but that doesn't mean we never plan to shack up. Should we ever decide to sign a lease, we've agreed on just one condition— we'll have made plans to sign a marriage certificate first. ✦

Brown, R., and Crain, E. (1998, September). "Are You Thinking of Living Together? Then You Need to Read This." *Cosmopolitan*, 225(3), 272–275.

4b

Living Together Is Good Preparation for Marriage and for Life

Robyn Brown

I'm "living in sin" and loving it. About a year ago, my boyfriend, Tom, and I moved in together. While we suspected that marriage might be in our future, neither of us was chomping at the bit to make me a Mrs. So we decided to try living together. And I've since discovered that in addition to making great financial sense—one apartment is a lot cheaper than two—there are plenty of other reasons cohabitation is nonmarital bliss.

You wouldn't buy a car without taking it for a test-drive, and it's no different with a man. Tom and I dated for three years before we shacked up, and I've learned more about him this past year than all the others combined. Living together is like taking a crash course in all of each other's quirks. And let's be honest—do you really want to wait until you're married to find out he goes berserk if he sees a single crumb on the kitchen counter? And doesn't he deserve to know that you have a pathological obsession with [your favorite television show]? Believe me, if you're going to share everything, everything matters.

You may know the man you're dating, but you don't necessarily know what he's like to live with. Some men make good boyfriends but lousy husbands. My friend Meredith says that living with her fiancé, Scott, for a few months saved her from a marriage that she's certain would have ended in disaster. Meredith says Scott was always a dream date—courteous, sweet, and dripping with class. But after they moved in together, he turned into a Neanderthal.

> His half-eaten salami sandwiches were in every room, and he absolutely refused to clean up after himself—even after we found bugs in the house,

Meredith recalls. "That's when I realized that my husband-to-be wasn't classy, just a spoiled slob." One morning, Meredith poured herself cereal for breakfast and noticed little larvae in the bowl. Her bags were packed by noon.

Living together is like flooring the gas pedal on your relationship—its 24-7 intensity accelerates whatever is going to happen next, for better or for worse. My friend Stephanie, for instance, says that moving in with her longtime lover was the best decision she ever made because it drove her to dump him. "Our so-so relationship would have dragged on indefinitely if we hadn't decided to push it and see," says Stephanie.

> Spending all that time together gave me the chance to see the real, nondate him—and the real him was an emotionally distant jerk.

Part of the reason living together shifts your relationship into fourth gear is that it guarantees you'll get a peek at each other's less attractive sides. He'll see you turning in for the night with your face covered in Clearasil. You'll walk in on him lip-synching in the bathroom mirror. Sharing these dirty little secrets can bring the two of you even closer together or send you screaming into the night.

I know, I know. He won't buy the cow if he can have the milk for free. But who decided Bessie was even for sale? My friend Rebecca says that she loves living with her boyfriend, Lionel, and has no intentions of tying the knot anytime in the near future. "I love that our lives are entwined but still separate," Rebecca explains. "Someday in the future I may want to be married, but for now, I'm still really enjoying my singleness."

On the other hand, my friend Alexis never lived with her boyfriend Paul until they had a wedding so expensive it would have made Donald Trump cry. A month later, she called me and told me she was getting a divorce—turns out marriage wasn't anything like she had imagined it. "The first couple weeks were really fun. It was just like playing house," recalls Alexis.

But after a while the novelty wore off, and we started to see marriage for what it really is—a lot of hard work. Whose job is it to balance the checkbook?

Should we invest some of our savings in the stock market? Our romantic relationship just was not ready to withstand that kind of strain.

The only thing perfect about marriage is the airbrushed wedding photo. Living together helps you see past romanticized notions and clue in to what marriage will really be like. If my boyfriend and I ever decide to tie the knot, it will mean even more, because we'll both fully understand the vows that we're taking. When they say "Do you promise to love, honor, and cherish," we'll know what they're really asking. Can you be patient when he calls for the third time to say he still hasn't left the office? Do you truly want to be with a man who refuses to eat a single green vegetable? Can you live a lifetime of sleeping with the TV on? Well, if it means I get to wake up every day next to him, I do. ✦

Brown, R., & Crain, E. (1998, September). "Are You Thinking of Living Together? Then You Need to Read This." *Cosmopolitan, 225*(3), 272–275.

Issue 4: Questions to Consider

1. Why do you think scholars are in such disagreement regarding the effect that cohabitation has on marriage and future divorce? Are they interpreting the research data differently? Do they have their own worldviews and social agendas? How might you determine the social agendas of scholars?

2. What factors would determine your decision about whether or not to cohabit?

3. Do you think, as Rindfuss and VandenHeuvel suggested, that the focus on individualism in the United States might be contributing to the increase in cohabitation? If individualism were a contributing factor, how would you explain the high rate of cohabitation in cultures such as Sweden that are not known for their individualism?

4. What are your predictions about the future of marriage? The future of cohabitation?

5. Is cohabitation good preparation for marriage or is it no preparation for marriage (or even preparation for divorce)?

6. Make a list of what you consider to be good reasons for cohabiting. Make another list of what you consider to be good reasons for not cohabiting. Compare your lists. What conclusions can you draw? ✦

Issue 5: Introduction

Does Distance Make the Heart Grow Fonder or Go Wander? Can Long-Distance Romance Work?

Living apart from one's partner or spouse is an increasingly common experience that is likely to become even more common in the future, not just for college students but for married adults of all ages. Dual-career couples often find it necessary to reside apart for professional reasons, sometimes for relatively short periods and sometimes as a way of life.

In the study that follows, Arditti and Kauffman examine how college students maintain long-distance relationships. They wanted to find out how couples who live apart manage to stay close. As you read this study, think about the challenges and barriers to maintaining a long-distance romantic relationship. Some challenges are mentioned by the people in this study, but it is likely that there are others faced by couples who live apart. Think also about ways to overcome these barriers and challenges. Are there ways to bridge the distance that college students in this study did not use? ✦

5a

Staying Close When Apart: Intimacy and Meaning in Long-Distance Dating Relationships

Joyce A. Arditti and Melissa Kauffman

In recent years long-distance romantic relationships have become increasingly common. For example, about one-third of premarital relationships in university settings may be long-distance in nature. Job mobility as well as educational pursuits have created a need for many romantically involved couples to be geographically separated.

Long-distance relationships (LDRs) may suffer because they lack the support of shared social networks, and partners cannot easily communicate or be affectionate with each other. Physical separation also increases the potential for individuals to mislead each other. On the other hand, LDRs may provide a context whereby individuals are free to think about themselves, their partners, and their relationships in new and creative ways.

The purpose of this study was to explore long-distance dating relationships. Little information is available describing how couples maintain intimacy while geographically separated. What little we do know is based on research on commuter marriages that may not apply to single romantic partners. The main questions guiding the study were: How do long-distance couples stay close? What shared meanings do individuals have with their long-distance romantic partners? Why do individuals stay in long-distance relationships? Ten college students that had dated their partners for at least six months in long-distance relationships were interviewed.

How do LDRs stay emotionally connected? Every person we interviewed used the telephone to varying degrees, most used e-mail, and some planned regular visits with their distant partners to stay close. There was a wide range of tolerance for disconnection, and there were differences in how frequently they needed to contact their partners in order to feel close to them.

Every person relied on the telephone as the primary link with their partner, although individuals varied in the frequency of phone use. For some, the need to talk to their partner was more important than anything—finances, school, work, whatever. One woman said that she had to talk with her boyfriend every night and, if they missed a night, they talked even longer the next night. Sam, a teaching assistant, and his girlfriend called each other daily and talked as long as they wanted, ignoring expenses.

However, not everyone was interested in talking with their partners daily. For students who emphasized school, the LDRs met their relationship needs but they also gave each other enough "space" to do their work. For example, Kim and Amanda talked by phone with their partners about once a week, stating that they felt they needed to stay completely focused on academics. Kim explained that difficult engineering courses left her little time for leisure and therefore planned weekly phone conversations, supplementing them with short daily e-mails. She seemed satisfied with this mutually agreed-upon schedule. Amanda needed to spend hours on horticulture projects and said she lacked the free time to get distracted by calling her boyfriend. She was satisfied with having little contact with her boyfriend while she finished her degree:

> I almost don't want him up here. I would be too distracted, I wouldn't be able to concentrate as much on my school work. . . . Yeah, in a warped sort of way it is kind of good that he is not here. We stay close when we are apart by calling a lot, sending a lot of e-mails, just reinforcing that we are thinking about each other even though we are separated and things are a little bit different, but it is not really. You can still talk to each other and communicate about things when you need to.

Other couples had "rules" about limiting phone calls because of expenses. Most LDRs supplemented phone calls with e-mail to cut down on costs. Darren and his girlfriend creatively used a free internet program:

> We talk a lot on the phone, especially recently, because on the Internet you can make free phone calls, so we usually talk to each other at least every other day.

In addition, planning visits provided comfort during the physical absence. Of course, there were constraints concerning how often they were able to visit each other, such as money, academic schedules, proximity, and their willingness/ability to travel. Some participants were able to see each other every weekend, while others, separated by greater distances, had to wait until major school breaks.

Some students set up their academic schedules so that they could frequently visit their partners. For example, Marcus, who lived 300 miles from his partner, said:

We have been seeing each other every 2 weeks . . . I set up my schedule so that I don't have anything on Friday at all. So I leave Thursday and I get back late Monday.

Sam and his girlfriend both loved road trips, so they viewed the five-hour drive separating them as an "inconvenience," but not a defining feature of the relationship:

> We have seen each other every single weekend. . . . It doesn't really feel like a long-distance relationship to me. It is a distance inconvenience, not a time inconvenience. We don't go long periods of time without seeing each other, because we are both willing to travel.

Both of these men demonstrated a willingness to travel frequently despite the distance. Having control over one's time and resources was connected with the ability to travel frequently. A positive view about the situation—minimizing the importance of geographic separation—also seemed to facilitate visiting and relationship satisfaction.

What shared meanings do individuals have with their long-distance romantic partners? Geographic distance was not related to how close partners felt. Instead, the meanings attached to their situation, regardless of how often they talked to or saw their partners, seemed to be most important. For example, meanings such as *not being distracted from academics* or the *importance of staying connected despite costs* made it easier for them to cope with separation.

Age, maturity, distaste for the "dating scene," and a desire to settle down and get married in the near future were attributes that the students felt contributed to their desires to be committed to their partners. These attributes also served to keep them out of new relationships that could threaten the LDRs. They took their relationships seriously and seemed to know what they were seeking in a lifetime partner. Sam emphasized his belief in committing to one person and his lack of interest in casual dating:

I don't believe in dating other people. . . . If you date other people, you are obviously not in love and you are just kind of looking for . . . somebody to have sex with, somebody to hold your hand, or have some kind of affection.

Several others shared Sam's attitude about dating other people. They thought that it would have been acceptable at the beginning of their relationship to date other people because they had not explicitly committed themselves to their partners, but they felt a growing commitment over time. These individuals admitted that they neither had the time nor the desire to date others.

In fact, only one person still thought they had the option of dating other people.

We talked about it a little bit and we just both decided that since we are both separated so much it would be better if we did date other people, if we wanted to. I haven't, and I didn't really ask him if he has. We did talk about it, but it is not something that we discuss all the time. . . . We date other people if either one of us wants to, but it is definitely more of a casual thing dating. It is not as if I think he would go out and find somebody that he would prefer over me. . . . We have known each other for so long . . . it is not something that is really a big deal.

Overall, these students were committed to their partners. They felt trust and exclusivity were central to their relationships. The issue of trust was particularly meaningful—several thought that without trust, LDRs would never work. For example, Lucy said: "I trust him. I mean that is the bottom line. I trust him, and I know he trusts me. I mean there is not even a question. We have established that." Despite this, she admitted that sometimes "her mind played tricks on her," and she felt insecure.

The predominant view of the separation was that it was an *investment for the future*. Most felt that changing academic plans in order to be geographically closer to their partners was not feasible. Academic and career plans were deemed essential to either their or their partners' professional growth.

This was a critical part of the shared meaning system for some couples. Amanda's comments reflect her unwillingness to change her academic study for the relationship:

I would not compromise my education, I wouldn't sacrifice anything . . . and he has such a good job . . . so I don't think he would move back up just until I finish school.

Most of them focused on the temporary nature of the separation. Having an end in sight made it easier for couples to deal with the long-distance status of their relationships. Jaime reflected this,

We realized that it would be a temporary situation, and it is okay as long as I know we are going to be together after I do this. It is like a Christmas present, you know it is there, you are just waiting to open it.

Similarly, Darren, realizing that a two-year separation would create greater career potential:

I look at it as a positive thing in the future, because we are both going to school for reasons, I guess to have better careers in the future, so in that way it would be better.

In addition to defining the separation as *necessary and temporary*, perceiving the separation as a factor that made them feel even closer to their partners made the experience more acceptable. Specifically, "not taking their partner for granted" and "developing a stronger connection through non-physical communication," were two issues that emerged from all of the interviews. This suggests how important it was for them to think positively about the situation. Marcus explained that after coming to school he realized how "great his girlfriend was. It's just the more I was down here, the more I realized what I missed." Sam also mentioned that being away from his girlfriend had made him cherish her more:

It has made us stronger. When you are constantly around somebody, you tend to take them for granted. I see a lot of that among my friends.

Not everyone felt that absence made their hearts grow fonder—for some the lack of physical intimacy was a negative part of the separation.

Why do individuals stay in long-distance relationships? Despite the sense of commitment to their partners, several people identified difficulties they had in maintaining the relationship. Among these were fear and uncertainty about being apart, the potential to "grow apart," and loneliness.

Lucy feared that the separation might affect the closeness she felt toward her partner if it was for a much longer period of time. She was unable to focus on the separation as temporary because she was not certain about when the separation would end, thus making her situation more ambiguous than the other respondents.

> As I start looking at this more closely, the longer we stay separated, that may cause a strain if we don't see one another. 'Cause there is a chance that we may grow apart.

Jaime admitted that the separation had negatively impacted both her and her boyfriend. "I am not as secure in our relationship because he is so far away, [and] I don't think either one of us are really as happy overall." Jaime was upset about the distance because she was unhappy about her boyfriend's decision to move away and get a job suggesting a lack of agreement about the need for the separation. Kim also clearly viewed the separation negatively. She initially stated that the distance did not really hurt that much, but deeper probing revealed that she believed the separation had kept the relationship from progressing. Kim admitted that she wished she had dated her boyfriend for longer before they were separated and was not convinced that she would be able to continue to connect as well with him from a distance. She explained:

> I don't think it is a good thing. . . . If we had started out earlier . . . before he left, it would have been better. I would know more about him, things like that, now he is far away, and it's kind of hard, you know.

It seemed that ambiguity regarding the length of the separation and the absence of an "end date" contributed to uncertainty about future plans and difficulty with the long-distance experience. Both Lucy and Kim were uncertain about how long they would be separated from their boyfriends. It is worth noting that Jaime was the only participant whose partner *left her* to go to a geographically distant location. The other nine participants were the ones who *left their partners*. The issue of who leaves and why has bearing on relationship satisfaction and on ways individuals handle the separation. If both members of a couple do not view the separation the same way, it seems more likely that the separation would contribute to either or both partners' unhappiness. The leaver may be less attached to the partner than the one who was left. It makes sense that the more attached an individual is to their romantic partner, the more distressed they will be when separated.

All of the respondents were occasionally lonely and sad over the lack of physical intimacy caused by separation. They discussed various ways that they dealt with these feelings, including thinking about the partner or by doing something to take their minds off their loneliness. Several of them coped by developing a "positive personal philosophy" about LDRs in general and about the specific effects of the separation on their relationships. Skip jokingly refuted the old adage, "Absence makes the heart grow fonder," by saying, "That is just a crock in my opinion!" His philosophy, *it's just one of those things*, made the separation into a "minor inconvenience." He felt that other problems in his relationship had been more difficult than the separation. "You know the distance is . . . nothing, a long-distance relationship is a cakewalk."

Personal philosophies about what constituted "good relationships" helped individuals cope by focusing on the positive aspects of their relationships. Lucy explained her philosophy: "I think when you both trust each other and you both love each other then you have a solid foundation. We have that foundation." Passionately explaining his philosophy on LDRs, Sam stated:

> If they fail, I think it is due to lack of effort, laziness, lack of character. If two people decide that they want something, then the only way it is not going to happen, is if they let it not happen. So if we broke up there is nobody to blame but ourselves. You can't blame the distance, you can't blame the time, you can't blame any of that, because if you truly love somebody, it is not an issue. . . .

Sam's personal philosophy emphasized working hard on the relationship and not giving up.

In summary, trust was cited as an essential aspect of satisfying LDRs. The mostly positive views about LDRs were helped by emphases on the temporary and necessary nature of the separations. Overall, respondents accepted their situations, although those who had been "left behind" or who were uncertain about when the geographic separation would end were less positive overall. Most believed that the distance did not affect how well they knew their partners. This may have been because they all considered their partners to be good friends, and they attributed the success of their relationships to this. Although admitting that LDRs could be difficult, they believed that their partner was "the one" for them—this belief helped support them being sexually faithful. Idealizing the partner may help the relationship continue by minimizing the possibility of meeting other potential mates and by justifying the separation as valid. ✦

Arditti, J., and Kauffman, M. (2001). *Staying Close When Apart: Intimacy and Meaning in Long-Distance Dating Relationships*. Unpublished manuscript. Reprinted by permission of Joyce Arditti and Melissa Kauffman.

Issue 5: Questions to Consider

1. How did the students in this study manage to feel close to their partners even though they lived apart? Would these strategies work as well for older adults (for example, married people)?

2. What about being apart bothered the people in this study? Can you think of other challenges that might face people in long distance relationships?

3. Have you ever had a long-distance relationship? What factors made it work or not work? If you have not had an LDR, would you ever have one? Why or why not?

4. Arditti and Kauffman speculate that the individuals in their study might be less accepting of their long-distance relationships if they did not think they would be together in a fairly short time. Do you agree or disagree with this speculation? Do you think that long-distance relationships that are permanent arrangements (those that have no specific end date) face different problems than the ones found in this study? ✦

Issue 6: Introduction

'Goin' to the Chapel and . . .': Does Marriage Matter?

Most adults in our society marry, but in recent years a rapid rise in cohabiting relationships, growing numbers of births to unmarried women, and a significant increase in the age of first marriages have alarmed some people. There appears to be a widespread rejection of marriage, or at least many individuals are delaying marriage. Social observers, scholars, policy-makers, and community leaders wonder what these trends mean. They worry that marriage as a social institution and as a relationship is in serious trouble, and may not survive (see Issues 4 and 19 for further discussion of this).

Others think that the meaning of marriage is changing. They argue that individuals expect a great deal of personal fulfillment from marriage and are willing to forgo marriage unless such expectations are met. People who hold this view often believe that other relationships (cohabiting relationships, for instance) are acceptable alternatives to marriage.

Still other social scientists contend that we are witnessing a temporary retreat from marriage due to changes related to expectations regarding equality between men and women. These social scientists think that marriages will make a comeback as young people adjust to egalitarian expectations of marriage (Nock, 2001).

It is not clear if the meaning of marriage is changing, or if marriage is gradually losing its desirable status, becoming simply one option out of many types of close relationships, or if marriage is temporarily less desirable to men and women struggling to figure out how to be equals. Whatever the case, marriage currently is seen as having high costs, especially by women (Nock, 2001).

Two very different papers examine the issue of whether marriage is a desirable or an undesirable status. In the first selection, journalists take a look at why women are leaving their marriages, avoiding marriage altogether, and, in general, acting as if they could take it or leave it. In contrast, sociologist Linda Waite reviews several large national data sets to document "why marriage matters" to women and men. As a researcher and a scholar, she clearly thinks that is it an advantage to be married and that people need to be informed of the benefits of marriage.

As you read these articles, make two lists—one of reasons why women avoid marriage and the other of the advantages of marriage for women. Examine your lists to see how much overlap there is between them. Which list is longer? Which list most closely reflects your thinking regarding whether or not to marry?

Reference

Nock, S. (2001). The marriages of equally dependent spouses. *Journal of Family Issues*, 22, 756–777. ✦

6a

Flying Solo

Tamala M. Edwards with Tammerlin Drummond and Elizabeth Kauhnan, Anne Mofiet, Jacqueline Savaiano, and Maggie Stager

More women are deciding that marriage is not inevitable, that they can lead a fulfilling life as a single. It's an empowering choice, but for many not an easy one.

Jodie Hannaman grew up in Houston, a city as fond of formal weddings as of barbecues and rodeos. So it was saying something at Duschene Academy, her Roman Catholic girls' school, that Hannaman was chosen as Most Likely to Be Married First. But her teenage fantasies of butter cream frosting and silky bridesmaids' dresses first began to crack with her high school sweetheart. He dated her for more than a decade before she finally got tired of waiting for a marriage proposal that was never going to come. There were other men after that, but it was Hannaman who repeatedly decided against a life built for two. Marriage, it began to dawn on her, wasn't an end in itself but rather something she wanted only if she found the right guy.

Now Hannaman, 32, spends 60 hours a week in her job as project manager for Chase Bank of Texas in Houston in an office decorated with art museum magnets and *Cathy* cartoons. She extends her business trips into the weekends for solo mini-vacations, enjoys the social whirl of the Junior League volunteer circuit and has started looking for a house. While she would love a great romance that would lead to marriage, she no longer feels she has to apologize for being single. "I've finally matured enough to acknowledge that there's more to life than being married," she says. "I'd like to get married and have kids, but something in the past few years has changed. I'm happier being single."

Hannaman might seem to have little in common with the four lead characters on TV's *Sex and the City*, single women who discard men quicker than last season's bag and shoes—and look good doing it. Her sex life isn't nearly as colorful, for one thing. All of them, nevertheless, are part of a major societal shift: Single women, once treated as virtual outcasts, have moved to the center of our social and cultural life. Unattached females—wisecracking, gutsy gals, not pathetic saps—are the *heroine du jour* in fiction, from Melissa Bank's collection of stories, *The Girls' Guide to Hunting and Fishing*, to Helen Fielding's *Bridget Jones's Diary*, the publishing juggernaut that has spawned one sequel and a movie. The single woman is TV's It Girl as well, on a growing number of network shows focused on strong, career-minded single women.

The single woman has come into her own. Not too long ago, she would live a temporary existence: a rented apartment shared with a girlfriend or two and a job she could easily ditch. Adult life—a house, a car, travel, children—only came with a husband. Well, gone are the days. Forty-three million women are currently single—more than 40 percent of all adult females, up from about 30 percent in 1960. (The ranks of single men have grown at roughly the same rate.) If you separate out women of the most marriageable age, the numbers are even more head snapping. In 1963, 83 percent of women 25 to 55 were married; by 1997 that figure had dropped to 65 percent. "Are you kidding? An 18 percent to 20 percent point change? This is huge," says Linda Waite, a sociologist at the University of Chicago.

To be sure, the rise in single women encompasses some other important trends. An estimated 4 million of these unmarried women are cohabiting with their lovers, and a growing number are being more open about gay relationships. Nevertheless, single women as a group are wielding more and more clout. A Young and Rubicam study labeled single women the yuppies of this decade, the blockbuster consumer group whose tastes will matter most to retailers and dictate our trends. The report found that nearly 60 percent of single women own their own home, buying them faster than single men; that single women fuel the home-renovation market; and that unmarried women are giving a big boost to the travel industry, making up half the adventure travelers and two out of five business travelers.

Equally important is the attitudinal change. The dictionary once defined a spinster as an unmarried woman above a certain age: 30. If you passed that milestone without a partner, your best hope was to be seen as an eccentric Auntie Mame; your worst fear was to grow old like Miss Havisham, locked in her cavernous mansion, bitter after being ditched at the altar. Not anymore. "We've ended the spinster era," says Philadelphia psychotherapist Diana Adile Kirschner, who has made single women a focus of her practice.

> Women used to tell me about isolation, living alone, low level of activity, feeling different. Now there's family, lots of friends, they're less isolated and more integrated into social lives.

More confident, more self-sufficient, and choosy than ever, women no longer see marriage as a matter of survival and acceptance.

They feel free to start and end relationships at will—more like, say, men. In a Yankelovich poll for *Time* and *CNN*, nearly 80 percent of men and women said they thought they would eventually find the perfect mate. But when asked, if they didn't find Mr. Perfect, whether they would marry someone else, only 34 percent of women said yes, in contrast to 41 percent of men. "Let's face it. You don't just want a man in your life," says author Bank, 39. "You only want a great man in your life."

Single by choice—it's an empowering statement for many women. Yet it's not a choice that all women arrive at easily or without some angst, and it raises a multitude of questions. Are women too unrealistic about marriage—so picky about men that they're denying themselves and society the benefits of marriage while they pursue an impossible ideal? Does the rejection of marriage by more women reflect a widening gender gap—as daughters of the women's movement discover that men, all too often, have a far less liberated view of the wife's role in marriage? Do the burgeoning ranks of single women mean an outbreak of *Sex and the City* promiscuity? And what about children? When a woman makes the empowering decision to rear a child on her own, what are the consequences for mother and child?

Society, to be sure, is far more accepting of single women than it was even a few years ago. When Barbara Baldwin, the director of Planned Parenthood in Tennessee, divorced her husband in 1981, she needed her father's help before anyone would give the then 29-year-old single mother a car loan and a credit card. Beverley Dejulio, a divorced Chicago mother who hosts *Handy Ma'am*, a weekly home-improvement show on **PBS**, says she dreaded the hardware store for years, because sales people kept asking, "Where's your husband?" And the Stone Age year when Anne Elizabeth, a Chicago artist, then 35, had to fight to not be listed as spinster on the mortgage application for her lakeside home? It was 1984.

Business has wised up. Now some auto manufacturers train salespeople to aim their pitches at women, going for the softer sell rather than the hard-nosed, macho wrangling of yesteryear. More than 100 travel companies have started to take women-only trekkers across deserts, up mountains and into volcanoes. Ace Hardware (where the slogan "Home of the Helpful Hardware Man" has been replaced by "Home of the Helpful Hardware Folks") now offers drills that are lighter with easy-grip handles, greenhouses full of flowers, and walls painted in pastels. They also run special seminars for women, who make up at least half their customers.

About a fifth of all home sales last year were to unmarried women, up from 10 percent in 1985. "Lenders don't presume single women can't make the mortgage anymore," says Mark Calabria, a senior economist at the National Association of Realtors. Orna Yaary, 42, a single mother and an interior designer, recalls that in the 1980s her single-women clients typically viewed their home as a temporary way station on the road to marriage. "It was like these single women with suitcases at the door, they wanted something but not anything permanent," says Yaary. Now she's decorating apartments for women like the 35-year-old investment banker who ordered built-in furniture and reconstructed the bathroom of her apartment. "She's doing what she wants. None of this attitude of 'I'll need to take it with me when I meet a guy.' "

Meanwhile, more single women—especially those watching their biological clocks run down—are resorting to solo pregnancies, sperm donors, or adoption agencies. While the birthrate has fallen among teenagers, it has climbed 15 percent among unmarried thirtysomethings since 1990. In the *Time/CNN* poll, fully 61 percent of single women ages 18 to 49 answered "yes" when asked whether they would consider rearing a child on their own.

Playwright Wendy Wasserstein recalls the clamor raised against her 1989 Pulitzer-prizewinning play, *The Heidi Chronicles*, because it concerns a woman who decides to have a baby alone. One female critic returned more than once to trash the play. "She said this was a cop-out, my saying women could be happy having a baby alone," the playwright says. Last year Wasserstein, still single at 49, gave birth to a daughter, Lucy Jane, conceived with the sperm of a friend she won't identify. "If I put Heidi out now, people would just say, 'Yeah, that's true,' " she says, shrugging.

And while many women who have embraced the single life are, like Wasserstein, well educated and economically independent, they cross social and class lines. Last year the National Marriage Project at Rutgers University released a report showing that the marriage rate among women had fallen one-third since 1970 and that young women had become more pessimistic about their chances of wedding. "The reality is that marriage is now the interlude and singlehood the state of affairs," says Barbara Dafoe Whitehead. For this summer's study, Whitehead chose to focus on blue-collar women in their 20s and expected more traditional attitudes. However, she found these women too were focused more on goals like college degrees, entrepreneurship, and home ownership than on matrimony. "They wanted to be married, yet they were preparing as if that was not going to be the case," she says. "There was a sense they couldn't count on men and marriage."

The embrace of singlehood is, in some ways, a logical result of the expanding possibilities for women brought on by the women's movement. "Women get addicted to the possibilities of their lives, the idea that on any given day you have the freedom to do this or that," explains Melissa Roth, author of *On the Loose*, a chronicle of a year in the life of three thirtysomething women. And so, while still looking for love, many women today are slow to let go of their space and schedules for the daily compromises—and sacrifices—of marriage.

Debra DeLee, 52, who is divorced and the director of a nonprofit group in Washington, is so taken with her life—a gorgeous Capitol Hill town house, trips all over the world, and a silver blue BMW roadster—that she's reluctant to change it even for the man of her dreams, Arnie Miller, 59, an executive recruiter who lives in Boston. "We talk about getting married, but this is so good right now," says DeLee, who ran the Democratic Convention in 1996. "Two minutes before he leaves, I think it's so hard to see him pick up and leave. But 2 minutes after he's gone, I think, *Ahh*, I've got my house back." Miller likes the arrangement too. "Why should this be offputting? I'm high-powered too," he says. "We both like our space. And three days later, we're racing to be back together."

At the same time, there's been a change in attitude toward love and marriage. Previous generations of women made their barter as much around the need for male protection and financial help as affection. And if at some point the sizzle went south, well. . . . But women today have a very different wish list from their mothers. "My single friends have their own life and money to bring to the table," says Sarah Jessica Parker, the star of *Sex and the City*.

It's the same as the characters on the show: My friends are looking for a relationship as fulfilling, challenging and fun as the ones they have with their girlfriends.

The choice to be single involves more than just rejecting the inevitable boors and slouches. More often, women speak of affairs with men they in many ways loved. But after much turmoil and tears, they ended things, deciding that being on their own was simply better than the alternative—being stuck with a man, and in a marriage, that didn't feel right.

"I totally adored him," says Lila Hicks, 32, a media producer, of the investment banker with whom she ended a seven-year romance not long ago, deciding life with him would be too limiting. "But I wasn't happy. I didn't think I could make him happy and retain my spirit, what makes me shine." Shawna Perry, an emergency-medicine doctor in Jacksonville, Fla., recently ended a ten-year relationship with a man whom she loves but feels is behind her in personal and professional growth. "His ups and downs were affecting our relationship and my security," she says. "I realized we were not building a life together and that

this was not a good place to be considering marriage."

In many cases, women who choose the single life have looked at those around them and vowed not to make their mistakes. "My mother married her first boyfriend. All my relatives stayed in marriages that are really tough," says Pam Henneberry, 31, an accountant who lives in Manhattan. "When I looked at the unhappiness that was in my parents' marriage, I said, 'I can't do that.'" If Cynthia Rowe, 43, a Los Angeles area store manager and divorcee, gets depressed, she thinks of her five closest girlfriends. "They are all just existing in their marriages," she says.

Two of them got married when they were young. Twenty years later, they had outgrown each other. One has not got over her husband's affair. Two friends aren't even sleeping in the same bedroom with their husbands anymore. Their personal happiness is placed last, and their kids know they are miserable.

Some women, of course, have learned from their own life. "At 28, I was terrified of the world," says Mary Lou Parsons, a Raleigh, NC, professional fund raiser, recalling her 1980 divorce. "I'd been raised a Southern woman, sheltered and protected by my family, then by my husband." In the ensuing 20 years she learned to raise her kids on her own—and how to start her own business, buy a town house, move to Alaska and back and, most of all, relish life on her own.

I had to get beyond that thinking in a lot of women's minds that aloneness is not O.K. But now I find solitude exhilarating.

Marcelle Clements, author of *The Improvised Woman: Single Women Reinventing the Single Life*, notes that there are many women, like Parsons, who were

taken by surprise. They were in relationships that broke up, hit what they thought was catastrophe, only to find that they were O.K., and [they] adopted an attitude that said, I'm fine. I don't need to be with anyone else.

Not surprisingly, many conservatives are disturbed at this growing acceptance of singlehood and its implied rejection of marriage. Danielle Crittenden, author of *What Our Mothers Didn't Tell Us*, argues that women have set themselves up for disappointment, putting off marriage until their 30s only to find themselves unskilled in the art of compatibility and surrounded by male peers looking over their Chardonnays at women in their 20s. "Modern people approach marriage like it's a Bosnia-Serbia negotiation. Marriage is no longer as attractive to men," she says. "No one's telling college girls it's easier to have kids in your 20s than in your 30s."

Women who have chosen the single life sometimes have their own qualms. Singlehood does not yield itself to a simple, blithe embrace. It's complicated, messy terrain because not needing a man is not the same as not wanting one. Even women who generally reflect on their choices with assurance may find themselves sometimes in the valley of what-ifs: What if I made the wrong choice to walk away, What if singlehood turns out to be not a temporary choice but an enforced state? "My sister knows that I'm good for a call every couple of months just crying, 'What's wrong with me?'" says Henneberry.

> I'm not willing to accept someone who is going to make me unhappy. But there are days when I have a physical need to go to sleep and wake up with someone there.

Mary Mayotte, 49, has a successful bicoastal career as a public-speaking coach. But she admits the occasional pang of regret. "There was a point when I had men coming out of my ears," she says.

> I don't think I was so nice to some of them. Every now and then I wonder if God is punishing me. Sometimes I look back and say, 'I wish I had made a different decision there.'

Some feel women are on an impossible search for the perfect man, the one who not only makes you feel, as Julia Roberts said of meeting Benjamin Bratt, "hit in the head with a bat," but also better for it. "Marriage is not what it used to be, getting stability or economic help," says the National Marriage Project's Whitehead. "Marriage has become this spiritualized thing, with labels like 'best friend' and 'soul mate.'" Some sociologists say these lofty standards make sense at a time when the high divorce rate hisses in the background like Darth Vader. But others suggest the marriage pendulum has swung from the hollowly pragmatic to an unhealthy romantic ideal.

Michael Broder, a Philadelphia psychotherapist and author of *The Art of Living Single*, decries what he calls the "perfect person problem," in which women refuse to engage unless they're immediately taken with a man, failing to give a relationship a chance to develop. "Few women can't tell you about someone they turned down, and I'm not talking about some grotesque monster," he says.

> But there's the idea that there has to be this great degree of passion to get involved, which isn't always functional. So you have people saying things like, 'If I can't have my soul mate, I'd rather be alone.' And after that, I say, 'Well, you got your second choice.'

Single women are used to hearing this complaint, and most don't buy it. "Some in my family think I'm not stopping till I find perfection," says Henneberry. "I don't feel like that. I just want the one who makes me go, 'Finally.'" Harvard sociologist Carol Gilligan notes, "There's now a pressure to create relationships that both men and women want to be in, and that's great. This is revolutionary." Even Ellen Fein, coauthor of the notorious 1996 dating guide *The Rules*, says her man-chasing disciples don't settle for just anyone. "Most of my clients have jobs; they can pay the rent; they can take themselves out to dinner," says Fein. "They want men to value them."

Many women can tell the story of a friend or relative who looked at her and said, "If you really wanted to be married, you'd be married." The comment can sometimes slap like a wet towel, in part because it is true and in part because of its implicit message: You could have compromised, perhaps settled, and been among the married. And so, the logic follows, you have no one to blame but yourself.

But these women have fought for years to be themselves—self-reliant, successful, clever, funny, willful, spirited—and for all the angst that the single life can bring, they're not willing to give it up for any arrangement that would stifle them. "It would be great if I found a relationship that allowed me to be as I am and added something to that," says documentary producer Pam Wolfe, 33, sitting in her one-bedroom condo in New York City. "But I'm not going to do anything to attract a person that means changing. I've worked long and hard to be myself." ✦

6b

Why Marriage Matters

Linda J. Waite

What are the implications, for individuals, of increases in nonmarriage? If we think of marriage as an insurance policy—which it is, in some respects—does it matter if more people are uninsured or are insured with a term rather than a whole-life policy? I argue that it does matter, because marriage typically provides important and substantial benefits. In this paper I focus on benefits to individuals.

Healthy Behaviors

Risk taking find[s] virtually no difference between men and women, but [we] still see much lower levels of unhealthy behaviors among the married—and the widowed—than among the divorced. Umberson (1987) examines a series of negative health behaviors, including marijuana use, drinking and driving, substance abuse, and the failure to maintain an orderly lifestyle. She concludes,

> on every dependent variable except marijuana use, the divorced and widowed are more likely than the married to engage in negative health behaviors and less likely to experience an orderly life style. (1987: p. 313)

Marital disruption appears to substantially increase stress (Booth and Amato, 1991) and decrease well-being (Mastekaasa, 1992), and thus may result in negative health behaviors. Umberson (1992) finds that the end of marriage increases men's cigarette and alcohol consumption, lowers body weight for both men and women at the lower end of the weight distribution, and reduces hours of sleep for women. The transition from unmarried to married, however, shows few effects on health behaviors except a decline in women's alcohol consumption. Umberson concludes that some of these changes result from the stress associated with the end of marriage, but that others appear to be more permanent consequences of being unmarried.

How does marriage affect healthy behaviors? Researchers in this area argue that marriage provides individuals—especially men—with someone who monitors their health and health-related behaviors and who encourages self-regulation (Ross, 1995; Umberson, 1987, 1992). In addition, social support by a spouse may help individuals deal with stressful situations. Also, marriage may provide individuals with a sense of meaning in their lives and a sense of obligation to others, thus inhibiting risky behaviors and encouraging healthy ones.

Mortality

Married men and women exhibit lower levels of negative health behaviors than the unmarried. Perhaps as a result, a good deal of research evidence suggests that married men and women face lower risks of dying at any point than those who have never married or whose previous marriage has ended. Once we take other factors into account, for both men and women, the married show the highest probability of survival and, of course, the lowest chances of dying. Widowed women are much better off than divorced women or those who have never married, although they are still disadvantaged when compared with married women. But all men who are not currently married face higher risks of dying than married men, regardless of their marital history.

How does marriage reduce the risk of dying and lengthen life? First, marriage appears to reduce risky and unhealthy behaviors. Second, marriage increases material well-being, income, assets, and wealth. These can be used to purchase better medical care, better diet, and safer surroundings, which lengthen life. This material improvement seems to be especially important for women. Third, marriage provides individuals with a network of help and support, with others who rely on them and on whom they can rely: This seems to be especially important for men. Marriage also provides adults with a readily available sex partner.

Partnered Sex

Married [people] report levels of sexual activity about twice as high as the single, even after we take into account other characterists that might affect this behavior. Married men report [an average] frequency of sexual activity of 6.84 per month and single men [an average] of 3.63 times per month. Married women report [an average] of 6.11 times per month and single women [an average] of 3.23 times per month. Cohabiting men and women also report high rates of sexual activity—7.43 and 7.20 times per month, which suggests that on this dimension, cohabitation equals marriage in its benefits to the individuals involved. These figures reflect reports of sexual activity with the primary partner. Insofar as single and cohabiting men and/or women are more likely than married persons to have multiple partners, the difference between these groups in level of sexual activity with all partners may be different than reported here.

So marriage and cohabitation mean more sex, at least with the primary partner, but are single individuals more satisfied with their sex lives? This could be the case,

for example, if each act of partnered sex was more passionate or more satisfying, and would be in keeping with the perception that married sex—or even sex with the same partner again and again—becomes boring and unsatisfying. The evidence suggests the opposite. Levels of physical satisfaction are somewhat higher for men than for women, but married men report significantly higher levels of physical satisfaction with their sex lives than either single or cohabiting men. For women, physical satisfaction does not differ by marital status.

Both married men and married women report more emotional satisfaction with their sex lives than do those who are single or cohabiting. Although cohabitors report levels of sexual activity as high as the married, both cohabiting men and women report lower levels of satisfaction with this activity. In all comparisons where we see a difference, the married are favored over the unmarried.

How does marriage improve one's sex life? Marriage and cohabitation provide individuals with a readily available sexual partner with whom to have an established, ongoing sexual relationship. This reduces the costs of any particular sexual contact, thus leading to higher levels of sexual activity. Laumann et al. (1994) state that the greater the commitment to a sex partner (defined as a long time horizon for the relationship and for its sexual exclusivity), the greater the incentive to invest in skills that are "partner-specific," including those which enhance the enjoyment of sex with that particular partner. Then sex with the partner who knows what one likes and how to provide it becomes more satisfying than sex with a partner who lacks such skills.

I would argue that more than "skills" are at issue here. The long-term contract implicit in marriage facilitates emotional investment in the relationship, which should affect both frequency of and satisfaction with sex. So the wife or husband who knows what the spouse wants sexually is also highly motivated to provide it, both because sexual satisfaction of one's partner brings similar rewards to oneself and because the emotional commitment to the partner makes satisfying him or her important in itself. Sex helps keep marriages healthy; it brings couples closer emotionally and helps them weather the inevitable strains of life with another person.

Cohabitation differs from marriage, especially in provision of sexual satisfaction, in important ways. First, although this is not a generally important motivator, some individuals choose to cohabit because it requires less sexual faithfulness than marriage (Bumpass, Sweet, and Cherlin 1991). Laumann et al. (1994) argue that sexual nonmonogamy leads to a less satisfying sexual relationship with any one partner. In addition, partners in cohabitation frequently bring different levels of commitment to the relationship, with different expectations for its future (Bumpass et al., 1991). Both the lower levels of commitment and differences in commitment between partners may affect the sexual satisfaction of those in cohabitations.

Assets and Wealth

In addition to having more sex, the married have more money. Median household wealth—estimated by Smith (1994) from the Health and Retirement Survey—for married couples, the separated, the divorced, the widowed, and the never married shows the tremendous disparity between married-couple and single-person households. Smith (1994) finds that the wealth advantage of married couples remains substantial even after taking into account other characteristics that affect savings. Also, although married couples have higher incomes than others, this accounts for only 28 percent of the savings disparity between married-couple households and other households.

How does marriage increase wealth? First, economies of scale mean that two can live as cheaply as one—or maybe one and a half. Married couples can share many household goods and services, such as TV and heat, so the cost to each individual is lower than if each one purchased and used the same items individually. Thus, the married spend less than would the same indi-

viduals for the same style of life if they lived separately. Second, because of specialization of spouses in marriage, married people produce more than would the same individuals if single. Each spouse can develop some skills and neglect others, because each can count on the other to take responsibility for some of the household work. The resulting specialization increases efficiency. Married couples save more at the same level of income than do the single. The desire to provide for one's spouse and to leave bequests for children may encourage saving by the married, but I think that the requirements and expectations of married (versus single) life encourage people to buy a house, save for children's education, and acquire cars, furniture, and other assets.

Labor Force and Career

Both black and white men receive a wage premium if they are married: 4.5 percent for black men and 6.3 percent for white men (Daniel, 1994). Black women receive a marriage premium of almost 3 percent. White women, however, pay a marriage penalty, in hourly wages, of over 4 percent. Men appear to receive some of the benefit of marriage if they cohabit. For women, marriage and presence of children together seem to affect wages. Black and white single women with children pay no marriage penalty. Black married women receive a sizable bonus if married and childless; this bonus diminishes with the number of children. Among white women, only the childless receive a marriage premium. Having any children makes the effect of marriage on white women's wages negative, with large negative effects for those with two children or more.

Why should marriage increase men's wages? Daniel (1994) argues that marriage makes men more productive at work, thus leading to higher wages. Wives may assist husbands directly with their work, offer advice or support, or take over household tasks, freeing husbands' time and energy for work. Also, being married reduces negative health behaviors such as drinking and substance abuse, which may affect productivity. Finally, marriage increases men's incentives to perform well at work, so as to meet obligations to family members.

To this point, all the consequences of marriage for the individuals involved have been positive—better health, longer life, more sex and more satisfaction with it, more wealth, and higher earnings. But the effects of marriage and children on white women's wages are mixed at best. Marriage and cohabitation clearly increase women's time spent in housework (South and Spitze, 1994); married motherhood reduces their time in the labor force and lowers their wages. Although the family as a unit might be better off with this allocation of women's time, women generally share their husbands' market earnings only when they are married. Financial well-being declines dramatically for women and their children after divorce or widowhood; women whose marriages have ended are often quite disadvantaged financially by their investment in their husbands and children rather than in their own earning power. Recent changes in divorce law seem to have exacerbated this situation, even while increases in women's education and work experience have moderated it (Bianchi, 1995).

Does Marriage Cause These Outcomes?

The obvious question, when one looks at all these "benefits" of marriage, is whether marriage is responsible for these differences. If all, or almost all, of the benefits of marriage arise because those who enjoy better health, live longer, or earn higher wages anyway are more likely to marry, then the effects of marriage simply may be due to selectivity.

The positive effect of marriage on well-being is strong and consistent, and the selection of the psychologically healthy into marriage or the psychologically unhealthy out of marriage cannot explain the effect. We have been too quick to assign *all* the responsibility to selectivity, and not quick enough to consider the possibility that marriage *causes* some of the better outcomes for the married.

What is it about marriage that causes some portion of the [positive] outcomes? Four factors are the key. First, the institution of marriage assumes a long-term contract, which allows the partners to make choices that carry immediate costs but eventually bring benefits. The long time horizon implied by marriage makes it sensible—rational choice is at work here—for individuals to develop some skills and to neglect others because they count on their spouse to fill in where they are weak. Thus married couples benefit from specialization. The institution of marriage helps individuals honor this long-term contract by providing social support for the couple as a couple and by imposing social and economic costs on those who dissolve their union.

Second, marriage assumes sharing of economic and social resources and what we can think of as co-insurance. Spouses act as a sort of small insurance pool against life's uncertainties, reducing their need to protect themselves by themselves from unexpected events. Third, married couples benefit—as do cohabiting couples—from economies of scale. Fourth, marriage connects people to other individuals, to other social groups (such as their in-laws), and to other social institutions, which are themselves a source of benefits. It provides individuals with a sense of obligation to others, which gives life meaning beyond oneself. It may change the psychological dynamics of the relationship in ways that bring benefits. Some consensus exists that marriage improves women's material well-being and men's emotional well-being, in comparison with being single.

Cohabitation has some but not all of the characteristics of marriage, and so carries some but not all of the benefits. Cohabitation does not generally imply a lifetime commitment to stay together. Cohabitants seem to bring different, more individualistic values to the union than do those who marry. Goldscheider and Kaufman (1994) believe that the shift to cohabitation from marriage signals

> declining commitment within unions, of men and women to each other and to their relationship as an enduring unit, in exchange for more freedom, primarily for men.

Perhaps as a result, some scholars view cohabitation as an especially poor bargain for women.

Cohabitants are much less likely than married couples to pool financial resources, more likely to assume that each partner is responsible for supporting himself or herself financially, more likely to spend free time separately, and less likely to agree on the future of the relationship (Blumstein and Schwartz, 1983). This uncertainty makes both investment in the relationship and specialization with this partner much riskier than in marriage, and so reduces them. Whereas marriage connects individuals to other important social institutions, such as organized religion, cohabitation seems to distance them from these institutions.

Some warnings are in order. First, for most outcomes, I presented information only on the average benefits of marriage. Some marriages produce substantially higher (and others substantially lower) benefits for those involved. Some marriages produce no benefits and even cause harm to the men, women, and children involved. On average, however, marriage seems to produce substantial benefits for men and women in the form of better health, longer life, more and better sex, greater earnings (at least for men), greater wealth, and better outcomes for children.

If marriage produces all these benefits for individuals, why has it declined? First, because of increases in women's employment, there is less specialization by spouses than in the past; thus benefits to marriage are reduced. Clearly, employed wives have less time and energy to focus on their husbands, and are less financially and emotionally dependent on marriage, than wives who work only in the home. In addition, high divorce rates decrease people's certainty about the long-run stability of their marriage, and thus may reduce their willingness to invest in it. Also, changes in divorce laws have shifted much of the financial burden for the breakup of the marriage to women, making investment in marriage a riskier proposition for them. Men may find marriage and parenthood less attractive when divorce is common, because they face the loss of contact with their children if their marriage dissolves. Further, women's increased earnings and young men's declining financial well-being have made women less dependent on men's financial support and have made young men less able to provide it. Finally, public policies that support single mothers and changing attitudes toward sex outside marriage, unmarried childbearing, and divorce have all been implicated in the decline in marriage. This brief list does not exhaust the possibilities.

References

Bianchi, S. M. (1995). Changing economic roles of women and men. In R. Farley (Ed.), *State of the Union: America in the 1990s, Vol. 1: Economic Trends* (pp. 107–154). New York: Russell Sage.

Blumstein, P., and Schwartz, P. (1983). *American couples*. New York: Morrow.

Booth, A., and Amato, P. (1991). Divorce and psychological stress. *Journal of Health and Social Behavior, 32,* 396–407.

Bumpass, L. L., Sweet, J., and Cherlin, A. (1991). The role of cohabitation in declining rates of marriage. *Journal of Marriage and the Family, 53,* 913–927.

Daniel, L. (1994). *Does marriage make workers more productive?* Working paper. The Wharton School, University of Pennsylvania.

Goldscheider, F. K., and Kaufman, G. (1994). *Fertility and commitment: Bringing men back in.* Presented at the Workshop on Expanding Frameworks for Fertility Research in Industrialized Countries, National Research Council, Woods Hole, MA.

Laumann, E. O., Gagnon, J., Michael, R. T., and Michaels, S. (1994). *The social organization of sexuality*. Chicago, IL: University of Chicago Press.

Mastekaasa, A. (1992). Marriage and psychological well-being: Some evidence on selection into marriage. *Journal of Marriage and the Family, 54,* 901–911.

Ross, C. E. (1995). Reconceptualizing marital status as a continuum of social attachment. *Journal of Marriage and the Family, 57,* 129–140.

Smith, J. P. (1994). *Marriage, assets, and savings.* Working paper, RAND.

South, S. J., and Spitze, G. D. (1994). Housework in marital and nonmarital households. *American Sociological Review, 59,* 327–347.

Umberson, D. (1987). Family status and health behaviors: Social control as a dimension of social integration. *Journal of Health and Social Behavior, 28,* 306–319.

——. (1992). Gender, marital status, and the social control of behavior. *Social Science and Medicine, 34,* 907–917. ✦

Waite, L. (1995, November). Does marriage matter? *Demography, 32,* 483–507. Reprinted by permission of Population Association of America.

Issue 6: Questions to Consider

1. What is the state of marriage today? Is marriage an outdated social institution that imprisons men and women or is marriage a solution to the problems of modern life, a haven?

2. Are we moving toward a society in which multiple forms of male-female relationships are acceptable, and even considered to be comparable to each other? (See Issue 4 on Cohabitation and Issue 8 for papers that examine this issue in regard to homosexual marriages.) Or are we witnessing a transition period in which marriage as a relationship and as a social institution is undergoing change?

3. Do you plan to marry? If so, why? If you do not plan to marry, or if you are not sure, why not?

4. What do you think about Waite's contention that marriage provides a form of social insurance? If marriage is a form of social insurance, can you explain why so many men and women reject it?

5. Waite identifies a number of benefits of marriage for men and women, although she notes that men may benefit more than women do, at least in some areas. Why would this be the case? Does the article by Edwards and her colleagues shed any light on this?

6. Some social scientists think that individuals will stop retreating from marriage (delaying it or cohabiting rather than marrying) once we learn how to live in egalitarian relationships (that is, husbands and wives are equal partners). Do you have egalitarian expectations for your marital relationships? How can we improve the chances of egalitarian expectations being met?

7. Waite uses associational data (two or more variables co-occur) to draw causal conclusions about the benefits of being married. Scientists do not usually make causal conclusions from data that are associated because it is usually impossible to know if either variable causes the other— they may even be associated because of a third (causal) variable. For instance, when researchers find that marital status and depression are related, the explanations that depressed people may be less likely to get married or to stay married are just as plausible as the explanation that being married helps prevent a person from being depressed. Consequently, most researchers simply state that variables are related without inferring causation. What are other possible explanations for the associations between marital status and well-being reported by Waite? ✦

Part Two

Controversial Marriage Issues

Issue 7: Introduction

When Should Women Marry?

Unlike some cultures around the world, in which parents or community elders arrange marriages between young adults, most individuals in Western societies choose their own spouses. Of course, these marital choices are not random—individuals are influenced in whom they marry by the attitudes and behaviors of friends, parents, and others in the community. In general, individuals tend to marry people that are acceptable to others in their social networks. Marital choices are also affected by laws, cultural and community values, and the media, all of which contribute to societal norms about marriage. Norms are guidelines that influence how we think and act.

One norm related to marriage concerns the age at which people are expected to marry. Every culture has expectations about when in the life course events such as marriage are normally or typically experienced. Age-related norms in any society change gradually in response to social, economic, and historical events. Of course, not everyone follows their culture's age norms, particularly in societies like the United States that highly value individual rights and freedoms. Therefore, the age at which one marries, and even *if* one marries, varies within cultures as well as between cultures. When people say things like, "Isn't it about time you thought about settling down and getting married?" they are reflecting the effect of norms on expectations about when people should marry.

The average age at marriage has increased significantly in the last two decades. Between 1970 and 2000 the median age at first marriage for women increased by 4.3 years to 25.1 years; for men, the increase was 3.6 years to 26.8 years (http://lists.census.gov/mailman/listinfo/public-news-alert). Opinions differ regarding whether this is a good or bad trend for individuals and relationships. In the following essays, Crittenden and Pozner debate the issue of when women should marry. As you read, think about age-related norms regarding families and other close relationships. Are there expectations about the best time to choose a partner, have children, retire from a career? ✦

Women Who Marry When They Are Young Will Be Happier

Danielle Crittenden

A beleaguered male friend of mine once joked, "It's not what the modern girl wants that matters—it's what she's going to have to settle for." He was complaining, of course, about the women he dated and how he never managed to measure up. In another era, my friend wouldn't have just measured up—he would have been snapped up. He's nice looking, has a good job and a gentle nature. But in our time people don't just reach a certain age and "settle." Indeed they're encouraged to do the opposite —to postpone marriage and family in pursuit of independence and that gleaming brass (not gold) ring.

For women, this approach to romance brings short-term pleasure (and not always that) at the expense of long-term gain. And this is because it is based on a faulty assumption of what we want out of life and how to get it. For nearly two generations women have been taught to deceive themselves about what it is they want. In the name of independence and equality, we've been told by our more feminist elders to deny our natural feelings—not to care too deeply (about the men we sleep with), to suppress our longing for commitment, to delay our desire to have children, to not trust or depend too much upon the men to whom we finally pledge our hearts. When we do have children, we are encouraged to sacrifice them for our jobs. And if we find ourselves unhappy and dissatisfied we've been taught not to blame the wisdom of these teachings but others—the men who have hurt us, the society that discriminates against us, the politicians who have not responded to every one of our personal needs. It is, however, the modern wisdom itself that is to blame.

We frequently hear that there is no going back, that women have gained too much and changed too much ever to be satisfied mainly with the unworldly comforts of hearth and motherhood. But there is no going forward, either, until we establish what exactly it is we want to gain. The previous generation of women succeeded in shattering the previous assumptions about women's lives. But in the shattering, they left behind a new round of unanswered questions beginning with: How can we be astronauts and lawyers and fighter pilots—and mothers. How can we be sexually independent—and wives? How can we demand to be treated identically to men—except for the times when we don't want to be? And how are men supposed to react to all this?

Feminists like to insist that "old-fashioned" values—as garden-variety morality now is called—and the social institutions that supported them are inconsistent with modern life. Yet while it obviously is true that you can't go back in time, it's not true that the teachings and principles that have guided humans since the beginning of civilization suddenly have become irrelevant. The problem we face as modern people—and particularly as modern women—is how to reconcile the old with the new. So while young women today may take for granted the professional respect their mothers craved, they no longer can expect marriage, stability, and children when they want them—or any special respect from men.

These young women confront the daunting task of trying to plan their lives from scratch, with very little in the way of guidance about how to reconcile their modern ambitions with the old institutions of marriage and motherhood. On the one hand they wish to be free, strong, and independent; on the other, to eventually wed husbands who will be devoted and monogamous and who financially will support them when they need it. They want to have interesting fulfilling jobs—and yet also be involved, committed mothers. The resulting relationships often are incongruous and flimsy, like the neotraditional houses you see springing up in suburbs across America. Traditional structure is not so readily reconciled with modern convenience, and yet modern convenience is something few people today will go without.

So we may pledge to love each other until death do us part—but we blanch at the first hint of sacrifice. We may express strong views on the sanctity of marriage—but we would not impose social sanctions upon those who betray their vows or even upon couples who refuse to take those vows in the first place. As women, we may be willing to accept most of the duties of child care—but we certainly won't take sole charge of the housekeeping and will snap at our husbands if for a moment they expect otherwise. Many of these changes, like the advent of refrigeration and modern plumbing, seem progressive: Why should anyone stay in a marriage that is unhappy? Why should women compromise their ambitions to raise children? But, like the drywall and plywood of modern houses, these attitudes have made our institutions much flimsier, and over time they endure less well.

Rather than believing in a utopian vision of equality, based upon the sexes being not just equal but the same—whether it's in the jobs they take on or the roles within marriage—we perhaps should accept that women now have achieved equality in every important way—politically, legally, and within the workforce. Our new goal should be happiness.

Edith Wharton once wrote, "I have sometimes thought that a woman's nature is like a great house full of rooms." Our souls are large enough to accommodate many roles. And if we are lucky, these days most of us will live long enough to attempt everything we want. What we must now do is give serious thought as to the arrangement of these rooms. Modern feminists would have us put a great deal of ourselves away in the attic or basement, possibly for future use, and otherwise decorate one or two rooms (so long as it's not the kitchen!) to suit ourselves. But if our homes are going to be comfortable, expansive places, echoing with the sounds of children, with the smell of good cooking, a warm husband in our beds, and of course a quiet room of our own in which to work or retreat to, then we are going to have to start planning our lives much better than we currently do.

To begin with, we are going to have to accept that simply pushing every important decision—marriage, children—to the middle of our adult lives is not only impractical, but self-defeating. Right now women are leading lives that are exactly backward. We squander our youth and sexual passions upon men who are not worth it, and only when we are older and less sexually powerful do we try to find a man who is worth it. We start our careers in our twenties, when we are at our most physically fertile and yet are neither old enough nor experienced enough to get anywhere professionally. Then we try to have babies when our jobs are finally starting to go somewhere, but our bodies—and our schedules—are less receptive to pregnancy.

It would, of course, be considered extremely regressive for a woman of 22 or 23 today to get married and promptly have a baby; I don't know any woman who has done it. But I wonder if it wouldn't be the most radical and even progressive act an ambitious woman could commit. Let's say she started thinking about it at the time she went to college. She could date a number of men in her late teens and early twenties and feel less pressure to sleep with them if she knew that soon she would be choosing one of them. And by taking marriage more seriously at an earlier age, she would be less likely to waste her time, or her heart, upon men with whom she couldn't imagine spending the rest of her life. If other young women followed her example, the shrinkage in the number of sexually available young women would have its effect on men: Sexual conquests would be harder, depriving them of their current easy ability to persuade women to share their beds without sharing their lives. By marrying earlier rather than later, a woman also could have her children when she's most physically ready for them and without too much disruption to her career later on, if she plans to have one.

To a modern woman, this surrender of youthful freedom might seem unimaginable. But look what she gains on the other end: By the time her second child is toddling off to nursery school, she'd still be only 29 or 30. She could have a third child if she liked or she could enter the workforce in a job with amenable hours or go to graduate school with a clearer conscience because her children would need her less than before. By the time her children were in school for a full day, she'd have just begun to hit her stride at work. She would not have to make the agonizing choice at 32 or 33 to stop everything now and drop out for a few years to have a baby.

From her employer's viewpoint, too, the time and money invested in her training would not be spent only to see her leave at the moment she became an asset. And most of all, she would have avoided joining the hordes of thirty-somethings speaking worriedly about such things as biological clocks, career versus motherhood, the cost of day care, infertility clinics, and the sudden shortage of available husbands.

Here's another unconventional idea: By marrying earlier, a woman probably would make a better marriage. There is actually little evidence to support the wisdom of our time that waiting until one is older and wiser leads to happier marriages. Marriages last not just because the people within them love each other but because of the time they have spent together, the children they share, the accommodations and sacrifices they have made for the other, and the depth of their intimacy and comfort with each other that make marriage to anyone else seem impossible.

Maybe what we should learn from the feminist experiment upon a generation of women is that you can't escape the consequences of your own actions. Generations of women may have had no choice but to commit themselves to marriage early, and then, with few other options outside the home available to them, they felt imprisoned by their lifelong domesticity. So many of our generation have decided to put it off until it is too late, not foreseeing that career isn't everything and that lifelong independence can be its own kind of prison. As my male friend might say, it's time for us gals to settle. ✦

Crittenden, D. (1999, February 22). "By Marrying Young, Women Will Be Happier as Wives, Mothers, and Employees." *Insight on the News*, 15(7), 24, 26–27. Reprinted with permission of *Insight*. Copyright © 1999 by News World Communication, Inc. All rights reserved.

7b

Women Should Marry When, and If, They Are Ready—Fools Rush In . . .

Jennifer Pozner

Brace yourself, because I'm about to reveal a shocking truth about feminists: *We like men.* Feeling skeptical? Not surprising, since antifeminists have spent the last three decades branding women's-rights activists "male bashers," "manhaters," and "feminazis." In reality, though, feminists believe that men have the capacity for compassion, loyalty, decency, and respect—which is why we demand no less in their behavior toward the women in their lives. Ironically, when it comes to their roles within the family, feminists have much greater faith in men's potential as attentive husbands, dedicated fathers, and loving partners than do many conservative women.

Certainly we give men more credit than does Independent Women's Forum leader Danielle Crittenden in her book *What Our Mothers Didn't Tell Us.* On the surface, Crittenden's "New Traditionalist" treatise appears to be strictly antifeminist—she says women can attain happiness only by abstaining from out-of-wedlock sex and by

> modernizing the traditional idea of getting married and having babies when our grandmothers would have, in our early twenties, and pursuing our careers later, when our children are in school.

At first glance, it would seem that her argument stems from straightforward social conservatism based solely on the notion that women are not well-served by professional and social equality. However, a closer look at Crittenden's prescription for female behavior betrays an oversimplification of the differing desires and socioeconomic conditions of women and a depressingly low opinion of the moral character and emotional depth of men.

Crittenden asserts that feminism, in general, and female sexual independence, in particular, have robbed women of

> the birthright of every previous generation of women: Children, a home life and a husband who—however dull or oppressive he may have appeared to feminist eyes—at least was *there.*

According to this argument, men are shallow, callous creatures who will never feel the need to commit to anyone, at any time, as long as they can get no-strings-attached sex from sexually liberated young women. Ergo, the feminist quest for independence leads women to an inevitable emotional dead end because regardless of how much a woman has achieved, she *will* feel profoundly meaningless without a husband and children. Why, you may ask, are independence and marriage mutually exclusive for women but not for men?

Because, Crittenden insists, since men are handsome and virile into their fifties, their "sexual staying power" outlasts that of women, whose attractiveness will dwindle with their first wrinkle. It is with this dim view of the heterosexual mating dance that she posits women's chances for lasting love:

No matter how intelligent, intriguing, caring or witty a woman might be, few men will find her appealing enough to marry once she feels mature enough to settle down.

Of course, she'll only have "less sexual power" to marry a man vapid enough to value her for her youthful sexuality. Why any woman would want to spend her life with someone uninterested in her mind, her heart, or her dreams is not a question that concerns Crittenden, for whom *the act of marriage* (rather than the quality of that lifelong partnership) is enough to ensure a woman's eternal happiness.

The intellectual stance of the so-called New Traditionalists seemingly assumes that modern men as a class are irresponsible because feminism and no-fault divorce have conditioned them to become cavalier about commitment. Americans used to blame a "midlife crisis" when a man abandoned a graying wife for a "pretty young thing." Now, the New Traditionalists blame feminism. They even blame feminism for deadbeat dads! And, their argument goes, if a modern woman manages to manipulate a man into marrying her and fathering her children, she will never feel secure that her husband won't leave her once her perkiest parts begin to sag or the pressures of parenthood become a drag. As Crittenden tells it,

> Even a beautiful woman's looks are not enough to hold a man forever; there are always more beautiful or younger or less demanding women coming along. And if a man does not feel like staying, there is none of the old social pressure on him to do so.

So, since shame no longer works, what's a modern gal to do? According to Crittenden, the answer seems clear: For any woman to transform an eligible bachelor into a suitable and dutiful husband all women must lure proposals from men by refraining from sexual activity until their wedding nights, effective immediately.

> If women as a group cease to be readily available—if they begin to demand commitment (and real commitment, as in marriage) in exchange for sex—market conditions will shift in favor of women.

In other words gender relations, she writes, simply can be summarized by the cliche, "Why buy the cow when she's giving away the milk for free?" As unflattering as this bovine metaphor might be for women who imagine they have more to offer the world—and any potential partner—than the use of their bodies, Crittenden's invocation of this adage is quite telling. When certain seventies feminists derided the traditional construction of marriage as "socially acceptable prostitution," it was this very commercialization of women's sexuality that they protested. Feminists understood then and now that a woman is more than the sum of her prettiest parts, just as a decent husband has merits that extend beyond the girth of his wallet.

At the heart of the egalitarian marriage under attack here is the belief that men, like women, are complex individuals who long for mates with whom they are intellectually, emotionally, and physically compatible. If we do not demand more from marriage than simple sexual access and monetary reward, we must resign ourselves to tenuous relationships devoid of mutual interest, love, respect, and trust. Yet, here we are again, reading another conservative pundit rhapsodizing about "market conditions," cows for sale and free milk—as if sex and love are nothing more than products to be purchased like so many hot stocks. So much for "family values."

There is nothing "new" about New Traditionalism. If we were all to follow what Crittenden considers "radical," "progressive" advice, husbands would reclaim their role as sole breadwinners and wives would care for children, hearth, and home full time. In an amazing leap of faith, Crittenden states that postponing work until the kids are fully grown would benefit women professionally, because it makes little sense for women to start careers in their early twenties when they are "neither old enough nor experienced enough to get anywhere professionally." Let's test this theory: A typical 23-year-old genX'er named Chelsea follows Crittenden's path and marries at 25, has her first child at 26 and her second at 29. When her second child enters first grade,

Chelsea will be 35; when he enrolls in high school, she'll be 43. Leaving aside the twin obstacles of age discrimination and the gender-based wage gap, let's follow Chelsea as she travels through her job search. How much sense does it make for a 35-year-old to apply for a part-time internship better suited to a recent college graduate? And how well will a woman of 43 with no credible work history compete in a free-market economy against skilled employees with two decades' experience under their belts?

Despite these considerations, Crittenden insists women who "neglect their children" in day-care programs are "selfish" because she believes women work primarily for emotional fulfillment rather than economic necessity. Further, she writes,

> When I hear a (married) woman say that she would like to have a baby but can't afford to leave her job, what she is really saying is that her husband is unwilling to support them if she does.

Working mothers don't "need" their incomes? Middle-class men are "unwilling" to support their families on one salary? Try the word "unable." Every day the business press carries another story about merger mania, corporate downsizing, unemployment, and the plight of the average American worker, who has to put in increasing hours for the pleasure of bringing home a smaller paycheck and fewer (if any) benefits. Job security has become as obsolete as Ozzie and Harriet. Ever since men's real wages began to drop in the early 1970s, more and more women began working not only to become more affluent but to keep up with housing, inflation, the skyrocketing cost of college and often, to keep their families above the poverty line. It not only is so-

cially regressive to suggest that women must forgo the pursuit of work outside the home—it is an impossibility for all but the most affluent of families (certainly it is beyond impractical for single mothers, widows, and the working class). These are the real "market conditions" American women face.

In conceptualizing middle-class women's increasing financial need for work, Crittenden asks, "Why have we come to consider taking care of our kids as a perk of the rich, like yachting?" It's a good question, and for women who wish to be with their children full time but cannot afford to do so it is a crucial one. But another question begs an answer as well: If societal help for middle-class women to raise their kids is a good idea, why do conservative antifeminists oppose public assistance to poor women who wish to stay home with their kids? Does it make sense to condemn middle-class working mothers for "neglecting their children" while simultaneously condemning stay-at-home mothers on welfare as lazy and irresponsible?

Which brings us back to the question of the hour: "Is early marriage the best path for American women?" The answer is obvious: If we ask women to subvert their desires for social, sexual, and economic independence to compensate for the supposed inherent moral deficiency of men, it not only limits what women can achieve—it demeans us all. ✦

Issue 7: Questions to Consider

1. The age at first marriage for men and women is increasing in recent years. Is this a positive or negative indicator for women and men, for marriages in general, and for society?

2. Why do these articles focus on women only?

3. Do the arguments made by Crittenden and Pozner apply to women who do not plan to have children? Why or why not?

4. Could Crittenden and Pozner argue the same points about the ages at which men should marry?

5. Take a position that men should either marry when they are younger or when they are older. Support your position.

6. Pozner and Crittenden's views are based on assumptions about women, men, and marriage. What are these assumptions?

7. Some social critics have claimed recently that the divorce rate has dropped because people are older when they marry now than 20 or 30 years ago. What do you think about this claim? Can you find research to support your position?

8. Why does Crittenden think women should marry young? Can you think of other reasons that she did not mention? Why does Pozner think women should not marry young? Can you think of other reasons that she did not mention?

9. Survey 10 students. Ask them "At what age should women marry?" "At what age should men marry?" Calculate the average age that the students in your sample think that women and men should marry. Is the average age for women to marry older, younger, or the same as the average age for men? Compare your findings to other students in your class. What do you think your "findings" mean?

10. Interview your parents and grandparents or other married relatives. At what age did they marry? What reasons do they give for marrying at that age? How do their reasons fit with Crittenden and Pozner's arguments? ✦

Issue 8: Introduction

'I Now Pronounce You Husband and . . . Husband?' Legal Marriage and Same-Sex Couples

In 2001, the Missouri legislature passed a bill, signed by the governor, that prevents the state from recognizing homosexual marriages that were formed in other states. Only marriages between a man and a woman will be considered to be legal marriages in the state. It was already the law in Missouri that two men or two women cannot marry each other. Since there is currently no place in the United States in which same-sex couples can legally marry, neutral observers may wonder why such a bill, called the Defense of Marriage Act, was needed.

Few of us seem to be neutral on the question of whether gays and lesbians should be allowed to marry. This issue has been hotly debated for more than a decade. Advocates and opponents of homosexual marriage bolster their positions with arguments that include legal, moral, religious, psychological, political, financial, and genetic considerations.

Advocates for homosexual marriage frequently point to earlier laws that prohibited interracial marriage as another example of laws and public policy based solely on prejudice. Opponents fear that allowing gays and lesbians to marry will erode what they see as an important social institution that is under attack and must be protected (see Issues 4, 6, and 19 for further discussion of the condition of marriages).

The fierceness of the debate over homosexual marriage belies the fact that only a small proportion (i.e., about 10 percent is a frequently cited estimate) of the population is homosexual. Regardless of the number of people affected, however, legislative bodies, policy makers, social critics, and advocates have spent much time and energy on this issue.

In the essays that follow, William Bennett and Scott Miller briefly present some of the main points of the cases for and against legal homosexual marriages. As you read these essays, note the rationale used to support each position, and see if you can think of other reasons that could be offered to support these differing views. ✦

8a

A Man and a Woman Are Needed for the 'Honorable Estate'

William J. Bennett

We are engaged in a debate that, in a less confused time, would be considered pointless and even oxymoronic: the question of same-sex marriage. But we are where we are. The Hawaii Supreme Court has found a new state constitutional "right"—legal union of same-sex couples.

Unless a "compelling state interest" can be shown against them, Hawaii will become the first state to sanction such unions [Editors' note—Vermont became the first state to legally recognize homosexual civil partnerships]. If Hawaii legalizes same-sex marriages, other states might have to recognize them because of the Constitution's full faith and credit clause. Some in Congress have introduced legislation to prevent this.

Now, anyone who has known someone who has struggled with his homosexuality can appreciate the poignancy, human pain, and sense of exclusion that are often involved. One can therefore understand the effort to achieve for homosexual unions both legal recognition and social acceptance. Advocates of homosexual marriages even make what appears to be a sound conservative argument: Allow marriage to promote faithfulness and monogamy. This is an intelligent and politically shrewd argument: It might benefit some people. But I believe that overall, allowing same-sex marriages would do significant, long-term social damage. Recognizing the legal union of gay and lesbian couples would represent a profound change in the meaning and definition of marriage. It is not a step we ought to take.

The function of marriage is not elastic; the institution is already fragile enough. Broadening its definition to include same-sex marriages would stretch it almost beyond recognition—and new attempts to broaden the definition still further would surely follow. On what principled grounds could the advocates of same-sex marriage oppose the marriage of two consenting brothers? How could they explain why we ought to deny a marriage license to a bisexual who wants to marry two people? After all, doing so would be a denial of that person's sexuality. In our time, there are more (not fewer) reasons to preserve the essence of marriage.

Marriage is not an arbitrary construct; it is an "honorable estate" based on the different, complementary nature of men and women—how they define, support, encourage, and complete one another. To insist that we maintain this traditional understanding of marriage is not to put others down. It is simply an acknowledgment and celebration of our most precious social act.

Nor is this view arbitrary or idiosyncratic. It mirrors the accumulated wisdom of millennia and the teaching of every major religion. Among cultures worldwide, where there are so few common threads, it is not a coincidence that marriage is almost universally recognized as an act meant to unite a man and a woman.

To say that same-sex unions are not comparable to heterosexual marriages is not an argument for intolerance, bigotry, or lack of compassion (although it will be considered so by some). But it is an argument for making distinctions in law about relationships that are themselves distinct.

Even Andrew Sullivan, among the most intelligent advocates of same-sex marriage, has admitted that a homosexual marriage contract will entail a greater understanding of the need for "extramarital outlets." He argues that gay male relationships are served by the "openness of the contract," and he has written that homosexuals should resist allowing their "varied and complicated lives" to be flattened into a "single, moralistic model."

But this "single, moralistic model" is precisely the point. The marriage commitment between a man and a woman does not—it cannot—countenance extramarital outlets. By definition, it is not an open contract; its essential idea is fidelity. Obviously that is not always honored in practice. But it is normative, the ideal to which we aspire precisely because we believe some things are right (faithfulness in marriage) and others are wrong (adultery). In insisting that marriage accommodate the less restrained sexual practices of homosexuals, Sullivan and his allies destroy the very thing that supposedly drew them to marriage in the first place.

There are other arguments to consider against same-sex marriage—for example, the signals it would send, and the impact of such signals on the shaping of human sexuality, particularly among the young. Former Harvard professor E. L. Pattullo has written that "a very substantial number of people are born with the potential to live either straight or gay lives." Societal indifference about heterosexuality and homosexuality would cause a lot of confusion.

A remarkable 1993 article in *The Washington Post* supports this point. Fifty teenagers and dozens of school counselors and parents were interviewed. Teens said it has become "cool" for students to proclaim they are gay or bisexual—even for some who are not. Not surprisingly, the caseload of teenagers in "sexual identity crisis" doubled in one year. "Everything is front page, gay and homosexual," according to one psychologist who works with the schools.

> Kids are jumping on it . . . [counselors] are saying, 'What are we going to do with all these kids proclaiming they are bisexual or homosexual when we know they are not?'

If the law recognizes homosexual marriages as the legal equivalent of heterosexual marriages, it will have enormous repercussions. Consider just two: sex education in the schools and adoption. The sex education curriculum of public schools would have to teach that heterosexual and homosexual marriages are equivalent. "Heather Has Two Mommies" would no longer be regarded as an anomaly; it would more likely become a staple of a sex education curriculum. Parents who want their children to be taught (for moral and utilitarian reasons) the privileged status of heterosexual marriage will be portrayed as intolerant bigots; they will be at odds with the new law of matrimony and its derivative curriculum. Homosexual couples will also have equal claim with heterosexual couples in adopting children, forcing us (in law at least) to deny what we know to be true: that it is far better for a child to be raised by a mother and a father than by, say, two male homosexuals.

The institution of marriage is already reeling because of the effects of the sexual revolution, no-fault divorce, and out-of-wedlock births. We have reaped the consequences of its devaluation. It is exceedingly imprudent to conduct a radical, untested, and inherently flawed social experiment on an institution that is the keystone in the arch of civilization. That we have to debate this issue at all tells us that the arch has slipped. Getting it firmly back in place is, as the lawyers say, a "compelling state interest." ✦

Bennett, W. J. (1996, May 23). "A Man and A Woman Are Needed for the 'Honorable Estate.'" *St. Louis Post Dispatch*, 7B. Reprinted by permission of William J. Bennett.

8b

State Has No Compelling Reason to Bar Same-Sex Unions

Scott Miller

In 1775, Thomas Jefferson said it was necessary for the American colonies to write a Declaration of Independence "to place before mankind the common sense of the subject, in terms so plain and firm as to command their assent." As we now face another crisis in our country's growth—the battle over equal rights for gays and lesbians—it seems common sense is the commodity in smallest supply. People on both sides need to stand back and look at the situation rationally, without insults, without false accusations.

Most Americans would agree with the Declaration of Independence that all people are created equal and deserve equal rights—unless there's a compelling reason to deny them rights (for instance, people convicted of crimes do not enjoy all the rights of other citizens). So all the clamor about gay marriage and other gay issues boils down to one concept: Gays and lesbians should have the same rights as straight people, unless there's a compelling reason to deny them those rights. In other words, there's no need to formulate arguments in favor of gay Americans having equal rights; they're Americans, after all. It's only necessary to figure out if arguments against equal rights for gays are legitimate.

Many of the religious extremists' arguments against equal rights for gays are based on one central idea, that the Bible says homosexuality is wrong. First, not all Americans are Christians or believe in the Bible. Even though our founding fathers were Christians, they were very careful in the Constitution to make our government a secular one, completely separate from the church. No matter what your moral beliefs, same-gender marriage and other gay issues are about the laws of America, not the laws of God. The Bible has nothing to do with passing laws, and Bible quotes are irrelevant in this arena. No one is asking for moral approval of gay marriage. No one is demanding that churches perform gay weddings (though thousands already do). We're only asking for legal recognition of something that already exists. It's not a moral issue. It's a legal one.

Yet even for those who don't accept that argument, another one is just as important: Only certain Christians believe homosexual acts are wrong. And though religious extremists attack gays invoking Leviticus, they conveniently ignore the other rules in Leviticus about putting to death adulterers and children who talk back to their parents, the detailed instructions on animal sacrifice, the rules against wearing more than one kind of fabric or paying workers less often than every day and much more. Apparently, they follow the Bible only when it suits them.

Another argument against gay equal rights is that homosexuality spreads AIDS. This one's a no-brainer. Homosexual acts do not breed disease; unsafe sex breeds disease, for anyone of any orientation. Worldwide, far more heterosexuals than homosexuals are infected with HIV today. In 1993, 48 percent of American AIDS cases were gay men. That percentage is much lower today. And because lesbians almost never contract AIDS, that means more than half of American AIDS cases were heterosexuals.

Some politicians are trying to induce panic by warning that, if we allow gays to marry, soon people will be marrying in threesomes or marrying their pets. Some folks even predict we'll soon have to legalize pederasty and bestiality. This is a smoke screen at best, rampant paranoia at worst.

The truth is simple. Right now in America, some couples can already get married and others can't, the distinction based only on their gender—a woman can marry a man, but a man can't. That certainly mucks up "and justice for all," doesn't it? Since there is no group of citizens who can currently marry in threes or who are legally allowed to molest children, no one is asking for those things to be legalized. Gays and lesbians aren't asking for a new right; they're asking for a right 90 percent of the population already enjoys.

Two of the most bizarre arguments are that gays will recruit children and, along with that, if gays marry and adopt children, their children will turn out gay. For those who believe people can choose to be gay or can be "recruited" into being gay, I have one question—who would ever choose this?

Today's society makes it tough to be gay. It's easier than it was 20 years ago, but it's still no picnic. Even if gays wanted to recruit, how could they? To quote a gay comedian, "What are the selling points?" We have no rights, and everybody hates us. Sign up here. The people who make these arguments just aren't thinking.

There's one point everyone seems to miss about children growing up in a gay household. Almost all the gays and lesbians living today grew up with straight parents. One look at the real world proves that straight parents are much more likely to raise gay kids than gay parents are.

The most often articulated of the arguments is that gay marriage will destroy the family and the institution of marriage—though no one has ever made this claim and actually backed it up. The extremists make the doomsday prediction that gay marriage will literally destroy society, but they can never say how this will happen because they don't know. And because it won't happen. People said the Emancipation Proclamation and the legalization of interracial marriage would both destroy America. Neither did.

To many people, homosexuality is about sex: But it's not. Being gay isn't just about sex any more than being straight is. Gays and lesbians don't have stronger sex drives. They don't have sex more often than straight people. Straight folks also have bars where they go to find sex. Straight people have pornographic videos, movie houses, magazines. In fact, 99 percent of child molestation is committed by heterosexuals. Many of the high-profile religious leaders today seem to have an almost adolescent preoccupation with sex. Everything boils down to sex for them—equal rights for gays, Hollywood, the Internet, the media, you name it. And they think everyone else is similarly obsessed. We're not.

Gays and lesbians want to be as free as their heterosexual friends to be open about their love. We want to wear wedding bands, have pictures of our spouses on our desks at work, bring our spouses to work functions, parties, award dinners, etc. When straight people wear wedding rings, talk about their spouses and kids, do we criticize them for flaunting the fact that they have straight sex? Does anyone ever ask them why they don't "leave it in the bedroom where it belongs"? No, marriage isn't about sex; it's about commitment. Whether it's gay or straight. Period. It's just common sense. ✦

Miller, S. (1996, May 23). "State Has No Compelling Reason to Bar Same-Sex Unions." *St. Louis Post-Dispatch*, 7B. Reprinted by permission of Scott Miller.

Issue 8: Questions to Consider

1. It is ironic that some gays and lesbians want to marry, whereas at the same time heterosexual men and women appear to be avoiding marriage or at least delaying entry into marriage (see Issue 4 on cohabitation and Issue 6 on whether marriage matters anymore or not). How do you explain these contradictory trends?

2. Some people contend that homosexuality is a lifestyle *choice*. Others think that homosexuality is genetically determined. Right now, the scientific evidence on a genetic cause of homosexuality has not been widely accepted. Does the case against legalizing homosexual marriages change if a genetic cause for homosexuality is found? Why or why not?

3. In Issue 21 the subject of covenant marriage is discussed as a way of reducing the number of divorces and improving marriage quality. Opponents worry that covenant marriage laws create different degrees or "levels" of marriage. How does this relate to the issue of legalizing homosexual marriages?

4. Miller and Bennett present a number of reasons for and against legalizing marriage between homosexuals. What other reasons can you think of that either support or oppose legalizing marriage between homosexuals?

5. Recently, the state of Vermont passed a law recognizing gay and lesbian *domestic partnerships*, and in Hawaii and a few city governments, homosexual partners are allowed to receive some employee benefits that used to be limited to married couples (e.g., pensions, health-insurance coverage). Opponents of homosexual marriages argue that many concerns expressed by advocates can be resolved by making wills (inheritance), owning property jointly, and through other legal actions that are available to all citizens. They say marriage, therefore, is not necessary. Investigate the claims that the benefits of marriage can be addressed in other ways. Are opponents of homosexual marriage correct or are there some problems that can be solved only via marriage? ✦

Issue 9: Introduction

Love and Marriage Go Together Like . . . ?

Is love the basis for marriage? If so, should it be? For most of human history, people married for mostly practical reasons, such as survival or to preserve or add to wealth and power. For example, royal families contracted marriages of their children to expand their landholdings, sometimes even when their children were infants. Love and marriage were not associated with each other until relatively late in human history. Now, however, "I married him because I love him" is not only the most common reason given for marriage, it often is the sole reason. We seem to take it for granted that individuals who get married do so *because* they love their partner. In fact, we may look at other reasons as superficial ("Because she is cute"), irrelevant ("Because he is from a prominent family in town"), or insufficient as a reason by itself ("Because we have a lot in common."). Music, movies, literature, and culture in general seem to support the idea that love is *both* necessary and sufficient for a satisfying marriage.

The following articles about the interconnections between romantic love and marriage were written originally for therapists and physicians who work with couples. However, the messages in these articles are relevant to anyone who is married or who thinks they might marry, and almost everyone in the United States does marry—at least once. Both Grunebaum and Silverman seem to agree that most people believe that love is the basis for marriage. However, their perspectives on the wisdom and effectiveness of this belief are quite different.

Silverman examines what he calls fallacies regarding the connection between love and marriage. His thinking is based on Rational Emotive Behavior Therapy (REBT), a psychotherapeutic approach developed by psychologist Albert Ellis. One of the premises of this approach is that a lot of what people believe to be true is untrue *and* irrational. When people act on these irrational beliefs, they make poor decisions, have unrealistically high expectations, and engage in self-defeating behaviors. Therapy consists, at least in part, of learning to think rationally about problems and how to solve them. Silverman treats love and marriage just as any subjects would be handled from the perspective of REBT.

Grunebaum, a physician and family therapist, takes a different stance on love. Grunebaum's views are similar to those of most people regarding the connection between romantic love and marriage, that love is a basis for marriage. He presents insights from his clinical experience in working with couples and individuals. ✦

Thinking About Romantic/Erotic Love

Henry Grunebaum

Romantic/erotic love is a powerful force in the lives of ordinary men and women. Indeed, many, if not most, people hope to find and to experience romantic love, to find a partner whom they love and desire. The ideas I will discuss here are based on my clinical experience of more than 30 years of working with couples. My purpose in this essay is to explore and identify some of the salient characteristics of romantic/erotic love.

What Is Romantic/Erotic Love?

A review of the literature yields no agreed-upon definition of being in love as distinguished from other emotional bonds such as friendship, affection, or sexual desire. Moreover, the part this kind of love plays in a person's life differs widely from individual to individual, depending on the importance they give it. The definition of romantic/erotic love used here is based on my clinical experience. It identifies three main features:

1. Feelings of longing for the other, including the desire to be intimate with them both sexually and psychologically, and feelings of loss and loneliness during separations.

2. The experience of the beloved as special, idealized, necessary for one's happiness. There is often a desire to know and share many details about the other.

3. The preoccupation with and over evaluation of the loved one. Lovers place great importance on appearance and may spend many hours looking in each other's faces.

I have deliberately linked romantic with erotic love because in life they are usually linked. Because romantic/erotic love exists in all cultures for which we have adequate data and because it does not appear to vary in its characteristics as a function of age or mental health, it is likely that romantic/erotic love is an emotional experience based on a biological propensity.

Characteristics of Romantic/Erotic Love

Romantic/erotic love has certain features that clearly differentiate it from other kinds of loving feelings. Based on my clinical experience, the following characteristics of romantic/erotic love are of the greatest significance for the therapeutic process.

We Do Not Have Control Over Our Feelings of Romantic/Erotic Love

We cannot choose whom we love, nor predict when the feelings will occur, and we usually cannot recapture the feeling when it has disappeared. That we use the expression *falling in love* suggests how precipitately the event can occur. I have surveyed a number of groups of people in long-term committed relationships, asking how long it took to know that the person they were to become involved with was a special person. More than half of them said they knew during the first or second meeting, and some said they knew immediately. Many added that it was not just a matter of attraction to the other person but a case of "actually falling in love." Since people cannot choose whom to love, they may find themselves loving at inopportune times or with inappropriate partners. And people cannot make themselves love appropriate partners.

Falling out of love is also a not uncommon clinical problem over which the individual has little control and the therapist, in my experience, little influence. For instance, Bill and Janet were an unusually successful, attractive, and likeable pair who had been married for three years and had no children. Sex before the marriage had been satisfactory, but afterwards it went downhill. Bill had expected marriage to make for increased variety, while Janet had hoped it would make Bill sensitive to her more conventional desires. Therapy had no impact on these expectations. Both remained hurt, and they separated; but neither was able to proceed with a divorce. They continued as best friends and could not go on with their lives. Their feelings of romantic love could not be resurrected.

Therapy cannot create feelings of love; it is also of little use in quenching them. Unrequited love is a uniquely painful, and often long-lasting, experience. John fell wildly in love with Sandra. She was passionate, exciting, just the opposite of his ex-wife, whom he experienced as unemotional. Never had sex been so wonderful. Unfortunately, Sandra had not ended her relationship with her former lover and finally went back to him, leaving John bereft. It took several years of therapy for him to regain his emotional stability. When he remarried 5 years later, he continued to miss the passion he had once known, although his life as a whole was much happier. In my clinical experience, when romantic/erotic love is lost, it is almost always gone for good.

We Are Likely to Experience Romantic/Erotic Love Only a Few Times in a Lifetime

Although one retains the capacity for romantic/erotic love throughout one's life, it is my clinical and personal experience that these feelings arise relatively infrequently. Since I found nothing in the literature

about the frequency of romantic love, I carried out a small, informal questionnaire study of a sample of 30 middle-class health care professionals. My respondents believed that the usual frequency of romantic/erotic love was about three to six times over a person's life.

My clinical experience suggests that one is likely to experience romantic/erotic love perhaps once in high school, once in college, once or twice more before marriage, and perhaps once after the loss of a spouse due to divorce or death. Typically, then, one experiences romantic/erotic love between three and six times over all. Precisely because most people experience romantic/erotic love relatively infrequently, we do not have much experience in assessing what it means and what course of action to take.

Because love is rare, people consider it precious, enduring much to stay with a beloved other. In addition, people not infrequently even search out a former beloved after years of separation and attempt to renew the relationship.

A Third Characteristic of Romantic/Erotic Love Is That It Is Regarded by Most People as a Good, a Positive Value

This good can and often does come into conflict with other values, and the criteria for resolving this conflict are themselves problematic. Love is a good, but it is not the only good. It often comes into conflict with other goods such as reason, personal goals, family, and ethical obligations. And the power of romantic/erotic love can lead one—even knowingly—into a relationship fraught with conflict, into moral and emotional minefields. Some of these conflicts are external, arising when a love relationship impacts negatively on other bonds and loyalties, particularly those involving one's family of origin, one's friends, and sometimes one's spouse and children. Still other conflicts are internal, focusing on the potential effect that loving a certain person will have on one's own values and what one needs to enjoy life.

The challenge in thinking about the consequences of romantic/erotic love is to determine what criteria to employ. For instance, some Jewish families treat as dead any member who marries outside the faith. How does one weigh the joy of being with the loved one against the positive and negative effects this love may have on oneself and on others?

What values should be considered when deciding what to do about a loveless marriage? Steve was not sure he wanted to marry Ann. He married her, but during the 20 years of that marriage, Steve had numerous affairs. At some point Steve met Myra, a passionate affair ensued, and they left their spouses and built a fulfilling life together.

The issues posed by affairs complicate and obscure the value that most people give to love. For while extramarital affairs sometimes involve love, they almost always involve lies, deceit, and betrayal. Thus the conflicts about the value of love may be better illustrated by cases in which affairs have not occurred. After her first date with Jonah, Virginia predicted to her mother that he would propose to her and added that she did not love him. She did not want to marry Jonah because she felt no real passion for him, but he pursued her so ardently that she finally yielded to his entreaties. Twenty years later she is still married to Jonah but feels no love for him and does not really want to live with him. On the other hand, they have a child, and her life is financially secure. She looks curiously at friends who do love their partners even though she is well aware of the difficulties in their marriages. She wonders, in therapy sessions, if spending the rest of her life without experiencing love is to have lived a good life.

Romantic/Erotic Love Is Regarded Today as an Essential Element for a Happy Marriage

Although falling in love and romantic/erotic love are wonderful, other capacities are necessary to sustain a long-term relationship. The characteristics which foster enduring romantic/erotic love in marriage are the ones which lead to strong relationships generally and are those of the mature person. By enduring romantic/erotic love I do not mean that couples remain in a state of romantic bliss, but rather that they know they love each other and feel romantically and erotically toward each other from time to time.

There are no easy solutions available to the clinician whose clients are experiencing problems with romantic/erotic love. There are no easy solutions because love itself is complicated and perplexing. We desire to have another to love, for without one we will be lonely and there will be no one who truly knows us. We desire to become one with the other, to be selfless, and to lose ourselves in sexual intimacy. But we are also afraid of losing ourselves, for we know that the person we love is other, independent, and that we can never truly know him or her. This is the predicament of love.

What makes matters even more challenging is the fact that we ask a great deal of marriage, of any serious intimate relationship. Perhaps the greatest demand we make is that it should combine passion and stability, romance and monogamy, transports of tenderness and excitement from the person who will also perform the many mundane tasks of daily living—in other words, meld everyday love with romantic/erotic love. Somehow, most of the time for most women and men, this seems to work. And when it does, it is love at its best. ✦

Grunebaum, H. (1997). "Thinking About Romantic/ Erotic Love." *Journal of Marital and Family Therapy, 23,* 295–307. Copyright © 1997 by American Association for Marriage and Family Therapy. Reprinted with permission.

9b

Fallacies About Love and Marriage

Joseph S. Silverman

This article, originally written for physicians in order that they are better prepared to deal with their patients' concerns about relationships, sheds interesting light on myths and misconceptions underlying problems in dating, mating, and separating. Behavioral specialists, and probably family physicians as well, sometimes consider with their patients questions about romance and marriage. As in many areas where physicians are consulted, professionals' wisdom is often based on their life experience. Authoritative sources are not readily available.

In reviewing these topics with patients and others, I have found an actual prevalence of what I believe to be misconceptions. Perhaps the following discussions, based on limited research but ample theory and clinical experience, will be of interest and value to other physicians and counselors.

Fallacy #1. Being in love is the best reason for getting married. Historically, romantic love as a basis for marriage has not for very long been the decisive factor. Indeed, in many parts of the world right now arranged marriages are the long-established cultural tradition.

What is this thing called love? Freud described romantic love as what evolves when an attractive and valued member of the opposite sex elevates one's self-esteem, routing personal insecurities. Romantic love, as someone has said, is therefore mainly nervousness—or, more precisely, nervousness relieved. There is no doubt that the fortu-itous cycle that Freud described produces glorious reassurance. But as a mechanism for reaching the most important decision of one's life romantic love is a poor substitute for rational evaluation—or, at least, for accurate intuition of one's fundamental emotional needs.

In decision-making of any kind, a certain amount of excitation intensifies commitment. And where a society lacks a tradition of marital commitment (e.g., prohibition of divorce), then heightened commitment to a relationship is a good thing. But a surer route to decades of satisfaction and harmony lies through such qualities as compatibility, particularly in areas of values, genuine liking of the other person, respect for that person, joy in sharing experiences, and concurrence on family goals (number of children; the ratio of togetherness to apartness; assignment of domains—who is in charge of what).

Fallacy #2. Having fallen out of love is a good reason for getting divorced. Because of this overestimation of the importance of romantic love, some persons, especially those with a strong histrionic element in their personalities, feel deprived, hollow, empty if excitement, particularly romantic excitement, evaporates as the years roll by. T. Byram Karasu, a noted psychoanalyst, taught a course at a national psychiatric meeting a few years ago. The audience was to be limited to 40 persons. One thousand psychiatrists applied for the course. Obviously what Karasu would have to say, clear-headed conclusions drawn from years of experience, was highly valued by his fellow psychiatrists. But during the coffee break halfway through the seminar Karasu found himself in the midst of a small group of young women, members of the convention's temporary staff: When Karasu, in informal light conversation, discoursed about the unimportance of romantic excitement in marriage, these young women greeted him with stony disbelief. In their young lives they had had abundant exposure to the notion that love is the primary issue in marital relationships; they were not ready to relinquish that cherished belief, no matter how prestigious the tutor. Some understandings require a certain amount of life experience and a certain amount of personal maturation.

Fallacy #3. Love is a feeling, a wonderful feeling. In its highest expression, love is not passive (how you feel about someone else) but rather active (how you display loving behavior toward others—kindness, concern, timely assistance). Infatuation is frequently confused with mature love. Infatuation is typically triggered by unconscious stimuli, the mystery of its appearance adding to its enchantment. The ancients pictured love as Cupid's arrow, zinging in out of nowhere to strike the unsuspecting victim. There is some validity to that metaphor, since the workings of the unconscious, at least initially, surpass our ordinary understanding.

Fallacy #4. Adultery is a good reason for divorce. Learning of one's mate's romantic involvement with someone else, a person will usually suffer a heavy blow to vanity and maybe even self-esteem. "What is wrong with me that he chose her over me?" (On another level there may well be hurt feelings over the deception involved or over a promise broken, the promise of loyalty). Blows to the ego are universally unappreciated, yet the rational response to such a trauma is the recognition that one's loved one is not one's property but is a free agent.

It would be preferable if the "violated" mates, rather than falling into self-pity and viewing themselves as injured parties (male victims have been termed cuckolds, for in-

stance), recognized that a partner's infidelity does not necessarily imply dissatisfaction with the marriage. Infidelity *does* indicate that there are some desires that the marriage does not satisfy, but then how can even the most important relationship in one's life fulfill every desire of both partners? The crucial issue is whether the couple has a problem and whether it can be remedied. A conflict may require resolution. A need that has gone unmet may crave gratification.

Fallacy #5. There is a 'right package' for you out there and when you find it (her, him), you get married. Many persons form a mental image of the ideal life partner. Typically the image is visual. The loved one must be attractive in whatever way the individual conceives attractiveness. Particular physical features may seem important. This Package Theory of mate selection is flawed because it overlooks one thing: it is the *interrelationship* of two people, how they feel with each other and how they feel about themselves when together with the loved one, that is critical—not any particular qualities of the romantic stimulus.

I propose the Color Theory of mate selection. If, for example, the male is represented by the color yellow and the female by blue, then let the mixing of hues to produce a particular shade of green symbolize the nature of the relationship. One partner may look at that green and find it pleasing. The other partner may look at the same green, finding it unpleasing. It takes two strong affirmatives to produce a decision to unite.

Fallacy #6. There is a perfect Someone out there for everyone. Two principles seem to me to be valid: There is no perfect partner; and no partner is perfect for you. Still, persons with a good deal of tolerance and flexibility in their makeup could successfully marry a number of people whom they encounter in the course of their lives.

Most people—including individuals who are grossly overweight, unusually tall or short, unprepossessing of face and/or figure—end up with a mate, at least at one point in their lives. Luckily, all do not share the same image of dreamgirl or dreamboy.

In any case, marriageability seems to be much more related to personality than to physique. But not everyone can or will mate successfully. Some people simply do not "partner" well. Fortunately, not everyone needs to mate. Some people do better single.

Fallacy #7. Jealousy is natural and normal. Jealousy shows that you care. Jealousy of one's mate, suspicion that the mate is having an affair, may indicate more than anything else the insecurity of the suspicious one. Jealousy also reflects an attitude that the mate is property rather than that the mate is a partner. One can rail against someone taking one's property without one's permission. But surely one's partner must decide for himself or herself about whether to enter into a romantic relationship outside of marriage. Love, in its noblest expression, involves valuing one's partner's happiness almost as much as one's own. This is the High Road, a road definitely less traveled in my experience. From the rational viewpoint, if you lose your mate to another whom your mate sees as for some reason more desirable, you are entitled to regret the loss. But if you truly esteem your mate, then you want that person to be happy even if happiness is purchased at the expense of the current union.

Fallacy #8. Lose a highly valued partner and your life will be second-class forever after. In matters of romance, things always work out for the best. In general, a relationship between two people will not survive for long unless both parties regard it positively. If now there is one disgruntled party, eventually there will probably be two; marital dissatisfaction felt by one partner breeds dissatisfaction in the mate. Relationships gone sour are abandoned, typically with a good deal of relief. But when finally two people commit to each other, reaffirming their mutual fulfillment repeatedly over time, each party is blessed indeed.

Note that I am not contending that there is no virtue to *remaining* in a flawed and disappointing marriage. Sometimes the reasons for staying together surpass reasons for separation and divorce. Not every marriage has to be violins and roses. There is a place for a marriage of convenience, a marriage continued because the advantages of staying together outweigh the disadvantages of staying together. ✦

Silverman, J. S. (1998). Fallacies about love and marriage. *Journal of Rational-Emotive and Cognitive Behavior Therapy, 16*, 225–229. Reprinted with permission of Kluwer Academic/Plenum Publishers.

Issue 9: Questions to Consider

1. What are the essential elements for a happy marriage, according to Silverman and Grunebaum? Would you add or delete anything from what they have identified as necessary conditions for sustaining a satisfying marriage?

2. Is love an essential element for a happy marriage? Can people be satisfied in their marriages if they do not feel romantic/erotic love for their spouses?

3. Grunebaum contends that we do not have control over our feelings of romantic/erotic love. In contrast, Silverman argues that "love is not ... how you feel about someone else ... but ... how you display loving behavior towards others." How much control over feelings of love do people have? Is love an uncontrollable emotion or something that we do (behavior)?

4. What would Silverman's views be on the topic of soul mates? Do you agree or disagree with the notion that everyone has a soul mate somewhere in the world, and the task is to find that certain someone?

5. Grunebaum thinks that "there are no easy solutions available to the clinician whose clients are experiencing problems with romantic/erotic love. There are no easy solutions because love itself is complicated and perplexing." How would Silverman respond to this statement?

6. Grunebaum illustrates points with examples from couples that he has known. In one of these cases, Virginia wonders in therapy "if spending the rest of her life without experiencing love is to have lived a good life." If you were a friend of Virginia, and she raised this question to you, what would you tell her? What would you advise her to do?

7. One of these authors describes love as a rare occurrence, while the other suggests that love could be quite common. How do you see love? What is your definition of romantic/erotic love?

8. Both of these authors are therapists. If you had a friend who was having some problems regarding love and/or marriage, which one of these therapists would you recommend to your friend. Why? ✦

Issue 10: Introduction

Why Do Men Batter Women? Two Perspectives

Domestic violence is a gender-neutral term—both men and women can be either perpetrators or targets of violence in families. However, most domestic violence consists of women being physically abused by men (husbands, boyfriends). Up to 12 million women in the United States are terrorized by husbands or other male partners (Taylor, Magnusson, and Amundson, 2001). About half of those women are also sexually abused.

Although many people accept men's violence against the women they profess to love as normal, most consider this behavior to be reprehensible and degrading to both women and men. To most of us, physically hurting someone you love makes no sense. Similarly, why women stay with men who physically hurt them is also puzzling to many people. Consequently, many different theories have been developed to try to explain the phenomenon of men battering women.

In the next two selections, explanations from two different theories are presented. Marin and Russo examine feminist perspectives on male violence against women, and Anderson and Schlossberg discuss family systems perspectives. Both of these theories are used widely to explain all kinds of behaviors, including violence in relationships. Researchers, educators, and clinical practitioners who work with couples and families are among the groups of professionals who view violence through the lenses of these theories.

Feminist theories are a collection of theories that focus mainly on women and that generally advocate for women's well-being.

Feminists do not see either intrapersonal or interpersonal reasons as primary causes for why men batter women. They discount personality as a cause ("He has a temper and can't help himself"), genetic reasons ("Men are driven by testosterone to be violent"), and relational explanations ("They lack the skills to disagree without resorting to violence"). Instead, they see male abuse of women being due to cultural beliefs regarding gender roles and to patriarchal values that are supported by social institutions (e.g., legal system, media). Perhaps, most importantly, they do not "blame the victim" (the woman being battered) for her plight. Feminists do not excuse woman battering as being the end result of a woman pressuring a man or asking too much of him.

Family systems theory is actually a school of related theories developed originally by family therapists. In these theories families are seen as social systems embedded in larger contexts such as neighborhoods, communities, and societies. Family systems theories rarely focus on individuals. Instead, emphasis is placed on understanding relationships from a holistic view. That is, the whole of a relationship is greater than the sum of its parts. The actions of individuals in relationships, such as a husband battering a wife, are seen as occurring in an interactional context. Family systems theories would not explain men's violence against women in close relationships as being the result of the characteristics of either partner nor would they likely look for a single causative factor. Instead, explanations include multiple causes that may include personal characteristics, relational patterns within the couple and the larger family system, and influences of other social systems. As you read these two theoretical explanations of why men physically abuse women, take notes on the evidence offered.

Reference

Taylor, W. K., Magnusson, L., and Amundson, M. J. (2001). The lived experience of battered women. *Violence Against Women, 7,* 563–585. ✦

Feminist Perspectives on Male Violence Against Women

Amy Marin and Nancy Felipe Russo

It was not until the late 1980s that [partner] violence was identified as the leading public health risk to adult women by the Surgeon General of the United States. The invisibility of partner violence is remarkable given it is the most common source of injury to women aged 15 to 44, more frequent than muggings, auto accidents, and cancer deaths combined (Dwyer, Smokowski, Bricout, and Wodarski, 1995). Physical assault against both married and unmarried women continues to be a widespread problem, crossing racial, sexual orientation, age, and socioeconomic lines. Research on national samples suggests that 20 to 30 percent of all women will be physically assaulted by a partner or ex-partner at least once in their lives (Frieze and Browne, 1989). Researchers have estimated that these reports may be as much as 50 percent lower than actual incidence rates (Browne, 1992).

The recognition of the widespread, multifaceted, and dynamic nature of partner violence is a tribute to the effect of feminism on U.S. society. Feminists have done more than simply bring attention to the problems of male violence against women. Feminists have organized shelters, developed public education programs, advocated new laws and policies, promoted change in the criminal justice and health care systems, and fostered the development of a new knowledge base that reflects the realities of diverse women's lives.

Feminist writing and theorizing have changed the way that researchers and scientists conceptualize and study male violence against women. From a feminist perspective, male-perpetrated violence against women is considered to be a form of social control used to maintain a subordinate status for women. Feminists have emphasized the social construction of male violence, not the biology or pathology of the individual.

Another significant contribution of feminist theorizing has been a shift toward viewing violence against women as an outgrowth of male power and privilege. Feminists view partner violence as reflective of a larger patriarchal structure that functions to subordinate women. Major institutions (e.g., criminal justice, health, military, athletic, and religious institutions) are seen as reflecting patriarchal values and encouraging and maintaining violence against women. A list of patriarchal values that have become institutionalized in our laws and cultural practices is found in Table 10a-1.

Violence: Naming Its Multiple Forms and Identifying Common Roots

A key contribution of feminist analyses has been the development of complex and sophisticated conceptualizations of violence. Feminists have emphasized the importance of conceptualizing and naming

> ### Table 10a-1
> ### Patriarchal Values Related to Partner Violence
>
> 1. It is the natural, God-given right of men to have power over women.
> 2. The male head of a household should be in charge, hold all power, make the decisions, and be responsible for determining the actions and behaviors of those within the household.
> 3. Masculinity should be defined by powerful characteristics: Strength, agency, independence, power, control, and domination.
> 4. Women pose a threat to male power and therefore need to be controlled. Femininity should be defined by weakness, passivity, dependence, powerlessness, and submissiveness.
> 5. Female sexuality is a particular threat to male power and therefore should be under the control of men, specifically fathers and/or husbands.
> 6. Sexual harassment, rape, physical violence, and any other fear-inducing tactics are legitimate and effective means of enforcing male entitlements and controlling women.

violence in ways that reflect women's experiences. Labels that do not fully encompass physical, sexual, and psychological aspects of violence can exclude the experiences of some women and may downplay the role of men as perpetrators. For example, use of the terms *wife battering* and *marital violence* fails to recognize the large numbers of unmarried or lesbian women who are assaulted by their sexual partners. The terms *intimate violence* and *domestic violence* do not specifically recognize women as targets and men as perpetrators. However violence is defined and named, women are most likely to be the victims, particularly when the violence is severe.

From the point of view of victims, it must be recognized that the threat of violence can be as effective as physical violence as a form of social control. Many feminists thus view acts experienced as threat, coercion, abuse, intimidation, or force used by men to control women as forms of violence. Thus, instances where the situation involves a threat of violence, such as stalking, and sexual terrorism are also forms of male violence against women.

Male violence against women can take many forms, and treating these forms as discreet categories can mask the realities of violence in women's lives. Women who experienced childhood sexual abuse report higher rates of partner violence (Russo, Denious, Keita, and Koss, 1997). Furthermore, dividing battering and rape into distinct and separate categories may obscure the overlapping nature of battery and rape in women's experiences (Russo, Koss, and Goodman, 1995). Similarly, separating violence in the home from violence in the workplace may be a distinction that does not reflect actual experiences. It may be more helpful to think of violence against women as a continuum rather than as discreet categories.

Some common themes emerge from the literature on male-perpetrated violence. First, regardless of the form violence takes, it is a pervasive, tenacious, everyday event in many women's lives, an event that crosses the lines of race, ethnicity, national origin, class, religion, age, and sexual orientation.

Second, in all forms of violence between intimates, men are most likely to be the perpetrators and women are most likely to be the targets. This suggests that understanding gender-role constructions is key to predicting and preventing violence. We need to know more about how these constructions vary—ethnicity, age, and region of the country are just a few examples of sources of variation in such constructions.

Third, understanding the relationship of violence to power dynamics is key. The sociocultural context encourages the use of violence to maintain inequitable power relationships in the workplace, home, and community. Fourth, the majority of women who experience violence are abused by people with whom they live and work. This suggests that relational expectations play roles in shaping and perpetuating violence.

Fifth, social institutions tend to trivialize or ignore women's experiences of violence. Coaches, judges, law enforcement officials, social service workers, religious leaders, teachers, and even mental health professionals have contributed to the prevailing cultural attitudes that serve to maintain and foster male violence. Our social structures themselves often reflect inequitable gender relationships that serve to maintain the legitimacy of male violence (relationships between female workers and male employers, wives and husbands, female patients and male doctors, female athletes and male coaches, share structural and ideological features in which women are subordinate to men). Inequities reinforce the patriarchal world-view that male domination over women is normal, natural, and expected.

Health care systems, schools, workplaces, and courts exhibit systematic support for male violence against women. The attitudes and practices of doctors indicate that many are failing to play a role in the prevention and treatment of men's violence against women. For example, partner violence often is ignored as a potential cause of problems in female patients seeking medical treatment in emergency rooms.

Legal and judicial systems enforce existing power relationships and thereby perpetuate partner violence. Studies of police response to partner violence indicate that levels of arrests are low, protection of women is often withheld, and the attitude of the state reflects a desire to stay out of family disputes and let the family members work the problems out privately. Some research suggests that police officers may discourage women from filing formal charges against a violent spouse (George, Winfield, and Blazer, 1992). In one study of 1,870 partner violence reports over a 12-month period, less than 28 percent of cases ended in arrest. Although men were more likely to be identified as batterers, women identified as batterers were more likely to be charged with a serious crime (Bourg and Stock, 1994). Even if the male perpetrator is ar-

rested, there are additional biases and problems in our legal system. Legal outcomes in court cases of partner violence are highly dependent on the attitudes of individual judges rather than on firm legal standards. Investigations examining situations in which the justice system has failed to provide protection to female victims of partner violence have exposed several problems: the trivialization of women's experiences by law enforcement officials and judges, problems with arrest policies, and a myth that both partners are equally responsible for the violent behavior. The inability of the justice system to deal effectively with partner violence continues to be a major factor in the perpetuation of violence.

Sixth, feminists have exposed the destructive effects of male violence to the woman, her family, and society. Women who have been victimized suffer both immediate and long-range consequences to their physical and mental well-being. Effects of partner violence can extend beyond physical wounds to include a variety of psychological consequences. The after-effects of partner violence may look very much like those experienced following any severe trauma—feelings of fearfulness, anxiety, confusion, anger, and powerlessness (Herman, 1992). Reactions of shock, denial, depression, and withdrawal also may occur. Women victims of partner violence also may exhibit the symptoms of PTSD (post-traumatic stress disorder), which include dissociation, flashbacks, sleep disturbances, and irritability.

Partner violence can have far-reaching as well as indirect effects on women's lives. Some of these consequences include high-risk sexual behavior and sexually transmitted diseases (Nelson, Higginson, and Grant-Worley, 1995), and drug and alcohol abuse (Dutton, 1992). Partner violence also is linked to unwanted pregnancy (Gazmararian et al., 1995).

One of the major indirect consequences of male-perpetrated violence is the effect it has on children who may witness or be involved in the abuse. Even when children are not abused, witnessing partner violence may have far-reaching consequences. Male children who have witnessed a father batter a mother are more likely to use violence in their adult lives than are male children from nonabusive homes (Straus, Gelles, and Steinmetz, 1980). Partner violence in the home is predictive of children's general psychopathology (McCloskey, Figueredo, and Koss, 1995).

In conclusion, feminists have emphasized that male violence against women is a complex phenomenon that takes multiple forms and is rooted in patriarchal social structures and cultural roles of women and men. Feminists have documented widespread and long-lasting effects of violence to the woman, her family, and society, providing irrefutable justification for the argument that society cannot afford to define partner violence as a private issue. Understanding, predicting, and preventing such violence will require a complex and comprehensive approach that intervenes at individual, interpersonal, and structural levels.

We need to identify the factors that suppress or inhibit violent tendencies and that reduce the probability that a man will be violent toward his partner. Given exposure to so many violent models in society, knowing how some learn to inhibit and redirect that potential is as important as knowing what creates and perpetuates violent inclinations in the first place. Explanations of male violence against women must address two questions: "Why are males violent and why is it that the women closest to them are primarily the targets?"

Macrosocietal Explanations

It is important to recognize that society is a reflection of every aspect of societal functioning, including material artifacts, language, beliefs, values, norms, skills, habits, customs, laws, and institutions. If we are to understand how battering might result from historical patterns in America, it is important to take this broader view of the larger sociocultural context.

In considering macro-level strategies to inhibit violence, we have yet to see a thorough economic analysis of who benefits

from violence and what tactics are used in the service of those interests. Who benefits from cultural beliefs that the world is threatening and that we need to purchase firearms to defend our homes? We suspect that a primary prevention strategy attempting to foster a cultural norm of nonviolence (through a media campaign or school-based interventions, for example) would be actively undermined by economic interests that depend on weapon sales. This is an example of how an aspect of our material culture (in this case, the prevalence of weapons) can contribute to normalizing the idea of violent behavior, as well as increasing the risk of injury and death associated with partner violence.

Another hypothesis that is strongly emphasized by feminist perspectives is the focus on unequal power relationships. We need to know more about how traditional patriarchal values in our culture have become reflected in our organizational and institutional structures, which in turn legitimize and maintain male violence against women. Clergy, physicians, and others implicitly and explicitly have supported and perpetuated male violence. In fact, insofar as any institution undermines women's economic independence from men, that institution contributes to unequal power relationships between men and women, thereby aiding and abetting intimate violence directly and indirectly. Institutional structures can perpetuate male violence in ways not obviously related to patriarchal values or gender-based inequalities in power. For example, lack of low-cost housing has forced some battered women to choose between staying in an abusive relationship or becoming homeless. Women's lack of economic resources thus makes lack of access to low-income housing a battered women's issue. In exploring how societal structures support violence against women, it is important to consider that there may be interactive effects between institutional structures and economic factors that create inadvertent support for that violence. In considering cultural supports for patriarchal values, however, it should be remembered that a culture perpetuates patriarchal values through more than its social structures and institutions.

Recent societal changes regarding expectations and realities in women's lives have produced men's fears about loss and increased violence toward women. Some authors have suggested that insofar as power over women becomes a defining quality of manhood, men will go so far as to use violence to preserve it. This hypothesis merits further exploration. However, we believe that it should be expanded to include male expectations for entitlement and privilege. Although power may be self-reinforcing and may become a part of manhood's definition, an understanding of men's use of power requires understanding the patriarchal values it serves.

This hypothesis needs to be crafted with care because if it constructs women's changing roles as a "cause" for violence, it may provide legitimization for male violence against women and lower inhibitions against violence. Batterers already have been found to point to "unwifely behaviors" as a defense for their violent acts. Even among college students, women viewed as provoking their batterers are perceived less sympathetically than women who are perceived as not provoking their batterers (Pierce and Harris, 1993). We cannot permit men to make the attribution that their violence is "caused by" women's changing roles. Males must take responsibility for their violent behavior. Focusing on women's behavior rather than male patriarchal values and beliefs puts the male perspective at the center of the analysis and perpetuates the status quo.

Although research is clearly needed, a full understanding of the relationship between changing roles of women and partner violence will require taking into account both facilitating and inhibiting factors. Interpreting any relationship between women's changing roles and their experience of violence must take into account the changing population base of violent families. Insofar as greater economic independence of women's changing roles enables them to leave violent situations, any portrait of the relationship between women's roles and violence that is based on the women who remain in such relationships will be incomplete. The dynamics of violence and the psychological characteristics of women in violent relationships may be very different in battered women who have the economic resources to leave violent relationships, but have stayed, compared with women who do not have the economic resources to leave.

Biology-Related Explanations

Research on the relationship of genes, hormones, and other biological differences to men's violence against women suffers from problems that commonly arise whenever biological explanations of behavior are proposed. There is confusion between correlation and causation, and failure to appreciate that behavior is a product of the interaction between biology and environment. It is important to recognize that biology is not equivalent to heredity; it is a product of heredity interacting with environment.

We suspect that the most promising avenue of research into the contribution of biological factors to aggressive behavior in general, and violence against women in particular, will be research that examines how biological and cognitive processes interact to influence emotion, particularly the emotion of anger. For example, Lazarus (1991) suggested that whether anger is the emotion an aroused person responds with in a particular situation depends on the person's cognitive appraisal of the *meaning* of the situation. Anger results when a person perceives a threat to his identity or basic values, which leads to an appraisal of a personal insult. Anger becomes linked to ideas of retaliation and vengeance because they offer ways to repair a damaged ego. Insofar as cultural norms lead males to expect entitlement and privilege, anger may result when those expectations are violated.

These theories provide a bridge between biological and social-role theories of male violence toward women. To these we now turn.

Gender-Role–Related Explanations

Gender-role socialization provides for the transmission of the cultural values of patriarchy, including male entitlement, privilege, and domination. All gender-related behaviors, including male violence against women, can be conceptualized as reflections of gender roles rather than individual traits. The masculine gender role includes qualities of leadership, power, and control. Males are encouraged and expected to engage in inequitable power relationships with females. Violence is often viewed as a means to exert power and maintain control.

Although batterers have been found to hold misogynistic attitudes toward women, the relationship of such attitudes to battering behaviors is not understood. We suggest that such attitudes function as disinhibitors, legitimizing women as a target for violent behavior and paving the way for the translation of arousal into anger and aggression directed toward women if other factors are present.

Theories of emotion that consider the interaction of biological, cognitive, and relational processes have promise for exploring how batterers interpret their experiences and express their emotions. Is male violence toward women an expression of anger at the erosion of male entitlements or is it an expression of frustration in other domains (e.g., employment) redirected toward a target that has been legitimized by patriarchal values? Understanding the cognitive processes of batterers may be the key to understanding the development and transformation of their emotional experiences.

Patriarchal attitudes are transmitted and reinforced through the mass media. Although there has been an increased awareness of male violence against women in the media, this awareness has not always yielded favorable outcomes. As news coverage of partner violence has increased from the 1970s to the present, so too have popular TV and Hollywood movies on the subject. Unfortunately, many of these films have served to reinforce existing ideologies that emphasize individual choice and free will. Larger structural forces are often ignored in media portrayals of male violence against women. In addition, repeated exposure to violent media has been shown to desensitize participants to partner violence. Ratings of sympathy for partner violence victims and ratings of the severity of their injuries have been found to decrease after repeated exposure to such films (Mullins and Linz, 1995).

Male lack of empathy and sensitivity to others is of concern here because such feelings are important inhibitors of violence against women. For example, research suggests that whether male fantasies about sexual aggression are actually expressed depends on how sensitive they are to others' feelings (Dean and Malamuth, 1997). Indeed, empathy has been found to moderate the relationship between physiological measures of sexual arousal and aggressive behavior. Such arousal predicts aggression when empathy is low, but not when empathy is high. Insofar as male gender-role socialization fails to instill a capacity for empathy in general, and for women in particular, it increases the likelihood of male violence.

Gender-role socialization also must be considered in the context of socialization into the larger culture, because other cultural values may have facilitating or inhibiting effects on gender-role dynamics. For example, the cultural value of individualism may result in drawing attention away from the structural factors that foster gender violence. However, it also may provide a counterforce to patriarchal values, fostering recognition of women as people with the full rights and responsibilities accorded to all citizens. A comprehensive approach should examine how specific gender-role values and expectations are reinforced and contravened by other cultural values and expectations, and how factors (e.g., individualism) may have effects in more than one direction.

Inter-Gender Relational Explanations

Although we agree that differential socialization of males and females contributes to male violence against women, we do not believe that differences in patterns of communication related to instrumentality and expressiveness are a major factor in the potential for that violence. We prefer to focus on the fact that gender-role socialization includes learning patriarchal relational scripts that can promote interpersonal violence. There is a basic heterosexual cultural script that legitimizes male dominance and eroticizes sexual inequality. The idea that women should seek out male partners who are older, taller, stronger, bigger, more educated, higher in status, more experienced, and more highly paid transforms female inequality into a romantic ideal. Male-centered objectification of women that emphasizes women's physical attractiveness and ability to satisfy men's desires provides another powerful buttress to inequality in the heterosexual script. We need to know more about how such scripts shape male-female communication and undermine the development of mutual respect and understanding between men and women.

Specifically, we need to learn more about how dating and other relationship scripts foster values, beliefs, and expectations that facilitate and inhibit violence. We know that destructive dating scripts can be acquired early. One study found that 57 percent of girls and 65 percent of boys reported that it was acceptable for a man to force a woman to have sex if they had been dating for more than 6 months ("Teens Express Themselves," 1988). We suspect that the idea that it is all right to use force to get a partner to do something generalizes beyond sexual intercourse. Once permissible violence becomes an acceptable part of the heterosexual script, then whether or not such violence is used probably depends on the number and the strength of the inhibiting factors present.

Males are taught to expect entitlement and privilege, along with the respect and subservience that go along with those characteristics. These expectations may lead to patriarchal scripts for interaction that, when violated, lead to the emotion of anger, and if inhibiting factors are not present, that anger in turn may lead to violence.

Although we agree that psychological abuse is probably a precursor to physical violence, we do not believe that women's alleged superiority in verbal warfare plays a significant role in that escalation. We suspect that psychological abuse provides a means for batterers to identify women who will tolerate abuse and be unable to defend themselves. Women who avoid relationships with abusive men are thus selected out of the batterer's pool of targets. Psychological abuse also may have a disinhibiting effect on violent behavior. We argue, however, that the idea that the verbal skills of battered women threaten their partners and that battering is a means to restore masculine identity or diminished self-esteem is a faulty construction of the dynamics. We agree that battering is a means to enforce male entitlements, manifest a batterer's sense of masculine identity, and buttress self-esteem, but the woman's behavior has little to do with it. No matter how hard a battered woman tries to please her husband, he can still find excuses for battering her.

Partner Violence Through a Feminist Lens

Explaining partner violence from a feminist perspective involves an understanding of how patriarchal values become institutionalized and communicated. Many broad theories of violence fail to explain why male violence is directed at women, or why partner violence is so common compared with other forms of male violence. Feminist approaches to partner violence seek to explain why women are often the victims, and men the perpetrators. They also seek to understand why the consequences of male violence become denied and trivialized, and the functions that male violence serve in the larger society. Patriarchal values serve as a starting point for understanding gendered violence dynamics.

At the macrosocietal level, our legal system, institutions, and other societal structures reflect and perpetuate these values. These patriarchal values are passed down from generation to generation through direct instruction as well as observational learning. Many families communicate these values through actual physical force, which may explain why children from abusive homes often end up abusing their own partners and children. At a cultural level, the mass media reproduces and reinforces patriarchal values. Finally, at the individual level, patriarchal values can become incorporated into everyday thought and action as men who expect to be able to control the women in their lives resort to physical violence, sexual violence, or both when their privileged status is threatened. Eliminating male violence against women requires working at all of these levels. In the final analysis, however, striking at the core of male violence—at the androcentric assumption that males have a natural or God-given right to privilege and entitlement over women that justifies the use of force to achieve male goals—will be the key to preventing male violence against women.

References

Bourg, S., and Stock, H. V. (1994). A review of domestic violence arrest statistics in a police department using a pro-arrest policy: Are pro-arrest policies enough? *Journal of Family Violence, 9,* 177–189.

Browne, A. (1992). Violence against women: Relevance for medical practitioners. *Journal of the American Medical Association, 267,* 3184–3189.

Dean, K., and Malamuth, N. (1997). Characteristics of men who aggress sexually and of men who imagine aggressing: Risk and moderating variables. *Journal of Personality and Social Psychology, 72,* 449–455.

Dutton, M. A. (1992). Assessment and treatment of PTSD among battered women. In D. Foy (Ed.), *Treating PTSD: Cognitive and be-*

havioral strategies (pp. 69–98). New York: Guilford.

Dwyer, D. C., Smokowski, P. R., Bricout, J. C., and Wodarski, J. S. (1995). Domestic violence research: Theoretical and practical implications for social work. *Clinical Social Work Journal, 23,* 185–198.

Frieze, I. H., and Browne, A. (1989). Violence in marriage. In L. Ohlin and M. H. Torrey (Eds.), *New approaches to social problems: Applications of attribution theory* (pp. 79–108). Chicago: University of Chicago Press.

Gazmararian, J. A., Adams, M. M., Saltzman, L. E., Johnson, C. H., Bruce, F. C., Marks, J. S., and Zahniser, S. C. (1995). The relationship between pregnancy intendedness and physical violence in mothers of newborns. *Obstetrics and Gynecology, 85,* 1031–1038.

George, L. K., Winfield, I., and Blazer, D. G. (1992). Sociocultural factors in sexual assault: Comparison of two representative samples of women. *Journal of Social Issues, 48,* 105–125.

Herman, J. L. (1992). *Trauma and recovery.* New York: Basic Books.

Lazarus, R. S. (1991). Cognition and motivation in emotion. *American Psychologist, 46,* 352–367.

McCloskey, L. A., Figueredo, A. J., and Koss, P. (1995). The effects of systemic family violence on children's mental health. *Child Development, 66,* 1239–1261.

Mullins, C. R., and Linz, D. (1995). Desensitization and representation to violence against women: Effects of exposure to sexually violent films on judgements of domestic violence victims. *Journal of Personality and Social Psychology, 69,* 449–459.

Nelson, D. E., Higginson, G. K., and Grant-Worley, J. A. (1995). Psychical abuse among high school students. Prevalence and correlation with other health behaviors. *Archives of Pediatric Adolescent Medicine, 149,* 1254–1258.

Pierce, M. C., and Harris, R. J. (1993). The effect of provocation, race, and injury description on men's and women's perceptions of a wife-battering incident. *Journal of Applied Social Psychology, 23,* 767–790.

Russo, N. F., Denious, J., Keita, G. P., and Koss, M. P. (1997). Intimate violence and black women's health. *Women's Health: Research on Gender, Behavior, and Public Policy, 3(3–4),* 315–348.

Russo, N. F., Koss, M. P., and Goodman, L. (1995). Male violence against women: A global health and development issue. In L. L. Adler and F. L. Denmark (Eds.), *Violence and prevention of violence* (pp. 121–127). Westport, CT: Praeger.

Straus, M. A., Gelles, R. J., and Steinmetz, S. (1980). *Behind closed doors: Violence in the American family.* Garden City, NY: Anchor.

Teens express themselves (1988). *The state* [Columbia, SC], p. 2A. ✦

10b

Family Systems Perspectives on Battering: The Importance of Context

Stephen Anderson and Margaret Schlossberg

The problem of men battering women is a complex issue, and no one perspective has yet been able to explain the phenomenon fully. Much of the available literature has emphasized individual or societal perspectives. Individual perspectives emphasize the characteristics, personality traits, and level of psychopathology of the individual batterer. Sociological and feminist perspectives highlight the sanctions that society fails to place upon men's use of violence or the sociopolitical climate that reinforces an unequal, patriarchal power structure that favors men's dominance over women and supports male aggression and violence as acceptable norms. Systems theories, in contrast, emphasize an *interpersonal perspective* that focuses upon the social and relational contexts and the unique patterns of interaction that recur within relationships. Systems perspectives highlight the unique histories of each partner and the situational factors that characterize a given relationship.

Some have suggested [that] family systems theorists have denied or minimized the problem of battering. We contend that systems perspectives have a great deal to offer the study of battering. Research consistently has pointed to the importance of the relational context and the pattern of interactions that occur over time in violent relationships. Attention to family systems formulations can raise additional questions

for study that have remained relatively unaddressed.

Two hypotheses provide the organization of this paper: (1) Men's violence toward women can be understood only by examining the social and relational contexts within which it occurs and (2) understanding male-to-female violence requires an examination of the patterns of interaction that characterize battering relationships.

We use the term *battering* to describe male-to-female violence. Battering is the systematic use of physical aggression or the threat of physical aggression to intimidate, subjugate, and control another human being. This definition incorporates forms of psychological or emotional abuse when these behaviors involve strategies intended to coerce the woman's freedom, it distinguishes the kinds of physical aggression enacted by women toward men from those enacted by men toward women (rarely do women systematically use physical aggression to subjugate or control men), and this definition emphasizes that abuse is a pattern that occurs within a relationship over time.

The following research findings support our view of the importance of systems perspectives in understanding battering. First, men are able to control their violence, because the majority of batterers are not violent against others outside their families. This, combined with the fact that violence is usually perpetrated against the batterer's own children and wife, suggests that the locus of violence is in the relational context rather than within the individual. Second, although it is important to consider the cultural and political contexts within which violence occurs, these dimensions are not sufficient to explain violence, because batterers are not violent 24 hours a day, seven days a week.

Third, there is no consistent psychological or sociocultural profile of the battered woman. As Hotaling and Sugarman (1990) noted after reviewing 400 empirical studies and the reanalysis of some national data,

> there is no evidence that the statuses a woman occupies, the roles she performs, her demographic profile, or her personality characteristics consistently influence her chances of becoming a victim of wife assault. (p. 393)

Instead, what appears to be more predictive of the woman's risk for repeated assault are situational variables such as a woman's financial dependence upon her partner, fear of threats of retaliation toward her or her children, hope based upon his promises that he will change, shame associated with reporting the violence, and avoidance or victim blaming by helping professionals or significant others. Such situational factors point to the relational and broader social contexts as critical factors in understanding the woman's participation in a battering relationship.

Fourth, despite consistent findings of significant correlations between male violence and variables, such as drug and alcohol problems, low self-esteem, inexpressiveness, dependency, jealousy, and rigid and traditional attitudes toward women, there is growing consensus that no conclusive single batterer profile exists. This also suggests that the relational context may be a critical factor in understanding differences in the types of batterers.

Fifth, studies have shown that physically aggressive and nonaggressive marriages can be differentiated on the basis of interactional variables. For example, violent couples differ from nonviolent couples in their level of positive communication skills and problem-solving styles. Several studies have found that the behaviors of physically aggressive spouses were highly contingent upon the behaviors of their partners. When one spouse exhibited angry or contemptuous affect, the partner was likely to reciprocate that behavior. This pattern was more consistent and lasted longer for violent couples than for nonviolent and nondistressed couples (Burman, John, and Margolin, 1992). The interactional patterns and styles of communication that couples enact to deal with interpersonal problems and situational stresses are central issues in systems perspectives.

Sixth, the majority of violent couples stay together (Lloyd, 1996). Placing full responsibility for the abuse upon the man does not alter the need to understand the dynamics that operate in these systems. This information is essential if we are to develop more effective treatments to alter repeating interactional cycles that serve as the context for abuse.

Seventh, assigning blame for the violence to the perpetrator may, in fact, perpetuate the woman's perception of her own ineffectiveness and victimization, based on research that has found that most battered women attribute responsibility for the violence at least partly to themselves, especially in the early stages of a violent relationship (Cantos, Neidig, and O'Leary, 1993). Assigning blame to one or both partners fails to focus on the issue of both people having inadequate skills. A systemic view of female battering must take into account the actions of the batterer, the responses of both partners, and the unique context within which the violence occurs. Neither partner must be seen as a victim. Both are capable of changing their behavior. The woman can learn how to protect herself and her children, and the batterer can learn to control his violent behavior.

Some of the criticisms leveled against systems perspectives are valid, whereas others are not. For instance, systems perspectives *describe* violent interactions and emphasize questions such as "How do violent men relate to their wives?" and "How do wives respond when their husbands become violent?" Systems theories do not provide causal explanations for the question, "Why do men batter their wives?" It is inconsistent to use systems theories to *explain the cause* of family violence because systems theories do not address cause and effect. It is inconsistent to use systems theory to assert that violence results from the partners' need to maintain a pattern or that violence is the product of an interaction between an "over-adequate woman" and an "under-adequate man" who uses violence to reestablish the equilibrium in the relationship. Such interpretations use interactional concepts in a manner inconsistent with systems perspectives.

A common criticism of systems perspectives is that they implicitly blame the victim and absolve the batterer by seeing the relationship, rather than the batterer, as the focus of study. Drawing a blaming/nonblaming distinction is again inconsistent with systems perspectives, which are more concerned with "how persons are involved in a battering relationship" than with "who is to blame." A systems perspective does not absolve batterers of responsibility for their violence nor does it blame the victim. It does take into account the complex set of influences that define each interpersonal encounter and holds each partner responsible for actions that contribute to abusive interactions.

Systems theorists have been criticized for ignoring the social, political, and cultural contexts that reinforce a patriarchal social system, protect men's dominance, maintain women in subordinate positions, and ignore women's victimization. Although valid, it should be stressed that systems perspectives always have espoused the importance of multiple levels of context in understanding family dynamics and behavior. These include biological, psychological, societal, and even broader ecological levels.

Finally, perhaps the most compelling argument against systems theories has been their inability to address the power politics of traditional gender roles, the family's division of labor, and the status of women in society and in the family. By emphasizing pattern, context, and circular interaction, systems perspectives are said to be unable to address concepts such as power. Although there is some merit to these arguments, it is not entirely the case that systems perspectives are unable to address power.

One way to conceptualize power is in terms of an interpersonal bargaining process by which one achieves intended effects over another. This process is governed by prevailing societal norms (e.g., the gender roles of men and women), a couple's established communication patterns, the level of trust in the relationship, and each partner's assessment of the costs and rewards associated with a given course of action.

Power is not a property of a person nor is it the inevitable by-product of a particular social or cultural context. Rather, power is determined by a variety of contextual variables (e.g., societal norms, public policies, availability of economic resources, family-of-origin experiences, and outcomes of the couple's previous interactions) and by the ongoing process of negotiation that has been established between the partners. It is these factors that explain the individual batterer's violent actions and the partner's responses. Both participants are viewed as exerting interpersonal power (influencing or attempting to influence the other) and both are, at the same time, influenced by external forces over which they have limited or no control. This is perhaps both the strength and limitation of systems perspectives. They provide no help in defining the causes of oppression, status inequality, gender discrimination, or family violence.

It should be clear that the two most important contributions of systems perspectives are in understanding the context within which battering occurs and in understanding the interactional patterns that occur within battering relationships. We now examine these two dimensions in more detail.

Contextual Factors Related to Battering

Research on battering has identified a number of factors that may compose the context within which battering occurs. The context within which battering occurs differs for each relationship or family system. Each is the product of unique individuals, with distinct personal traits, abilities, histories, and past relationship experiences. We review the factors that have been associated with battering to highlight critical variables and to emphasize the complexity involved in understanding battering. This includes socioeconomic variables, alcohol and drug use, stress, isolation and the absence of social support, societal norms, earlier family-of-origin experiences, and marital conflict.

Socioeconomic factors, such as the batterer's level of education, occupational prestige, and income, are thought to be one element of the context of battering. Violence is more likely to occur when the husband has fewer perceived or actual resources than his wife, because he may feel threatened by his wife's status relative to his own (Yllo and Bograd, 1988). The context of battering frequently involves the use of alcohol or other drugs on the part of the batterer. Drugs and alcohol may act as a disinhibitor for those prone to violence or provide a justification or excuse for violence. Sometimes the substance abuse becomes a topic of contention between the batterer and his wife. Battering is more likely to occur among individuals experiencing higher levels of stress. Stress results when the demands upon the individual or family system are beyond the system's resources for coping. Violence is one response or strategy for coping with stress and frustration. For instance, if a husband cannot meet his family responsibilities and role expectations because of inadequate education, a low status job, or low income, the level of stress is enhanced and the likelihood of violence increases. *Isolation* from community, extended family, and other social supports exacerbates the effects of stress and marital conflict by removing potential coping resources, such as emotional support, information, and legal and professional assistance, from the woman. Batterers often attempt to limit the wife's outside contacts, and such isolation diminishes the likelihood that societal sanctions will be imposed upon the batterer and the likelihood that interventions will be sought to teach him more effective coping strategies to replace the violence. *Societal norms*, such as role stereotypes that support men as rational, aggressive, and dominant, and women as emotionally expressive, irrational, accommodating, and dependent, constitute another contextual factor. Such sex-role differences reinforce societal tolerance of battering and the use of violence as a viable solution to conflict and other problems.

The context within which violence occurs also includes the experiences of partners in their own *families of origin*. One of the most common research findings is that adults who were abused as children, or who witnessed marital abuse as children, are more likely to be abusive with their partners as adults (Doumas, Margolin, and John, 1994). Family-of-origin experiences establish a legacy that affects identity development, attitudes and beliefs about women, and strategies to deal with significant others. Consistent with systems perspectives, researchers have concluded that violence in one's family of origin is neither sufficient nor necessary for violence in one's current intimate relationship (Pagelow, 1992).

A high level of conflict and *marital distress* are additional contextual factors that are significantly related to battering (Stets, 1990). Distressed couples experience higher levels of stress than satisfied couples, and they tend to blame each other, complain, criticize, and put each other down. It is important to keep in mind that not all conflicted or distressed relationships experience violence. Furthermore, not all violent relationships are characterized by marital distress.

From a systems perspective, the contextual factors, representing social, cultural, extended family, and individual levels, are thought to be moderated by the patterns and dynamics that operate within the family system. Although it must accommodate its cultural environment, the family and its members actively screen, interpret, and modify cultural standards to fit with the family's identity, their system and rules for relating. The family's relationship rules and role expectations are further defined by the qualities, traits, and abilities of its members. The context influences the strategies the family develops to manage its daily tasks; regulates the emotional environment; establishes the identity of each member and the family as a whole; and regulates the boundaries between individual members and subsystems, and between the family and the outside world. Socioeconomic factors, alcohol or drug abuse, stress, social isolation, societal norms, one's family-of-origin experiences, or marital conflict are not thought to cause battering. Rather, they enhance the likelihood that men will use violence and that the family will organize around the battering as a strategy for relating.

Interaction Patterns Associated With Battering

On the whole, we know little about interactions that occur during battering episodes. Much of our knowledge comes from retrospective self-reports of those engaged in battering episodes. Observational studies with couples who have acknowledged battering have shown that batterers engage in higher levels of threat, blame, criticism, and other negative behaviors than husbands in nonviolent marriages. Both husbands and wives in violent marriages enacted fewer positive behaviors (approval, smiling, paraphrasing) and greater levels of disagreement, criticism, and put downs than did partners in nonviolent marriages. They also were more likely to exhibit rigid patterns of interaction in which hostile, angry behaviors by one partner would trigger hostile responses by the other (Burman, John, and Margolin, 1992). Violent couples have been

found to differ from nonviolent couples in their level of communication and problem solving skills (Sabourin, Infante, and Rudd, 1993). When husband and wife are both deficient in communication ability and the husband is less powerful, there is a greater risk of battering (Babcock, Waltz, Jacobson, and Gottman, 1993). Overt verbal hostility and passive aggression are precursors to battering (O'Leary, Malone, and Tyree, 1994).

It is not the presence of conflict that distinguishes the battering relationship from others. Conflict is inevitable in any intimate relationship. The critical factor is how conflict is negotiated within the relationship. Couples differ in the degree to which their strategies are effective or ineffective in managing conflict. Positive strategies promote mutual understanding, resolve differences, and foster intimacy. Destructive strategies are oriented toward "winning at all costs" or exerting control over another. Systems perspectives assume that partners in a battering relationship lack skills for constructively handling conflict. This, combined with contextual factors (e.g., family-of-origin experiences, substance abuse), increases the risk of battering. Violence escalates as a result of failed attempts to resolve conflicts through less negative strategies.

Some may read this assessment as holding the battered woman responsible for the battering and minimizing the responsibility of the batterer. A counterargument could be raised that women do nothing to provoke their partners and have been found to demonstrate effective social and interpersonal skills in intimate relationships with other men after being separated from the batterer. More recent research has not supported this latter view, finding instead that both men and women reenact similar roles (batterer, battered) and relational strategies in subsequent relationships (Kalmuss and Seltzer, 1986). Furthermore, many women respond in ways that escalate or reinforce the pattern of violence (Flynn, 1990).

Future Research Questions Derived From Systems Perspectives

Systems perspectives offer considerable promise in helping unravel the complex processes that occur within battering relationships. We list a number of questions that we believe warrant further empirical examination.

1. Can Relational Typologies Be Developed to Describe Previous Research on Battering Relationships More Accurately?

Holtzworth-Munroe and Stuart (1994) hypothesize three subtypes of batterers that were consistent with previous research. *Family-only* batterers, the most common type, were least violent and were violent only with family members. They were the least likely to have psychological, legal, or substance abuse problems, or to have witnessed violence in their families of origin. Family-only batterers also were described as having more satisfying and less conflictual marriages. They were most likely to feel remorse and shame over the battering. *Dysphoric borderline* batterers were described as more emotionally unstable and violent primarily within the family, but also sometimes outside the family. They were described as engaging in more severe violence that included physical, psychological, and sexual violence [and] as having extreme dependency upon their wives, showing high levels of jealousy, marital dissatisfaction, and ambivalence about their relationships. *Generally violent* batterers were described as the most violent, the most likely to treat their wives as objects, the least likely to show remorse, and the most likely to blame their partners for the battering. They were most likely to have social personality disorders, be criminally violent outside the home, have alcohol or drug abuse problems, and to have witnessed violence in their own families of origin. We propose that such batterer typologies might be a useful starting point for developing relational typologies that describe different relationship dynamics within each group. For instance, couples in the *family-only* group may be more likely, because of poor communication and problem-solving skills, to engage in escalating cycles of verbal conflict and physical aggression. Wives in such relationships may be more likely to "fight back," given the less severe nature of the marital problems and the generally lower level of physical danger. Relational themes of intense possessiveness, jealousy, loyalty, control, rejection, abandonment, enmeshment, and poor individuation that have been identified in the literature may be more likely to occur in the *dysphoric borderline* typology (Lloyd, 1996). Such relationships also may be the most dangerous for wives to leave and the most likely to include patterns of stalking or other forms of intense surveillance and control of women's behavior. In contrast, themes of impulsivity, unpredictability, volatility, extreme oppression, and depersonalization may characterize the *generally violent* group. Wives in these relationships may be the most likely to report unprovoked assaults and to feel the most terrorized, traumatized, and fearful of fighting back. Our hypotheses are intended only to illustrate an avenue for future research.

2. What Are the Characteristics of the Interaction Patterns in Couples Who Successfully Terminate Violence in Their Relationship?

Research has suggested that as many as one half of battering relationships cease to be violent over time (Woffordt, Mihalic, and Menard, 1994). Yet we know little about the couples who succeed in maintaining their relationship and successfully terminate the battering. For instance, do couples who overcome violence differ significantly from those who do not in the types or severity of contextual variables influencing their relationship (e.g., severity of alcohol use, stress, isolation from the community or extended family, and family-of-origin experiences)?

Do they differ in their level of communication, or problem-solving skills, or in their strategies for negotiating power issues within the relationship? Answers to such questions should assist in the development of more effective prevention and treatment strategies.

3. What Are the Interactional Dynamics That Occur Within Family-of-Origin Experiences That May Account for the Intergenerational Cycle of Violence?

Are there particular patterns of interaction that occur within the family of origin that can help explain how some individuals who are exposed to family violence during childhood perpetuate this pattern into their adult relationships and some do not? There appears to be a greater likelihood of becoming involved in a violent relationship in adulthood when one witnesses violence between significant others as opposed to experiencing it directly, but, what are the mechanisms by which this occurs? Caesar (1988) presented some anecdotal evidence to suggest that batterers were more likely to become caught up in their parents' marital conflicts and to be enlisted by one parent or the other as an ally or a mediator. In contrast, those who did not become batterers as adults were more likely to remain disengaged from the family conflicts. These same patterns have been observed even in children who witness marital conflicts between the parents that do not involve physical violence. We still know little about family processes, earlier childhood and their relationship to adult family violence.

4. What Is the Relationship Between Violence in the Marital Relationship and the Functioning of Other Subsystems in the Family, Such as the Parenting Subsystem?

Systems perspectives assume that stress or conflict in one part of the family affects functioning in other parts of the system. Studies have begun to address the question of whether the impact of battering on children is the direct result of witnessing traumatic events or an indirect result, affecting parents' ability to parent their children effectively in a hostile environment. Results suggest that battering is related to children's adjustment indirectly through impaired parenting strategies that involve a complex set of variables, including the parents' and child's gender, the responses of the child to each parent, and the responses of each parent to the other parent's actions toward the child (Margolin, John, Ghosh, and Gordis, 1996). Additional research is needed to unravel relationships between battering and different subsystems within the family.

5. What Role Do Current Family-of-Origin Relationships Play in Perpetuating or Ending the Battering?

We know of no research that has examined the role of parents, siblings, and other extended family members in encouraging or discouraging the current battering relationship.

6. Do Battering Relationships Follow a Developmental Course?

Studies have shown that at least some battering relationships follow a pattern of progressively more frequent and severe episodes of battering over time (O'Leary, Malone, and Tyree, 1994). We know that over time, abuse tends to erode the quality of the relationship. Cantos, Neidig, and O'Leary (1993) found that mutual aggression that was not in self-defense was most common in young married couples who generally used lower levels of aggression and reported less dissatisfaction with the relationship. However, women in more severely violent relationships often reported high levels of marital discord and reported that their physical aggression was often in self-defense. Early on, wives are more likely to attribute blame or responsibility for the battering to themselves, but as the severity increases, they are more likely to hold their partners responsible (Cantos et al., 1993). These findings suggest a pattern of systematic changes in the relationship over time. However, we do not know yet whether specific stages of development of a battering relationship can be identified, whether specific patterns of interaction characterize each stage of relationship development, or whether different typologies of battering relationships follow different developmental paths.

It is extremely difficult to specify the situations in which battering will occur, because the meaning of the specific situation is known only to the participants in the interaction. The particular cues, or trigger events, to which each batterer responds are subjective and may vary from time to time. These triggers are undoubtedly a product of past experiences in the family of origin, cultural messages about the roles of men and women and the acceptance of violence, the couple's unique relationship history, level of earlier unresolved conflict in the relationship, the previously established strategies for resolving conflict, and the outcomes of previous battering episodes.

For instance, what is the focus of the man's attention at the moment he decides to become violent? Is he responding to the hurtfulness of his wife's previous comment or anticipating greater pain from her next comment? Does he respond to what would appear to an outsider to be an apparently insignificant event, such as the evening meal not being prepared on time, because he experiences this as a loss of control over his environment? Does he associate the current situation with others in which he has felt vulnerable, inadequate, or threatened?

What is the focus of the woman's attention at the moment of attack? Is she primarily concerned with keeping her children safe even at personal cost to herself? Has she come to accept that she has, in fact, done something to warrant the kind of attack she receives? Have her family-of-origin experiences consistently exposed her to violence so that she now accepts battering as an unavoidable, expected occurrence? Has she determined that she will not tolerate this kind of abuse and responds with psychological abuse or physical violence in turn? Has she decided that she has had enough and that she must leave this relationship?

We have argued here that systems perspectives have much to offer in understanding the variability and complexity that characterize battering relationships. Some couples are able to negotiate differences in their relationship successfully by allocating legitimate power and authority to each partner in different spheres of their relationship, whereas others are characterized by strategies that rely upon the use of power, domination, and control. It has been suggested that no single profile of the male batterer exists and that some men are violent only within their families, whereas others evidence a more generalized pattern of aggression. Some couples manage to eliminate violence from their relationship on their own, whereas others follow a pattern of increasing severity from verbal to physical abuse. These and other findings point to the importance of systems perspectives' emphasis on context and pattern in helping to explain male-to-female violence.

References

Babcock, J. C., Waltz, J., Jacobson, N. S., and Gottman, J. M. (1993). Power and violence: The relation between communication patterns, power discrepancies and domestic violence. *Journal of Consulting and Clinical Psychology, 61,* 40–50.

Burman, B., John, R., and Margolin, G. (1992). Observed patterns of conflict in violent, nonviolent, and nondistressed couples. *Behavioral Assessment, 14,* 15–37.

Caesar, P. L. (1988). Exposure to violence in families-of-origin among wife abusers and maritally nonviolent men. *Violence and Victims, 3,* 49–63.

Cantos, A., Neidig, P., and O'Leary, K. D. (1993). Men and women's attributions of blame for domestic violence. *Journal of Family Violence, 8,* 289–302.

Doumas, D., Margolin, G., and John, R. (1994). The intergenerational transmission of aggression across three generations. *Journal of Family Violence, 9,* 157–175.

Flynn, C. P. (1990). Relationship violence by women: Issues and implications. *Family Relations, 39,* 194–198.

Holtzworth-Munroe, A., and Stuart, (1994). Typologies of male batterers: Three subtypes and the differences among them. *Psychological Bulletin, 116,* 476–497.

Hotaling, G. T., and Sugarman, D. B. (1986). An analysis of risk markers in husband to wife violence: The current state of knowledge. *Violence and Victims, 1,* 101–124.

——. (1990). A risk marker analysis of assaulted wives. *Journal of Family Violence, 5*(1), 1–13.

Kalmuss, D., and Seltzer, J. (1986). Continuity in marital behavior in remarriage: The case of spouse abuse. *Journal of Marriage and the Family, 48,* 113–120.

Lloyd, S. (1996). Physical aggression, distress, and everyday marital interaction. In D. Cahn and S. Lloyd (Eds.), *Family violence from a communication perspective* (pp. 177–198). Thousand Oaks, CA: Sage.

Margolin, G., John, R. S., Ghosh, C. M., and Gordis, E. B. (1996). Family interaction process: An essential tool for exploring abusive relations. In D. Cahn and S. Lloyd (Eds.), *Family violence from a communication perspective* (pp. 37–58). Thousand Oaks, CA: Sage.

O'Leary, K. D., Malone, J., and Tyree, A. (1994). Physical aggression in early marriage: Prerelationship and relationship effects. *Journal of Consulting and Clinical Psychology, 62*(3), 594–602.

Pagelow, M. D. (1992). Adult victims of domestic violence: Battered women. *Journal of Interpersonal Violence, 7,* 87–120.

Sabourin, T. C., Infante, D. C., and Rudd, J. E. (1993). Verbal aggression in marriages: A comparsion of violent, distressed but nonviolent, and nondistressed couples. *Human Communication Research, 20,* 247–267.

Stets, J. E. (1990). Verbal and physical aggression in marriage. *Journal of Marriage and the Family, 52,* 501–514.

Woffordt, S., Mihalic, D. E., and Menard, S. (1994). Continuities in marital violence. *Journal of Family Violence, 9,* 195–225.

Yllo, K., and Bograd, M. (Eds.). (1988). *Feminist perspectives on wife abuse.* Newbury Park, CA: Sage. ✦

Issue 10: Questions to Consider

1. According to feminist theories, why do men batter women in close relationships? According to family systems theories, why do men batter women in close relationships?

2. Compare the main points presented in these two papers. Is there anything about male violence against women in which feminists and systems theorists agree? What are the primary differences between these explanations?

3. Choose one of the two theories and think about how public policy might be affected if it was guided by the theory you have chosen.

4. What do feminists mean by "gender role constructions?" How do gender role constructions contribute to violence against women? What would family systems theory have to say about this?

5. What do feminists mean by "patriarchal values"? How do patriarchal values contribute to male violence against women? What would family systems theory have to say about this? ✦

Part Three

Controversial Issues Regarding Parenting

Issue 11: Introduction

Should Parenting Require a License?

If you want to legally drive a car, you must show proficiency in the skills necessary to drive safely, and you must demonstrate on a written examination that you know the basics of driving safety and the rules of the road. You also must be at least a certain minimum age, have adequate vision to pass an eye exam, and have enough money to pay the licensing fee. If you want to get legally married, you need to be of a certain minimum age (16 to 18, depending on local laws), be able to provide identification of who you are, and have enough money to pay the licensing fee. If you want to become a parent, you can do so as long as you are fertile—there are no tests of skill or knowledge, no minimum age (beyond physiological limitations), and no licensing fees. Does it make sense that it is easier to become a parent than it is to become an automobile driver?

David Lykken, Professor Emeritus of Psychology at the University of Minnesota, doesn't think so. Lykken, a respected scholar and educator, makes a strong and controversial case for parental licensure in the first essay that follows. He argues,

> If every American child were raised by both biological parents who are mature, married, and self-supporting, the rates of social pathologies of all kinds would rapidly decline.

He believes that biological parents should be required, by means of a licensure statute, to meet the same minimal qualifications that are required of adoptive parents.

Sound absurd? Sound like something that would not be tolerated in a free country (see Scarr's rebuttal)? Perhaps not, but in several recent cases in the United States, judges have ordered men who have not fulfilled their obligations to their children to not have any more children (*Milwaukee Journal Sentinel*, 2001). It appears that at least a few judges are creating policies that mirror the parental licensure laws advocated by Lykken. In short, we may not be as far away from passing such laws as you might think.

Lykken argues that fathers who live with their children and parents who are married are needed to help raise children, particularly when they live in dangerous or socially impoverished environments or when the children have difficult temperaments. He proposes a social engineering program on what he calls "eumemics," the science of maximizing good environmental influences and experiences for children.

Sandra Scarr and Judith Harris rebut various parts of Lykken's proposal for parental licensure. Scarr opposes the restrictions to personal freedom such statutes would embody. She proposes an alternative social engineering program, Positive Procreation, in which individuals would be encouraged to become parents voluntarily. Scarr also criticizes Lykken's emphasis on marriage.

Harris takes a different approach. She criticizes what she calls the "nurturance assumption" that what parents do matters to how children develop. Instead, she believes that the social environment and genetic effects are more important influences on children than parents' behaviors. She criticizes Lykken's emphasis on fathers.

These papers are rich with complex arguments designed to support the respective authors' positions. The authors support their views with research findings, demographic and crime statistics, and anecdotes about children and families. There are many ideas to which you should attend as you read these papers. Foremost among them are the policy implications of these suggestions. As you read, note the public policy suggestions and see if you can identify both the *intended consequences* and *unintended consequences* of such policies. In addition, these authors differ on the relative importance of fathers and on how fathers make contributions to their children. Note these various arguments as you read. You may want to read issues 16, 19, and 20 for other discussions of the value of fathers and compare these authors' rationales.

Reference

Milwaukee Journal Sentinel. (2001, July 16). Deadbeat dad decision divides court, children. A2. ✦

11a

Licensing Parents—A Controversial Cure for Crime

David T. Lykken

Jack Westman (1994), editor of *Child Psychiatry and Human Development*, has made a strong case for parental licensure. If every American child were raised by both biological parents who are mature, married, and self-supporting, the rates of social pathologies of all kinds would rapidly decline. On the basis of this assumption, it is argued that we should give Westman's proposal serious consideration—to require, by means of a licensure statute, the same minimal qualifications for biological parenthood that we now require of adoptive parents.

The fact is that we have experienced an unprecedented increase in crime and violence that began in the early 1960s. The recent modest downturn has been attributed to several causes: Most cities have expanded police forces and adopted proactive policing, turf wars between drug dealers have diminished as territorial boundaries have become established, [and] the increase in the number of perpetrators who have been taken off the streets to serve long terms in prison. As recently as 1970, there were fewer than 200,000 people in state and federal prisons but that number has risen to more than 1.3 million. The United States keeps a higher proportion of its citizens imprisoned than any other major nation except for Russia. Because felons commit an average of 12 crimes during the year prior to conviction (Blumstein, Cohen, and Farrington, 1988), imprisoning an additional million predators produces a signifi-

cant, if temporary, reduction in the crime rate. The rates of violent crime *should have decreased* substantially over the past 20 years for two reasons: (1) the proportion of the population that are elderly has increased, while (2) the proportion of young males, the group that furnishes most of the violent criminals, has sharply decreased.

Violent crimes committed by offenders under age 18 have increased in recent years. The number of juveniles arrested for aggravated assault in the United States, per 100,000 juveniles in the population, increased more than 130 percent from 1973 to 1992 according to the FBI. More than 200,000 boys from 12 to 17 years old were arrested in 1992 in the United States for murder, forcible rape, aggravated assault, or robbery. By now, most of them are back on the streets. In the year 2000, there will be 50,000 more boys in this age range than there were in 1955.

Referring to our growing criminal underclass, Judge C. D. Gill (1994) asks:

Where do these monsters, predators, and 'punks' come from? Did they parachute from another country? Did they emerge from a spaceship from another planet? We know three things about these hated citizens. One, they were all born in American hospitals; two, they were all educated in American schools; and three, they were all reared by American adults. It is the rare predator who has had a successful childhood. The place to fight crime is in the cradle. Because all of these social misfits began life as innocent babes, most of whom could have become law-abiding, self-supporting citizens if the circumstances of their formative years had been somehow different, I think it is reasonable to think of them, like the objects of their malevolence, as victims too.

The Socialization of Children

How do most children avoid becoming social misfits? Through the monitoring and example of their elders. We are born with the capacity to develop a conscience that works to inhibit rule breaking. We can learn to feel empathy for our fellow creatures and to take satisfaction in acts of altruism. Most of us develop a sense of responsibility to our families and community, a desire to pull our own weight in the group effort for survival. We may be the only species that is motivated to emulate people whom we admire in order to feel good about ourselves.

These prosocial inclinations do not emerge as well-formed instincts but, like our inborn capacity for language, they require to be elicited, shaped, and reinforced by our interactions with other, older humans during our early development. Our poor success in rehabilitating persons who have reached young adulthood still inadequately socialized suggests that there may be a critical period for socialization. Unless it is evoked, sculpted, and made habitual in childhood, our human talent for socialization may wither and never develop.

Why Is Crime Increasing?

The sharp increase in crime since 1960 indicates that there has been a corresponding increase in the proportion of youth who are managing to grow up unsocialized. I have pointed out (Lykken, 1997) that there is a striking correlation, at least in the United States, between fatherless rearing and subsequent social pathology. Of the juveniles incarcerated in the United States for serious crimes, about 70 percent had been reared without fathers (Beck, Kline, and Greenfeld, 1988). If the base rate for fatherless rearing of today's teenagers is 25 percent (which is the best current estimate), then one can calculate that the risk for social pathologies ranging from delinquency to death is about seven times higher for youngsters raised without fathers than for those reared by both biological parents.

Correlation does not prove a direct causal connection. Fatherless children may be at higher risk because single or divorced mothers tend to have to live in bad neighborhoods. The biological parents of fatherless children may pass on to their offspring genetic disadvantages, lower IQ, or difficult temperaments. Women (and girls) who end up as single mothers may on average be less competent as parents, either because of their personal limitations or because parenting is simply too difficult and demanding for most individuals to accomplish it successfully alone. Harper and McLanahan (1998) analyzed the data from the National Longitudinal Survey of Youth (NLSY) to determine whether the increased crime rate among boys reared without fathers can be attributed to the facts that such children tend more often to be poor, Black, to live in central cities, or to have been born to teenage mothers. Even after controlling for all of these factors, family structure remained the strongest predictor of the boy's incarceration by age 30. It is interesting that the presence of a stepfather did not decrease the risk involved with mother-only rearing, whereas boys reared by single fathers were no more at risk for delinquency than those brought up by both parents.

Whatever it is that causes youngsters reared without fathers to be more at risk for social pathology than youngsters reared by both biological parents, the proportion of these high-risk people living among us has gone up at least 250 percent during the same time period, which has seen an increase of 300 percent in violent crime. Do fatherless youngsters so often fail to become socialized because of their parenting, their poverty, or their personalities?

Personality

Studies suggest the heritability for criminal conviction of about 40 percent (Cloninger and Gottesman, 1987), the heritability for Antisocial Personality Disorder was estimated to be 30 percent (DiLalla, Gottesman, and Carey, 1993), [and] adoption studies, in which criminality in adult adoptees is related to criminality in adoptive and biological parents, indicate a heritability of from 30 percent to 40 percent (Lykken, 1995). It can be misleading, however, to speak of the heritability of criminality as if this were a trait with its own DNA blueprint. One trait that contributes to crime risk is a low IQ (Wilson and Herrnstein, 1985), yet only a small fraction of persons with IQs of 92 (the mean for delinquents and adult criminals) become delinquent or criminal. Surely most of the genetic risk for criminality is carried by heritable traits of personality or temperament.

A wide variety of violent personality profiles can interact with an equally wide variety of developmental circumstances to yield a whole or partial failure of socialization. While certain traits—high levels of aggression, impulsiveness, fearlessness—can be problematic, it may be that almost any [genetic] trait can interact with certain environments to produce a pathological result. Thus, while there are no known "criminal genes," there can be no doubt that some children, for genetic reasons, are more difficult to socialize than others.

To explain the rapid increase in the rates of crime, we need a causal variable that has increased in parallel with the crime rate. Can we suppose that the proportion of hard-to-socialize children is now three or four times what it was in the 1960s? Lynn (1995) has demonstrated a tendency in England for criminals to father more children than do noncriminal parents. Although no systematic studies are available, it is a reasonable conjecture that parents of babies born out of wedlock and of children left fatherless by early divorce tend on the average to have more deviant personality profiles than parents who rear their children in amicable partnerships. Therefore, it is also rea-

sonable to suppose that each successive U.S. birth cohort since 1960 may have included a somewhat higher proportion of "difficult" children than the one before. But this increase cannot have been high enough to account for the increase in crime. Thus it seems reasonable to conclude that the majority of current prison inmates began life as innocent babies who could have been adequately socialized by the right developmental milieu. It is also reasonable to ask whether increasingly large fractions of each cohort have been deprived of adequate socialization experiences.

The Nurture Assumption

Harris (1995) attempts to refute the widely held assumption that children are shaped and socialized primarily by the guidance and modeling of their parents. Harris argues that the nurture component of the nature-nurture process consists primarily of influences experienced by children outside of their homes, in their neighborhoods, and with their peers. Young children, she points out, are inclined to be drawn to and to interact with other young children, rather than adults. Young children, along with their age peers, tend to emulate older children and so on upwards toward the ultimate role models, the adults of the community.

Harris emphasizes children's capacity for being able to adopt one set of behavior precepts in the home and quite a different set in the broader community environment. It is the latter set of values and behavior tendencies, rather than the ones modeled and shaped within the home environment, that gradually evolves into that child's adult personality and behavior patterns.

In ancestral times, it truly did take an entire village to raise a child. The children of extended-family groups of hunter-gatherers learned to behave, not like their parents, but like the other children of their age and gender, while all the children looked to the example of the older children, who ultimately, emulated the community adults. The biological parents took primary responsibility for the feeding, care, and shelter of their offspring but the socialization of those children was a community function.

So it is in modern times, Harris insists. Most parents provide the basic nurturing that is necessary for their child's survival but, beyond that, the only contribution that the biological parents make to their offspring's individuality is completed at the great genetic lottery that takes place at conception. Notice that Harris is not saying that parents do not influence their children's behavior. Harris's claim is that parents have little differential effect on how children "behave the way they do in the world outside the home—the world where they will spend the rest of their lives."

I think Harris makes a powerful case. Yet I believe that some parents play an important role in either maximizing their children's good qualities and chances for success or helping their children overcome disadvantages. And I believe that some parents are truly bad—incompetent, uncaring, or downright malignant—so that children in their care are at great risk to become unsocialized adults. If the many studies of parenting or socialization provide little evidence either to support these claims or to refute Harris, what sorts of new and different research designs might stand a better chance?

The Good Parent Conjecture

I contend that 10 percent to 20 percent of parents really make a difference in the adult lives of the children whom they raise. The *good parent conjecture* says that some parents are able to help their children make more of their genetic proclivities, and to overcome their genetic handicaps, than are the general run of parents. A child with Down's syndrome, for example, should prove to be happier, better adjusted, and more independent when reared by a good parent than a similarly afflicted child reared by an average parent. A child who displays unusual timidity at age 2, if raised by a skilled parent, should be a more confident and effective adult than a similar child reared by ordinary parents.

One result that most parents strive for is to socialize their children, both for the children's sake and for the parents' own peace of mind. This most basic responsibility of parenting is often easily accomplished but it can be a real challenge if the child has a difficult temperament. With daring, adventurous, or aggressive children who rebel at discipline, for example, average parents are inclined either to back off, thus reinforcing that behavior, or to intensify punishment, thus tending to antagonize or alienate the child (Patterson, Reid, and Dishion, 1992). A more skillful parent works to instill in such a child, while still very young, a prosocial self-concept.

Suppose we could match children in infancy for talent and temperament and assign them at random to be raised by a representative sample of parents. Then, two decades later, we could allocate scores to these parents based on the relative achievements, adjustment, and socialization of their foster child compared to all the others in the matched control group. Our assessment of parental skill would be better yet if we had several matched groups of foundlings—a group of Down's children, a group of slow ones and another matched for derring-do, a group of average kids, and another of children with IQs of 150—and then place one of each group in each foster home. Then we could claim to be able to assess good parenting as a general trait.

But we cannot do this experiment and so we must rely on dribs and drabs from real-life studies. The best evidence for the good parent conjecture probably is limited to case histories like that of Donald Thornton, a laborer, and his wife, Tass, a former chambermaid. This African American couple were determined that their six daughters would grow up to be women of accomplishment and the products of their endeavors included one nurse, one court stenographer, one lawyer, one oral surgeon, and two physicians. There are numerous accounts of single mothers, stranded in poverty and a bad neighborhood, who manage somehow to rear successful children. In such instances, unsocialized peer groups were assuredly available so that the youngster's success cannot be attributed to the extra-familial environment. We cannot assume either that these children were fortified by unusual genetic advantages.

Harris insists that children adopt the values and mores of their peer group more readily than those of their family. One way to identify effective parents, therefore, would be to assess the relative strengths of the child's commitment to parents versus peers. A good parent should be able to influence the kinds of peers a child is exposed to and also the choice that child makes of the peers that are available. Ideally, there should not be a great difference between the values of the peer group and the aspirations that the parents have for their child. Where there are differences, the child of the more effective parents should be leaning more in their direction than in that of his or her friends.

Do the parents know their child's friends? Do the friends feel comfortable in the child's home, and is the child comfortable in the joint presence of parents and peers? Feeling free to bring one's friends home is not enough to prove that one's parents rank among the select few at the top of the bell curve of parental competence, however. Nushawn Williams, the 21-year-old who is said to have infected as many as 100 young women with HIV, apparently felt free to bring his crack-dealer friends home. After all, his mother and his grandmother were crack addicts and his 17-year-old sister was accepting money for sex. Nushawn never had to worry about Dad being around, because neither Nushawn nor his mother ever knew who Dad was—or who fathered the sister's new baby.

The Bad Parent Conjecture

The Williams family illustrates the other end of the bell curve of parental competence. It can be argued that our job, as a society, is not to punish but to break the vicious circle. For example, one might see it as society's responsibility to ensure that Nushawn's sister's child is not required to grow up in such a family. Yet present law prevents us from rescuing that child be-

cause its elders have not actually broken its bone or burned it with cigarettes, and because present law and social work theory is dedicated to "family preservation" (MacDonald, 1994). Even if we were to find a decent foster home for that infant, there is nothing to prevent Nushawn's sister from having another and another.

It is difficult to identify with certainty parents at the high end of the bell curve of parental competence because their well-socialized, successful children usually grow up among socialized, successful neighbors and share their parents' easy-to-socialize genes. At the low end of the competency curve, it seems to me that the problem is much easier. I do not believe that Nushawn or any of his relatives were genetically doomed to lives of crime, vice, and social dependency. His sister did not learn prostitution from her peers; she learned it from her mother when she was only 13. This family was the fount of its own problems.

Suppose we moved the Williams family to middle-class neighborhoods and gave them two unrelated foundlings to adopt. Would those children grow up [to] be at grave risk? Would it not be wrong to place foundlings in the care of such families? Yet we did not think it wrong to permit Nushawn's mother to raise him and his sister nor did we hesitate to raise the family's welfare income when the sister had a child of her own.

The Nurture Presumption

I shall assume that Harris is correct in thinking that success in socializing children does not vary greatly over the broad midrange of parental competence. But I shall also presume that some unusual parents have greater success than most caregivers would in socializing the difficult cases, while other parents are so bad—so inept, overburdened, immature, or unsocialized themselves—that almost any child in their custody will become a victim of social pathology. Finally, I shall argue that the current epidemic of crime and violence is due largely to the growth in the numbers of families like Nushawn's. Out-of-control families headed by single mothers (or by single grandmothers), living in poverty and in bad neighborhoods, spawn additional families of the same sort. And the generations are short because the daughters begin having babies in their mid-teens. The boys start doing serious crimes also in their mid-teens.

Psychopaths and Sociopaths

People like Nushawn, and most of his close relatives, I call sociopaths—people with broadly normal genetic characteristics, including their temperament, who have arrived at young adulthood unsocialized because of a failure of socializing agents, usually the parents. *Psychopaths*, in contrast, are people whose genetic tendencies, including their temperaments, make them so difficult to socialize that the kinds of parents and neighborhoods that succeed in socializing the vast majority of youngsters do not succeed with them. It will be apparent that these categories are distinct only at the extremes because many children who have the worst parents and peer groups were also handicapped by their inheritance of tendencies making them relatively unresponsive to the usual socializing influences.

Parental Competence

[Imagine] the socialization of three boys with different genotypes. Pat, whose innate temperament makes him easy to socialize, is bright, nonaggressive, moderately timid, with a naturally loving disposition. He starts out life essentially unsocialized and, if his parents are totally incompetent, his neighborhood a war zone, and his peers all little thugs, Pat might remain marginally socialized. But boys like Pat tend to avoid conflict and chaos, they are attracted by order and civility and they tend to seek out socialized mentors and role models. With even poor parenting, the Pats of this world tend to stay out of trouble.

Bill, a boy with an average genetic makeup, [is] moderately aggressive, moderately adventurous. Because he is average, we can safely anticipate that average parents, living in an average neighborhood,

will be able to raise Bill to be an average, law-abiding citizen. Incompetent parents, however, living in a disruptive neighborhood, will not succeed with Bill who, like Nushawn Williams, will remain a sociopath.

Mike is difficult to socialize; he may be fearless, or hostile and aggressive. The majority of parents would find Mike too much to cope with, a perennial source of worry and disappointment. Talented parents or, more likely, a combination of parent, neighborhood, peer group, and subsequent mentors, can sometimes socialize even these hard cases. One reason I believe in the Good Parent Assumption is that many heroes, on whose fearlessness and danger-seeking inclinations our civilization has always depended, have the same temperaments that make some youngsters too hard for ordinary parents to handle, youngsters who often grow up to be psychopaths.

The Bills in each generation, because they are average, are vastly more numerous than either the Pats or the Mikes. Most youngsters have average genetic temperaments like Bill and, therefore, even though only a minority of parents are incompetent, the total number of Bills who reached adolescence and adulthood still unsocialized—who become criminal sociopaths—is much larger than the number of psychopaths like Mike. Moreover, because unsocialized people tend to become incompetent parents, the number of sociopaths is growing faster than the general population, faster than we can build reform schools and prisons.

Poverty

Nushawn Williams and many other exemplars of the criminogenic underclass of American society grew up in relative poverty. It is fair to ask whether any parents, no matter how dedicated, could be reasonably expected to successfully rear children in, say, the Henry Horner Housing Project in Chicago.

I would argue that someone living in such circumstances should not have children, not until and unless they are able to get up and get out of that pernicious environment. I would regard someone as lacking parental competence if, living in such circumstances, he or she was to ask to adopt a baby. Should one not make the same judgment if that person elects to be a birth parent?

It is a natural reaction for many citizens to suppose that the best solution to such problems is a more generous welfare system. But the War on Poverty's solution of improved welfare benefits has been a failure in reducing the size of the sociopathic underclass. Even intensifying that "war" would not work. Suppose that we were to somehow provide every poor person over 19 with a tax-free stipend of $20,000 a year, and every single-mother of minor children with $40,000 annually: Surely that should reduce the poverty problem, but would it solve the social problem? Would those mothers move to better neighborhoods and begin to nurture, monitor, and socialize their children? Would their boyfriends be less likely to abuse their younger children? Would the teenage boys quit their gangs and buckle down to their homework? Would the teenage daughters defer motherhood until they had finished high school and established a relationship with the prospective, self-supporting father?

Proposed Responses to the Current Epidemic of Social Pathology

Educator William Kilpatrick (1992) urges teachers and parents to provide children "with good books that transmit moral values." But most of the parents and children we consider here can barely read at all and they are not interested in books. Nor are they interested in midnight basketball or any of the other well-intentioned nostrums that have been suggested. But many inadequate parents cannot or will not participate in such programs.

Even if we had an adequate system of parental training, professional foster care, kibbutzim-like day care, group homes, and boarding schools, many children would still fall through the cracks and the production

of victims needing rescue would continue. Addressing the growing incidence of child abuse and neglect from the perspective of a child psychiatrist, Westman (1994) has proposed what seems to be the radical but workable solution, parental licensure. Among other arguments Westman discusses the cost of all these needed programs. Conservative estimates indicate that each youngster who never becomes socialized, who grows up to be like the Williams', costs us $50,000 for each year of his or her life, or $2 to $3 million for each lifetime. Because there are millions of them, these costs amount to real money.

The Adoption Model

Although laws and practices vary from one jurisdiction to another, we do now, as a rule, set reasonable requirements to be met by anyone wishing to rear someone else's child through adoption. Teenagers, crack addicts, prostitutes, criminals, and persons unable to provide for themselves are likely to be unsuccessful should they apply as potential adoptive parents. We have these standards because we understand that the child's rights to a fair start in life must far outweigh the rights of would-be parents.

Yet for some reason we set no standards for those who would acquire babies biologically. According to Danfield (1998), for example, some 120,000 babies are born each year in the U. S. to mentally retarded mothers who cannot read or tell time, women who cannot be entrusted with the safe care of an infant without constant supervision.

Suppose we were to establish these same minimum requirements for maintaining custody of one's future biological children. At the same office where one now obtains a driving license, most of today's parents could apply for and obtain a license to have a baby. That is, they could show that they were both over 21, married, self-supporting, and that neither had been convicted of a violent crime. When we finally establish 3-month parental practicum courses in our system of community colleges, a certificate of completion of such a course might be an additional requirement. Applicants who had divorced a former spouse while any child of that marriage was less than 12-years-old might have to convince a Family Court judge that their new union was more likely to endure. Wealthy professional women, such as actress Jodie Foster, who wish to become single mothers, or gay and lesbian couples, and others not meeting these basic requirements, but who can make a good case for their ability and commitment, could also resort to Family Court to request an exemption.

A pregnant woman unable to meet these simple requirements, but who intends to carry the baby to term, would be required to name possible fathers who, in turn, would be required to submit to paternity testing so that the father could be charged the costs of the maternity. At the discretion of the Family Court, the mother-to-be might be confined during her pregnancy to an agreeable maternity home where she would receive good nourishment and medical attention, counseling and training where appropriate, and where her fetus would be safe from drugs, alcohol, infection, or illness. One assumes most citizens would agree that "parental rights" do not include the right to bring to term a baby with congenital venereal infection or disabilities produced by maternal substance abuse. The infant would be removed at birth and placed for permanent adoption. If either parent had participated previously in an unlicensed pregnancy, he or she would have to submit to a long-acting contraceptive implant.

One of the many arguments raised against a proposal for parental licensure is that it would impact differentially on certain minorities and especially on African Americans. The large Black underclass stems from the same roots as its White counterpart. The Black and the White crime problems have the same causes and the same cures. The Black problem is proportionately greater now because the disruption of families and the upsurge of illegitimacy began 30 years earlier in the Black community than in the White. If every American child, Black and White, were to be born to pairs of parents who meet the minimal criteria for licensure outlined above, both the Black and White underclasses would shrink in size and the Black and White crime rates would be reduced to tolerable and equivalent levels.

Eumemics Rather Than Eugenics

What I am proposing is not a program of eugenics. Eugenics is the science of good breeding, its purpose to maximize the production of socially useful genetic characteristics and to minimize socially destructive ones. But we do not know enough about which genetic characteristics are useful and which are not over the long term nor do we know confidently how to breed for them. *The Bell Curve* (Herrnstein and Murray, 1994) documented the fact that members of society's underclass are less intelligent on average than middle class citizens. Herrnstein and Murray argue that this IQ deficiency accounts for the higher rates of crime, illegitimacy, and welfare dependency that are characteristic of this bottom stratum. They do not propose a solution to this social problem, probably because the only real solution, if their analysis is correct, would be some form of eugenic program designed to prevent the breeding of persons with low IQs or other evidence of genetic defect.

My thesis is different and less pessimistic. I argue that the solution to the crime problem requires us to realize that parenthood is both a privilege and a responsibility. The privilege of parenthood would not be determined by test scores or family trees but by behavior. Whatever your test scores or genetic background, if you wish to have a child, all you have to do is to grow up, keep out of trouble, get a job, and get married.

The correct name for the program advocated here is a new term "eumemics," coined by the anthropologist, Vincent Sarich, and based on another new word, "meme," coined by Richard Dawkins (1976). Just as the gene is the unit of genetic influence upon the development of the individual, so the meme is the unit of experience or environmental influence. Then "eumemics" is the science of maximizing the good memes and minimizing the bad ones in the developmental experiences of our children.

It has been my argument that high upon the list of good memes that we all want for all children are the experiences that conduce toward the three components of socialization: The avoidance of antisocial behavior, the disposition toward prosocial behaviors, and the acquisition of the work ethic and the capacity for economic independence. Because these memes are primarily the responsibility of parents to provide, this proposal is to license only those potential parents who are both able and likely to provide these socializing experiences. We can try to ensure good rearing environments for the increasing fraction of American children who are being brought into this world by immature, overburdened, sociopathic, or otherwise incompetent parents. If we demanded the same minimal requirements for biological parenthood that we require for adoptive parenthood—a mother and father committed enough to be married to each other, who are mature and self-supporting, neither criminal nor incapacitated by mental illness—then the source of most crime and violence would dry up.

More important, parental licensure would acknowledge a moral principle that all reasonable people will accept once they confront it: Every baby born has an inalienable right to life, liberty, and the pursuit of happiness, a right that outweighs the rights of unfit would-be parents. We do not know enough to define parental fitness by statute except in terms of a few minimal requirements such as those outlined above. Some licensed parents would prove to be bad parents; like any law, parental licensure would never be a fail-safe measure. But most of the Americans now in prison might have become citizens, taxpayers, and welcome neighbors if the circumstances of their growing-up had included licensable parents.

A Challenge to Critics

The "cure" for crime and other social pathology is assuredly controversial. My chief purpose is to set out certain alarming facts that I believe are not reasonably in dispute. My hope is that colleagues will acknowledge the implications of the premises summarized below and, if they believe that the licensure proposal is unnecessarily draconian or unfeasible, that they will offer alternative solutions. The facts with which we have to deal are as follows:

1. The violent crime rate in the United States now is four times what it was in 1960.

2. Other social pathologies, including school drop-out, teenage pregnancy, child abuse, teenage runaways, juvenile delinquency, and social dependency, have increased concurrently and in similar degree.

3. The proportion of American males aged 15 to 25 who were either born out of wedlock or who were reared without the active participation of their biological fathers because of early divorce, has risen in proportion to the increase in the crime rate.

4. More than two-thirds of incarcerated delinquents, of high school dropouts, of teenage runaways, of abused or murdered babies, and of juvenile murderers, were reared without their biological fathers. Although studies have not been done, it is likely that this "rule of two-thirds" applies to criminals, drug addicts, and healthy welfare recipients.

5. Criminals tend to be higher than noncriminals in the factors of negative emotionality (especially aggression) and lower in constraint. Many of these traits are correlated only weakly between parents and offspring.

6. Many children at risk for antisocialism because of temperament and poor parenting can be adequately socialized if reared in a community of socialized peers.

7. Suppose we began a study of 10,000 infants born to licensable parents and an equal number whose parents could not meet the requirements. In 20 years the children reared by the unlicensable

parents would evidence a much higher rate of delinquency and other social pathology than would children born of mature, married, self-supporting parents. Critics should explain their disagreement. Those who oppose parental licensure should suggest another social policy that would mitigate this social problem.

8. American society now can claim that young persons who graduate from high school with grades appropriate to their abilities and without criminal convictions, babies, or drug addictions, can reasonably aspire to further training or employment and to economic success consonant with their talents and energies, without regard to gender or ethnicity.

9. Most, although not all, of the men incarcerated in American prisons, and many of the millions of American children with incompetent or unsocialized parents, were or are being cheated of their birthright to life, liberty, and the pursuit of happiness.

Westman has proposed what seems to me to be a workable solution. I look forward to suggestions of other viable alternatives. There is much to think about.

References

Beck, A., Kline, S., and Greenfeld, L. (1988). *Survey of youth in custody, 1987.* Washington, DC: Bureau of Justice Statistics.

Blumstein, A., Cohen, J., and Farrington, D. P. (1988). Criminal career research: Its value for criminology, *Criminology, 26,* 1–37.

Cloninger, C. R., and Gottesman, I. I. (1987). Genetic and environmental factors in antisocial behavior. In S. Mednick, T. E. Mofitt, and S. A. Stack (Eds.), *The causes of crime: New biological approaches* (pp. 92–109). Cambridge, UK: Cambridge University Press.

Dawkins, R. (1976). *The selfish gene.* Oxford: Oxford University Press.

Danfield, R. (1998, October 22). Outgrowing your parents at 8. *New York Times Magazine,* 32–35.

DiLalla, L. F., Gottesman, I., and Carey, G. (1993). Assessment of normal personality traits in a psychiatric sample: Dimensions and categories. In L. J. Chapman, J. P. Chapman, and D. Fowles (Eds.), *Progress in experimental personality and psychopathology research* (pp. 145–162). New York: Springer.

Gegax, T. T. (1997, November 10). The AIDS predator. *Newsweek,* 52–59.

Gill, C. D. (1994). In the Foreword to J. C. Westman, *Licensing parents* (p. viii). New York: Plenum.

Harper, C. C., and McLanahan, S. S. (1998, August). *Father absence and youth incarceration.* Paper presented at the 1998 annual meeting of the American Sociological Association, San Francisco, CA.

Harris, J. R. (1995). Where is the child's environment? A group socialization theory of development, *Psychological Review, 102,* 458–489.

Herrnstein, R., and Murray, C. (1994). *The bell curve.* New York: The Free Press.

Kilpatrick, W. (1992). *Why Johnny can't tell right from wrong: Moral illiteracy and the case for character education.* New York: Simon and Schuster.

Lykken, D. T. (1995). *The antisocial personalities.* Hillsdale, NJ: Erlbaum.

———. (1997). Factor of crime. *Psychological Inquiry, 8,* 261–270

Lynn, R. (1995). Dysgenic fertility for crime. *Journal of Biosocial Science, 27,* 405–408.

MacDonald, H. (1994, Spring). The ideology of 'family preservation.' *The Public Interest,* 45–60.

Patterson, G. P., Reid, J. B., and Dishion, T. J. (1992). *Antisocial boys.* Eugene, OR: Castalia.

Westman, J. (1994). *Licensing parents: Can we prevent parental abuse and neglect?* New York: Plenum.

Wilson, J. Q., and Herrnstein, R. J. (1985). *Crime and human nature.* New York: Simon and Schuster. ✦

Adapted with permission from Lykken, D. T. (2000). "The Causes and Costs of Crime and a Controversial Cure." *Journal of Personality, 68,* 559–605. Copyright © Blackwell Publishers.

11b

Toward Voluntary Parenthood

Sandra Scarr

Lykken presents a scholarly analysis of sociopathic youth as the disastrous products of neglectful and abusive parenting. He charts the enormous costs to our society of millions of unwanted, unsocialized youngsters, whose educational failure, criminality, and single parenthood are legion. These children are not genetic failures, he says, but the unfortunate products of irresponsible parenting.

The facts are compelling: Single-parent households produce most of the nation's social pathology, and generations of irresponsible parents produce communities of lawless, drug-addicted criminals, who continue the cycle of thoughtless reproduction and irresponsible parenthood. He refutes the ideas that poverty alone or below-average IQ can be blamed for the massive parenting failure. Rather, he presents convincing evidence that the failure to socialize children to the norms of society is correlated with, but not identical to, poor personal and economic resources. Single parenthood is the real villain in Lykken's scenario. Marriage is an important part of his remedy.

The facts about poor socialization and social pathology are the same for all races, but the larger proportion of unmarried mothers among African Americans produces a higher proportion of unsocialized youngsters in that community. Mistrust between Blacks and Whites in the United States is aggravated by disparate proportions of criminal youth, who prey on law-abiding citizens in both communities, more frequently on Blacks than Whites.

To intervene in this cycle of human waste, Lykken proposes that parents be licensed. Licensure would be based on achievement of a minimal status of social adjustment and economic promise. Only married parents would be licensed. Unlicensed parents would lose their children to adoption. Two questions arise immediately: Would licensing parents reduce the number of "feral" children? And at what price to our society? The answers are "Yes" and "Too high."

Eugenics and Eumemics

Lykken uses a term, eumemics, to mean the science of selecting good rearing environments for children. By contrast, eugenics is the science of selective breeding to reduce the frequency of undesirable genetic traits. Let us be clear about the likely success of both genetic and environmental selection programs. Yes, we could reduce the number of mentally retarded and mentally ill people through selective breeding, just as we successfully breed other animals to reduce the frequency of undesirable traits. Yes, we could successfully reduce the number of unsocialized children through licensing only married parents who are likely to provide good home environments. There is no question that both programs would reduce the number of young criminals, but what kind of society would well-socialized youngsters inherit?

It is hard to imagine a proposal that confronts our civil liberties more directly than Lykken's. The idea that some agency of government could decide who can rear their biological offspring is anathema to most Americans. Just as Planned Parenthood fought to get the government out of the bedroom in contraceptive use and out of women's bodies in the abortion debate, most Americans would fight to keep the government from legislating whether or not we can rear our own children. As a woman who has reared four children to successful adulthood, mostly as a single mother, let me assure Lykken that I would be on the front lines in this battle.

Confronting Constitutional Rights

To intervene between a mother and her newborn, the society must have a very compelling reason. In cases of demonstrated abuse and neglect, there are legal mechanisms to adjudicate removal of children and their placement in more responsible homes through foster care and adoption. The key legal issue here is demonstrated abuse and neglect. Under the United States Constitution, one cannot be deprived of civil rights on unproven, probabilistic ground.

Lykken argues that the probability of a single mother producing an unsocialized deviant is so high that single mothers should not be permitted to rear their offspring. But how high is high enough to deprive all single mothers of rearing rights? If 100 percent of children reared by single mothers turned out to be unsocialized monsters, and none reared by married parents did, perhaps one could argue for the development of a constitutionally compatible procedure to remove them at birth. There is not a perfect correlation, however, between marital status and socialization of children, as demonstrated by my high-achieving, single-reared children and the solid two-parent family of President Reagan's would-be assassin, David Hinkley.

Can the government in the United States act preemptively to deprive all single mothers of their babies? Certainly not! The U.S. Constitution, I am happy to say, prohibits any such rash infringement of our rights.

Other proposals to identify prospective delinquents in the preschool years and potential sex offenders fall into the same constitutional trap. In the United States, the government cannot act preemptively against its citizens. However rational and efficacious they may seem, both forced eugenics and eumemics destroy the basic premise of citizenship in a free, democratic society—the civil society Lykken says he wants to save.

Another Proposal to the Same End

The key to a kind of social engineering that works in the American constitutional context is informed choice, not government coercion. Let me share a fantasy. It is quite farfetched, but it illustrates a reproductive intervention that respects individual liberties.

I believe that everyone deserves the right to control his or her own reproduction. Ideally, each of us decides how many children we will have and when they will be conceived. This is a fundamentally different position from that of Lykken, who proposes that external criteria be used to permit parenthood, whereas I propose personal choice.

I believe that most inadequate adults, who would fail as parents to socialize their children, would not freely choose to become parents. This statement applies more fully to women whose reproductive capacities are limited and who typically have more child-rearing responsibilities than men do. Women want to be selective about when they bear young and how many children they have. If some women are unable or unwilling to devote time and effort to socialize children, they would choose to have none or fewer children than they now have, if they were able to control their reproduction. The problem is how to give them realistic reproductive choices, when the least adequate women have the most difficulty with contraceptive planning and abortion decisions.

Positive Procreation

To make reproduction a positive choice, we should ideally start from an infertile state. We should have to take specific action to become fertile. My fantasy is that a harmless contraceptive that acts on both men and women could be put into drinking water and food supplies and be unavoidable in daily consumption. Everyone in the population would be infertile. The antidote to the universal infertility treatment would be freely available to anyone who wished to use it. For a very small fee, one could purchase the antidote over-the-counter at any pharmacy and supermarket. Each person could decide when and how often he/she wished to reproduce.

If conception required a positive act to occur, every woman could have the number of children she desires (multiple births aside). If everyone was infertile and conception required a positive act, the effect would be nondiscriminatory by race, social class, and country of origin. Furthermore, such a policy would empower all citizens to act in their own reproductive interest, without government interference in so precious a human right as procreation. I believe that the positive effects on the next generation of parents would be quite similar to the effects of the coercive measure Lykken advocates.

Surveys of reproductive aspirations for many decades have shown that women's desired fertility is correlated positively with their economic well-being. On average, better educated, more affluent women aim to have more children than less educated, less affluent ones do. Yet, completed family size is negatively correlated with socioeconomic status, because less educated women have more children than they intended. If all women could reliably determine their reproductive outcomes, social status would correlate positively with number of children. The solution is to start with infertility and require positive action to restore fertility.

The imagined implications of Positive Procreation abound. Social conservatives would try to limit the access of teens to the ubiquitous infertility treatment—make them drink privately bottled water and eat only untreated foods—in a vain attempt to limit sexual activity without procreative consequences. But they would fail, because in this utopia teens have only to turn on the tap to get the infertility treatment. Surveys would show that 99 percent of teens want the infertility treatment and only 0.2 percent want to try the infertility antidote. Just some fantasies from a world of personal choice.

Misplaced Emphasis on Marriage

Let me take further umbrage at Lykken's focus on marriage as a solution to poor parenting. Not all adults who choose to be parents are married, nor do I think marriage is essential to socialize children well. Having two committed parents makes child-rearing easier, to be sure, but many resourceful single mothers manage to rear wonderful children with help from relatives, friends, hired workers, and communities that support parenthood. Women who have good personal and economic resources can be excellent parents. Divorce can be negotiated by mature adults to preserve relationships between both parents and their children. A growing number of single mothers-by-choice are proud parents of well-socialized, high-achieving children. Lykken's focus should not be on parents' marital status but on the adequacy of individuals to fulfill the parental role.

Inadequate Adults

For a psychologist who has spent many years studying psychopathy, Lykken puts little emphasis on the personal inadequacies of parents who fail to socialize their children. Inept, inadequate parents may not be genetically deficient, but their inability and unwillingness to socialize their children is a defect of the parent as a person. The historical cause of the defects may be the inadequacies of their own parents, but the poorly socialized individual carries inadequate parenting into the next generation.

Lykken fails to mention that more than half of child neglect cases that come to official attention involve mentally retarded mothers. Perhaps requiring all retarded mothers to be married (some are already married, of course) would ameliorate some neglect, because a spouse might be a more adequate caregiver. The root cause of child neglect, however, is the inability of many mentally retarded mothers to understand and respond appropriately to the needs of infants and young children.

Requiring inadequate persons to be legally married to receive permits to rear their own children does not address the proximal cause of their poor child rearing. How does marriage constitute an intervention for personal inadequacy? Perhaps the answer is that such persons will not marry or stay married long enough to become parents under the proposed permit. If they reproduce without a permit, and behave irresponsibly as parents, their children will be wrenched from them—hardly a pretty picture in a democratic society. Successful prevention of poor socialization is far more likely under the Positive Procreation plan than under a marriage requirement. It may be a far-fetched fantasy, but at least it respects the constitutional rights we are entitled to enjoy as U.S. citizens.

Welfare Reform as Social Engineering

Lykken is certainly correct that never-married young mothers are the highest risk group for child abuse and neglect and for poor socialization of their children. Thus, it is interesting to explore ways to reduce their reproduction without denying them parental licenses. Surprisingly, Lykken does not cite the large effect of welfare reform on unmarried mothers' birth rate. Indeed, since serious discussions about welfare reform began in 1995, the teen birth rate has dropped by 25 percent, and overall births to unmarried women have declined substantially. Moving mothers from welfare to work is successful in most states, because unemployment is currently low. In early 1997, the latest date for which figures are available, federal cash assistance to welfare families had dropped from its peak by 22 percent. In

April 1999, President Clinton announced in his weekly radio address that the number of welfare recipients had declined by more than 45 percent from the peak in 1994. Employment is likely to reduce reproductive rates of former welfare recipients still further, if they respond as other groups of women have to economic improvements.

The current wave of reform may not address the least able, most addicted, welfare dependents, but the overall effect is very positive for participants and society. Welfare reform should be seen as a massive empowerment movement through which millions of poor women have gained more control of their economic and reproductive lives. As poor women experience greater economic independence, they feel better about themselves, and they may even provide better environments for their children.

Conclusions

David Lykken is a compassionate person who cares about the plight of our most vulnerable and defenseless children. No child should be exposed to parental antisocial behavior, persistent substance abuse, and serious child abuse. Removing children from grossly neglectful and abusive homes should have priority over maintaining "intact" families, which are seldom stable units with two married parents. The economic and social costs of ignoring the unsocialized underclass is extremely high and growing. We do not differ in our assessment of the problem.

On the solution we differ markedly. Any parental licensing scheme would fail to pass the constitutional test, however strong the empirical results of the monitoring study Lykken hopes to conduct.

It is more feasible to help women who are unfit for motherhood not to become mothers in the first place. My fantasy about a system of Positive Procreation may not be feasible or socially acceptable, but it sets an ethical and moral goal of self-determined childbearing. We can approach the goal of voluntary parenthood through making effective contraception and abortion services easily available to all women.

As a society, we cannot afford, and should not tolerate, anti-choice terrorists who reduce the availability of safe reproductive services. What could be more self-defeating for a society than to mandate parenthood for those least able to control their reproduction and least able to socialize their children? It is immoral to use childbearing as punishment for sexual activities and to sacrifice children on the altar of an unrealistic (and certainly unrealized) goal of unmarried sexual abstinence. Like Lykken, my goal is to make all homes safe and nurturant for children who are born. The majority of Americans approve of voluntary parenthood; we can outvote the sexual hang-ups of the Far Right, if the issue is clearly drawn.

I have faith in the power of individuals' self-interest. Given effective control over their reproduction, women will sort out when and how often to procreate and rear children. Voluntary parents are far more likely than unwilling ones to socialize their children for productive roles in society. Women who have control over their lives are more effective people and parents.

Adapted with permission from Scarr, S. (2000). "Toward Voluntary Parenthood." *Journal of Personality, 68,* 615–623.

11c

The Outcome of Parenting: What Do We Really Know?

Judith Rich Harris

Lykken would like every child to have two parents with the means and the know-how to be good parents. He would like every child to be reared in a well-run home in a nice neighborhood. Who can quarrel with those goals? Not I.

Therefore, I will not directly address Lykken's proposal for parental licensure. Instead I will examine the premise on which it is based: The idea that children are socialized by their parents—or, to put it another way, that parents have the power to influence their children's behavior outside the home as well as within it. This premise is accepted by most psychologists as a "given," but it is a hypothesis that deserves the same kind of dispassionate, rigorous testing that is routinely accorded to less popular hypotheses (Harris, 1998).

The Case of the Fatherless Child

Lykken links the rise of crime over the past 40 years to the increase in the proportion of children reared in homes headed by a single mother. Almost all psychologists and sociologists believe that being reared without a father is bad for children, and that children reared in such homes are less likely to turn into well-behaved adolescents and well-adjusted adults. A mountain of evidence supports this belief. There is no question that children reared by divorced or never-married mothers are more likely to commit crimes, become sexually active at

an early age, drop out of high school, and fail in their own marital relationships (Lykken, 1997; McLanahan and Sandefur, 1994). The problem with this mountain of evidence is that correlations between parents and their biological children, with no way of separating the effects of the environment the parents provide from the effects of the genes they provide, and no way of separating the effects of the home environment from the effects of the environment outside the home, is ambiguous.

Most psychologists and sociologists interpret the ambiguous evidence on the basis of their faith in what I call "the nurture assumption" (Harris, 1998)—the assumption that the most important aspect of the child's environment is the child's parents. Even sophisticated researchers are unwilling to give up their conviction that at least some of the correlation between fatherless rearing and an unsuccessful outcome must be due to what happens, or what fails to happen, to the child at home.

In their 1994 book *Growing up with a Single Parent* McLanahan and Sandefur laid out the case against fatherless rearing: Compared to those reared by two biological parents, children reared without fathers are less likely to graduate high school and more likely to be unemployed; the girls are more likely to become mothers while still in their teens. But the evidence in McLanahan and Sandefur's book contains a number of counterintuitive findings. First, the presence of a stepfather does not improve the child's chances, even though the children in stepfather families are given as much supervision (their whereabouts monitored, their homework checked) as those living with their biological fathers. Second, the presence of another biological relative, such as a grandparent, is also ineffective, even though children in such families are left alone less often than those in two-parent families. Third, the ill effects of fatherless rearing are largely confined to children whose fathers are absent but alive. For children reared by widows, the ill effects are greatly attenuated or, in some studies, absent entirely. Finally, it does not matter how old the child was when the father left—the children whose fathers stuck around till they were on the brink of adolescence were no better off than those whose fathers showed their heels on the same day they deposited their sperm.

Putting together all the evidence, I concluded (Harris, 1998) that three major factors are involved in the adverse correlates of fatherless rearing. The first is neighborhood. Single mothers are an economically disadvantaged group; many of them are forced to rear their children in economically disadvantaged neighborhoods because they cannot afford to live anywhere else. Neighborhoods vary in the proportion of adolescents who commit crimes, drop out of school, and get pregnant. All else being equal, adolescents' chances of getting into trouble will go up or down depending on where they live.

[For example, a] study of neighborhood effects looked at aggressive behavior in elementary school children. The researchers focused on children who were considered to be "high risk" on the basis of family composition (no father in the home), race (African American), and family income (low). They found that children with these risk factors who lived in mostly Black, low-income neighborhoods were highly aggressive, but those who lived in mostly White, middle-class neighborhoods were "comparable in their level of aggression" to their middle-class peers (Kupersmidt, Griesler, DeRosier,

Patterson, and Davis, 1995). This is the effect of the neighborhood culture.

The second factor associated with the absence of the father is changes of residence. Children who do not live with their biological fathers are more likely to experience multiple moves. This is the primary reason why children in stepfather families fare no better than children in single-parent families even though they are better off economically. Children in stepfather families suffer more residential moves than those in any other family constellation (McLanahan and Sandefur, 1994). Each time they move their peer relationships are disrupted; each time they must reestablish their status in the peer group and start all over from the bottom; each time they must adapt to new neighborhood norms. Children who are subjected to multiple changes of residence, whether or not they have fathers, have more social, behavioral, and academic problems than children who stay put (Eckenrode, Rowe, Laird, and Brathwaite, 1995). And yet most researchers who study the effects of divorce on children make no attempt to parse the effects of moving from the other consequences of divorce.

McLanahan and Sandefur (1994) found that changes in residence plus low income could account for about three quarters of the difference in outcome between children living with two biological parents and children living with one. But some difference still remained. The researchers attributed this difference to the effects of the father's presence or absence in the home—his "involvement" in the child's upbringing.

But McLanahan and Sandefur did not consider what I consider to be the third major factor involved in the correlation between fatherless rearing and unsuccessful outcome: Genetic influences. They did not consider the effects of the father's genes. Lykken does consider it; he considers it very carefully. As a behavior geneticist Lykken is well aware of the evidence of the importance of the genes, and equally aware of the evidence of the importance of the home environment (Scarr, 1992).

There is good evidence that criminal behavior is indeed heritable in the usual sense—that it does, to some extent, "breed true." The evidence comes, not from twin studies, but from adoption studies. A large study of Danish adopters (Mednick, Gabrielli, and Hutchings, 1987) showed that the biological children of fathers who had committed crimes were more likely than other adoptees to commit crimes, even if reared by law-abiding adoptive parents (as most of them were).

The other interesting finding of the Danish adoption study was that 29 percent of the adoptees' biological fathers had a criminal record, versus 8 percent of men in that age group in the general population (Mednick et al., 1987). There was a statistical association between criminal behavior and behavior that resulted in the birth of a child placed for adoption. A number of personality characteristics might predispose individuals both to criminal behavior and to irresponsible reproductive behavior, and at least some of them—for example, a lack of conscientiousness—are known to have substantial additive heritabilities (Bouchard, 1994). There is a modest difference in outcomes between children reared in fatherless homes and those reared in two-parent homes, after differences in family income and number of residential moves are partialed out (McLanahan and Sandefur, 1994). I attribute this difference to heritable differences in personality. On average, fathers who depart are likely to differ in personality from fathers who remain, and the evidence suggests that some of these differences can be passed on to their children. The genetic factor explains why the children of dead fathers fare better than children whose fathers are alive and healthy but somewhere else.

Very, Very Good Parents

There is another shortcoming of the behavior genetic evidence: The fact that the studies do not draw their samples from the entire population but only from part of it, which means that the conclusions drawn cannot be applied to the entire population. Lykken is willing to concede that over the middle range of parenting ability—a range that includes 80 percent of parents—the function relating parenting skill to how well the child turns out is flat. Pretty good parents do not produce better children than average parents or pretty bad parents. But Lykken still maintains that very good parents will produce better children than average parents, and that very bad parents will produce worse ones.

What Lykken is saying is that over the entire range of families for which we have data, there is no relationship between quality of parenting and quality of offspring. It is only in the small part of the range for which we do not yet have data that he claims there is a relationship. His faith is a testimony to the power of the nurture assumption.

To examine this claim more closely, I will begin by looking at the upper 10 percent of the parenting distribution: the very good parents. According to Lykken

> A child who displays unusual timidity at age 2, if raised by a skilled parent, should be a more confident and effective adult than a similar child reared by ordinary parents.

Lykken may be basing this prediction on statements made by Kagan. According to Kagan (1997), some children who were born to be timid do not turn out that way, and he gives their mothers credit for the improvement. The data he cites in support of this interpretation are meager, however; they come from a group of infants who were followed only to the age of 21 months (Arcus, 1991).

If it were true that skillful parents had the ability to turn a timid 2-year-old into a confident adult, then the results of this training should show up in behavior genetic studies. A pair of monozygotic twins both born timid, if reared by skillful parents, should both become less timid—why should the parents' skill work on one identical twin but not the other? Twins in the same household should resemble each other on personality dimensions. But twins reared together are no more similar in personality than those reared in separate homes (Bouchard et al., 1990). Any similarities between them are due to their identical genes; there is no evidence that their parents' skillfulness, or lack thereof, has had any effects.

Finally, there is no reason to suppose that the children of exceptionally skillful parents are underrepresented in behavior genetic data. These parents should be more likely than any other group to send their children to college, and college students are well represented in these data. One would have to assume that this highly skilled group of parents, if they exist at all, must make up only a tiny fraction of the population. I remain skeptical. If they exist, show me the data.

Very, Very Bad Parents

On the other hand, it is quite true that the children of very, very bad parents are likely to be underrepresented in the behavior genetic data. Thus, the possibility remains that parents can be bad enough to have lasting deleterious effects on a child's personality or mental health. Before we can conclude that such damage occurs, however, we must rule out other possible sources of the deficits often noted in the children of abusive or otherwise "dysfunctional" parents.

When the children of abusive parents are compared to children who have not been abused, they always come out worse. They are more aggressive, they have more trouble making and keeping friends (Dodge, Pettit, and Bates, 1994), they have more trouble with their schoolwork (Perez and Widom, 1994), and when they grow up they are more likely to abuse their own children (Wolfe, 1985). All these findings are accepted at face value, but all these findings are ambiguous. There are no controls for genetic influences, despite the plausibility of a genetic explanation (DiLalla and Gottesman, 1991) for a correlation between aggressive parents and aggressive offspring. There is no way to distinguish the parents' effects on the child from the child's effects on the parents, although it has been observed that some children who are moved from their abusing homes are abused again by their foster parents (Vista, 1982). And there is no way to distinguish what happens

to the child within the home from what happens outside of it.

Within an abusive home, abuse is often focused on one child in the family while the other children are treated reasonably well. We know some of the factors that can make a child more likely to be targeted as a scapegoat: slow development, a difficult temperament, an unattractive appearance—these same characteristics also jeopardize a child's standing in the peer group. When researchers find that children who have been abused by their parents tend to be unpopular with their peers, their knee-jerk response is to attribute the child's peer problems to the treatment he or she received at home. But if the parents and the peers are behaving in a similar way to this child, it is going far beyond the data to say that the parents' behavior is the cause and the peers' behavior an effect. It is also going beyond the data to conclude that the psychological problems that mar the adulthood of this unfortunate individual are due to the experiences with parents and not to the experiences with peers. The problems seen in adulthood could logically be attributed to parental abuse, to abuse or rejection by peers, to pre-existing characteristics that the individual was born with, or to some combination of these factors. The nurture assumption blinds researchers to the ambiguities in their data and causes them to prefer one explanation over all the others.

I cannot disprove Lykken's assertion that some parents are bad enough to inflict permanent damage on their children; I suspect he is right. There are environments so terrible that no mortal can hope to escape from them unscathed.

Are Some Children Unsocialized?

When adolescents break the law, their parents often get the blame. Some communities are even threatening to fine the parents of the malefactors. It is presumed that the parents must have failed to socialize their children—that is, they failed to teach their children not to lie, not to steal, and not to harm other people. But psychologists have [long] known that children who are law-abiding at home—who do not break family rules—may lie or steal when they are not at home. Similarly, children who are honest in the classroom or the playground may break rules at home. In a given context, children tend to behave similarly to the way their peers and siblings behave in that context.

The group or small community, not the parents, socializes the child. That is why the African American children from low-income, single-parent homes were no more aggressive, outside the home, than the White, middle class peers they went to school with (Kupersmidt et al., 1995). That is why the children of immigrants, transplanted to a neighborhood of native-born Americans, adapt to their new culture and acquire a new language, and in adulthood are indistinguishable from the children of native-born Americans (Harris, 1998).

Social norms differ from one neighborhood or subculture to another. In some subcultures the norm is to be aggressive and to break laws. The children and adolescents who belong to these subcultures do what children and adolescents do everywhere: They adapt their behavior to that of their group. We may not like the way these young people behave, but that does not mean they are unsocialized. They are conforming to the norms of their group, which do not conform to the norms of ours.

Other Possible Sources of the Increase in Crime

Lykken links the increase in crime over the last 40 years to the increase in the proportion of children reared in fatherless homes. But many things have changed over the last 40 years. How do we know that the increase in crime is not due to the increased use of computers or the decreased consumption of fat? We do not know, but the nurture assumption predisposes psychologists to seek an explanation inside the home whenever something goes wrong outside of it.

I suggest two other possible explanations for the increase in violent crime. The first is the vast increase in the amount and vivid-

ness of the violence depicted in movies and television shows. According to group socialization theory (Harris, 1998), the influence of the media does not operate directly on the individual child but is transmitted by way of the peer group, in the same manner as other acts of the culture. Children accept what they see on television as representing the way people are expected to behave in their society. Television influences the norms of the peer group and thus can affect the behavior of all children in the group, even if some do not watch these shows.

A second possibility is that the increase in crime—in particular, the crime among African Americans—is due to the decline and fall of the Cold War and the fact that Americans no longer have a common enemy to unite them. In the absence of a common enemy, large groups—that is, large social categories such as "Americans"—tend to split up into smaller ones, and these smaller groups or social categories tend to develop contrasting norms. Group contrast effects are clearly visible in schools that serve heterogeneous communities. What often happens is that one group will adopt the role of the "goody-goodies" and its members will follow school rules and strive for academic achievement, and the other group will go in the opposite direction and develop antischool and antisocial attitudes. The contrast might involve White, middle-class students versus White, working-class students, or White students versus Black students, or Black students whose parents immigrated from Jamaica or Haiti versus Black students whose parents have been Americans for many generations. These contrast effects are beneficial to the group pegged as goody-goodies—the descendants of Jamaican immigrants have been outstandingly successful—but extremely harmful to the group pegged as baddy-baddies, and harmful to the society in which they live.

A common enemy would unite us, but perhaps at too great a cost. Drastic solutions like an attack by extraterrestrials or a law to license parents might not be necessary, however. Group contrast effects also cause adolescents to contrast themselves with adults. The result is that each generation wants to be different from the one that came before it. When it is no longer possible to be different by being more outrageous, the pendulum tends to swing back the other way and the younger generation asserts its uniqueness by becoming more conservative. The recent decline in crime rates might be a sign that such a change is brewing. Let us hope so.

References

Arcus, D. M. (1991). *Experiential modification of temperamental bias in inhibited and uninhibited children.* Unpublished doctoral dissertation, Harvard University.

Bouchard, T. J., Jr. (1994, June 17). Genes, environment, and personality. *Science, 264,* 1700–1701.

Bouchard, T. J., Jr., Lykken, D. T., McGue, M., Segal, N. L., and Tellegen, A. (1990, October 12). Sources of human psychological differences: The Minnesota study of twins reared apart. *Science, 250,* 223–228.

DiLalla, L. F., and Gottesman, I. I. (1991). Biological and genetic contributors to violence—Widom's untold tale. *Psychological Bulletin, 109,* 125–129.

Dodge, K. A., Pettit, G. S., and Bates, J. E. (1994). Effects of physical maltreatment on the development of peer relations. *Development and Psychopathology, 6,* 43–55.

Eckenrode, J., Rowe, E., Laird, M., and Brathwaite, J. (1995). Mobility as a mediator of the effects of child maltreatment on academic performance. *Child Development, 66,* 1130–1142.

Harris, J. R. (1998). *The nurture assumption.* New York: Free Press.

Kagan, J. (1997). Temperament and the reactions to unfamiliarity. *Child Development, 68,* 139–143.

Kupersmidt, J. B., Griesler, P. C., DeRosier, M. E., Patterson, C. J., and Davis, P. W. (1995). Childhood aggression and peer relations in the context of family and neighborhood factors. *Child Development, 66,* 360–375.

Lykken, D. T. (1997). Factory of crime. *Psychological Inquiry, 8,* 261–270.

McLanahan, S., and Sandefur, G. (1994). *Growing up with a single parent: What hurts, what helps.* Cambridge, MA: Harvard University Press.

Mednick, S. A., Gabrielli, W. F., Jr., and Hutchings, B. (1987). Genetic factors in the etiology of criminal behavior. In S. A. Mednick, I. E. Moffitt, and S. A. Stack (Eds.), *The causes of crime: New biological approaches* (pp. 74–91). Cambridge, UK: Cambridge University Press.

Perez, C. M., and Widom, C. S. (1994). Childhood victimization and longterm intellectual and academic outcomes. *Child Abuse and Neglect, 18,* 617–633.

Scarr, S. (1992). Developmental theories for the 1990s: Development and individual differences. *Child Development, 63,* 1–19.

Vista, R. (1982). Physical child abuse: A dual-component analysis. *Developmental Review, 2,* 125–149.

Wolfe, D. A. (1985). Child-abusive parents: An empirical review. *Psychological Bulletin, 97,* 462–482. ✦

Issue 11: Questions to Consider

1. What criteria for becoming a licensed parent does Lykken propose? What evidence does he offer to support the choice of these criteria?

2. Parental licensure and the notion of eumemics have serious implications for African Americans and other racial minorities. Critique these concepts from the perspectives of racial and ethnic minorities.

3. Harris and Lykken both cite research findings on genetic influences on children's behavior. Which author's interpretation of these studies made the most sense to you? Why?

4. All of these authors write that they want to achieve the same outcomes for children, families, and society. They clearly differ on how to reach those outcomes. Generate a list of other ways that these goals might be achieved.

5. Write your own Counterpoint essay to rebut Lykken's proposal (or prepare an oral rebuttal). Do not include the points raised by Scarr and Harris (in short, create your own).

6. Scarr proposes Positive Procreation as a way to increase the proportion of good parents. Write a Counterpoint essay to her ideas or prepare an oral rebuttal.

7. Harris argues that parents' child rearing practices have relatively little effect on children's development. Write a Counterpoint essay to her ideas or prepare an oral rebuttal.

8. What are the intended consequences of parental licensing statutes? What might be some unintended consequences if such a law was passed?

9. What was your reaction to Scarr's suggestion of perhaps putting a contraceptive in the water supply so that women wanting to get pregnant would have to do something proactive to do so? Is this a good idea? Would it reduce the number of unwanted pregnancies? Would it lead to wanton sexual behavior among adolescents? Why or why not? ✦

Issue 12: Introduction

Parenting by the Book—But *Whose* Book? Race, Ethnicity, and Parenting Styles

Most self-help parenting books frame advice for what parents should do in raising their children from the standpoint of middle-class white families of European descent. This may reflect the author's white middle-class status or it may be the result of limited research on parents and children from other racial and ethnic groups. Self-help authors may have little scholarly information to draw upon that is not based on white families.

Is there a best way to raise children? The authors of the following paper think that the most appropriate parenting style for any family depends on its social and cultural environment. In particular, they believe that in order to understand parents of racial and ethnic minority groups, it is nec-essary to understand the *context* of the parents' behaviors. Space limits preclude a presentation of all racial and ethnic groups, so the authors present Latino and African American families as examples. As you read this paper, think about what you know about raising children and about your values regarding parenting.

Editors' Note

Linda Halgunseth is the daughter of an immigrant Mexican American mother. The personal experiences in the Latino section of the paper are hers. Catherine Cushinberry and Tashel Bordere are African Americans, and their personal experiences are shared in the African American section of the paper. ✦

12a

Race, Ethnicity, and Parenting Styles

*Linda Halgunseth, Catherine Cushinberry,
and Tashel Bordere*

Take a minute to answer these questions from your personal perspective. Then read the responses given that match how some parents within African American or Latino cultures might respond. How similar were your responses to the ones here? What would your parents have done in these situations?

You are in a grocery store with your child. As you walk down the cereal aisle she sees a brand of cereal that she wants. She grabs the cereal and you say "no." In response, she cries, screams, and throws a tantrum. How would you handle this situation?

An African American parent may discipline the child verbally or with a spanking. A public spanking is not to humiliate the child, but to provide immediate and swift punishment for unacceptable behavior. There are ongoing debates about the appropriateness of spankings, but many African American parents spank their children, not out of anger, but as a disciplining tool. All spankings are not child abuse, and not all children require spankings.

A Latina mother might attempt to make the child feel guilty for being selfish—money would be better spent on food for the whole family instead of on luxury items for the child. The mother may tell the child, "I make the money and the decisions on how to spend the money in the grocery store. If you do not like the things I buy, you can go live with another family or make your own money and buy your own grocery items."

Feeling shunned from the family will make the child feel guilty for being selfish and realize that she really does need her family (economically and emotionally) more than she needs a certain brand of cereal. A Latino parent will not spank or yell at the child. They may simply give a disapproving look to indicate to the child that the behavior is unsatisfactory.

Self-help books might recommend a time-out as a punishment for a child who has thrown a tantrum.

> Using physical punishment, such as spanking, as a method of limit-setting has generally fallen out of favor, as parents have come to recognize its destructiveness and search for more effective techniques . . . A time-out occurs when you interrupt inappropriate behavior and have your child sit quietly in a certain place for a specified period of time. Time-outs represent a reasonable and relatively simple way to make your point, and they are generally quite effective with children under the age of 12 . . . By removing the child from the scene, you deprive him of the opportunity to get attention for his misbehavior, and this gives him a chance to quiet down on his own. The time-out offers the added benefit of laying the groundwork for learning emotional self-reliance and self-control . . . Used properly, time-outs should eliminate your need to scold or be upset with your child about what has happened. (Kashani, Mehregany, Allan, and Kelly, 1998, p. 79)

You have a 13-year-old daughter who wants to spend a school night with a friend. How would you respond to this request? Why?

Latin American parents may say "no" whether the daughter wanted to spend a school night or a non-school night at a friend's house. Time with family is important and encouraged. A Latina mother may say, "Why? Don't you like your own family?" or "You are from this family, and you should sleep here. Jessica has her own house and family, and she sleeps there." The point is that being with your family should be your first priority (Buriel, 1993). A child wanting to spend time away from home may indicate to the parents that the child may be trying to pull away from the family. On the other hand, Latin American parents might say yes to the child's request on the condition that the child completes her or his housework and any other chores for the family before leaving (Buriel, 1993).

A white middle-class parent would not object to the child spending time away from the family, but they would object to a "sleep over" on a school night (e.g., "You need to be well-rested so you perform well at school. You can stay with your friend Friday or Saturday night"). If the daughter argues, self-help books would suggest:

> When adolescents resist limit-setting, you can explain your logic to them and reach a compromise on minor points. Again, if you remain calm, firm, and persistent, gradually you will begin to see a decline of the unwanted behavior. (Kashani et al., 1998, p. 78)

Your 8-year-old has just come into the house crying. He runs in and tells you that another child pushed him to the ground and called him a derogatory name. What would you do?

A typical response of an African American parent may be to tell the child to fight back. A friend shared his story of growing up in a dangerous inner-city environment. He was afraid of the older boys who taunted him as he walked to school. His mother responded to his tearful request for help that he should fill his pockets with rocks each morning. If the boys taunted him, he should throw rocks at them—a solution that worked! (The friend may not have actually thrown any rocks, but their presence comforted him and made him feel safer.) Although parenting books are unlikely to suggest rock throwing as a skill to be inculcated in children, in this case, it made sense. The boy was less afraid, and walking to school was not as traumatic. He later became a college professor, so his "pockets full of rocks" clearly did not translate into later violent behavior.

A typical response of a Latin American parent would be to teach the child to seek help from an authority figure (e.g., teacher) or to inform the bully's parents. Latino parents do not typically teach their children to physically fight back or to take matters into their own hands. Instead, Latino children are taught to elicit help from others in times of need and to maintain harmonious relationships, reflecting their interdependent orientation. Rotheram-Borus and Phinney (1990) found that in situations of peer conflict, Mexican-American children relied more on authority figures for solving problems, and African American children were more action-oriented and expressive.

In general, most parents, regardless of race or ethnicity, have similar hopes for their children—that they be safe, healthy, happy, and that they grow up to have satisfying lives. A quick visit to any bookstore will reveal shelves of books written to help parents reach those goals, and there are thousands of web sites with advice to parents. Unfortunately, many of these sources take a one-size-fits-all approach to parenting. That is, they ignore the reality of family contexts. European American middle-class parenting tends to focus on individuation and eventual separation from the family. Those terms are not even a part of the Latino vocabulary.

A one-size-for-all approach may cover the "middle ground" of parenting—those aspects of raising children in which nearly all agree (i.e., keeping children safe and healthy). However, they do not adequately describe the parenting styles of racial and ethnic minorities, nor do they fit the needs of minority families. Just as siblings who share the same parents and the same house experience home life differently, racial and ethnic groups experience society in different ways. The histories of various racial and ethnic groups in North America are quite diverse, as are the social and cultural contexts within which they now live. Consequently, parents from racial and ethnic minorities often use distinct methods of raising their children that are particularly suited to helping them become functional members of society, given the social realities under which they live. Their approaches to parenting are guided by cultural values and by past and current social conditions.

In this paper, we address Latino and African American parenting styles. We answer commonly asked questions about the parenting behaviors of Latino and African American parents.

Latino Parents

Why Are Latino Parents so Strict? They Don't Allow Their Children to Do Anything but Work Around the House

At very early ages, both daughters and sons work inside and outside the house. For example, at 10 years of age a daughter may do all of the ironing or dusting. You may also see a son waking up at the crack of dawn to help his father. To some non-Hispanic White Americans it may seem that Latino parents are either mean or lazy. However, from the perspective of the Latin American parent, they are promoting familism, a sense of attachment and identification with the family. Latino parents believe that they are helping their children attain a sense of family membership and cohesiveness by teaching their children familial responsibility and the importance of contributing to the family. Latino parents enforce the idea that if every member contributes to the functioning of the family, the family will remain strong.

Collectivism or interdependency is an orientation that promotes individuals contributing to a society rather than promoting

self-interests. The Latino culture has been characterized as collectivistic or interdependent, and the cultural value of familism stems from this orientation. The underlying tenet is that members of a group (society or family) work together and rely on each other. This interdependent orientation was obvious in my childrearing. Whenever I complained about having to clean the house, my Latina mother would emphasize that she provides me with food and shelter and that "we all have a role in this family."

Interdependence is taught at an early age. Latino parents often use modeling to teach their children instead of the commonly used "inquiry and praise" used by non-Hispanic White Americans. For example, if a child is learning how to set a table, a Latino parent will teach the child by demonstrating, whereas a non-Hispanic White American parent may inquire ("Where do you think the glass goes?") and then provide praise ("Very good. You did that all by yourself."). Doing things "all by yourself" does not hold the same value as it does for non-Hispanic White Americans. The Latino parenting style fosters interdependence and relational learning whereas the non-Hispanic White American parenting style emphasizes independence and self-initiated learning (Zuniga, 1992).

Interdependence is even noticeable in Latino infant caretaking. Latino parents encourage dependence in their infants through high amounts of nurturing and what others might call spoiling. Latin American parents are not as concerned with their infant/toddlers achieving developmental milestones (i.e., a child should walk by age 1) as are non-Hispanic White American parents. They are more concerned with their infants/toddlers developing positive character and interacting with other family members. In fact, a 4-year-old still drinking out of a bottle is not a reason for concern for Latin American parents. However, for most non-Hispanic White American parents, a 4-year-old drinking out of a bottle reflects negatively on the parents (negligence; too lazy to wean the child) and may be seen as a sign of a developmental delay in the child's learning of independence (Zuniga, 1992).

Do All Latin American Parents Teach Their Sons to Be 'Macho' and Their Daughters to Be Subservient 'Stay-At-Home Moms'? In Other Words, Do They Encourage Their Children to Enact Gender-Stereotyped Behaviors?

This stereotype in part stems from the infamous concept of "machismo" that has characterized Latin American men for decades. Machismo is a system of behavioral traits marked by exaggerated manliness (e.g., aggressiveness, courage, domination of women, and sexual conquests). It is commonly believed that because Latinos have the dominant role in a marital relationship and Latinas have the subordinate role of housekeeper and child-bearer, Latin American parents prepare their sons to be "macho" or independent and their daughters to be subservient.

The origin of these stereotypes has its roots in the 1500s, when Spanish conquerors set out to find gold and the fountain of youth. In countries such as Mexico, Peru, and Puerto Rico, the Spanish forced the natives to adopt their language and religion, and they also exploited the native women, forcing them to have sex and treating them like slaves. The native women's children by the Spanish conquerors were called mestizos (i.e., being half Indian and half Spanish). Because they grew up in an environment where their father had power and their mother was equivalent to a slave, the mestizos (i.e., both sons and daughters) learned that males were dominant and females were subordinate. As generations passed, Latin American men and women continued to fulfill those roles set by their ancestors (Penalosa, 1968).

Of course, this stereotype does not characterize all Latin American parents. Traditionally, these pronounced gender roles have been more prevalent in middle class families where it was not necessary for the mother to work (Penalosa, 1968). Working class mothers were less likely to experience the patriarchal hierarchy because they had less time to cater to their husbands and attend to the house and children. Unlike the middle class, working class mothers had some power because they provided income to the family. In addition, fathers whose wives worked outside of the home shared more of the household chores and caretaking, much as is true in modern European American families (Cromwell and Ruiz, 1979). The prevalence of machismo is slowly diminishing as increasing numbers of Latinas enter the work force and attain higher levels of education. Many mothers share at least equal power with fathers in making familial decisions and in disciplining their children.

Are changes in gender role influencing Latino child-rearing practices? Are the boys still socialized to be "macho" and the girls to be subordinate? The answer to this question depends on how traditional Latino parents are in enforcing cultural values and how recently and from where they emigrated to the U.S. In very traditional families boys are socialized to be independent (i.e., manly), and girls are socialized to be dependent and nurturing. Recent Latin American immigrants, particularly those from rural areas, have received less exposure to North American ideals and are more likely to raise their children to adopt gender-stereotyped behaviors and attitudes (Penalosa, 1968).

For Latino mothers who work outside the home and share family decision-making responsibility, socialization of children has become less gendered. And over time, successive generations of Latino family members often become acculturated, adopting the prevailing values of the majority culture. This is not true of all, however. Some families retain their traditional cultural values while acquiring some of the values of their new home—these families are said to become bi-cultural.

Why Are Latin American Parents Apathetic About Their Children's Education?

The stereotype that Latin American parents do not care about their children's education is a gross misinterpretation. Latin American parents report valuing their children's education and believing that home-work is important for their children's learning process (Bempechat, Graham, and Jimenez, 1999). However, Latin American parents who do not speak English fluently or who have not completed high school may feel inadequate in helping their children with homework or other school projects. Because of language problems they also may not attend school functions as often as other parents, and they may be reluctant to contact school officials (see Issue 13 on child language brokering). Relatively new immigrants and those that are poor are particularly likely to avoid contacting their children's teachers. Unfortunately, this behavior is interpreted as apathy or disinterest. Given that many Latinos are poor, the unfortunate tendency is to assume that *all* Latino parents are uninvolved or apathetic toward their children's education (Garcia Coll, Meyer, and Brillon, 1999).

It should also be recognized that the definition of education encompasses more than academics for Latin American parents. A well-educated (*bien educado*) child according to the Latin American culture is one who is calm (*tranquilo*), respectful (*respetuoso*), and obedient (*obediente*). To be disrespectful is to be disobedient; the two words are synonymous. Respect to others, especially to elders, is strongly reinforced. Latino parenting strategies and child discipline are designed so that children will interact with others in a respectful manner. Parents monitor their children's verbal and nonverbal displays of respect to others. A child who is loud or antagonistic is immediately corrected and punished for being disrespectful. For example, there were severe consequences when I talked back to my mother. My nonverbal communication (i.e., body language) was also closely monitored. My mother made me leave the room if I looked like I was in a bad mood, even if I had not said anything. Latino parents reinforce body language and facial expressions that show respect, such as smiling and nodding, and they correct body language that they consider disrespectful (e.g., eye contact avoidance or other gestures that show that the child is not paying attention). As a re-

sult, Latin American children acquire acute field-dependent skills or are sensitized to the nonverbal communication cues and responses of others (Zuniga, 1992). Parents do not have to yell at their children or swat them to get attention, the children will know they have misbehaved by reading their parents' body language.

Personalism and interpersonal relatedness are two qualities that are also included in a "well-educated" Latino child. Personalism refers to self-dignity and a pleasant disposition. My cousin from Mexico is so proud that her baby daughter smiles often and seldom cries because this shows that she *"tiene un buen caracter"* (i.e., has a pleasant personality or disposition). To have *"un buen caracter"* differs from the Euro-American notion of a "happy baby" in that *"un buen caracter"* emphasizes the positive reactions of others to the baby. In addition, interpersonal relatedness, the ability to interact with others in a harmonious manner that fosters a mutual respect between parties, is valued in children. Being able to develop and maintain harmonious relationships is characteristic of the collectivistic Latino culture, in which the goal is to contribute to the group rather than to the individual.

Why Don't Latin American Parents Try to Help Their Children Integrate Into Mainstream Society?

Latino parents may choose to shelter their children from the mainstream society for two reasons: (1) to promote familism, and (2) in response to racism. Familism originated from economic necessity but later became a cultural value in itself. Familism facilitates interpersonal attachment, and this attachment may be particularly helpful for Latin Americans who reside in a society where racism is prevalent. Having people say that, "you do not belong in this country," that "you should go back to your own country," or "if you are going to live in this country you need to speak our language," are not only cultural attacks but personal attacks as well. Being hated or disliked because of one's culture is obviously irrational, but it can create fear or anger within Latinos/as. Unfortunately, some Latinos (adults and children) have learned that as nice as they try to be or as hard as they work, they continue to be viewed negatively because of their cultural heritage. Latino parents in the United States thus may encourage their children to stay close and spend time with them; they feel safe and accepted when they are together. Second and third generation Latin Americans may not know if they are more "Latino" or more "American," but they will always know they are part of a family.

African American Parents

Why Are Black Parents so Hard on Their Children?

In an undergraduate psychology course that included both black and white students, we were asked to break into small groups and list defining characteristics for various parenting styles. My (Bordere) group quickly agreed that authoritative parenting was mostly used in White families—that parents utilizing this style are caring, warm, and communicate rules and expectations to children by talking to them and allowing feedback. That authoritative parents raise their children in a rational, issue-oriented manner, frequently engaging in discussion and explanation over matters of discipline (Hill and Sprague, 1999), seemed to fit my classmates' perceptions of the style of European American parents. On the other hand, my peers thought that minorities, especially Blacks, prefer authoritarian parenting—strict, controlling, discouraging autonomy, expecting children to mind without questioning. My classmates also thought that Black parents yell a lot and spank their children rather than talking to them. Their perceptions of Black parenting techniques were quite negative.

Authoritarian parenting, also referred to as no-nonsense or power-assertive parenting, is one of many methods used by African American parents to help their children become competent adults. It entails direct, often physical forms of discipline that can

be interpreted as harsh. However, the umbrella concept of African American parenting is probably respect—and respect is shown when children don't challenge their parents' authority and are obedient. Some speculate that cultural values of respect required of children (Hurd, Moore, and Rogers, 1996), may come from strong religious roots among African Americans and may be based on religious beliefs. Regardless of the reason, African American parents who use forceful disciplining techniques and demand respect are trying to prepare their children for a world that may be unfair and prejudicial towards them. Black parents have to prepare their children for overt racism (e.g., racial profiling, name calling) and for more subtle judgments of others that can profoundly affect their lives.

To offset racism, Black parents believe it is important for their children to learn to respond to them as authority figures. Asking "Why?" when given a directive by a parent is unacceptable in many African American homes. We (Cushinberry and Bordere) know from experience that when Black parents say move, their children better move! Questioning the authority of parents is seen as a clear sign of disrespect. Black parents know that children labeled as troublemakers or as disrespectful of authority are likely to run into a lot of difficulty and perhaps danger in the dominant culture. Because African American children may suffer greater consequences than children from other cultural backgrounds for questioning authority, this "rule" serves a protective function.

Children's understanding of their parents' expectations for respect and obedience was revealed by two perceptive preschoolers during interviews in a study investigating their choices when given conflicting instructions by parents (sit on the floor while opening birthday present) and teachers (sit on the sofa while opening birthday present). When asked whose instructions would be followed, one white child replied, "My teacher." He then paused, seemingly pondering the dilemma. "Well," he continued, "if I listen to mom, my teacher will be mad at me. My mom will be mad too if I do what my teacher says, but me and mom, we'll work it out somehow." This child's response clearly reveals the negotiation and high level of communication characteristic of authoritative parenting. In contrast, the responses of one African American child were matter-of-fact and straightforward. With a serious expression on his face, the 5-year-old responded to each dilemma with a blanket statement, "My Mom . . .'cause she's the BOSS!" The response of this child shows his understanding that his mom is an authority figure who is not to be questioned.

Although African American children, like all children, have at some point thought of their parents as mean, they understand that their parents care about them and have their best interests in mind. Authoritarian parenting has worked for many African American families. However, children reared in other cultures may interpret authoritarian discipline differently and, therefore, experience different outcomes.

Of course, not every Black parent prefers to yell and insist on obedience nor does every Black child fare best when yelled at. Nor does every European American child benefit from negotiated parenting. The method of discipline depends on a number of factors, including the child's age and temperament, the parent's personal values, and the context (Bradley, 1998; Hill and Sprague, 1999).

Why Are African American Children so Close to Their Parents? How Do Black Children Ever Become Independent?

The African American culture is defined by interpersonal connectedness. This means that family ties or kinship bonds are strongly valued, not only with immediate family members, but with extended kin as well. The high level of connectedness in African American families is evidenced in the emotional closeness of their relationships, which can be observed physically. That is, they often live in close proximity, and a high level of contact is maintained with relatives who do not live nearby as well. One way that this sense of connectedness has been preserved within the African American culture

is through the promotion of emotional closeness in the parent-child relationship. These parent-child ties foster reliance on the family and keep the children physically close. For example, many African American children, even as adults, rely on their parents for approval when making important decisions. This may seem odd to individuals living in families that emphasize independence and individualism (e.g., European American families). However, the functionality of emotional dependence within the African American culture has been supported by research (Fuhrman and Holmbeck, 1995).

Why Do African American Children Seem More Accepting of People in General and of Diversity Than Other Racial Groups? Is This a Value That Black Parents Teach Their Children?

Blacks may be less willing to exhibit discriminatory behaviors toward others because of the bigotry and racism they have experienced. They know how damaging this can be. However, research support for greater tolerance among Blacks is mixed (Galanis, 1987). There is some evidence that Blacks are more accepting of groups of people that are persecuted due to no fault of their own, but they are not more tolerant than other racial or ethnic groups of deviance in general.

A Caution

When examining parenting styles, it is important to distinguish between race and social class. Some parenting styles have been attributed to race or ethnicity when they actually are related more to social class. For example, an African American mother who lives in a low-income, violent neighborhood may be more protective of her child and stricter in what she allows the child to do outside of the home than would be the case with a middle class African American mother. In addition, parenting reflects the style of previous generations of parents, the parents' personal choice, the parents' education level, and their knowledge of child development. The personality and temperament of the child is also a factor, as is the context. These factors influence the parenting practices of all parents regardless of race or ethnicity. Parenting is challenging in American society and the family—immediate, extended, and in the case of African Americans, fictive kin—has been a source of strength for African American and Latino families. Their challenges and strengths may differ from those of the mainstream culture, but they are merely different, not dysfunctional. Strong parents produce resilient children. We need a better understanding of what supports strong parenting for all of the various groups making up American culture.

References

Bempechat, J., Graham, S., and Jimenez, N. (1999). The socialization of achievement in poor and minority students: A comparative study. *Journal of Cross-Cultural Psychology, 30(2),* 139–158.

Bradley, C. R. (1998). Child rearing in African American families: A study of the disciplinary practices of African American parents. *Journal of Multicultural Counseling and Development, 26,* 273–281.

Buriel, R. (1993). Child rearing orientations in Mexican American families: The influences of generation and sociocultural factors. *Journal of Marriage and the Family, 55,* 987–1000.

Cromwell, R., and Ruiz, R. A. (1979). The myth of macho dominance in decision-making within Mexican and Chicano families. *Hispanic Journal of Behavioral Sciences, 1,* 355–373.

Furhman, T., and Holmbeck, G. N. (1995). A contextual-moderator analysis of emotional autonomy and adjustment in adolescence. *Child Development, 66,* 793–811.

Galanis, C. M. (1987). When stigma confronts stigma: Some conditions enhancing a victim's tolerance of other victims. *Personality and Social Psychology Bulletin, 12,* 169–177.

Garcia Coll, C., Meyer, E., and Brillon, L. (1999). Ethnic and minority parenting. In M. Bornstein (Ed.), *Handbook of parenting vol. 2: Biology and ecology of parenting* (pp. 189–209). Mahwah, NJ: Lawrence Erlbaum Associates, Inc.

Gonzales, A. (1982). Sex roles of the traditional Mexican family. *Journal of Cross-Cultural Psychology, 13(3),* 330–339.

Haight, W. L. (1998). "Gathering the spirit" at First Baptist Church: Spirituality as a protective factor in the lives of African American children. *Social Work, 43,* 213–221.

Hill, S. A., and Sprague, J. (1999). Parenting in Black and White families: The interaction of gender with race and class. *Gender and Society, 13,* 480–502.

Hurd, E. P., Moore, C., and Rogers, R. (1996). Quiet success: Parenting strengths among African Americans. *Families in Society, 76,* 434–443.

Kashani, J., Mehregany, D., Allan, W., and Kelly, K. (1998). *Raising happy children: A parent's guide.* New York: Three Rivers Press.

Penalosa, F. (1968). Mexican family roles. *Journal of Marriage and the Family, 30,* 680–689.

Rotheram-Borus, M. J., and Phinney, S. (1990). Patterns of social expectations among Black and Mexican American children. *Child Development, 61,* 542–556.

Silver, N. (2000). *Rules for parents.* New York: Berkely Books.

Steinberg, L. (1999). *Adolescence.* Boston: McGraw-Hill.

Zuniga, M. E. (1992). Families with Latino roots. In E. W. Lynch and M. J. Hanson (Eds.), *Developing cross-cultural competence: A guide for working with young children and their families* (pp. 151–179). Baltimore: Paul H. Brookes. ✦

Halgunseth, L., Cushinberry, C., and Bordere, T. (2001). *Racial and Ethnic Differences in Parenting.* Published by permission of the authors.

Issue 12: Questions to Consider

1. How would you resolve the parenting situations that were presented in the opening of this paper? How do your responses compare to those that might come from a Latino parent or an African-American parent?

2. Can you remember times when your parents' typical parenting style changed dramatically? If so, what was the context?

3. Do you think there is a best way to raise children or do you agree with the authors' contention that effective ways to raise children depend on the social context in which they live?

4. Trace the history of parenting advice offered in self-help books and government pamphlets over the past 75 years or more. Examine the trends on specific parenting behaviors such as spanking, weaning, or bedtime regimens. Write a report on your findings and be prepared to discuss your findings in class.

5. Do a search of parenting books targeted for specific groups of parents such as the two presented in this paper (i.e., African American and Latino). Do a brief review of one of the books and contrast the advice given with the advice from a "mainstream" parenting book. ✦

Issue 13: Introduction

'Mama, He Says . . .': Children as Language Brokers for Their Parents

Almost 20 percent of children in the United States speak a language other than English at home (http://www.census.gov). Spanish is the first language for nearly 70 percent of these children, and it is projected that by 2050, the U.S. population will be about 25 percent Latino. In 2000, foreign-born Americans made up about 11 percent of the U.S. population, only slightly less than the 15 percent that was foreign-born in 1900. North America has been and continues to be racially, ethnically, and linguistically diverse, which means that Child Language Brokering, the subject of the following papers, will be an issue for years to come.

The authors of the three papers are young professionals who are second-generation Americans. Each had at least one foreign-born parent whose native language was not English. Linda Halgunseth's mother emigrated from Mexico, Adriana Umaña-Taylor's parents emigrated from Colombia, South America, and Susan Santiago's parents emigrated from Puerto Rico. Each woman had some personal experience with language brokering, but the first two papers are based on the research literature and do not necessarily reflect the authors' personal opinions. The third paper, on the other hand, is written from personal experience. As you will see from reading the paper, this personal experience had a mixed effect on the writer. As you read these three articles, think about what life would be like with parents who did not speak English. How would it feel to be a *language broker*? How would it feel to know personal information about one's parents that most children do not know? How would you have reacted to the responsibility of relaying correct health information and diagnostic information between your parents and physicians? ✦

13a

Language Brokering: Positive Developmental Outcomes

Linda Halgunseth

Language brokering is when a third party (i.e., a bilingual child) mediates communication between two different linguistic/cultural agents; for example, a non-English-speaking parent and an English-speaking postal worker. Language brokering (LB) is different than translating and/or interpreting for three reasons: It is informal, the goal is to mediate communication rather than merely transmit it, and there exists an unequal power relationship between the broker and the agents, usually one in which the broker (i.e., a bilingual child) is normally under the authority or supervision of one of the beneficiaries (i.e., non-English-speaking parent). Child language brokers (CLBs) fulfill important functions for their families. Their particular experiences as a mediator between their non-English-speaking parent/s and the English-speaking world shape their development. Prolonged LB positively contributes to the cognitive, social, emotional, and cultural development of CLBs.

Before discussing the positive developmental effects of LB, however, it is important to first understand why LB even exists. One complaint often made in regard to LB concerns the immigrant parents of CLBs, "Why don't they just learn English?" Or "If they are going to live in our country, why don't they speak our language?" The complaint may seem logical; however, it also assumes that non-English-speaking parents do not want to learn or have made the con-scious decision not to learn English. This is far from the truth.

Non-English-speaking adults who immigrate to the United States face cognitive obstacles in learning English. Lenneberg (1967) explains that the nervous system loses flexibility with age, so that by puberty, the organization of the brain is fixed, making language learning difficult. Children, on the other hand, acquire second languages with comparably more ease and efficiency. Thus, immigrant children will learn English with much less effort than their immigrant parents. Immigrant proficiency in English is related to the age at which immigrants arrive in the United States, not to the number of years lived in the United States (Johnson and Newport, 1989). Those immigrating before the age of 7 develop grammatical proficiency comparable with that of native English speakers. Thus, due to the difficulty that adults face in learning a new language and the relative ease for children, parents immigrating to the United States are often forced to rely on their children's help to communicate in English—to language broker.

Prolonged LB contributes positively to the cognitive development of CLBs. From as early as 10 years of age, CLBs mediate communication between parents and various English-speaking professionals such as postal workers, lawyers, teachers, utility service representatives, landlords, and/or doctors. In order for CLBs to effectively assist their parents, they must learn guidelines and terminology for a variety of professional settings. As a result, CLBs acquire school-related vocabulary that may help build their lexicons and enhance their school performance.

CLBs develop strong interpersonal skills as a result of LB. In communicating with various adults in the community, CLBs learn to modify and adapt their social and communicative skills. Communicating with adolescent peers differs from communicating with professional adults; however, CLBs make this transition daily. CLBs not only learn social skills, but they learn to apply them appropriately according to the context. This helps them develop strong feelings of social self-efficacy.

Many situations in which children broker are in the context of negotiation (i.e., non-English-speaking parent and business associate). CLBs realize quickly that the information mediated between their parents and a business associate can determine the outcome of the business endeavor. Therefore, in order to influence a positive outcome, the CLB may present information in a manner that is pleasing to the listener. For instance, Harris and Sherwood (1978) report that CLBs often temper outbursts of a parent when communicating to another agent.

> Father to CLB: *'Digli che e un imbecille!'* (Tell him he's a nitwit). CLB to 3rd party: 'My father won't accept your offer.' (Harris and Sherwood, 1978, p. 157)

Understanding the perspectives of various party members and mediating information between them to influence a positive outcome requires the interpersonal skills of a U.S. ambassador; however, these skills are used often by CLBs as early as 10 years of age (McQuillan and Tse, 1995).

According to social exchange theory, behavior is motivated by self-interest and personal profit. In examining the behavior required of CLBs, many tangible rewards come to mind. For example, CLBs may broker because they benefit from household bills getting paid, the electricity getting turned on, and the family being financially supported. However, there are also many intangible rewards—feeling important and independent, enhanced self-esteem—from language brokering. It is these intangible rewards that may contribute most to the emotional development of CLBs.

In knowing two languages, CLBs perform a unique function for other family members. Their brokering skills provide great utility and may enhance feelings of importance and usefulness in CLBs, as well as feelings of self-confidence and self-worth (McQuillan and Tse, 1995). Feelings of maturity and independence, which are especially important in adolescence, may also result from interacting in adult contexts (e.g., lawyer's office). In addition, family members may exhibit more respect and appreciation to CLBs due to their valuable service, which may lead to a "move up" on the family hierarchy.

A less obvious and less direct emotional benefit of LB is the fact that CLBs prevent potentially embarrassing situations (Tse, 1995). When in public, transactions between a non-English-speaking parent and an English-speaking-only third party go more quickly when a CLB is there to facilitate. Negative stimuli such as stares, sighs, criticisms, and racial slurs are less likely to occur when a third party who is fluent in the language of a host country is in charge of the transactions. Children, especially in adolescence, are not only sensitive to their own social acceptance, but also do not want their parents to be socially criticized or embarrassed. I remember often feeling uneasy when my Hispanic mother and I would approach the drive through at fast food restaurants: "What? Two what? Two hamburgers? What?" It seemed easier and less painful for me to lean over and speak for my mother than to hear the frustration in the voices of both parties and the honking of cars behind us.

In addition to providing English interpreting and translating skills, CLBs also relate cultural information to their immigrant parents. CLBs are usually their parents' only source of information regarding the American culture. While bearing the responsibility of explaining and socializing their parents on American cultural values and norms, CLBs are also becoming acculturated to the United States. Acculturation is the process of learning or borrowing elements from other ethnic groups (Berry, Trimble, and Olmedo, 1986). For example, if a non-English-speaking parent does not understand why school is cancelled on the third Thursday in November, the child will need to learn about the cultural tradition of Thanksgiving in order to explain it to his/her parent. Therefore, even though CLBs can be considered acculturating agents for their parents, it is also true that the LB experience accelerates the acculturation process for CLBs.

In addition to acculturation, the LB experience strengthens feelings of biculturalism (i.e., the integration of competencies and sensitivities associated with two cultures within a person) in CLBs. Tse (1995) reported that one reason CLBs appreciated LB was because it allowed them to maintain fluency in the language of their native country. Thus, LB is an invaluable experience because it allows the CLB to continue to feel connected to their native culture, while functioning within their host culture.

In conclusion, parents who immigrate to the United States are often forced to rely on their children for help in communicating to the English-speaking world. CLBs have the unique experience of bridging these two linguistic and cultural agents and as a result, are positively affected cognitively, socially,

emotionally, and culturally. These children have the benefit of providing an invaluable service to their parents and of knowing the "ins and outs" of two distinct cultures.

References

Berry, J., Trimble, J., and Olmedo, E. (1986). Assessment of acculturation. In W. Lonner and J. Berry (Eds.), *Field method in cross-cultural research.* (pp. 291–394). Newbury Park, CA: Sage.

Harris, B., and Sherwood, B. (1978). Translating as an innate skill. In D. Gerver and H. W. Sinaiko (Eds.), *Language interpretation and communication* (pp. 155–170). New York: Plenum Press.

Johnson, J., and Newport, E. (1989). Critical period effects in second language learning: The influence of instructional state on the acquisition of English as a second language. *Cognitive Psychology, 21,* 60–99.

Lenneberg, E. (1967). *Biological foundations of language.* New York: Wiley.

McQuillan, J., and Tse, L. (1995). Child language brokering in linguistic minority communities: Effects on cultural interaction, cognition, and literacy. *Language and Education, 9,* 195–215.

Tse, L. (1995). Language brokering among Latino adolescents: Prevalence, attitudes, and school performance. *Hispanic Journal of Behavioral Sciences, 17,* 180–193. ✦

Language Brokering as a Stressor for Immigrant Children and Their Families

Adriana J. Umaña-Taylor

As Halgunseth stated in the previous article, child language brokering (CLB) involves children acting as translators for parents and relatives who exhibit limited English proficiency. Research on Latino, Chinese, and Vietnamese children of immigrants indicates that nearly all of the children had served as a CLB for their families (Tse, 1995; Valenzuela, 1999). Children broker for their families in many ways. They may translate government documents, mail, television news programs, and messages from school; explain to their parents how to file taxes or how to interpret legal issues related to immigration; and advocate on behalf of their parents in interactions with outsiders that do not speak their language (Valenzuela, 1999). Although some researchers argue that CLB is a positive experience for children—it helps them develop language competence in both English and their family's native language and they gain valuable experiences in interpersonal relations (Tse, 1995)—it can also have negative effects.

Role Reversals

Family relations can become strained when children broker for their parents because of the role reversal that takes place when parents become dependent on their children for communication with people outside the family. This dependency can foster resentment on the part of parents who feel uncomfortable entrusting adult business to their children (Baptiste, 1993). Furthermore, the social order of the family, and the adults' assumed authority over the children can be disturbed when children gain private information about parents during a translation (Cohen, Moran-Ellis, and Smaje, 1999). Parents may find it disrespectful for children to ask about adult matters such as their employment status or health concerns, even though they expect their children to serve as LB during transactions that involve adult matters (e.g., filling out job applications, visiting a physician). Over time, this may foster feelings of resentment within immigrant parents toward their children. Clinical evidence also suggests that children who often serve in an adult role, such as being a language broker, resent being shifted back to a child's status at other times (Baptiste, 1993).

Increased Anxiety

When a child must convey confidential information, both the parents and the child may become anxious and stressed. For example, when translating information between their parents and a physician, there is incredible pressure for a child to correctly translate to the doctor parents' symptoms as well as translate to the parent the doctor's questions, diagnoses, and recommended treatments. Compared to adults, children have limited vocabularies and cognitive reasoning skills. Thus, when a child has to relay information that requires a more advanced vocabulary than is developmentally appropriate for them, it can be stressful. This stress is compounded when the content involves important information regarding the parents' health. The parents' health and well-being could be at risk if the child incorrectly translates commands. Moreover, brokering in a medical setting may expose children to their parents' pain and/or fear, which is frightening for children and which may result in them taking on even more responsibility for the parent (Cohen et al., 1999). Parents' anxiety during language brokering in a physician's office may result from the humiliation of disclosing intimate information (e.g., sexual activity, history of depression) to their child and the fear that they might not be accurately diagnosed and treated by the physician because of limits to children's understanding or language skills. These interactions can put pressure on vulnerable young children.

Poor Educational Outcomes

Another potentially negative consequence of CLB is that children who broker may be at risk for lower academic or educational outcomes. Although research that examines the influence of brokering on educational achievement and outcomes is limited, existing work indicates that many children broker for their parents in situations involving their own education (and without their parents' knowledge). For example, children often report that they are entrusted with handling school matters for themselves and for their siblings (Tse, 1995; Valenzuela, 1999). They also report that they often don't show notes from school to their parents, that they sign many, if not all, of their own permission slips, and that they take on the sole responsibility of making educational decisions for themselves and

their siblings. They also can write their own absent/tardy notes ("Please excuse Maria from school yesterday. She was very ill") and have their parents sign it, telling them it is something else (Valenzuela, 1999). Making decisions without the benefit of their parents' experience and knowledge can negatively affect the children's academic potential and educational outcomes (Tse, 1995). For example, some schools give students and their families a choice of whether the student will participate in a "General" academic plan comprised of basic courses that are required for graduation or an "Advanced" academic plan comprised of college preparation courses. Without discussing these options with their parents, students may be inclined to choose the General plan because it is easier and/or allows more flexibility, even though the Advanced plan might be more appropriate for them.

CLBs may also limit children's educational and occupational opportunities because of perceived family responsibilities to continue brokering. They may feel guilty dropping the brokering function to pursue their own educational and career goals, even after they become adults. They may turn down college scholarships, for example, because they feel obligated to stay close to their parents and continue language brokering.

Inhibited Identity Formation

CLB also has implications for individuals' identity formation. When most children are exploring their identity and concentrating on who they want to become, CLBs are performing adult tasks (e.g., mediating at Social Security offices, negotiating at their parent's place of employment). There are negative consequences to skipping adolescence and going straight to adulthood. Adolescents need time to explore their identities and examine various roles that they might assume. If CLBs are continually fulfilling adult tasks for their parents (or other family members) during their teenage years, the identity process may be compromised.

In sum, although there may be advantages to children who language broker for their families in terms of language acquisition and development of interpersonal skills, there are also limitations to consider. To temper these limitations, organizations that serve or employ immigrants (e.g., government agencies, health care, education) should attempt to provide translation services for adults who are not proficient in English. Although employing additional workers to translate may increase institutional costs, in the long run it may be cost effective. For example, health care professionals working through professional translators rather than a child could more quickly and privately gain information about the patient's symptoms, and make a diagnosis that would save physicians' time, allowing them to see more patients and generate more revenue. Employers decrease the strain that is put on the family and especially the employee, by providing translation assistance. Mental health can greatly affect employees' productivity; thus, it is in the best interest of companies to limit the stressors that are placed upon their employees. It is time that having translators on staffs becomes institutionalized in the United States. It is unreasonable to continue to expect immigrant children to assume stressful adult responsibilities.

References

Baptiste, D. A. (1993). Immigrant families, adolescents and acculturation: Insight for therapists. *Marriage and Family Review, 19,* 341–363.

Cohen, S., Moran-Ellis, J., and Smaje, C. (1999). Children as informal interpreters in GP consultations: Pragmatics and ideology. *Sociology of Health and Illness, 21,* 163–186.

Tse, L. (1995). Language brokering among Latino adolescents: Prevalence, attitudes, and school performance. *Hispanic Journal of Behavioral Sciences, 17,* 180–193.

Valenzuela, A. (1999). Gender roles and settlement activities among children and their immigrant families. *American Behavioral Scientist, 42,* 720–742. ✦

13c

Language Brokering: A Personal Experience

Susan Santiago

I was born in 1969 and raised in Philadelphia. My parents are dual citizens of the United States and Puerto Rico, a territory in North America. They lived on the island until the mid-1950s when they emigrated to the U.S.A. in search of economic opportunity. Their job options were limited because they each had less than a 6th grade education. My mother worked in a factory as a seamstress under horrible conditions in what is today termed a "sweat factory." My father followed his older brothers to Delaware to work on a farm where they were treated worse than the livestock. He and his older brothers managed to run away and settled in Philadelphia. My father found employment as a construction worker and later received training to become a welder.

My parents have never really mastered the English language, and because of this they tend to be extremely self-conscious when speaking to non-Latino persons, even after living on the mainland for almost 50 years. My siblings and I, as first generation Puerto Rican-Americans, experienced the duality of existing in a bicultural and bilingual home. My siblings are many years older than I am, and they experienced more teasing from classmates about their Spanish accent and timid ways than I did. Their teachers considered them model students as long as they did not speak Spanish or raise their voices too loud. This was during the 1960s when ESL (English as a Second Language) was not as popular—even in "progressive" East Coast cities—as it appears to be today.

My brother served as the interpreter for my parents until I was old enough to put a sentence together without using Spanish and English words interchangeably. My first memory of officially interpreting for my parents was after taking the California Scholastic Aptitude Test in 1st grade. I scored in the 95th percentile, and Ms. Jones raved to my parents about how smart I was. I explained to them that I was to be placed in the advanced reading class, but I recall how my parents didn't understand Ms. Jones, and they did not understand the significance of this transition for me. This may have been due to my inability to effectively language broker. However, by this time my brother had received his driver's license, was hardly ever home, and had lost interest in serving as interpreter for my parents. So I assumed the CLB role. I felt proud knowing that I was able to help my parents to a degree that most of my classmates had not reached, but there was sometimes stress as well.

Mostly, however, I remember feeling like an adult in my role as interpreter. In retrospect, I must have amused the store and office clerks as I rattled off my mother's request to them and then in turn, rattled off their response to my mother. I also recall that speaking on the phone with persons of authority, such as bank tellers or real estate agents, and being able to express my parents' requests, made me very happy. I usually felt so comfortable with this type of communication that I think I developed a certain maturity and patience at a young age that continues to serve me well in most situations.

I continued developing language-brokering skills, but I became aware over time of how I had begun communicating mainly in English to my parents just as my siblings had been doing for years. I was conscious of how odd this was because Spanish and English are not always easily translated and understood. Many messages became misconstrued because my parents spoke to us in Spanish, and we responded in English. I was becoming *acculturated*, and I believe that I chose to speak Spanish less often around age 9. I recall teachers commenting on how well I spoke English, which probably encouraged me to stop speaking Spanish. As a child I really did not understand how ethnocentric those kinds of comments were, and I internalized the notion that in order to be considered a "good" student, I should speak proper English and not Spanglish (a combining of Spanish and English words together) like I did at home and in my neighborhood. Although I don't remember for sure, I suspect that I was encouraged not to express my bilingualism in elementary school. As an adult, realizing this has caused me a great deal of concern. I feel as though I sacrificed mastering my native language in order to be accepted into mainstream culture.

However, as a teenager I was accepted into mainstream society largely because I expressed myself well in English. Nonetheless, I recall how awkward I sometimes felt because I was not sure which culture I really fit into. When I was growing up there was not much discussion of *biculturalism*. I existed in both worlds, and at times I sacrificed one for the other depending on the situation.

Even as an adult, I continue to serve as interpreter for my parents, albeit from a distance. For instance, when my father was diagnosed with prostate cancer and needed medical attention I served as the language broker between my father and his urologist. This was especially uncomfortable for my father because he had to reveal intimate details to me, but it was absolutely necessary to ensure that he received the proper medical attention. My mother has glaucoma. I assumed that she had continued going to the optometrist after I left home, but I recently found out that she has not been taking care of her eyes as she should. I telephoned her optometrist and explained that my mother would feel more comfortable if the facility had a Spanish translator because she feels as though she is often misunderstood, which is very frustrating for her. I also served as language broker for my parents when they became eligible to receive Social Security benefits. In general, my parents appear to be less uncomfortable with my assuming the role of language broker now than when I was a child.

I wonder how different I would be today had I received the support necessary to be a CLB. As an adult I understand the complexity of being a CLB. However, I believe that with proper support and guidance, CLBs can not only assist their families, but also have the potential to create a sense of language mastery that will be beneficial in their own development. On the other hand, if proper support and guidance is not provided, CLBs will experience conflict associated with the duality of this role, and they may not feel appreciated for the contributions they make to their families as language brokers. For me, being a CLB was a very mixed experience. ✦

Reprinted with the permission of Susan Santiago.

Issue 13: Questions to Consider

1. Should children be allowed to be Language Brokers or should most major institutions in the United States (e.g., hospitals and clinics, employment agencies, government agencies, schools) provide interpreters?

2. After reading these papers, is it your judgment that Child Language Brokering is a good thing or a bad thing? What information had the greatest effect on your decision?

3. How do you think your parents would have reacted to having to share private information about their health or financial situation with you when you were still a child? Would they have resented it, been embarrassed by it, not minded? How might this have affected your family relationships?

4. How do you think you would have reacted to the responsibility of being the communicator to the outside world for your family? Would this have helped build your self-esteem? Would you have resented the responsibility? Would you have been embarrassed by your parents' inability to speak English well?

5. If you were a Child Language Broker for your family, how did your experiences fit with what you read in the three papers? Why do you think this was the case?

6. What can institutions do to either facilitate Child Language Brokering or dispel it? ✦

Issue 14: Introduction

Are Companies Becoming Friendlier to Working Moms and Dads?

Work is the key to family income, and adequate family income is essential to family functioning. Without income, the family cannot be fed, housed, kept in good health, clothed, or even educated. Yet, we traditionally have thought of work as something separate from family life, and have often failed to notice the links between workplace practices and family functioning, between work hours and time for family, and between work environments and individual stress, which spills over into the home.

In spite of increased attention given to work/family stress, our lack of understanding of the relationship between work and family is still fairly profound. There are a number of reasons for this. One reason is that *the workforce has been rapidly changing*. Women have been entering the workforce at a steadily increasing pace, and now the percentages of men and women working are nearly equal, although women are much more likely than men to be working part-time. According to a March 2000 U.S. Department of Labor Women's Bureau report, women's share of the labor force reached 46 percent in 1994 and has remained at that level with a slight increase to 48 percent of the labor force anticipated by 2008.

A number of factors affect women's labor force participation. For example, there are ethnic and racial differences. Historically, Black women have participated in the labor force at a higher rate than White and Hispanic women, and that was still the case in 1999 (63.5 percent for Black women, 55.9 percent for White women, and 55.9 percent for Hispanic women). Education is also a factor. Women with more education are more likely to work than those with less education. The labor force participation of women is also affected by the ages of their children; the older the children, the more likely women are to work (i.e., 78.9 percent of women with children ages 14–17; 60.7 percent of those with children under the age of 3). Social class is another factor (Coltrane, 1998). Working-class women have always had to work outside the home to get by. Middle-class women's work was in the home rather than the marketplace but was believed to feed into the economy because they cared for their children and husbands (who were paid workers). Even though middle-class women are now participating in the workforce, the notion of women providing home care and men engaging in market work remains a part of our culture. This notion has been labeled "domesticity."

According to Joan Williams, law professor and the author of *Unbending Gender: Why Family and Work Conflict and What to Do About It*, "domesticity" is a gender system that separates market work and family, and it remains the entrenched, almost unquestioned, American norm and practice. Market work is organized around the notion of the ideal worker —one who is willing to work full-time and overtime and not let family interfere with the job. When work is structured this way, women do not fare well because they are typically the caregivers in their families. Over time, domesticity became the norm, and men were considered to naturally belong in the marketplace because they were aggressive and competitive and women, who focused on children and caregiving, were "naturals" for being in the home. John Gray's best-selling but highly criticized book, *Men Are from Mars, Women Are from Venus*, promotes domesticity by focusing on how men and women are "naturally" different.

Domesticity is harmful to women in that they are not viewed as "ideal workers." Therefore, they are not paid as well, and they are less likely to be given jobs of importance because they cannot work full-time and overtime, and they are unlikely to ignore their children and home life. This means that women who divorce (and nearly half of marriages end in divorce) are placed at a huge financial disadvantage in comparison to men. Even though a wife may have been supporting her husband's higher wages by doing the lion's share of the household labor, which enabled him to be an "ideal worker," her household work efforts are not considered worth anything when financial settlements are determined following divorce. Even after divorce, women continue to support their ex-husbands' ability to be "ideal workers" because they typically have physical custody and continue to provide most of the child care. This more than offsets any drain of child support from a man's income. Most states have a limit on how much child support the noncustodial parent (usually the man) is required to pay, but there is no limit on how much household labor the custodial parent must provide. This is not about male bashing, however. It is about how our society structures home and work.

Domesticity is harmful to men because "ideal workers" are exempt from child rearing and other household labor. This means men who are "ideal workers" often spend little time with their children. Just as women are marginalized in the marketplace, men are marginalized in the home. As a result, it may be difficult for men to form close relationships with their children, and if they divorce their children's mother, the relationships they have managed to forge with their children are sometimes seriously damaged or even dissolved.

Williams (2000) recommends that market work be restructured so that both par-

ents can be involved in their children's lives. She contends that we need to rethink *domesticity* and examine other ways to structure home and market work. For example, work/family policies vary by country and can include such things as parental leaves, provision for day care, family allowances, and tax structure. Sweden and Norway, for example, provide more policies that integrate work and family, and their cultures place great emphasis on egalitarianism. In the United States and Canada, the emphasis tends to be on individual freedom, and policies integrating work and family are nearly nonexistent. In addition, U.S. workers maintain the longest work week (in number of hours) and have the fewest days of vacation of any developed nation in the world. Rather than pitting men against women to argue over who is doing the dishes and laundry, perhaps we need to think at the societal level of how to fully and meaningfully include both men and women in work and family. Can we set aside our gendered notions of the home and workplace?

As you read the following three articles, think about the "flexibility" of the companies that Matt Peiffer and Rick Ollett work for. Is the flexibility adequate to maintain a work/family balance? Or is it just a small step in the right direction? How would you determine company policy regarding flexible hours to attend children's special events if you were interviewing? The third article, by Barbara Bergmann, questions the gendered nature of corporations' "family friendly" policies. Think about how the issues Bergmann presents might affect your career and family life. On which issues do you agree with Bergmann? On which do you disagree?

References

Coltrane, S. (1998). *Gender and families.* Thousand Oaks, CA: Pine Forge Press.

Williams, J. (2000). *Unbending gender: Why family and work conflict and what to do about it.* New York, NY: Oxford University Press. ✦

14a

Being There for the Children

Carol Lippert Gray

Matt Peiffer has a 7-year-old daughter, a working wife and a demanding calendar. But the vice president and CFO of the Dallas-based Forest Products International Exchange was inspired to schedule time at his daughter's school and sporting events after he heard the CEO and CFO at his former company "swapping stories about how many soccer games they missed," Peiffer says. "The conversation was memorable in that shortly after hearing this, the CEO, a father of three, was diagnosed with terminal cancer."

Like Matt Peiffer, 78 percent of married employees have spouses or partners who are also employed, up from 66 percent in 1977, according to a study by the non-profit Families and Work Institute in New York. And, like 46 percent of workers in the study, he has a child under 18 who lives with him. But he's lucky, because he works for a new company that's still setting its parameters.

"My employer allows me to take time off for my daughter's events: Soccer games, cafeteria duty once a month, and open houses," Peiffer notes.

> My company is a venture capital-backed firm currently with 40 people, and we're in the process of creating the company's culture. We work more than 60 hours a week, nights, etc., so taking hours out of the day for events isn't a problem. It also helps that our president has four children, and he does the same.

Peiffer says he and his wife trade coverage, so at least one parent is present at each activity. Technology facilitates this change in work style; with call forwarding, roaming cell phones and telecommuting, he's rarely out of touch.

Such flexibility is good for the Peiffers of the world and good for their companies, too, according to Ellen Galinsky, president of the Family and Work Institute and a co-author of the study. "Demanding and hectic jobs lead to negative spillover into workers' personal lives, jeopardizing their personal and family well-being," she says.

> And when workers feel burned out by their jobs, when they don't have the time and energy for their families, these feelings spill back into the workplace, reducing job performance.

> "But supportive workplaces offer some protection against this negative fallout from work," adds James T. Bond, Institute vice president and the study's principal author.

> And the more support employees receive on the job—the more flexible their work arrangements and supportive their supervisors—the higher their productivity, the more willing they are to go the extra mile and the more likely they are to stay with their current employers.

Still, the study shows 70 percent of all parents feel they don't spend enough time with their children, and both fathers and mothers say they have less time for personal activities. While it isn't easy to fit family obligations into business hours, when many of the milestones in a child's life occur, many financial executives are making the effort to watch their children don their cleats or toe shoes–or, simply be there as they eat their lunch.

Dr. Mindy Fried, project director of the National Work Life Measurement Project at The Center for Work and Family at Boston College and author of *Taking Time: Parental Leave Policy in Corporate Culture*, agrees that balancing personal and professional needs is critical to employee performance.

"People are more productive when there's more work/life balance, whether it's family or something else," she says.

> Their stress level is reduced. We're seeing that people for whom the company makes accommodations have a greater commitment level. By looking at the whole person, they'll see an employee who's grateful and willing to put out.

But, she cautions, that doesn't always happen.

> "The higher you get to the top, the more isolated you are. In any kind of chain situation, [family time] is viewed as your personal problem instead of a social issue,

she says. And she thinks there's a gender component as well. "Men at the top aren't scrutinized in the same way women are," she explains. "Women operate in a male-defined culture where it's more common to be on the job all the time. They need a structural support system to break away."

Whether a woman's breaking away is seen as a positive or negative, Fried adds, "depends on how she's viewed. It's a gender-loaded zone. Women are riding a fine line but can be committed to both."

Bob Petersen, managing director at Greater Community Financial in Clifton, NJ, thinks it all boils down to a question of priorities. "There are things more important than dollars and cents," he says.

> Work isn't everything and the workplace isn't everything. As long as what my staff is trying to get done gets done, I'm pretty flexible about time.

Petersen's sons are now 21 and 23. But, he says,

I used to coach baseball, which was fun. I'd leave early to do that. When they started to play organized sports at school, a lot of parents would show up. It's important for children to know that somebody really cares. It was a planned absence; I'd structure my time if I knew I had to be at an activity.

How important? While his boys never overtly expressed appreciation for the times Petersen was in the bleachers, he remembers, "The one or two times I didn't show up, they said, 'Where were you?' "

"Having your parents there shows that they care about you," agrees one 15-year-old. "And," this high school sophomore adds, "you want to show your parents how well you can do, and make them proud of you. It's definitely important."

When Rick Ollett, CFO of AFCO Credit Corp., the father of three boys and a girl, tried to attend soccer, wrestling, and track meets, "I'd check out around 1:30 or 2:00 to get there on time," he notes.

> I'd try to balance my time among each of them. It frequently became an issue of whose game did I go to last, not how well the team did last. I only get a chance to see them grow up once. There's a lot of my time and energy involved in what they do.

The bottom line is that employees today are trying to make it work, to restore the balance in their lives," Galinsky notes.

> Male and female roles are beginning to converge, and children are getting a little more time with their employed parents. But what workers need, and would really make it all come together for them and their employers, is improvements in the quality of jobs and more support in the workplace. ✦

Gray, C. L. (1999, July-August). "Being There." *Financial Executive, 15,* 47. Reprinted with permission from *Financial Executive,* July/August 1999. Copyright © 1999 by Financial Executives Institute, 10 Madison Avenue, PO Box 1938, Morristown, NJ 07962-1938.

14b

Friendly for Whose Family?

Betty Holcomb

One might assume that Lynnell Minkins, a single mother of three, would be thrilled to work for Marriott International. Last year, Marriott made *Working Mother* magazine's list of the best companies for working mothers, largely because it offers flexible work schedules, hot lines to help employees deal with child-care emergencies, and three on-site child-care centers. Minkins, a food server at the San Francisco Marriott, could use that sort of help. But it's not available to her. Instead, she never knows from week to week what her hours will be, making it hard to find and hold on to decent child care, let alone make plans. "How can I get doctor appointments if I don't know when I'll be working?" she asks. "A month ahead, the clinic says there are only these days. I take them, and then I have to work."

The irony is that, at least officially, Marriott offers flextime to its approximately 135,000 U.S. employees. Yet the one time Minkins tried it, her supervisors constantly pressed her to fix the "problem," and in her annual performance review that year she was described as being "challenged" by time management. "I should have called them on it, but I let it go," she says. "People who work in these jobs, they need the money. So you don't tell anybody what's going on." Senior managers, says Minkins, don't seem to suffer the same scrutiny.

> It doesn't look like their job is being challenged. The lower people, the people in the back of the house, they're having the problems.

So it goes for hundreds of thousands of lower-level workers at companies widely recognized for their "family-friendly" policies. In fact, research conducted by the Families and Work Institute shows that the workers who most need benefits such as child care and flexible hours are the least likely to get them.

Consider these facts from the study. Workers in low-wage jobs are:

- Half as likely as managers and professionals to have flextime.
- Less likely to have on-site child care.
- More likely to lose a day's pay when they must stay home to care for a sick child.
- Three times less likely to get company-sponsored tax breaks to help pay for child care.
- Less likely to be offered a paid maternity leave.

The types of benefits currently offered are also skewed toward higher-paid workers. Child-care help, for example, comes most often in the form of company-sponsored tax breaks or "resource and referral" hot lines. Both are useless to workers like Minkins, who don't make enough to pay much in taxes and can't afford the licensed child care the hot line refers them to.

The rare companies that offer on-site child care—about 5,000 of the nation's millions of employers—often do so only at headquarters, where managers and executives work, and the fees may still be too high for the clerical and office support staff. Just as much of a problem is that many benefits are offered only at the discretion of supervisors—who expect lower-level workers to stick to unbending schedules.

Even winning a temporary accommodation can be difficult. Consider the case of Tracey Kullman, an office technician for a large communications company in Albany, New York. Last summer, her disabled son was accepted for a 14-week program for special-needs kids. The only glitch: She'd have to pick him up at 4:30 every afternoon, which meant leaving work a half hour early. She figured she could work it out, given that her employer has a flextime policy and frequently wins awards for its family-friendly culture, and her job is a fairly independent one.

Yet when she approached her boss with several proposals, including taking a shorter lunch or coming in earlier, "I was told, 'Absolutely not. If we let you do this, everyone will want to do it,' " Kullman recalls. In the end, she was docked a half-hour's pay for every day her son was in the program.

Perhaps the biggest irony behind family-friendly benefits is that the workers most likely to get them don't need the help. Last year, the Hyatt Regency San Diego touted the success of a job-sharing initiative. Six women out of a workforce of 800 were sharing three jobs, and each of the women said they could afford to stop working if they had to.

Even more disturbing, the time bind is growing worse. Short-notice overtime, rotating shifts, and strict attendance policies are growing ever more common. Many workers like Lynnell Minkins and Tracey Kullman must choose between jeopardizing their paychecks or their children's safety—an unconscionable situation, especially at companies that wave the family-friendly banner.

It's not that corporate leaders haven't confronted the issue of equity. Most trumpet their efforts to make benefits universally available. In presentations, Marriott officials stress that family-friendly benefits are meant for everyone, from the most senior manager to the busboy in the company's restaurants. "We have a firm stake in the sand in seeing to it that our hourly employees are served well," says Donna Klein, vice president for diversity and workforce effectiveness, and chief architect of many of Marriott's family-friendly benefits. "We help with everything from finding child care, child-care subsidies, even immigration and housing issues."

The central question is whether management thinks of lower-wage workers as important to their companies, and therefore deserving of benefits. They'd broken ground by introducing flextime, part-time work with benefits, job-sharing, and on-site child care at their companies. And they were getting plenty of attention for their efforts. But now, they turned their attention to the workers who made their beds, served their food, and cleared their tables while they set workplace policies. "What about the chambermaids?" asked Arlene Johnson, a leading researcher on work-family conflict who was chairing the plenary session. "How are we meeting their needs?"

J. Thomas Bouchard, a senior vice president of IBM, who had championed the growing visibility of family-friendly benefits, now sounded a somber note. "I don't see how we can or will. Who's going to pay for it if we try to make these things universal?" In fact, he insisted, it was probably best to not even suggest that all workers might someday have access to child care and flexible schedules via their employers. "There's nothing worse than false hope," he insisted. Better to simply acknowledge that most companies don't want to add costly new benefits or change the way people work.

It can be a tough sell, especially since many top executives have never struggled with conflicts between showing up at work and taking care of their children. The benefits that companies offer tend toward low-cost or no-cost to them. Employers get their own tax write-off for providing child-care tax breaks. Flextime usually costs nothing, while it boosts productivity. Telecommuting can reduce the need for office space and improve productivity as well.

Many advocates of family-friendly benefits say we have to challenge the notion that work and family are separate spheres; the workplace has to bend to the demands of the home. But those are long-range goals. In the short term, advocates are trying to win over executives by making a business case for these benefits. They are trying to disprove the ideas that companies can't afford benefits for all. Studies have shown again and again that family-friendly policies help the bottom line.

In the end, the question is really one of power and privilege. Who has the power to change things, on what terms, and for whom? For the moment, the most progressive innovations arise out of the goodwill and good vision of a few corporate leaders. The truth is that professional, skilled workers are the ones corporations are trying to keep, and they do it with expensive benefits packages, among other things. Nonprofessional staff is more easily replaced, they believe, and thus not worth the financial investment. ✦

Holcomb, B. (2000, April/May). "Friendly for Whose Family?" *Ms.*, *10 (3)*, 40–45. Reprinted by permission of Ms. Magazine, copyright © 2000.

14c

Watch Out for 'Family Friendly' Policies

Barbara Bergmann

What could be better than employers adopting policies that give employees the resources, time, and flexibility to take care of their families? What could be wrong with that? What grinch could object? The best reply to these questions is another bunch of questions: Do family-friendly policies promote equality between men and women, or the reverse? Are some family-friendly policies "mommy tracks" that encourage, enable, pressure, and trap women (but not men) to adopt dead-end jobs and to sabotage their independence and their careers? Do family-friendly policies take the place of better solutions to the problems they are designed to help? Do such policies discriminate against employees who are not in a position to take advantage of them: Single parents, childless single people, childless gay people, cohabiting heterosexuals, people with low wages?

Back in the days when few wives held jobs outside the home, lots of time and labor were dedicated to home tasks. Children had the full-time attention of a nurturing adult who was presumed to love them particularly. There was time for mom to make apple pie from scratch. Unfortunately, that devotion of time and labor were the result of a caste system: A portion of the population was designated at birth as restricted to a particular occupation, namely housekeeping. Caste systems produce big status differences, and this one was no exception: Women had distinctly inferior sta-

tus. When a baby without a penis was born, they said, "It's a girl!", but they could just as well have said, right there in the delivery room, "It's a future housewife!" and "It's a person of very little brain, but real sweet!"

The movement of women, and particularly the mothers of young children, into paid work robbed the home of the worker who had been fully dedicated to tasks within it. Many, if not most, of these tasks are worthwhile, even necessary, despite the low status associated with doing them. Yet the march of women into the paid workforce was done without attention to how or whether the tasks they had previously done would be accomplished.

One reason for the pressure for family-friendly policies in companies—flexible time, job sharing, family leave to take care of a newborn or sick relative—has been the minimal change in the distribution of unpaid family work between spouses. More husbands benefit from the increased cash income from the paid work of wives, but they have not put out additional effort at home to any great extent. Wives also benefit from the increased income (and in some cases the increase in interesting activities and opportunities) but these benefits are partially counterbalanced by their greater workload.

One reason that husbands of employed women continue to withhold their labor from the tasks of running the household is the persistence of the ideology which declares certain tasks as appropriate for a person of a particular sex. Another is the low status associated with family work. Another is the still-discriminatory regime in the workplace, which deals men higher wages and better opportunities for promotion than women have, and makes the diversion of their energies and time to household tasks more costly. Another is wives' inability to enforce or motivate changes in their husbands' duties. Still another is the lack of public discussion about what the norm should be and our failure to visit shame on those violating it. (Oddly enough, the first and only group not predominantly female to make a public issue of men sharing housework is the Promise Keepers, who also make a public issue of men being the bosses of their families.)

The low amount of male help has greatly increased the strain on the wife, as the time she has devoted to the performance of work (paid and unpaid) has increased, and her opportunities for leisure and sleep-time have decreased. This increased burdening of the wife has been the major source of demands for workplace policies that accommodate family life.

Most family-friendly policies are on their face sex-neutral; men as well as women can take advantage of the leave provisions, or use flexibility arrangements. In theory, family-friendly policies might have the effect of getting men to do more domestic work. But this effect is probably very limited, because these policies do little or nothing to counter the influences on male behavior that make men withhold their labor from household tasks.

Thus the major effect of family-friendly policies has been to allow wives to partially resume those abandoned duties, or facilitate her doing them; in other words, they have strengthened the traditional caste system. Workplace policies which provide the opportunity for part-time work are likely to have this effect, particularly if the part-time status means low pay and benefits, routine duties, and little chance for promotion. Husbands are less likely to take this kind of work, and the wives who do are cementing the inequality of their status. It is cemented further by paid parental leaves that extend

well beyond the time necessary to overcome the disability caused to the mother by the child's birth, and which are designed to allow the parent to engage in child rearing.

But workplace policies can take several forms, some of which might promote greater equality. Reductions in work time, for example, can be given as reduced daily hours rather than as additional days of vacation. More days of vacation may be used by the husband to go off fishing with male companions, or the family may spend more time at a summer cottage, where the wife continues to do all the domestic tasks. But if both spouses work full-time, a shorter standard working day would probably encourage both partners to share more family duties.

Family-friendly policies also can promote paid substitutes for unpaid family labor. Workplace subsidies for child care, or setting up child care facilities at the workplace, probably would promote equality because they relieve the family of a function usually carried out by the wife. However, we have to ask whether it is wise to push employers to provide these services voluntarily rather than push for better public provision. The history of health insurance in the United States suggests that when employers provide expensive benefits, it is far from universal, is subject to withdrawal, and may discriminate among different kinds of workers. And the very existence of even inadequate employer-based health insurance has stood in the way of developing a system providing universal coverage. Out-of-home child care is a task of the same financial and managerial magnitude; employer provision may end up being counterproductive.

One final concern about "family-friendly" policies is their effect on the absolute and relative status of single people, with or without children, and those not in jobs, all of whom are more likely to be women than men. Shortening the work day, with a proportional drop in pay, may make life more difficult for lower-income female single parents.

In general, "family-friendly" policies, like "family values," can push us back. We cannot assume them to be benign. Policies that help one group may hurt others. Policies that appear to make life easier for women, and that may even be welcomed by a majority of women, may cement women's inequality. The equity of such policies deserves close scrutiny. ✦

Bergmann, B. (1998, January-February). "Watch Out for Family Friendly Policies." *Dollars and Sense*, 215, 10. Reprinted by permission of *Dollars & Sense*, a progressive economics magazine <www.dollarsandsense .org>.

Issue 14: Questions to Consider

1. How did your parents split work and home responsibilities? Did their method seem to work well for your family? What did you like or not like about it?

2. Do you think the men in the articles that you read are unusual or fairly common? Was your father able to come to your school and extracurricular events? Why or why not?

3. When corporations provide on-site facilities such as dry cleaning or even day care, they are accused of providing these services only so that employees have no excuse for leaving work. If day care is provided, the employees can work overtime because no one is really needed to pick up the children. Do you think there is validity to this criticism? Or do you think that corporations are really interested in families? What is your evidence of their interest or lack of interest?

4. Is there really a work/family conflict? Or is it that the marketplace is unfair to women, especially mothers? What choices should men and women have regarding work?

5. What is the relation between family policy and work/family conflict in countries such as Sweden that have established far more family policies than is true in the United States? How do those policies seem to work?

6. Why are benefits for lower-wage workers so much worse than for white-collar workers? Some have said that lower-wage workers are easily replaceable and it would cost too much to provide family-friendly benefits. Develop arguments both for and against that statement. ◆

Issue 15: Introduction

Does Day Care Make Children Mean? The New Debate Over Working Mothers

Most mothers of young children are employed. According to the U.S. Department of Labor Women's Bureau (2001), six out of every 10 mothers of children under age 3 were either in the labor force or were looking for work. That figure increased to seven of 10 mothers of children ages 3 to 5. For more than half of those children, their primary childcare provider is not a relative—32 percent are in center-based childcare programs, 16 percent are in family day care, and a babysitter or nanny in the child's home cares for 6 percent. A relative such as a grandmother cares for another 23 percent, and 24 percent are in parent care (e.g., parents work different shifts so one can always be with the children).

Despite the increasing number of hours mothers work outside of the home, in the past two decades employed mothers have spent about the same amount of time with their children as they always have, according to a 1997 Families and Work Institute National Study of the Changing Workforce. Perhaps even more surprising, mothers who do not work outside the home spend only seven more hours per week with their school-age children than do working mothers. Of course, mothers who are not employed outside the home spend far more time with their preschool children than do working mothers.

One fact about working mothers that comes through loud and clear is that there are a lot of them, and the numbers continue to increase. The increase is greatest for mothers with preschool children.

The effects of "working" mothers (those employed outside the home) on their children have been a topic of much debate and considerable research for over 40 years. As more and more mothers joined the workforce, the debate has shifted subtly from the effects of maternal employment on child outcomes to the effects of child care arrangements on child outcomes. Fathers have even received some attention as caregivers (see Issue 16), but clearly the main focus has been on mothers' responsibility for the care of children. Consequently, every new large-scale study of the effects of child care gets huge media attention, either raising or lowering mothers' guilt about working outside the home. As Laura Scott, assistant editor of the *Kansas City Star*, wrote,

> Mothers often are motivated by guilt. It just seems to come with the territory of raising children. . . guilt in mothers shows up most acutely when it comes to subtle and not-so-subtle references to the job they are doing with their children. (May 3, 2001)

A recent guilt-increasing press conference was held in the spring of 2001 at the biannual conference of the Society for Research in Child Development. At that press conference, the results of a national Early Child Care Study sponsored by the National Institute of Child Health and Human Development (NICHD) were announced. Quoted heavily was Jay Belsky, one of the researchers, who concluded that, "The moral of the story is maybe we should stay home more with our children" (Goodman, May 3, 2001). The NICHD study, a longitudinal project that entailed following 1,300 children at 10 locations since 1991, was started in response to an earlier study by Belsky (1988) in which he reported that infants whose mothers worked more than 20 hours per week in their child's first year of life were less likely to be securely attached to their mothers. Because research has indicated that insecure attachment is related to developmental problems in older children, concerns were voiced about these findings, and the NICHD study was launched.

Most of the headlines following the press conference focused on Belsky's negative conclusion, although other members of the research team conveyed opposing views. Perhaps Belsky's message resonated more with recent efforts by politically conservative groups opposed to day care and working mothers. Working and middle-class mothers are sometimes called selfish and uncaring if they work outside the home, and they are warned that leaving their children in the care of others might be harmful to them. At the same time, welfare reform policies have encouraged low-income mothers to go to work and get off welfare. Less concern has been shown about how poor children left in the care of others might be affected. Our society's split views on working mothers have been evident for years—during World War II, when women were needed to work, there were no guilt trips placed on them. They were seen as courageous and patriotic. Our views about working mothers and child care appear to be at least partially motivated by politics. Keep this in mind as you read the following two articles. The controversial findings of the NICHD study are reported in the two articles that follow this introduction, but the findings are presented from two quite different worldviews. As you read the articles, try to determine the values that underlie the stand taken by Charen as compared to values underlying Shonkoff and Phillips' comments.

References

Belsky, J. (1988). The 'effects' of early day care reconsidered. *Early Childhood Research Quarterly*, 3, 235–272.

Goodman, E. (May 3, 2001). With mothering comes guilt. *Kansas City Star*, B7. ✦

15a

Denying Reality Can't Change Day Care Facts

Mona Charen

There are times when you sense we are in the realm of "Mustn't Be True." On the day that the National Institutes of Health released its report showing that day care seems to have undesirable effects on the behavior of a significant percentage of kindergartners, scores of commentators, mostly women, were ready with what amounted to a "don't confuse me with the facts; my mind is made up" response.

"Aggressive according to whom?" demanded one female commentator who must not have read the study, which explained that aggressive means "gets into a lot of fights," "cruelty" and "explosive behavior." Marion Wright Edelman, tireless advocate of government solutions to problems, offered, "The last thing we need to do is to be scaring parents or alarming parents who have to work in order to put food on the table."

But this isn't just about poor parents. Certainly the parents whose children are being cared for by nannies, who were observed as part of this study, are not one step away from the poor house. The "Mustn't Be True" chorus next discounted the numbers. Seventeen percent of children who had spent time in day care showed aggressive and difficult behaviors in kindergarten, as compared to 6 percent who were raised by their mothers. "That means 83 percent were just fine," crowed another analyst. Besides, she added, "We really have to decide

whether we expect to raise our children the way our mothers raised us." And then, answering her own question, she said, "It's not happening anymore."

Several commentators whined that the study seemed aimed at provoking guilt only among mothers, not fathers. The study is just a study and not "aimed" at anyone. Others trotted out the hoary old rationalization that day care improves children's social skills. But the research seems to support the opposite conclusion. Some mentioned that moms do a better job with children when they are fulfilled in other ways—a dubious assertion. And still others took the occasion to demand better quality care subsidized by the taxpayers.

The study looked at all kinds of day care—large institutional settings, nursery schools, relative care, nannies, even dads—and found all were inferior to mother care. Children who spent significant amounts of time in care with people other than their own mothers were three times as likely as home-reared youngsters to be aggressive, defiant, impatient, and attention-demanding. These findings held true for girls as well as boys and for rich as well as poor, and almost without regard to the "quality" of alternative care they received.

Well, the critics say, we cannot know that day care is the culprit here. It could be a million other things. Possibly, but as Jay Belsky, one of the lead investigators and a former proponent of day care explained, "There is a constant dose-response relationship between time in care and problem behavior, especially those involving aggression and behavior." In other words, the more time away from mom in the early years, the more problems. The effects really begin to kick in when a child spends more than 30 hours a week in alternative care; the national average is 26 hours per week.

Critics are correct that social science can be tricky. It could be, as the *New York Times* speculated, that mothers who place their children in child care are more stressed than mothers who don't, and the stress rather than day care itself is the problem. Maybe, though with 65 percent of married mothers with children under age 6 in the workforce, and a presumably larger per-centage of unmarried ones, it seems doubtful that all are emotionally fragile.

It's also possible that in this era of working women, the ones who buck the trend are those most committed to doing right by their kids. If this is true, some of the moms who are placing their children in day care might wind up being worse for their children than day-care providers. And yet, the obvious conclusion of the study does seem the most plausible—young children do best with their moms. And if that's true, our best course is to figure out how to help more mothers do this job, rather than rail at reality. ✦

Charen, M. (2001, May). "Denying Reality Can't Change Day Care Facts." *Saint Louis Post-Dispatch*. Reprinted by permission of Creators Syndicate.

15b

Want Better Child Care? Hire Better Caregivers

Jack Shonkoff and Deborah Phillips

Here we go again. A new study reports that children who receive at least 30 hours a week of nonmaternal child care exhibit higher levels of aggressive and demanding behavior than those who spend 10 hours or less a week in comparable settings. Another study finds that child-care centers are losing well-educated staff at alarming rates. Academics and advocates argue about these data. And parents who entrust the care of their young children to others head off to work and agonize over the significance of these troubling findings.

What's a mother or father to do? How should a thoughtful policymaker respond? Whom can we trust to help us differentiate science from politics? Science is the result of the cumulative findings of multiple researchers. As each new study either confirms or challenges what we know, additional hypotheses or questions are generated that guide further research, and the process of learning continues. A recent 500-page report by the National Research Council and Institute of Medicine provides a comprehensive synthesis of hundreds of studies on early childhood development conducted over the past four decades.

The blue-ribbon committee that authored the report concluded that human behavior is influenced by many factors and complex interactions between both nature and nurture, and that early relationships are the active ingredients of the environment's impact on young children. Extensive research focused on early child care and education confirms the futility of searching for simple conclusions regarding their effects on young children. Most important, however, is the consistent finding that parents remain the most important influences on their children's development, despite the substantial time that many youngsters spend in nonparental child-care settings.

Furthermore, higher-quality programs are associated with greater gains in cognitive and language skills, especially for children whose circumstances place them at risk for failure. Reports of more aggressive behavior associated with greater hours of nonmaternal care demand the same thoughtful consideration as any other research findings. Thus, it is important to examine the data—not the rhetoric. For example, 83 percent of the children who received 30 or more hours of child care did not demonstrate elevated levels of aggressive behaviors. Moreover, the reported higher levels fall at the upper end of the normal range for young children and, therefore, do not constitute a behavior disorder.

Are these findings ominous? No. Should we view them as a wake-up call? If we are worried about the social and emotional risks of child care, we should be more concerned about the training and skills of the personnel in those settings. Science tells us that young children need nurturing relationships that are stable and predictable.

Pay benefits, and working conditions of child-care providers must be improved.

If we are troubled by aggressive behaviors at the upper end of the normal range, we should be providing more help for parents and providers of early care and education to deal with these behaviors before children enter school. If we are frightened about the early roots of anti-social behavior, we should use the extensive clinical knowledge available to treat young children with serious emotional disorders, who are often expelled from child-care programs and whose needs go unmet because there is no mental health system for them.

Kindergarten teachers tell us they have a harder time with children not ready emotionally or socially than with youngsters who don't know their letters or numbers. Yet new policies for children who are at risk are urging greater emphasis on teaching them to read and less on helping them cope with their feelings. The well-being of young children whose parents work is an important public concern that demands thoughtful attention and effective action. Are we using available science to inform enlightened policies or are we missing the point? ✦

Shonkoff, J., and Phillips, D. (2001, May 3). "If Our Kids Are More Aggressive, What Would Help? Better Caregivers." *St. Louis Post-Dispatch*. Reprinted by permission of Jack Shonkoff and National Academies Op-ed Service.

Issue 15: Questions to Consider

1. Shonkoff and Phillips raised an interesting question to consider, "How do you differentiate science from politics?" How would you respond to that question?

2. What more would you need to know about the NICHD study after reading these two brief articles to decide which side is right?

3. One of the concerns raised by conservatives reacting to the NICHD study is that 17 percent of the children in child care—day care, nannies, and other nonmaternal care—behaved aggressively (e.g., pushed, teased, fought, demanded attention, spoke out of turn) and only 6 percent of children in maternal care behaved this way. Why might this be true? Some have suggested that children are more likely to behave aggressively in the presence of other children

than in the presence of their mothers. What do you think about this?

4. The NICHD study indicated that the quality of childcare was critical to children's well-being. Why do we not have more high-quality child care in the United States? What political factors do you think might be at work? What parental factors might be at work? What other factors might be affecting the quantity of high quality care?

5. Why do you think that public funding for the education of children is not available until children are of kindergarten age (about 5 years old)? Why was this age chosen—because of research on children's learning and development, because of politics, or was it arbitrarily decided? Why do you think we do not provide public funding to educate all children younger than kindergarten age? ✦

Issue 16: Introduction

Do Fathers Matter?

Many children do not live with their fathers. Some children live with men who are not their fathers (e.g., grandfather, uncle, stepfather), and some reside in households headed by adult women (e.g., mothers, grandmothers). Countless other children spend part of the time with their mothers and part of the time with their fathers.

In recent years the media have paid a lot of attention to the role of fathers. Unfortunately, the messages conveyed are quite mixed. Fathers are more active in raising their children than they were a generation or two ago, but mothers still do most of the child care in families, even when both parents are employed outside the home. The latest census showed an increase in single fathers, yet more children are raised by grandparents than by lone fathers.

Parke and Brott argue that fathers contribute in important ways to children's development. They see fathers as mattering to children, and they cite studies to support their point of view. In contrast, Silverstein and Auerbach "deconstruct" the "essential" father in a review of research in which they frankly stated their intention of debunking the notion that fathers are essential for children to develop into satisfied, productive, and healthy adults. Silverstein and Auerbach clearly recognize the politics of interpreting social science data. Ironically, their review was criticized for being more political than scientific.

This article became the target of Dr. Laura Schlesinger, the radio personality who was so offended by their message that she protested its appearance in the respected APA journal *American Psychologist*. Her reaction was so loud and insistent that politicians in Washington and social pundits from many media sources decried what they described as the value-laden and political agenda of Silverstein and Auerbach. The authors stood firm, however, stating that they were presenting findings from studies that were ignored by those advocating the ideology that fathers were necessary.

Several other issues in this book show similar examples of political and personal values affecting how research data are interpreted (see Issues 11, 15, 20, 22). As you read these reviews of research on fathers, be aware of your values as well as the values of the authors. ✦

16a

Yes, Fathers Really Matter!

Ross Parke and Armin Brott

Every generation has its scapegoat for contemporary social ills: Communism, rock and roll, drugs, feminism, television. Now it seems to be the absence of fathers in the family. It's hard to pick up a newspaper or magazine without encountering a story about the deterioration of the American family and how the absence of a father is at least partly responsible. At the same time, new conceptions of what fatherhood is and creative visions of what it could be are gradually emerging.

This focus on fatherhood has given rise to a heated debate about how much fathers actually matter. "Fatherlessness is the most harmful demographic trend of this generation," writes David Blankenhorn.

> It is the leading cause of declining child well-being in this society. It is also the engine driving our most urgent social problems, from crime to adolescent pregnancy to child sexual abuse to domestic violence against women.

Others—especially men in the Fathers' Rights Movement—believe that fathers are so important that their mere presence in a family (or granting them custody of children after divorce) will do everything from decreasing alcohol and drug abuse and reducing welfare payments to single mothers to improving children's grades. Their implication? Dropping an involved father into every household would solve our most urgent social problems.

In the other corner are those who have tried to prove that fathers are not impor-tant. Children raised without dads are doing just fine, they say, and any problems kids suffer are the result of economic factors rather than the physical or psychological absence of a father.

Although diametrically opposed, the fathers-aren't-necessary and the father-as-panacea camps share one feature, views that are based more on politics than on research. As a result, both views are too simplistic to shed any light on the issue of the importance of fathers in their children's lives. While politicians change their views to suit the prevailing climate, academic researchers over the past two decades have been nearly unanimous in their findings: Fathers matter a lot.

We all know that babies are better off when they have two parents to love them, cuddle them, and contribute to their college fund. And even though mothers are the ones who breast-feed and undoubtedly change more than their fair share of a newborn's diapers, fathers play a unique and important role. Children benefit developmentally from the special ways their fathers interact with them.

So what exactly do fathers do? To start with, they tend to allow their infants more freedom to explore, while mothers are usually more cautious. Fathers encourage their children's independence by promoting exploration. They even speak to their children differently than mothers do. Overall, fathers seem more interested in doing practical, educational things rather than talking about them.

The area in which fathers' parenting style is most obvious and most important is play. Anyone who has ever watched new parents in action can attest that women tend to play more visual games with their babies and are often more verbal with them. Men, on the other hand, are far more physical, right from the time their kids are infants. Pediatricians Michael Yogman and T. Berry Brazelton found clear differences in the ways adults—mothers, fathers, and strangers—played with a group of 2-week-old to 24-week-old infants. Mothers spoke softly, repeating words and phrases frequently and imitating the infants' sounds more than either the fathers or the strangers. Fathers were less verbal but more tactile than mothers. They touched their infants with a rhythmic tapping more often than the mothers or the strangers. Father-infant play shifted rapidly from peaks of high infant attention and excitement to valleys of minimal attention; mother-infant play demonstrated more gradual shifts. As Brazelton observed:

> Most fathers seem to present a more playful, jazzing-up approach . . . it seems that a father is expecting more heightened, playful response from the baby. And he gets it! Amazingly enough, an infant by two or three weeks displays an entirely different attitude toward his father than to his mother.

Differences between fathers' and mothers' play styles are not lost on children, who generally respond more positively to play with their fathers than with their mothers. In fact, when given a choice of play partners, more than two-thirds of 2 1/2-year-olds choose their fathers over their mothers. This preference for the paternal play style is so strong that most children choose it—no matter whom they're playing with. Researchers observed a group of boys as they played with each parent in two different playrooms, one containing books and puzzles conducive to maternal play, the other containing large, soft balls and pillows conducive to paternal play. Boys reacted more positively to both their parents when their play style was more physical and active, resembling the typical paternal style.

Playing with dad is almost always fun for a child, but there are other benefits as well. Children who get along best with other children often have fathers who spend a lot of time playing physically with them. In addition, 3-year-olds who had good relationships with their fathers have better, longer-lasting friendships at age 5.

How is this possible? What could children learn from playing that would influence their friendships? On the most basic level, "while they're roughhousing with their fathers, infants are already learning some valuable lessons in self-control," says John Snarey, a professor of human development at Emory University. Fathers also help children learn how to express and manage their emotions, recognize others' emotional cues, and understand that biting, kicking, and other forms of physical violence are not acceptable.

Fathers influence their children's emotional lives in other ways. "The kids who did best in terms of peer relationships. . .were those whose dads validated their feelings and praised their accomplishments," writes John Gottman in *The Heart of Parenting*.

> These fathers were Emotion Coaches, who neither dismissed nor disapproved of their kids' negative emotions, but showed empathy and provided guidance to help their kids deal with negative feelings.

Gottman found that fathers' acceptance of and assistance with their children's sadness and anger at 5 years of age were related to children's social competence among their peers 3 years later. Kids with supporting and emotionally accepting fathers were less aggressive, had better relationships with friends, and had less trouble in school. Interestingly, the mothers' management of emotions was a less strong predictor of the children's later social success. Fathers, it seems, make an important but often unrecognized contribution to the development of their children's "emotional intelligence"—and it's a contribution that lasts a lifetime.

In the 1950s Robert Sears and colleagues examined the child-rearing practices of more than 300 parents when their children were 5 years old. Twenty-six years later, another group of researchers contacted some of the children from the original study to assess their level of empathy and compare it to Sears' original findings. The most powerful predictor of empathy in adulthood was paternal childrearing involvement at age 5. This proved to be a better predictor than several maternal predictors and was evident for boys and girls. In another follow-up, when the original children were 41, those who had better social relationships (a happy marriage; engaging in recreational activities) were the ones who had experienced more paternal warmth [as] children.

These studies should make us seriously rethink our views about the ways mothers and fathers influence their children. It has long been accepted that mothers are the emotional brokers in the family, while fathers play a mostly instrumental role. Clearly, though, fathers have a much larger and more complex impact on their children's emotional lives than anyone had previously thought. Besides being "emotionally intelligent," children of involved fathers tend to be smarter as well. "The evidence is quite robust that kids who have contact with a father have an advantage over kids without that kind of contact," says Norma Radin, a professor emeritus at the University of Michigan. These advantages are evident early in life. Radin found that children who were raised by involved fathers scored higher on verbal ability tests than children whose fathers were less involved. In another study, toddlers whose fathers took interest in childcare were consistently rated 2 to 6 months ahead of expected on development, problem-solving skills, and social skills. Radin believes that "there's a strong connection between kids' math skills and the amount of contact they have with their fathers."

Radin is far from alone in her findings. Kevin Nugent of Harvard University found that a father's level of caregiving during the first year of life was related to his baby's score on an infant IQ test given at 12 months. The more caregiving fathers did, the more advanced their babies' cognitive skills.

Interestingly, fathers' skills as playmates are excellent predictors of their children's intellectual development. Fathers who were good at ball toss and bouncing, for example, had more intellectually advanced children than those who couldn't keep their children interested in their games. Fathers also apparently contribute to their children's intellectual capacity by encouraging them to be independent. In one study, the earlier (within reason) the father expected his child to be able to handle a pair of scissors or take a bath alone, the more advanced the child's intellectual development.

Another way of assessing fathers' impact on their children is to examine what happens to kids who grow up in families without a father. The evidence is striking and clear: Children growing up in homes without a father tend to have poorer intellectual development. The risk of dropping out of high school is twice as high in father-absent families than in two-parent families. Adolescents from single-parent families had lower test scores, grade point averages, school attendance, than those from two-parent families. Young adults from single-parent families were less likely to enroll in college and less likely to graduate. In their twenties young men from these homes were more likely to be out of school and out of work than men from two-parent homes. Women in their twenties, especially those with children, show similar trends.

Even in intact families, fathers can be "absent." A classic study from the late 1960s demonstrated that fathers' availability, as well as their absence, affects their children's academic performance. Compared [were] four groups of third-grade boys, all of whom had average IQs, all were from working-class or middle-class backgrounds, and all had the same number and gender of siblings. Only their paternal situation was different. Simply put, the underachievers (kids who were working below their grade level) came from homes where the father had left before the child was 5. The superior academic performers were the boys whose fathers were present and available to them.

The boys who had lost their fathers after age 5 and those whose fathers were living at home but generally unavailable were functioning somewhat below grade level.

Highly available fathers can be models of perseverance and achievement motivation. The father can be an example of a male successfully functioning outside of the home atmosphere. Frequent opportunity to observe and imitate an adequate father contributes to the development of the boys' overall instrumental and problem-solving ability. Having a competent father will not facilitate a boy's intellectual development if the father is not consistently accessible to the boy or if the father-son relationship is negative in quality.

As all this research suggests, the quality of a father's involvement is crucial. Simply being there is not enough; being available and involved is what really counts. Too many fathers who are still in two-parent families are unavailable to their children because of their work schedule, travel, or lack of interest. Furthermore, kids whose fathers are cold and authoritarian, derogatory, and intrusive have the hardest time with grades and social relationships. They are, says Gottman, even worse off than kids who live in homes with no father at all. Kids with nonsupportive dads and dads who humiliate them were the ones most likely to be headed for trouble, he says. They were the ones who displayed aggressive behavior toward their friends, they had the most trouble in school, and they were the ones with problems often linked to delinquency and violence.

Interestingly, fathers don't treat—and thus don't affect—their sons and their daughters in the same way. Mothers also treat their boys and girls differently, but the difference is not so marked. Fathers tend to play and interact more physically with their boy infants than with their girls. Later on, fathers give their boys more encouragement to explore and be independent. Boys are allowed to cross the street alone at an earlier age, to stay away from home more, and to explore a wider area of their neighborhood than are girls. There's some speculation that these distinctions may make a difference. Lois Hoffman of the University of Michigan suggests that

> boys' greater experience in these independent explorations, which girls lack, very likely has considerable importance in the development of independent coping styles, a sense of competence, and even some specific skills.

These skills include such traits as curiosity, assertiveness, and a sense of adventure.

It's important to remember that despite differences in the way fathers treat sons and daughters, girls still have a lot to gain emotionally, socially, intellectually, and psychologically from greater contact with their fathers. Girls whose fathers play with them a lot tend to be more popular with their peers and more assertive in their interpersonal relationships throughout their lives. Other research has found that extremely competent and successful women frequently recall their fathers as active and encouraging, playful and exciting.

It's not completely clear why fathers treat boys and girls differently. Perhaps fathers are reacting to biological differences in the rates at which boys and girls develop. Girls generally acquire language earlier than boys, while boys are more physically active. Or fathers may treat boys and girls differently because of gender stereotypes concerning the appropriate ways to interact with sons and daughters (girls are more fragile, goes the logic, therefore they shouldn't be played with too much).

Biology may also have a role. Male monkeys, for example, show the same preferences for male infants and tend to respond more positively to bids for rough-and-tumble play in the same way that human fathers do. There's little doubt that cultural, ethnic, and environmental factors play a role too. Boys and girls in African-American families are treated more similarly by their fathers than boys and girls in white families.

Children aren't the only ones who benefit from spending more time with their fathers. Wives of active, involved fathers seem to gain as well. The more support mothers get from their husbands (including taking care of the children), the happier they are in their marriages and the better they perform their own parenting duties. This may be due in part to the fact that women who have involved partners are more likely to work outside the home. And women who are employed are generally more satisfied and less depressed than stay-at-home mothers—especially those who want to work. This, in turn, benefits fathers. Men whose wives are happy in their marriages tend to be happier themselves. And men who are happy in their marriages are generally more involved in their fathering role.

Conventional wisdom has it that a man's health is affected more by his work than by his family relationships. But according to Rosalind Barnett and Caryl Rivers, the opposite is true.

> Being a father who is deeply involved with his children is good for a man's health. The men who had the fewest worries about their relationships with their children also had the fewest health problems. Those who had the most troubled relationships with their children had the most health problems.

The benefits of involved fathering on fathers themselves last a lifetime. A father's involvement in child rearing during the first two decades of the child's life seemed to predict his occupational mobility at age 47 far more than any other factor, including his parents' occupations, his IQ, and whether or not his wife works outside the home. Involved fathers tend to have happier marriages and more successful careers.

Fatherhood also seems to promote men's abilities to understand themselves as adults and to care sympathetically for other adults. Men who take an active role at home are, by the time their children are grown, better managers, community leaders, and mentors. They're more concerned with the next generation than with themselves.

Although no one completely understands the processes involved, active fathering clearly benefits children, mothers, and fathers themselves. Encouraging fathers to be involved—and supporting them in their efforts to do so—is an investment that could yield important social dividends for all. Sadly, society has both wittingly and unwittingly erected a series of barriers that reduce men's involvement with their children and families. As a result, women, children, and men have suffered greatly. Until we stop supporting these barriers, we are unlikely ever to experience fully the positive benefits of involved fathering. ✦

16b

Are Fathers Essential? Maybe Not

Louise B. Silverstein and Carl F. Auerbach

In the past two decades, there has been an explosion of research on fathers. Overall, this explosion of research on fathering has increased the complexity of scholarly thinking about parenting and child development. However, one group of social scientists (e.g., Biller and Kimpton, 1997; Popenoe, 1996) has emerged that is offering a more simplistic view of the role of fathers in families. These neo-conservative social scientists have replaced the earlier "essentializing" of mothers with a claim about the essential importance of fathers. These authors have proposed that the roots of a wide range of social problems (i.e., child poverty, urban decay, societal violence. teenage pregnancy, and poor school performance) can be traced to the absence of fathers in the lives of their children. Biller and Kimpton (1997, p. 147) have even used the term "paternal deprivation" in a manner parallel to Bowlby's (1951) concept of maternal deprivation. In our view, the essentialist framework represents a dramatic oversimplification of the complex relations between father presence and social problems.

We characterize this perspective as essentialist because it assumes that the biologically different reproductive functions of men and women automatically construct essential differences in parenting behaviors. The essentialist perspective defines mothering and fathering as distinct social roles that are not interchangeable. Fathers are understood as having a unique and essential role to play in child development, especially for boys who need a male role model to establish a masculine gender identity.

In contrast to the neo-conservative perspective, our data on gay fathering couples have convinced us that neither a mother nor a father is essential. Similarly, our research with divorced, never-married, and remarried fathers has taught us that a wide variety of family structures can support positive child outcomes. We have concluded that children need at least one responsible, caretaking adult who has a positive emotional connection to them and with whom they have a consistent relationship. Because of the emotional and practical stress involved in child rearing, a family structure that includes more than one such adult is more likely to contribute to positive child outcomes. Neither the sex of the adult(s) nor the biological relationship to the child has emerged as a significant variable in predicting positive development. One, none, or both of those adults could be a father (or mother). We have found that the stability of the emotional connection and the predictability of the caretaking relationship are the significant variables that predict positive child adjustment.

We agree with the neo-conservative perspective that it is preferable for responsible fathers (and mothers) to be actively involved with their children. We share the concern that many men in U.S. society do not have a feeling of emotional connection or a sense of responsibility toward their children. However, we do not believe that the data support the conclusion that fathers are essential to child well-being and that heterosexual marriage is the social context in which responsible fathering is most likely to occur.

One of the cornerstones of the essentialist position is that biological differences in reproduction construct gender differences in parenting behaviors. This theoretical framework proposes that the biological experiences of pregnancy and lactation generate a strong instinctual drive in women to nurture. This perspective assumes that men do not have an instinctual drive to nurture infants and children.

The neo-conservative perspective relies heavily on evolutionary psychology to support this argument. Trivers' (1972) hypothesis states that all other things being equal, male mammals will maximize their evolutionary fitness by impregnating as many females as possible, while investing very little in the rearing of any individual offspring. Female mammals, in contrast, invest a great deal of energy in parenting.

Another cornerstone of the essentialist position is that the traditional division of labor characteristic of Western, industrialized societies has been true throughout human evolutionary history. [However], Zihlman (1997) has pointed out that for most of our evolutionary history, human societies were nomadic. This bioecological context required both men and women to travel long distances, hunt, gather food, and care for older children and other members of their community. Thus, the assertion that a rigid sexual division of labor existed over most of our evolutionary history is not supported either by what is known about human society in prehistory or by contemporary pre-agricultural cultures.

The neo-conservative perspective has also claimed that mothers are more "natural" caregivers than fathers. Yet, more than a decade ago, Lamb (1987) reported that research on mothers and fathers during the newborn period yielded no differences in parenting behaviors. Neither mothers nor fathers were natural parents. Because mothers tended to spend so much more time with their infants, they became much more familiar with their biological rhythms, visual and behavioral cues, and so forth. Many

subsequent studies have shown that when fathers assume the primary caretaking role, they are as competent and as sensitive as mothers (Lamb, 1987).

In summary, the neo-conservative position is simply wrong about the biological basis of observed differences in parenting behaviors. Cross-species and cross-cultural data indicate that fathering can vary from a high level of involvement to a total lack of involvement. Given these wide variations in paternal behaviors, it is more accurate to conclude that both men and women have the same biological potential for nurturing.

The neo-conservative perspective has argued that without a biological basis for nurturing in men, the best way to ensure that men will behave responsibly toward their offspring is to provide a social structure in which men can be assured of paternity (i.e., the traditional nuclear family). However, Smuts and Gubernick (1992) found that the amount of time and energy males invest in nurturing and protecting infants varies, depending on the mutual benefits that males and females have to offer each other within a particular bioecological context. Smuts and Gubernick (1992) have made a strong case for the power of the *reciprocity hypothesis* to predict male involvement among nonhuman primates. We argue that the reciprocity hypothesis does predict male involvement among human primates.

In cultures where women have significant resources to offer men in exchange for child care, paternal involvement should be higher than in cultures where women have fewer resources. In line with this prediction, paternal involvement in the United States, Sweden, and Australia is higher than in more traditional cultures, such as Italy and Spain, where women's workforce participation is less widespread (Blossfeld, 1995). Similarly, Haas (1993) reported that a survey of more than 300 Swedish families indicated that fathers participated more in child care if their partners made as much or more money than they did.

The least amount of father involvement in U.S. society has been observed in two groups of fathers: Poor, unmarried teenage fathers and upper-class fathers in traditional nuclear families. Teen dads in U.S. society are often undereducated and under-employed. Therefore, they cannot make a meaningful contribution to the economic security of their children. Poor teen fathers do not have meaningful benefits to offer their child's mother. As the reciprocity hypothesis would predict, these fathers are often minimally involved in the lives of their children.

In upper-class families, in contrast, it is most often the wives who have few benefits to exchange. The family's high income is the result of the husband's earning capacity. The wife's additional economic contribution is rarely meaningful to the family's economic security. Most of the wives do not participate in paid employment. Thus, the upper-class wives have few benefits to offer in exchange for direct paternal involvement. Within this context, the fathers in these families use their income to pay for other-than-mother child care but do little active caregiving themselves.

Working-class, dual-shift families are the context in which mothers and fathers are most evenly matched in terms of the resources they have to exchange. Both parents' incomes are significant to family stability. Because they work opposite shifts, involvement in child care by the at-home parent is necessary for child well-being. From the perspective of the reciprocity hypothesis, the parity of resources between husband and wife within this family structure generated the high level of paternal involvement.

In summary, these data on human parenting behaviors conform to the predictions of the reciprocity hypothesis. In social contexts where either the fathers or the mothers have few benefits to exchange, paternal involvement is low. When both fathers and mothers have benefits that contribute to family well-being, paternal involvement is relatively high. Thus, improving employment opportunities for women, as well as men, is crucial to increasing father involvement. These findings suggest that in our current cultural context, it is economics, not marriage, that matters.

The neo-conservative perspective has proposed that if men can be induced to take care of young children, their unique, masculine contribution significantly improves the developmental outcomes for children. From the essentialist perspective,

> fatherhood privileges children. Conversely, the primary consequences of fatherlessness are rising male violence and declining child well-being, and the underlying source of our most important social problems. (Blankenhorn, 1995, pp. 25–26)

These claims represent an oversimplification of the data. Father absence covaries with other relevant family characteristics (i.e., the lack of an income from a male adult, the absence of a second adult, and the lack of support from a second extended family system). McLoyd (1998) has pointed out that because single-mother families are over-represented among poor families, it is difficult to differentiate the effects of father absence from the effects of low income.

Another major limitation to this paradigm is that father absence is not a monolithic variable. Qualitative research has shown that relationships between absent fathers and their children can vary widely. Father involvement exists on a continuum, whether or not fathers live with their children. Fathers can be absent even when they reside with their children and can be present despite nonresident status.

Another aspect of the neo-conservative perspective is the argument that "key parental tasks belong essentially and primarily to fathers" (Blankenhorn, 1995, p. 67). Fathers are seen as essential role models for boys, relationship models for girls, and "protectors" of their families (Popenoe, 1996, p. 77). The essentialist perspective assumes that boys need a heterosexual male parent to establish a masculine gender identity. Pleck (1995) has demonstrated that empirical research does not support this assumption. Similarly, a significant amount of research on the children of lesbian and gay parents has shown that children raised by lesbian mothers (and gay fathers) are as likely as children raised in heterosexual, two-parent families to achieve a heterosexual gender orientation (Patterson, 1995). Other aspects of personal development and social relationships were also found to be within the normal range for children raised in lesbian and gay families.

We speculate that the larger cultural context of male dominance and negative attitudes toward women may interfere with the ability of many single mothers to establish an authoritative parenting style with male children. Within patriarchal culture, boys know that when they become adult men, they will be dominant to every woman, including their mother. This cultural context, unmediated by a male presence, may undermine a single mother's authority with her sons. Taken as a whole, the empirical research does not support the idea that fathers make a unique and essential contribution to child development.

If the essentialist paradigm is not supported by empirical data, why has it been so widely accepted? We believe that the appeal of the essentialist position reflects a reaction against the rapid changes in family life that have taken place in the past three decades. Since the 1960s, family-formation strategies have changed dramatically in Western, industrialized cultures. In this context of rapid change, the neo-conservative position reflects widespread societal anxiety about who will raise the children. Mothers are no longer at home, and society has not embraced other-than-mother care. The United States, in contrast to other Western countries, has not yet developed a social policy agenda designed to help women and men integrate their work and family responsibilities. Thus, many people believe that a return to the traditional nuclear family structure with its gendered division of labor would be preferable to large numbers of neglected and unsupervised children.

In addition to an authentic concern about the welfare of children, we believe that the appeal of the essential father also reflects a backlash against the gay rights and feminist movements. In the last two decades, the employment of women has dramatically increased, whereas the employment of men has declined significantly (Engle and Breaux, 1998). Many more women can now choose to leave unsatisfactory marriages or to have children outside of the context of a traditional marriage.

Many gay men and women who would previously have entered into a heterosexual marriage to have children, now see a gay family structure as a viable alternative for raising children. Parallel to these changes is the tendency emerging among heterosexual couples to live together and delay marriage until after a first pregnancy (Blossfeld, 1995).

These social changes require heterosexual men to relinquish certain aspects of power and privilege that they enjoyed in the context of the traditional nuclear family. Most men no longer have sole economic power over their families. Similarly, most men must accept some degree of responsibility for child care and household tasks. The majority of heterosexual men no longer have full-time wives to buffer the stress of balancing work and family roles. Within this new context of power sharing and role sharing, heterosexual men have been moved from the center to the margins of many versions of family life. In our view, the societal debate about gender differences in parenting is, in part, a reaction to this loss of male power and privilege. We see the argument that fathers are essential as an attempt to reinstate male dominance by restoring the dominance of the traditional nuclear family with its contrasting masculine and feminine gender roles. The emphasis on the essential importance of fathers and heterosexual marriage represents an attempt to reassert the cultural hegemony of traditional values, such as heterocentrism, Judeo-Christian marriage, and male power and privilege.

References

Biller, H. B., and Kimpton, J. L. (1997). The father and the social-aged child. In M. E. Lamb (Ed.), *The role of the father in child development*. (3rd ed., pp. 143–161). New York: Wiley.

Blankenhorn, D. (1995). *Fatherless America: Confronting our most urgent social problem.* New York: Basic Books.

Blossfeld, H. P. (1995). *The new role of women.* Boulder, CO: Westview.

Bowlby, J. (1951). *Maternal care and mental health.* Geneva, Switzerland: World Heath Organization.

Engle, P. L., and Breaux, C. (1998). Fathers' involvement with children: Perspectives from developing countries. *Social Policy Report: Society for Research in Child Development, 12,* 1–23.

Haas, L. (1993). Nurturing fathers and working mothers: Changing gender roles in Sweden. In J. C. Hood (Ed.), *Men, work and the family* (pp. 238–261). Newbury Park, CA: Sage.

Lamb, M. E. (1987). Fathers and child development: An introductory overview and guide. In M. E. Lamb (Ed.), *The role of the father in child development* (3rd ed., pp. 1–18). New York: Wiley.

McLoyd, V. C. (1998). Socioeconomic disadvantage and child development. *American Psychologist, 53,* 185–204.

Patterson, C. J. (1995). Lesbian mothers, gay fathers and their children. In A. R. D'Augelli and C. F. Patterson (Eds.), *Lesbian, gay and bisexual identities over the lifespan* (pp. 262–290). New York: Oxford University Press.

Pleck, J. H. (1995). The gender role strain paradigm: An update. In R. F. Levant and W. S. Pollack (Eds.), *A new psychology of men* (pp. 11–32). New York: Basic Books.

Popenoe, D. (1996). *Life without father.* New York: Pressler Press.

Smuts, B. B., Gubernick, D. J. (1992). Male-infant relationships in nonhuman primates: Paternal investment or mating effort? In B. S. Hewlett (Ed.), *Father-child relations: Cultural and biosocial contexts* (pp. 1–31). New York: Aldine de Gruyter.

Trivers, R. L. (1972). Parental investment and sexual selection: In B. Campbell (Ed.), *Sexual selection and the descent of man 1871–1971* (pp. 136–179). Chicago: Aldine-Atherton.

Zihlman, A. L. (1997). Women's bodies, women's lives: An evolutionary perspective. In M.E. Morbeck, A. Galloway, and A. L. Zihlman (Eds.), *The evolving female: A life history perspective* (pp. 185–197). Princeton, NJ: Princeton University Press. ✦

Silverstein, L. B., and Auerbach, C. F. (1999). "Deconstructing the Essential Father." *American Psychologist,* 54, 397–407. Copyright © 1999 by the American Psychological Association. Adapted with permission.

Issue 16: Questions to Consider

1. The importance of fathers to children and family functioning is an important one. Where do you stand on this issue? Do children need fathers?

2. Can other men substitute for absent fathers?

3. What do fathers contribute to children's development? Do they offer children something mothers cannot?

4. Do children need fathers, but only if they have certain qualities (e.g., are loving, caring, and nurturing)? Do children not *need* fathers, but benefit from their involvement?

5. The essentialist position that Silverstein and Auerbach take issue with is based partly on the notion that nuclear families are the best environments in which to raise children and partly on evolutionary theory. What evidence do they offer to refute this essentialist position?

6. Are there points about fathers on which these two sets of authors agree?

7. Silverstein and Auerbach assert that the co-mingling of political and personal values with scientific evidence on families and other relationships is common. Can you think of other topics on which science and politics compete? ✦

Issue 17: Introduction

Do These Genes Look OK? The Human Genome Project and Our Future

The Human Genome Project (HGP) is a massive undertaking that potentially may change the course of human health care, if not history. For several years, scientists have been engaged in mapping the human genome. A genome is all of the DNA in an organism, including its genes. Genes carry the information needed to make all of the proteins that determine such things as how we metabolize and behave and how we respond to infections and illnesses. The HGP started in 1990 and should be completed in 2003. Among its goals were to identify all 30,000 to 35,000 genes in human DNA and to determine the sequence of the 3 billion chemical bases that make up human DNA.

The HGP may yield many positive benefits. In one of the papers that follow, David Stipp describes a view of the future in which illnesses that are now fatal are cured via gene therapy, the effects of aging are slowed or eliminated, inherited problems in children are avoided through premarital genetic screening, and life spans increase dramatically. All of this, and more, are predicted to become reality during the lifetimes of most college students. If it sounds too good to be true, perhaps it is, at least according to Garland Allen.

Allen asks some disturbing questions about the HGP. He raises the specter of eugenics, a "science" designed to improve human beings through selective breeding. In the past, eugenicists argued that people with known mental, physical, or personality defects should not be allowed to reproduce and pass these problems along to future generations. Persons with such defects were sterilized (or worse). Although the HGP holds the promise of correcting detected mental, physical, and perhaps even emotional problems genetically, Allen fears that such information will be misused by insurance companies and others. Moreover, the new biotechnology holds the promise of parents being able to produce "designer babies," resulting in kind of a reverse eugenics. Allen worries that our scientific technology may be more advanced than our abilities to think through the ethical, legal, and moral problems that result from these biotech breakthroughs.

Scientists employed by the U.S. government, sponsor of the HGP, have long been concerned about ethical, legal, and moral issues related to the project. After reading the two articles in this volume, you may want to visit the U.S. government's web site on ethical and legal issues. The URL is <http://www.ornl.gov/hgmis/elsi/elsi. html>. ✦

17a

Blessings From the Book of Life

David Stipp

Sequencing the genome is often called "biology's moon shot." That's wrong: Getting to the moon was a joy ride to a dead end—it had no lasting effect on our everyday lives. Decoding the genome will trigger developments that will change our daily lives as much as westward expansion changed the U.S.

Biotech pioneers will seek out the genetic bad actors behind our worst scourges, from arthritis to Alzheimer's, which in turn will lead to hundreds of new therapies. They'll find genes underlying idiosyncrasies like aptitude for math or low pain threshold. They'll pinpoint the scant 1 percent or so of our DNA that separates us from chimps. They'll trek into deep time to investigate how ancient networks of genes taught themselves to assemble the fabulous jack-in-the-box of a newborn's brain and the monstrous one of a tumor cell.

Some of their forays may go awry, of course. Insecticidal genes placed in food plants may jump to other species, creating superweeds. Biotech may also yield the bitter pill of thwarted hope—if it turns out that a confusing multitude of genes, rather than a few clear-cut culprits, engender our major afflictions, the quest for cures may get mired in complexity. There's sure to be endless debate about the rising costs of biotech drugs. And genetic studies are likely to reveal patients' disease risks long before cures arrive, causing great frustration.

Here, then, are some guesses about where we'll all be going during the next few decades.

By 2010 . . .

We'll start winning the war on cancer. Say you experience back pain, night sweats, and loss of appetite, and then find an egglike swelling under your arm. Today a doctor would analyze biopsied cells from your lump with an instrument using 400-year-old technology, the microscope, and make an educated guess: You have non-Hodgkins lymphoma. You'd get one-size-fits-all chemotherapy that might work. If it doesn't, your doc would tell you not to despair—other drugs might save you.

In 2010 your doctor will scan your biopsied cells with a DNA array, a computer-chip-like device that registers the activity patterns of thousands of genes in cells. It will quickly establish that your lymphoma is actually one of six genetically distinguishable types of T-cell cancer, each of which is known to respond best to somewhat different drugs. Another gene-testing device called a SNP ("snip") chip will flag medicines that won't work in your case because your particular liver enzymes tend to break them down too fast.

Since your first round of therapy will hit your tumor cells square on, your odds of achieving lasting remission will be very good. You'll have years and years to stop and smell the roses—your favorites will be the bioengineered blue ones.

In a recent study with SNP chips made by Orchid Biocomputer of Princeton, NJ, researchers at the University of Cincinnati found that by examining a single DNA letter in a gene that helps regulate blood pressure, they could predict whether a patient with congestive heart failure was likely to decline rapidly on standard drugs for the condition, and hence might need more aggressive treatment.

As for that horticultural grail, the blue rose: Australia's Florigene is working on it—the biotech company has already created violet carnations implanted with petunia genes.

Health sites on the Web will try to grab you by offering inexpensive genotyping services that predict your responses to scores of drugs. For a sizable fee, they'll perform more extensive genotyping to estimate your future risks of developing heart disease, various cancers, and other major killers.

Reproductive clinics will offer prospective parents the ability to screen embryos generated through *in vitro* fertilization for hundreds of inherited diseases. Such tests will be conducted on cells culled from the embryos before implantation in a mother's womb, enabling parents to select babies-to-be that are free of genetic glitches that cause diseases such as cystic fibrosis.

Debate will intensify about whether prospective parents should be allowed to reject embryos because they carry gene variants only loosely linked to later disease, such as ones that pose a 30 percent higher-than-normal risk of diabetes.

"Many drugs fail in clinical trials because they turn out to be toxic to just 1 percent or 2 percent of the population," says Mark Levin, CEO of Millennium Pharmaceuticals, a Cambridge, Mass., genomics company. With genotyping, drug companies will be able to identify gene variants underlying severe side effects. That will let their occasionally toxic flops fly—the drugs will be safe to use with gene tests that tell doctors who shouldn't get them. Levin predicts such "pharmacogenomic" advances will more than double the FDA-approval rate of drugs that reach the clinic.

Researchers will decode hundreds of germs' genomes, enabling them to ferret out the bugs' Achilles' heels. That will lead to potent new antibiotics with novel modes of action, such as MedImmune's Synagis, whose bioengineered immune molecules ward off pneumonia in newborns. Gene-inspired drugs to blunt diseases of aging will begin arriving to help deal with the T. Rex of demographic trends: The baby-boomers' long goodbye. Cancer will loom as the killer issue for boomers, as heart disease did for their parents' generation. But just as drugs to control risk factors, plus cardiac surgery, have largely turned heart disease into a "manageable" chronic condition, biotech will push death from the big C ever further into old age.

Gene therapy will start delivering on its huge promise. Attempts so far to treat diseases by inserting corrective genes in patients' cells have proved disappointing, and the recent death of a patient in a gene-therapy trial at the University of Pennsylvania has whipped up concerns about side effects. This rocky road isn't too surprising. Most gene therapy to date has been "like taking a Swiss watch, cramming in a new gear, and hoping it meshes," says William Haseltine, CEO of Human Genome Sciences of Rockville, Md. Despite the bad news, though, researchers are beginning to get it right.

Several inherited diseases, such as hemophilia, will be curable by gene therapy. Arguing that a few injections of its new gene-fixing drugs can dispense with decades of costly chronic therapy, a biotech company that has spent a fortune developing them will price the medicines at $20,000 a dose.

Rising consumer resistance to bioengineered foods will peak and begin subsiding after 2005, when rice implanted with genes that make vitamin A precursors begins preventing vitamin deficiencies that annually blind up to 500,000 kids worldwide; fruits tweaked to deliver vaccines begin preventing infections that kill millions; and bioengineered grains with extra iron begin reaching the two billion people worldwide threatened with anemia.

Meanwhile, the rage for nutraceuticals—foods and dietary supplements laced with trace nutrients thought to stave off diseases of aging—will help sell biotech foods in the developed world.

By 2020 . . .

Researchers will begin clinical trials by giving safe, tiny doses of, say, half-a-dozen possible variations of a new medicine to volunteers. The drugs' effects on thousands of genes and proteins will be monitored and analyzed by computer to predict how higher "therapeutic" doses will affect people of various genotypes. That will enable researchers to select the optimal molecules and immediately begin large, pivotal clinical trials, skipping initial phases of testing that now often take years.

The result: Gene-based drugs geared to patients' genotypes will be available for most major killers. Some big diseases will be on the way out—rheumatoid arthritis and other autoimmune diseases such as lupus will be essentially curable by drugs that selectively switch off parts of the immune system that attack patients' own tissues. Potent new therapies will be available to treat once mysterious diseases, such as schizophrenia and narcolepsy, at the level of root causes.

Dozens of gene-inspired "lifestyle" drugs will be available, from rejuvenators of fading hair-pigment genes to his and hers libido boosters. You'll be able to afford treatments that let you look as if you've hardly aged during the past decade. If you're male, gene therapy shampoos will reverse your pattern baldness. If you tend toward obesity, drugs tailored to your genotype will let you benignly alter your energy metabolism and fearlessly chow down. Biofacials will rev up dermal genes that make antioxidants and DNA-repairing enzymes, slowing time's toll on your face.

Comprehensive drug-based personality tune-ups will be in vogue among the wealthy, just as psychoanalysis once was. If you feel bad, you won't blindly try one antidepressant after another—you'll undergo molecular neural analysis to guide the prescription of a cocktail of highly selective neurotransmitter modulators. You'll select the new inner you from a psychic-dimension menu whose options will include items like "desired obsessive-compulsive activation" and "preferred excitability level."

Reproductive clinics will begin cautiously testing biotech's equivalent of atomic fission: germ-line gene therapy. Its promise has long been obvious: Thousands of inherited diseases, such as cystic fibrosis, might be eliminated by patching faulty genes in reproductive cells, causing the fixes to be passed to future generations.

Web-based premarital counseling services will offer genome screening to help customers select mates. Before getting serious, couples will be able to check whether their children would be at high risk from combinations of disease-predisposing genes they carry. (We all carry such genes.) Dari Shalon, director of the Harvard Center for Genomics Research, predicts that bionerds will embrace a new fad in personals ads: Reference to possession of gene variants linked to mental acuity, a tendency to take risks, and other presumably desirable traits.

Genomic genealogy services will proliferate. You'll be able to order up genetic profiles of various family members that show how gene variants associated with things like perfect pitch, high excitability, and light spirits have passed from grandparents to certain of the grandkids.

Regenerative medicine will take off as researchers develop ways to create new tissues from biodegradable polymers and "stem cells," potent cellular generalists that give rise to the various specialized cells in our organs. There will be "living insurance" companies: Places where people deposit such cells for later use in generating immune-compatible tissues to patch or replace failing organs.

In 2020 your pancreas will be severely damaged by a rare autoimmune disorder. Luckily, back in 2014 you socked away some of your blood stem cells, culled from blood taken during a checkup, paying out of pocket to have them cryopreserved in your local cell bank. Your HMO has agreed to pay a company named RegenerUs Inc. to tweak the cells so that their gene-activation profiles resemble those of pancreatic cells, and then multiply them inside a biopolymer matrix to implant in your damaged organ. You're going to be just fine.

By 2040 . . .

Individualized preventive medicine will be the gold standard. Gene therapy, as well as more traditional gene-based drugs, will be available for most diseases. It will be possible to hold most cancers in check for many years. Alzheimer's disease, which will be detectable before symptoms appear, will usually be preventable.

The average life span in the developed world will top 90. Key genes involved in aging will be identified, and clinical trials of anti-aging drugs will be under way. A consortium of life insurers will help fund the trials, counting on the medicines to boost their profits by delaying boomers' life-insurance payouts.

Clinical trials of drugs to boost IQ, memory, and other mental powers will be under way. Heated debate will begin about whether the NIH should fund research on germ-line gene therapy to enhance future generations' cognitive performance.

Your heart will finally start to give out. Not to worry: The stem cells you banked more than two decades ago can now be used to generate a reasonable facsimile of your ticker, thanks to the latest advances in regenerative medicine. In fact, most of your tissues and a number of major organs can be similarly regenerated over periods of weeks to months. Such replicas will cost hefty sums though, making regenerative medicine the focal point of heated debate about unequal access to biotech's bounty by the rich and poor. ✦

Stipp, D. (2000, March 6). "Blessings From the Book of Life: Decoding the Human Genome Will Yield a Bounty of Biotech Miracles That Will Transform Our Lives in the Next 40 Years." *Fortune, 141 (5)*, 21. Stipp, D., *Fortune*, copyright © 2000 by Time Inc. All rights reserved.

17b

Designer Genes for All?

Garland E. Allen

The biological sciences have experienced unprecedented growth in the 20th century. Of all the branches of biology none has developed at a more spectacular pace than genetics. Beginning with the discovery of the work of the Moravian monk Gregor Mendel in 1900, genetics has advanced with leaps and bounds from major theoretical discoveries about the molecular structure and function of genes to agricultural and medical applications that promise boundless improvements in human welfare.

The rapid growth of genetics has also posed a number of major scientific, ethical, and legal problems. From genetically designed food to genetically designed babies, the questions arise with increasing frequency: Are we developing a technology faster than our ability to use it wisely and justly? What can we legitimately expect from genetics in the future? Is it the "magic bullet" some exponents claim, allowing us to solve the persistent problems of hunger, human health, and even behavior?

Proponents of the massively funded Human Genome Project are promising we can soon replace defective genes with functional ones, and even genetically alter behavioral and personality traits such as intelligence or a tendency toward violence. How realistic are such claims, and, even if they are technically feasible, how are they to be used, by whom and toward what ends?

History can provide some guidelines on these sorts of questions. In the early decades of the 20th century, when the new

Mendelian genetics were being applied with great success to animals and plants, a number of human genetics traits (the A–B–O blood groups, hemophilia, color blindness) were being identified. In conjunction with legitimate genetics, another movement—eugenics—sought to apply the new genetic knowledge to improving the hereditary quality of the human species through scientifically planned reproduction. Eugenicists thought it would be possible to eliminate not only specific medical conditions such as Huntington's chorea and hemophilia, but also more general personality and mental traits such as manic depression, alcoholism, prostitution, nomadism, "feeblemindedness," and pauperism. Noting that such conditions often ran in families, eugenicists argued that these traits were the result of defective genes. By preventing reproduction of people with histories of these traits, eugenicists thought they could significantly improve the quality of the human population in just a few generations.

On the basis of this supposedly "scientific" evidence, eugenicists in the United States lobbied successfully for passage of the Johnson Immigration Restriction Act in 1924, which established quotas for immigration from Europe. Quotas were heaviest for southern and eastern Europeans (Italians, Poles, Serbs, Jews) who eugenicists claimed were the most genetically defective. Eugenicists also lobbied at the state level for the passage of compulsory sterilization laws for the genetically defective in state mental institutions, orphanages, prisons, or hospitals.

Most of the laws were based on the "Model Sterilization Law" drawn up by Harry H. Laughlin, a former Missourian from Kirksville, who became Superintendent of the Eugenics Record Office at Cold Spring Harbor, N.Y., in 1910. More than 30 states passed eugenical sterilization laws by 1935, and by 1963 more than 60,000 people had been sterilized. Laughlin's model law was also used as the basis for Germany's massive sterilization law in July 1934, one of the first major pieces of legislation initiated by the new National Socialist (Nazi) government after its take-over in 1933. Eugenics provided the "scientific" rationale for more than 400,000 sterilizations in Germany prior to the onset of World War II.

Eugenicists in both the United States and Germany claimed it was illogical to allow the unfit to reproduce at will and then have to take care of their offspring for generations to come. It made more sense to prevent the problem in the first place, and it would save the state money. Most convincing, eugenics seemed to be scientific, unmarred by opinion or prejudice.

Some geneticists objected to eugenics, claiming the biology was naive and the legal consequences mean-spirited. The public and politicians got their views from the media, however, which gave much more space to the wonders eugenics would accomplish than to its problems.

Are we in danger of the new genetics turning into a brand of eugenics? It seems that we may be closer than we like to think. Consider first the scientific evidence. As in the early 1900s, many new human genetic traits (many of them diseases) are being identified, and for some, like Huntington's disease or cystic fibrosis, the actual gene has been located and its molecular structure determined. These are major advances, and the science behind them is sound.

At the same time, we hear claims that conditions such as manic depression, schizophrenia, alcoholism, intelligence, ho-

mosexuality, risk-taking, and the like are significantly influenced, if not totally determined, by genes. As in the old eugenics movement, the science behind these sorts of claims is not so sound. In the past decade, virtually none of the claims for the discovery of genes for complicated human behavioral or personality traits has stood the test of time. Many have been actively withdrawn when the original findings could not be duplicated.

Consider also the social and economic parallels. *In utero* genetic testing allows doctors to identify the presence of certain genes, such as Huntington's, cystic fibrosis, or Tay-Sachs. If insurance companies will not cover such individuals, or significantly increase premiums for their coverage, termination of pregnancy may be the only choice open to families when such conditions are diagnosed. While the decision to terminate pregnancy may be less morally problematic with severe newborn diseases like Tay-Sachs (where the child usually dies before the age of 2), it is more problematic with Huntington's or cystic fibrosis.

Huntington's is a late-onset condition, showing up only in an afflicted individual's 40s or 50s. We only need remember that folk singer Woody Guthrie had Huntington's to recognize that such reproductive decisions are highly problematic.

Some people with the cystic fibrosis genes show few or no symptoms. Yet, if we were to rely solely on genetic diagnosis for our information and let economic agencies like insurance companies dictate the decisions, we may end up with a kind of eugenic way of thinking without realizing it.

We can avoid our predecessors' mistakes by keeping two points in mind: Genetics is not a cure for social problems. Claims of a genetic basis for learning or behavioral problems are usually a cover-up for rectifying the environmental conditions that influence our actions far more than any genes. Second, we have to recognize that reproductive decisions have to be made on an individual and/or family basis, and cannot be determined by governmental or corporate (i.e., insurance company) policies. We would do well to develop a universal health-care policy that would allow families to make reproductive decisions in human, not economic terms. We can well afford that luxury. ✦

Allen, G. (1999, December 28). "Designer Genes and Babies-to-Order: Is a New Eugenics Afoot?" *St. Louis Post Dispatch*, D9. Permission granted by Garland E. Allen, Department of Biology, Washington University, St. Louis, MO.

Issue 17: Questions to Consider

1. If you could choose what your children would be like by using some kind of genetic intervention, what characteristics would you choose? Would you use genetic screening to help you choose a mate (and future parent of your children)? Why or why not?

2. African Americans, Jewish Americans, and other ethnic and racial groups have greeted the HGP with caution. Why do you think members of racial and ethnic minorities have expressed more concern than white European Americans about these biotechnological advances?

3. Genetic screening is potentially a positive prevention method to avoid inherited problems such as Tay-Sachs and cystic fibrosis. Allen has some concerns about genetic screening. What might be other concerns about the effects of genetic screening? For example, how do you think health insurance companies might react if they find out you have been screened for Huntington's?

4. Stipp predicts that gene replacement and organ rejuvenation therapies will extend the life span by many years. Most people welcome the thought of living a long, healthy life, but there may be negative consequences to extending the life span of humans by 30 or 40 years. Think about the potential societal and individual problems that could result.

5. Do you agree or disagree with Allen's reasoning that "designer babies" may be a bad idea?

6. Do you think there will need to be new laws regulating the use of genetic information about a person? Why or why not? If you think there should be laws, what will they regulate? ✦

Part Four

Controversial Issues Related to Family Diversity

Issue 18: Introduction

Is Love (Color) Blind?

Anthropologists and biologists tell us that race is a socially constructed label applied to people and not a set of genetic characteristics. Yes, there are biological elements to race, but behavioral differences between groups of people identified as different races have far more to do with social and cultural environments than to inherent genetic influences. In North America, race, and the meanings attached to racial categories, are important to a lot of people. We read and hear stories of racial pride and racial hatred nearly every day.

The United States is rapidly becoming more diverse racially and ethnically. Currently, non-Hispanic whites comprise about 72 percent of the U.S. population, but this proportion is expected to decrease to 53 percent over the next 50 years (Spencer and Hollmann, 1998). African Americans and people of Hispanic and Asian/Pacific Islander descent will increase in number and in proportion of the population.

One by-product of the increase in racial and ethnic diversity, according to the most recent census, is that more Americans than ever are marrying individuals of another race (<http://www.census.gov>). We can expect this trend to continue. There is still some prejudice against interracial relationships, but at least it is no longer illegal to marry someone of another race, as it was in some U.S. states.

An increase in interracial relationships means there are going to be more children with bi- or multiracial heritages. The 2000 Census for the first time in history allowed individuals to check more than one box for "race," and 3.3 percent of the population identified themselves as being a member of more than one race.

Given the importance of race in our society, how does this affect individuals who "belong" to two or more racial groups? In the final two papers in this section, a biracial man and a biracial woman write about their experiences. Susan Fales-Hill embraces both of her racial backgrounds with enthusiasm and pride. Don Terry is connected emotionally to both of his racial heritages, but identifies more strongly with being an African American. As you read these two papers, see if you can identify the reasons why Fales-Hill and Terry had such different experiences as biracial Americans.

Reference

Spencer, G., and Hollmann, F. W. (1998). Population projections of the United States by age, sex, race and Hispanic origin: 1995 to 2050. *Current Population Reports, Series P25–1130*. Washington, DC: United States Census Bureau. ✦

18a

My Life in Black and White

Susan Fales-Hill

I'm sick in bed watching Oprah one afternoon, and I want to scream—and not because I don't like what she's wearing. A sobbing biracial girl is being comforted by a midriff-baring Mariah Carey, the Oprah-annointed pop patron saint of "mulattos." Oprah asks Mariah and the disconsolate teen if hearing about their painful experiences will confirm the public's belief that the children of mixed marriages are doomed to suffer. "That's not true!" I find myself shouting at the screen. "Why didn't you ask me or any of my well-adjusted mixed friends?! I'm living proof that mixed does not mean mixed up! I'm doing fine!" (If that's true, why am I yelling at a television screen in the middle of the afternoon? you may ask.) So often have I heard people assume that being "mixed" is tantamount to misery, and so desperate am I to share my message of hope with the world that I briefly consider climbing up to my rooftop to shout it out. But since I live in a respectable Park Avenue co-op, right across the street from the Lenox Hill Hospital mental ward, I reconsider my approach.

We "mulattos" (I put the word in quotation marks because it comes from the Spanish word for mules) have always gotten bad PR. We've been denounced as Satan's spawn. To quote an old American adage: "God made the black man, and God made the white man, but the Devil made the mulatto." Then there's the brilliant question I'm often asked: "Your mother's black and your father's white. So what does that make you?" Human, last time I checked.

Contrary to popular belief, being born into a biracial home does not automatically condemn one to a life of isolation and ethnic schizophrenia, "torn between two races, feeling like a cafe au lait fool." (Just ask Tiger Woods.) For me, growing up biracial has been a privilege and an extraordinary adventure. My story may not be typical, but it is in a sense quintessentially American, and with its melding of immigrant, Afro-Caribbean, Puritan, and European cultures, quintessentially African-American.

My parents wed in 1958, when the anti-miscegenation laws still on the books rendered their marriage illegal in many states. My mother, the daughter of Haitian political exiles, was a singer and actress appearing on Broadway in the musical *Jamaica* with Lena Horne. My father worked as an executive at a shipping company. A mutual friend, Johnny Galliher, took my father to see the show. As my mother belted out the show stopping number "Leave de Atom Alone," my father decided he would never leave her alone. At the end of the performance, he said to his friend, "That's the mother of my children." Two months and scores of roses later, my mother agreed to a date. They were married April 15 of that year.

I first realized my parents were different "colors" when I was 5. I had spent the day with my father and was astonished at his mystical power over the city's taxis. He had only to raise his hand in the air and the lemon-yellow vehicles would come screeching to a halt. This to my childish eyes was akin to the parting of the Red Sea on the scale of miracles. I felt certain my father was a magician. It was so different from being out with Mommie. Three or four Checker cabs would speed past us before even one would stop. Or the OFF DUTY sign would suddenly illuminate when we came into view. Upon arriving home, I announced to my mother, "Papa's really good at getting cabs, and you're terrible." That was the first time my mother sat me down to explain the racial facts of life in America in 1968. The cabdrivers didn't want to pick her up, she explained, because she was black and they thought she was going to Harlem or some other "undesirable" neighborhood. Papa was white. They assumed he was going someplace nice. Though I've never forgotten that moment, it was far from devastating. Mommie presented the injustice to me as part of an ugly but not immutable status quo, like slavery, or her own experiences singing in clubs she couldn't attend as a patron in the fifties. Her message was one of hope. There was nothing wrong with us; it was society that was tragically misinformed.

In spite of the racial turmoil and upheaval of the period, our life was relatively free of strife. My brother and I were fully accepted in both our families. Summers we spent on my grandmother's estate in Gladstone, New Jersey, where black people were such a rare sight that the first time my mother set foot in the local convenience store they knew immediately she was "the one who had married into the Fales family." (Each time we saw a black person in town, my parents would excitedly point him or her out. I found this odd and uncouth until they explained their elation to me. It meant things were changing.) Though my mother, with her mahogany skin, pipe-cleaner-thin body, extravagant clothes, and false eyelashes, certainly stood out among the tweedy "hunt-club set," she absolutely refused to change who she was. I can see her now striding into the vegetable garden in her stilettos, full makeup, and a spaghetti-strap chiffon gown to pick fresh tomatoes for our evening meal. "Take me as I am," she seemed to declare to the WASP world. And it did. (My grandmother, a Colonial Dame of

America, accepted my mother fully. She became my grandfather's favorite daughter-in-law.) My mother's refusal to bow to someone else's standard of "correctness" taught me that I didn't have to spend my life seeking other people's acceptance or approval, that "fitting in," like virginity, was a highly overrated virtue.

In addition to the love of our families, we enjoyed the support of our parents' eclectic, multiethnic group of friends. In fact, we were part of a sort of ad hoc "mixed-marriage colony." Far from being oddballs, we knew many other children like us.

My parents dealt with the stereotyping in popular culture by creating a cult of "uniqueness." When Farrah Fawcett-Majors appeared, wiggling and jiggling on television, my mother would say, "Anyone can look like her; you look different, and that's wonderful." Those who preferred Fawcett-Majors' all-American look to my wild mane and cafe au lait complexion were, yet again, tragically misinformed. Sometimes my parents' attitudes verged on the delusional, as in 1976, when the press vetted the names of various Sloane Rangers as potential brides for Prince Charles, and my father insisted the Windsors could have no objection to the Prince's selecting me. Even at 13, I knew that my being black might prove a small sticking point. But my father's overriding message prevailed: I was the equal of any human being, white or black. In his eyes, I was fit for a king.

Though white, my father had an encyclopedic knowledge of black culture internationally. He was an ethnic chameleon who could fit into any group, be it a voodoo "church" in Brazil or a salon of French intellectuals. He would argue against accusations that blacks were an inferior breed by employing inexhaustible examples drawn from history and literature. More so than any professor, he showed me the interconnectedness of all the world's cultures, whether it was in the person of Alexander Pushkin (the Russian writer of Abyssinian descent) or in the decor of our home, in which a Malian sculpture might sit on a Hepplewhite table. My father was also far from naive about the challenges my brother and I would face. He didn't treat us like white children with a tan. Our parents explained that though we had a claim to both our heritages, America would classify us as black. And that was just fine because, whether or not America realized it, black was beautiful, varied, rich, and noble.

Harvard proved my real dose of being judged by the color of my skin rather than the content of my character. I didn't know I was "fair-skinned." I didn't know I was supposed to sit at the Freshman Black Table to prove what I already knew: That I was not and never would be white. Many of the black students assumed I identified only with the culture of DWMs (Dead White Males) and that I would date only LWMs (Live White Males).

There were days I belonged "everywhere and nowhere." When listening to certain African-American students talk about their belief in the innate racism of whites, I couldn't, for the life of me, identify. To me, the white race was not a hostile and alien monolith; it was my beloved grandmother and grandfather, my doting uncles, my cousins, my father. It was my blood. I did, however, feel equally alienated from insouciant Caucasian students who didn't believe their infractions would reflect poorly on their families or their people. They didn't know what it was to feel "When and where I enter, the whole race enters with me." Whether it was in a classroom or at a keg party, I always felt the weight of being a cultural ambassador of blacks and the offspring of mixed marriages. People teased me about my formal manner and my obsession with dressing well. I didn't have the luxury enjoyed by whites of walking around in torn jeans and being treated as an equal member of society. Still, I relished my undergraduate years.

Growing up, I was struck by an affliction common to many young African-American women from affluent backgrounds: acute BPG—Black Princess Guilt. "I've never lived in the 'hood,'" goes the self-flagellating mantra. "I've only driven through it in an expensive foreign car." By definition, Black Princesses haven't struggled, or wrestled the demon Poverty. Our stories of oppression begin with lines like "There I was at the cashmere-sweater counter . . ." These are not stories of being harassed by the police; they are stories of being treated like "less than a shopper" in expensive boutiques. And so, like many others suffering with BPG, I went out and found a boyfriend who would give me as hard a time as possible about growing up privileged. Lorenzo (name has been changed to protect the guilty), though he was also mixed, constantly berated me for being a "white girl in brown face." I couldn't sing like Mahalia Jackson or break into the vernacular. In short, I lacked soul. My academic achievements were all well and good, but did I know how to survive "on the street"? Well, I thought I did, but according to him, Bond Street and Madison Avenue didn't count. I was woefully unprepared for "real life." I wore this psychological hair shirt for several years, until one bright day it occurred to me that my parents were right. Being "authentically black" did not mean being authentically poor. Nor did it mean speaking fluent Ebonics or qualifying for membership in the Abyssinian Baptist Church Choir. Though Lorenzo's abdominals were chiseled to perfection, his ideas were nothing if not ill formed. Let's face it, in street parlance, they were wack! I bid him and BPG sayonara and began my quest for a true soul mate.

Over the years, I dated everyone from a rapper named after a breakfast cereal to WASP trust-fund babies. With my mixed friend Suzanne Kaye, I discussed marrying black or white. At the end of the day, it came down to marrying human beings who understood us. My husband, a black American of British West Indian descent who grew up in Hanover, New Hampshire (black population: his family), knows firsthand what it means to be a cultural mulatto, to fit in everywhere and nowhere. He immediately understood my West Indian side, relished my "WASPy" side, and celebrated my European side. He doesn't, in other words, try to condense my identity.

This year in the census, for the first time, I had the opportunity of checking more than one ethnic box. I did so, not in order to set myself apart but to declare who I am. (Truth is, most African Americans could check more than one box, and for all some whites know, so could they.) I will do so to acknowledge both of my families, and especially my parents, whose humor, love, madness, arrogance, and irreverence helped me, far more than economic privilege, to overcome the prejudices of our society. And so to those who would ask, "Your mother's black and your father's white. What does that make you?" I have only one reply: "Rich, baby." ✦

Fales-Hill, S. (2000, June). "My Life in Black and White." *Vogue*, 76, 78, 84. Reprinted by permission of Susan Fales-Hill. This article originally appeared in *Vogue*.

18b

Getting Under My Skin

Don Terry

When I was a kid growing up in Chicago, I used to do anything I could to put off going to bed. One of my favorite delaying tactics was to engage my mother in a discussion about the important questions of the day, questions my friends and I had debated in the backyards of our neighborhood that afternoon like, Who did God root for, the Cubs or the White Sox? (The correct answer was, and still is, the White Sox.)

Then one night I remember asking my mother something I had been wondering for a long time. "Mom," I asked, "what am I? What I mean is, you're white and Dad's black, so what does that make me?" "Oh, I see," she said. "Well, you're half-black and you're half-white, so you're the best of both worlds."

The next day, I told my friends that I was neither black nor white. "I'm the best of both worlds," I announced proudly. "Man, you're crazy," one of the backyard boys said. "You're not even the best of your family. Your sister is. That girl is fine." For much of my life, I've tried to believe my mother. Having grown up in a family of blacks and whites, I'd long thought I saw race more clearly than most people. I appreciated being able to get close to both worlds, something few ever do. It was like having a secret knowledge.

And yet I've also known from an early age that things were more complicated than my mother made them out to be. Our country, from its very beginnings, has been obsessed with determining who is white and who is black. Our history has been shaped by that disheartening question. To be both black and white, then, is to do nothing less than confound national consciousness.

My mother denies it, but it has also sometimes confounded our family. For as my mother was answering my bedtime question, my brothers, David and Robert, her children from an earlier marriage, were going to sleep in a house 15 miles away. My father was black. David and Robert's was white. They lived with my grandmother in an all-white neighborhood. I lived with my mother and my younger sister, Diane, in Hyde Park, a mixed neighborhood on the South Side of Chicago. We shared a loving parent, but we lived in separate Americas. We have spent most of our lives trying to come together.

My father, Bill Terry, was born in Covington, Ky., in 1921, the grandson of slaves. In his youth, he was a professional boxer. Later, he went to work as a bodyguard for the unions in Chicago, cracking scab heads. He was one black man who was not at all shy about standing up to authority. In his late 30's, he became an actor.

He was a lifelong integrationist, but the nonviolent civil rights movement was not for him. He could not understand how protesters could allow themselves to be roughed up and spat on at sit-ins and not defend themselves. Bill Terry didn't turn the other cheek; he threw the other fist.

My mother, Jeanne Katherine Ober, was born in 1918 and was reared on a dairy farm outside the village of Greenwood, Ill. She was sent to high school in Chicago and then, at 25, she returned home to marry the son of a wealthy farmer. It was a rocky union: her husband drank too much, and after eight years of marriage, my mother left, taking her two sons to Chicago—David was 8, Robert was 2. There, she opened a nursery school and became involved in civil rights work through her Unitarian church. Until then, she had never personally known a black person.

My parents met in 1956, at a party of racially mixed hipsters. He was 35; she was 38. As my mother tells it, she had been eyeing my father for much of the evening. He was the center of attention, with his boxer's grace and a smile that could light up the darkest corners of the room. Before long, my father asked my mother to dance. At 6 feet 2 inches, he towered over her. Soon, my parents were living together—along with David and Robert—in my mother's four-bedroom Colonial in Evanston, a Chicago suburb. Ten months after they met, I was born.

In 1959, my parents had a daughter, Diane. I remember how happy I was that we were all together. It was especially great to have my father around. If I bugged him enough, he would put down his paper and, like his hero, Paul Robeson, sing "Ol' Man River" for me. On hot summer evenings, when it seemed the whole neighborhood was out, my father would scoop me up in his arms and run with me through the warm evening air. I was home. My dad was with me; it was heaven.

Hyde Park itself played a major role in my happiness. The neighborhood, which is home to the University of Chicago, had been integrated since the late 1940's, despite the early resistance of the university. By the time I came along, having a black father and a white mother was common in Hyde Park. In fact, there were so many biracial children running around the neighborhood when I was a kid that it was almost hip to be "mixed," as we called ourselves then.

Most of the mixed kids in Hyde Park were pure-blooded mulattos, so to speak. All of them had black fathers and white mothers. With so many kids who looked like me and with so many parents who looked like mine, it was easy to feel completely comfortable saying I was simply half and half. My memory is one of togetherness.

That's not to say that even in this utopia the power of race was entirely absent from our lives. When I was a boy, my father would perform a ritual. He'd plop his long brown arm down on a table top and ask me if I could see the red tint in his skin. "See there," he'd say. "That's the Indian blood in me. You have it, too. All the Terrys do. We're a quarter Cherokee."

I'd carefully inspect his arm, turning it over in the light, but all I could ever see was the brown skin of a black man. I thought it was a strange game. He did not look like an Indian. His skin was brown. There was nothing red about him.

There was nothing red about me either. My complexion is the color of sand. The texture of my hair is somewhere between kinky and curly. I have my father's full lips, and my nose and thick eyebrows come from my mother. When I look in the mirror, it is easy for me to see Europe and Africa dancing across my face like lovers.

Other people, however, aren't sure what they see. When they ask, "What's your nationality?" I often suspect that they really mean: Are you on our side or their side? Can we trust you, brother? Are you dangerous, nigger? I'm not sure my answer can ever really change the interaction. These questions, these loyalty oaths, have followed me most of my life.

In 1962, our world changed. My parents got into a vicious argument. My father had been out carousing, and my mother was fed up with him drinking up what little money we had. In a flash, my father had his big hands wrapped around my mother's throat, squeezing as hard as he could, banging her head against the wall. After that, my parents separated for good. My father moved to New York City to pursue his acting career. My mother was left with two children in a crumbling apartment. We went on public assistance.

Biracial though I was, my first real memory of being called "nigger" was the same cruel rite of passage it has been for black children the country over. I was 7, and I was playing football with a group of white kids in a suburb 25 long miles from Hyde Park. A boy, about my age, saw me in a neighbor's yard and started jumping up and down. He pointed at me excitedly as he chanted: "Nigger. Nigger. Nigger."

A few years after the football game, I was walking down the street with a white friend. A well-dressed member of the Nation of Islam asked me if I wanted to buy a copy of Muhammad Speaks, the group's newspaper. "No thanks," I said. "Come on, brother, help your people out." "No thanks." "Man, you just want to be with Europeans," the Muslim said bitterly, pointing his paper at my friend. "My mother is a European," I said. "Brother, I'm sorry for you," the Muslim shot back.

Other moments also made it clear that a mixed family seemed foreign to the eyes of America. In the summer of 1972, when I was 15, my brother David, who collects old Packards, took me to Nebraska to pick up a 1956 Patrician. I was excited—it was my first out-of-town trip with one of my brothers. At the car owner's house, David introduced me to a white man in white shoes. He leaned against a white picket fence.

"This is my little brother, Donny," he said. The man and I shook hands. Then he stared at me. I had a huge Afro; David's straight brown hair was cut Young Republican short. The man winked at David. "You mean you work together?" he asked. "No," David said. "I mean this is my brother." "Oh, I get what you're saying," the man said. "The Bible says we are all brothers under the skin. It's good to see people taking the word of God to heart."

What a fool, I thought to myself then. Today I know: As a person of mixed race, it's the norm to have your closest relationships questioned at every turn.

Until I went to college, racial difference stood out for me precisely because it was the exception to the rule. In college, it became a defining force in my life.

What was wrong with me? I wasn't split in two—the world was. And yet I was the one expected to adjust. Being away from Hyde Park was a shock to my racial system. I felt even more out of step with most white students. For the first time, I was exposed to white people who had not known black people as friends, neighbors, or even classmates.

One night, I was visiting a white girl and her white roommate in their dorm. The door was open and we were just talking. Another black student was also there, flirting with the roommate. I was just about to leave when a white girl walking down the hall passed the open door and stuck her head in. She looked disgusted. "What's this," she asked, "a soul-brother session?" I was stunned. What did race have to do with anything? We were just two guys rapping to two girls and not getting anywhere. The girl I was visiting looked embarrassed. I wasn't sure if she was embarrassed about her rude neighbor—or that her rude neighbor had "caught" a couple of brothers in her room.

Fed up, I embraced blackness—as a shield and a cause. I signed up for a course on black nationalism. At last, I felt in touch with my rage that race, even at my "progressive" college, mattered so much; that I could not completely be who I was, Don Terry, an integrated man, with a white mother and a black father; that I would repeatedly be lumped in a broad racial category—black—and treated like a caricature instead of the complicated individual I knew myself to be. Disgusted by the world's refusal to see me as mixed and individual, I chose "blackness." My decision, I've come to believe, had as much to do with anger as anything else. I was afraid I was becoming a racist.

After college my first job was at the *Chicago Defender*, a small and struggling but historically significant black newspaper. I then went on to work for a number of larger papers in the Midwest before coming to the *New York Times* in 1988.

In just about every one of these jobs, my reputation was built as much around my race as my journalism; I was the black man with a big mouth, ready to get loud at the slightest racial slight—the brother with a boulder on his shoulder.

My mother had four children. David is a successful stockbroker. Robert is an artist and boat captain. My sister, Diane, has spent the past 22 years battling schizophrenia. Diane has a daughter, Wakara, who was reared mostly by my mother and me.

Though we are adults now in a more enlightened time, race can appear like a ghost, disrupting the life of our family. A few years ago, I was at David's house. Julie, then 12, announced to us that she had received an A on her seventh-grade social studies assignment. "Would you like to see my project, Uncle Donny?" she asked me.

Using old photographs, Julie had laid out 100 years of the family's history, culminating in the well-kept suburb where she and her family now lived. She handed me the three-ring notebook. There were pictures of everyone, except for Aunt Diane, Cousin Wakara and Uncle Donny, the black members of the family.

I could not believe that we had been left out. "I'm not in this," I said, closing the book and handing it back to Julie. "What's up with that?" There was only awkward silence.

Though I tried to let the incident go, I found myself one day raising it with David's son, Noah, who had just returned from the Navy. Noah listened to the story, and then told me one of his own. He was showing his photo album to a black shipmate. When the sailor turned to pictures of Wakara and me, Noah said: "The guy was happy. He patted me on the back. He said, 'We don't have to worry about Noah. He's part black.'" My nephew paused. "I told him I'm not part black," he said. "It didn't matter to him. He was still happy." And so was I.

My brother Robert lives in a small city in Washington State, largely isolated from the rest of the family. One day, Robert, Henry [my nephew], and I drove up to Vancouver, Canada. We spent a wonderful afternoon going to museums and eating fish and chips. In the evening, we headed home, with Robert driving and Henry and me sitting in the back. At the border, Robert pulled into the line of cars waiting to go into the United States. From the back seat, I could see the American border guard, a young black man, wave several cars through with hardly a word. When it was our turn, however, he walked slowly around our car, peering into the windows. Something was suspicious

about us. "Where are you going?" he asked Robert. "We're going home," Robert said. "Who's that in the back seat?" the guard asked, pointing at me. "That's my brother." "Your brother?" "We're half brothers." I cringed at the word "half." The guard looked at me again. He was on the verge of asking another question, when Henry leaned across my lap and, poking his head out the window, said, "He's my Uncle Donny, and we love him."

The young American still looked suspicious, but he stepped aside and waved us on our way home. Perhaps, I thought, that's the best we can hope to do—to insist upon our allegiance to one another, our brotherhood across the divide—and try to go home.

And my parents? My mother went back to college when she was in her 40's and has been a schoolteacher ever since. At 82, she teaches history and conflict resolution at an alternative school, Sullivan House, on the South Side of Chicago.

My father died of cancer in 1998 in New York City at age 76. I finally could not bear to go to the service, all those years late. My grief and anger over his abandonment was still strong. A friend brought me a videotape of the service. I was pleased to see a parade of mourners of all colors walk to the front of the room and say kind things about my father. One speaker was a stylishly dressed white man in his late 60's. He said he and my father had spent a lot of time talking about my father's childhood. The man started choking up and walked away.

The man, it turned out, was a psychologist my father had started seeing when he was 70. A few months after watching the tape, I called him. We talked about the fact that Bill had fathered seven children with four different women—three white, one black. With the obvious exception of my sister, I barely know any of them.

> He was repeatedly touching on the issue of white women as if he were trying to make rational in somebody else's eyes how he had lived his life,

the therapist said. "He couldn't see it as accidental that he had a succession of nonblack women in his life who gave birth to his children."

The therapist said that my father wanted to have racially mixed children in part to prove himself to his mother. By having lighter, mixed-race children, he was saying, the therapist concluded: "'Look at these beautiful children I've produced.' It was a search for approval."

The day after my father died, I wandered through his apartment. From under his bed, I pulled a small strongbox with a broken lock. It was full of documents. One was a copy of my birth certificate. I was surprised and touched that he had it. Then I noticed what he had done to it. The clerk's of-fice for Cook County, Ill., had recorded that my father was "Negro" and my mother "Caucasian." My father, however, using dark blue ink, had crossed out the references to race on my birth certificate, leaving just "father" and "mother."

On paper, at least, he tried to give me a gift that could not be fully realized in his life: The gift of family that transcends divisions of race. On paper, it was that simple. ✦

Terry, D. (2000, July 16). "Getting Under My Skin." *The New York Times Magazine*, 6, 32. Copyright © 2001 by the New York Times Co. Reprinted by permission.

Issue 18: Questions to Consider

1. What are the benefits of being in an interracial relationship? What are the costs?

2. If a pregnant friend of yours who was in an interracial relationship asked you for advice about raising a biracial child, what advice would you give to her, based on the experiences shared by the authors of these articles?

3. Do some library research on the history of interracial marriages. Why were they illegal in some states until nearly the end of the twentieth century? How do the arguments given in the past for banning interracial marriages relate to current arguments against gay and lesbian marriages?

4. Would you consider marrying a person of another race? Would you consider a serious romantic relationship with a person of another race? Why or why not?

5. Race is primarily a social construct. How do most people decide if someone is a member of one race or another? For instance, think about Terry and Fales-Hill's anecdotes about growing up—why did other people decide that they were black rather than white? Discuss the consequences for biracial children of using race as a social category.

6. To get a different perspective on race, read some of the novels of Amy Tan, an Asian American married to a European American. Her novels have many autobiographical elements. Are the experiences of Asian Americans similar to those of African Americans? If not, how do they differ? ✦

Issue 19: Introduction

Nuclear Family Wars:
The Status of American Families

The following two papers by David Pope-noe, sociologist, and Stephanie Coontz, family historian, present very different views of the state of modern American fami-lies. Popenoe sounds an alarm that Ameri-can society is in decay because the two-nat-ural-parent family is in decline. Coontz takes the more sanguine approach that American families overall are in far better shape now than was true at the beginning of the last century. Which one is right? How do you decide?

As you read these two articles, examine the language being used. For example, Popenoe says that there now can be little doubt that successful, well-adjusted chil-dren are more likely to come from two par-ent families—biological mother and father. Alternate family forms such as single parent and stepfamilies "have been demonstrated to be inferior." How did you interpret these statements? Did you understand them to mean that most well-adjusted children come from two-parent, first-married fami-lies? Did you interpret them to mean that single parent and stepfamily environments are generally bad for children? What evi-dence does Popenoe offer to support these statements?

Coontz presents quite a different picture of American family life at the beginning of the twenty-first century than did Popenoe. What evidence does she use to support her statements?

According to the Census Bureau Current Population Report issued in April 2001, in 1996 there were 71.5 million children under the age of 18 living in households. Of these children:

- 50.7 million lived with two parents (at least 10 percent were stepfamilies).
- 1.5 million lived in unmarried-couple families.
- 1.8 million lived with their father only.
- 1.3 million lived with their grandpar-ents in households with no parent pres-ent.
- 10.3 million children lived in an ex-tended household that contained at least one person who was not a parent or a sibling.
- 4.1 million lived in extended house-holds with grandparents.
- 11.8 million children lived in stepfami-lies.
- 4.9 million lived with a stepparent.
- 15.2 million children lived in house-holds with no siblings present.
- Among the 56.2 million children who lived with siblings, 9.5 million lived with at least one step- or half-sibling.

As you can see, children today live in quite diverse households —and this has al-ways been true. This report goes on to say that, "Today's family and household struc-tures are not unique." There was almost no change in children's living arrangements from 1880 until 1970. Figures that follow in parentheses are from 1970. In 1880, 83 per-cent (85 percent) of children lived with two parents, 8 percent (11 percent) of children lived with mothers only, 3 percent (1 percent) lived with fathers only, and 6 percent (3 percent) lived with neither parent. Between 1970 and 1990, however, there was a major change in the percentage of children living with two parents (73 percent in 1990) and with mothers only (23 percent). Few changes were noted between 1990 and 1996, when the data for the report were compiled. Think about these figures as you read the articles. ✦

19a

Can the Nuclear Family Be Revived?

David Popenoe

Based on accumulated social research, there now can be little doubt that successful and well-adjusted children in modern societies are most likely to come from two-parent families consisting of the father and mother. Alternative family forms which are attempted, such as single-parent and stepfamilies, have been demonstrated to be inferior in child outcomes. The recent movement away from the two natural-parent family has led to considerable social malaise among the young, not to mention social decay in general.

It can be argued that child well-being would be enhanced if families lived among caregiving relatives and in supportive communities, but this has become an ever-diminishing situation. Historically, a substantial stripping down has occurred of both the extended family and the cohesive neighborhood, and this trend is probably irreversible. The state has tried to fill the vacuum, but without much success. The two-parent nuclear family therefore may be more important today for children, and for society in general, than ever before in history.

Constituting one of the greatest dilemmas faced by modern societies, however, is the fact that nuclear families themselves are breaking apart at dramatically high rates. The chances in some societies are now less than 50-50, thanks mainly to divorce and out-of-wedlock births, that a child will live continuously to adulthood with both natural parents. This is despite the fact that, unlike in times past, parents now almost always live to see their children reach maturity.

One fundamental reason for the high break-up rate is that the nature of marriage has changed. Not so long ago marriage was an economic bond of mutual dependency, a social bond heavily upheld by extended families, and a religious bond of sacramental worth. Today, marriage is none of these. The economic bond has become displaced by affluence, by female economic pursuit, and by state support; extended family pressures on marriages have all but vanished; and modern societies have become increasingly secular. Marriage has become a purely individual pursuit; an implied and not very enforceable contract between two people; a relationship designed to satisfy basic needs for intimacy, dependency, and sex. When these needs change, or when a presumptively better partner is discovered, marriages are easily dissolved. Moreover, more of the everyday needs traditionally met by marriage can be met in other ways, such as through the marketplace.

With its surrounding and supporting social structure collapsing, can there be any hope that the nuclear family can be revived? Yes—the basis for hope lies in the fundamental biological and psychological makeup of human kind. If the evolutionary biologists are correct, human beings are a pair-bonding species. Unlike most other species, we have an innate predisposition to mate with one member of the opposite sex (homosexuals notwithstanding) and form a pair-bond for the purpose of raising children.

Pair-bonds are considered to be an evolutionary development of enormous impor-

218

tance to the human species, a major reason for our extraordinary success in the world of nature. Our predisposition to pair-bond appears to be a legacy of the fact that, in our ancestral environment of evolutionary adaptation, the mother-child bond alone was inadequate for favorable child outcomes. The most successful childrearing occurred when fathers were involved in the endeavor, bonding with the child's mother at least to the extent of providing the resources necessary for survival.

Human nature today still largely functions in these terms, but there is a joker in the deck. This pair-bond does not seem well matched with the marriage ideal of the modern nuclear family—sexually-faithful, lifelong monogamy in which husband and wife share love and companionship. Such monogamy, in fact, has been extremely rare in humankind. Most societies throughout history have had a strong propensity toward polygyny (one husband, several wives), or toward serial monogamy involving a high marital break-up rate, the system that we have in modern societies today. Moreover, adultery is found almost everywhere, certainly among men but to a lesser degree among women as well.

The Modern Nuclear Family

The largest single reason for the historical deficit of faithful, lifelong monogamy, it has been suggested, is the evolved male mind. Whereas women, who necessarily have to make a tremendous personal investment in each offspring, have a strong desire for one mate who will care for them during their time of childbirth dependency, men can sire numerous offspring with little personal investment. Men are therefore pulled in two directions, one toward pair-bonding and the other toward sexual promiscuity. In most societies, a whole variety of cultural factors has helped to prevent widespread promiscuity, including the desires and influence of women and the self-protective attitudes and actions of men toward one another. Where these cultural factors fail, however, the male promiscuity option wins by default. One could argue that the default

option is especially evident today in certain sections of America's inner cities.

It is important to stress the historical uniqueness of the modern nuclear family. Before its rise in the West several centuries ago, such monogamy as existed was typically maintained by extended family pressures, by strong economic dependencies between husband and wife, by the lack of legal alternatives, and by religious sanctions. The marriages in these families were quite unlike those of today. As the distinguished family historian Lawrence Stone has noted,

> until fairly recent times the purpose of marriage had nothing to do with romantic love, sexual passion, or even necessarily friendship.

Pre-modern marriages seem to have been mostly arranged partnerships for the purposes of economic production and extended family connection.

The modern nuclear family was a truly remarkable development in the history of human social organization, and probably the only example in history to which voluntary lifelong monogamy was widely practiced. This family form consists of a monogamous married couple living with their children, apart from other relatives, with the husband working outside the home and the wife being a mother and full-time housewife. The marriage partnership is freely chosen and based on love and companionship. First arising among the bourgeoisie in northwestern Europe, this family form endured as a dominant ideal in the West through the Victorian era and up until the 1960s. The linchpin of its success was the still strongly internalized norm of marital permanence. Especially in the Victorian era, in addition, the family form was maintained by other strict moral codes that involved substantial sexual repression and to some extent the subjugation of women.

Due to this remarkable family organization, and thanks to rapidly decreasing parental death-rates, by the 1950s more children in the industrialized nations were growing up with both of their natural parents than at any other time in world history. But after that, the modern nuclear family was diminished as a widespread cultural ideal by accelerating cultural, social, and economic trends together with new technological developments. In the realm of technology, new contraceptive techniques plus abortion permitted women for the first time in history to have active sexual lives without the near certainty of pregnancy and childbirth, and television and other mass communications media revolutionized the organized entertainment industry and, thereby, popular culture. Of seminal importance, also, was the unparalleled economic growth and affluence of the post–World War II years, which brought the possibility of unprecedented personal choice, for example in lifestyles, as well as rampant materialism heavily promoted by the advertising industry. Also important was the new mixing of men and women in the workplace, the decline of parental and adult authority, and the break-up of intact and culturally integrated neighborhoods and communities.

These trends were part of a larger ideological shift away from collective identities and toward an isolating and eventually destructive individualism. Even though the modern nuclear family had been built largely around individualism, the trend of individualism continued developing into the extreme form of a highly expressive or self-focused individualism. This differed from the individualism of the earlier era in which the purpose of self-development was more oriented to benefit the group and larger causes beyond the self. Several new cultural ideologies were involved in this shift, especially the therapeutic ideology with its goal of self-fulfillment, a Playboy-style sexual opportunism and rejection of responsibilities by males, and a radical feminism that looked at the modern nuclear family as an oppressive institution. Also implicated were the cultural relativism of the social sciences and the humanities, and extreme rights-oriented political movements.

In view of this barrage of forces, what can be done to nourish the cultural ideal that must be restored if we are to revive the nuclear family: Voluntary lifelong monogamy? First, let us realize that many things probably can't be changed. Among the

things we can't rid ourselves of, or change to any significant degree, are the following: the biological make-up of males and females; modern technologies; the isolated nuclear family (few people wish to return to the earlier system of living in extended families); women in the workplace (except for certain periods of their lives, such as child-rearing, women are in the workplace to stay); the nature of the marital relationship (no one wants to go back to arranged marriages, patriarchy, and gross economic dependence); and material affluence (despite the possibility of temporary economic recessions and depressions).

Our efforts must obviously be concentrated on those factors that can be changed, and they fall into two areas: cultural, moral, and religious beliefs and norms; and government policies, programs, and legislation. Of the two, the cultural realm is by far the most important. Some would argue that the culture cannot be changed, but they are wrong. Think of the dramatic changes in recent decades in our attitudes and beliefs about women, blacks, sex, the environment, the role of government, and perhaps even the option of war.

To repeat: If the nuclear family is to be revived, we *must restore the cultural importance of voluntary, lifelong monogamy.* Here are the three most important focal points for such efforts:

1. Counter the Sexual Revolution

- Promote sexual abstinence at least through the high school years. Most parents certainly favor this and probably most high school students do as well.

- Encourage women and men to lead their premarital sex lives with eventual marriage more strongly in mind. For example, what our grandmothers supposedly knew might well be true: if a woman wants a man to marry her, wisdom dictates a measure of playing hard to get.

- Rein in the organized entertainment industry. At one time the entertainment industry did have a moral conscience, so we know it is possible. The main levers today are mass protests and boycotts.

2. Promote Marriage

- Spread the word about the emotional, economic, and health benefits of life-long monogamy, and about how it is superior to other family forms. This can be done by high schools and universities, churches, voluntary associations, and even by federal and state governments.

- Educate people about the nature of modern marriage—that it is not merely finding the perfect mate and living a life of passion and romance. It is a long-term friendship between a man and a woman that requires constant effort and care plus a strong moral commitment to the institution, in addition to special communications skills.

- Widely promulgate the findings about how marriage failure damages children.

- Continue to privilege marriage through public policy and at the same time discourage the formation of alternative lifestyles.

3. Renew a Cultural Focus on Children

- Parents want to do what is best for their children. So do most adults. We should not let the age-old cultural priority on childrearing—the sentiment that children are our future—slip from our grasp, as now seems to be happening. A serious problem is that less than one third of households today contain children, down from more than three-quarters in prior centuries. The task will not be easy. ✦

19b

The American Family Today Is Not Worse Off Than in the Past

Stephanie Coontz

Many observers fear for the future of America's families. Our divorce rate is the highest in the world, and the percentage of unmarried women is significantly higher than in 1960. Educated women are having fewer babies, there's an epidemic of sexually transmitted diseases among men, [and] many streets in urban neighborhoods are littered with cocaine vials. Even in small towns, people have easy access to addictive drugs, and drug abuse by middle-class wives is skyrocketing. Police see 16-year-old killers, 12-year-old prostitutes, and gang members as young as 11. America at the end of the 1990s? No, America at the end of the 1890s.

The litany of complaints may sound familiar, but the truth is that many things were worse at the start of [the twentieth] century than they are today. Then, thousands of children worked full-time in mines, mills, and sweatshops. Most workers labored 10 hours a day, often six days a week, which left them little time or energy for family life. Race riots were more frequent and more deadly than those experienced by recent generations. Women couldn't vote, and their wages were so low that many turned to prostitution.

In 1900, a white child had one chance in three of losing a brother or sister before age 15, and a black child had a 50-50 chance of seeing a sibling die. Children's aid groups reported widespread abuse and neglect by parents. Men who deserted or divorced their wives rarely paid child support. And only 6 percent of the children graduated from high school, compared with 88 percent today.

Why do so many people think American families are facing worse problems now than in the past? Partly it's because we compare the complex and diverse families of [today] with the seemingly more standard-issue ones of the 1950s, a unique decade when every long-term trend of the twentieth century was temporarily reversed. In the 1950s, for the first time in 100 years, the divorce rate fell while marriage and fertility rates soared, creating a boom in nuclear-family living. The percentage of foreign-born individuals in the country decreased. And the debates over social and cultural issues that had divided Americans for 150 years were silenced, suggesting a national consensus on family values and norms.

Some nostalgia for the 1950s is understandable: Life looked pretty good in comparison with the hardships of the Great Depression and World War II. The GI Bill gave a generation of young fathers a college education and a subsidized mortgage on a new house. For the first time, a majority of men could support a family and buy a home without pooling their earnings with those of other family members. Many Americans built a stable family life on these foundations.

But much nostalgia for the 1950s is a result of selective amnesia—the same process that makes childhood memories of summer vacations grow sunnier with each passing year. The superficial sameness of 1950s family life was achieved through censorship, coercion, and discrimination. People with unconventional beliefs faced governmental investigation and arbitrary firings. African Americans and Mexican Americans were prevented from voting in some states by literacy tests that were not administered to whites. Individuals who didn't follow the rigid gender and sexual rules of the day were ostracized.

Leave It to Beaver did not reflect the real-life experience of most American families. While many moved into the middle class during the 1950s, poverty remained more widespread than in the worst of our last three recessions. More children went hungry, and poverty rates for the elderly were more than twice as high as today's.

Even in the white middle class, not every woman was as serenely happy with her lot as June Cleaver was on TV. Housewives of the 1950s may have been less rushed than today's working mothers, but they were more likely to suffer anxiety and depression. In many states, women couldn't serve on juries or get loans or credit cards in their own names.

And not every kid was as wholesome as Beaver Cleaver, whose mischievous antics could be handled by Dad at the dinner table. In 1955 alone, Congress discussed 200 bills aimed at curbing juvenile delinquency. Three years later, LIFE [magazine] reported that urban teachers were being terrorized by their students. The drugs that were so freely available in 1900 had been outlawed, but many children grew up in families ravaged by alcohol and barbiturate abuse.

Rates of unwed childbearing tripled between 1940 and 1958, but most Americans didn't notice because unwed mothers generally left town, gave their babies up for adoption, and returned home as if nothing had happened. Troubled youths were encouraged to drop out of high school. Mentally handicapped children were warehoused in institutions. Wives routinely told pollsters that being disparaged or ignored by their husbands was a normal part of a happier-than-average marriage.

Denial extended to other areas of life as well. In the early 1900s, doctors refused to believe that the cases of gonorrhea and syphilis they saw in young girls could have been caused by sexual abuse. Instead, they reasoned, girls could get these diseases from toilet seats, a myth that terrified generations of mothers and daughters. In the 1950s, psychiatrists dismissed incest reports as Oedipal fantasies on the part of children.

Spousal rape was legal throughout the period, and wife beating was not taken seriously by authorities. Much of what we now label child abuse was accepted as a normal part of parental discipline. Physicians saw no reason to question parents who claimed that their child's broken bones had been caused by a fall from a tree.

There are plenty of stresses in modern family life, but one reason they seem worse is that we no longer sweep them under the rug. Another is that we have higher expectations of parenting and marriage. That's a good thing. We're right to be concerned about inattentive parents, conflicted marriages, antisocial values, teen violence, and child abuse. But we need to realize that many of our worries reflect how much better we want to be, not how much better we used to be.

Fathers in intact families are spending more time with their children than at any other point in the past 100 years. Although the number of hours the average woman spends at home with her children has declined since the early 1900s, there has been a decrease in the number of children per family and an increase in individual attention to each child. As a result, mothers today, including working moms, spend almost twice as much time with each child as mothers did in the 1920s. People who raised children in the 1940s and 1950s typically report that their own adult children and grandchildren communicate far better with their kids and spend more time helping with homework than they did—even as they complain that other parents today are doing a worse job than in the past.

Despite the rise in youth violence from the 1960s to the early 1990s, America's children are also safer now than they've ever been. An infant was four times more likely to die in the 1950s than today. A parent then was three times more likely than a modern one to preside at the funeral of a child under the age of 15, and 27 percent more likely to lose an older teen to death.

If we look back over the last millennium, we can see that families have always been diverse and in flux. In each period, families have solved one set of problems only to face a new array of challenges. What works for a family in one economic and cultural setting doesn't work for a family in another. What's helpful at one stage of a family's life may be destructive at the next stage. If there is one lesson to be drawn from the last millennium of family history, it's that families are always having to play catch-up with a changing world.

Take the issue of working mothers. Families in which mothers spend as much time earning a living as they do raising children are nothing new. They were the norm throughout most of the last two millennia. In the 19th century, married women in the United States began a withdrawal from the workforce, but for most families this was made possible only by sending their children out to work instead. When child labor was abolished, married women began reentering the workforce in larger numbers.

For a few decades, the decline in child labor was greater than the growth of women's employment. The result was an aberration: the male-breadwinner family. In the 1920s, for the first time, a bare majority of American children grew up in families where the husband provided all the income, the wife stayed home full-time, and they and their siblings went to school instead of work. During the 1950s, almost two-thirds of children grew up in such families, an all-time high. Yet that same decade saw an acceleration of workforce participation by wives and mothers that soon made the dual-earner family the norm, a trend not likely to be reversed in the next century.

What's new is not that women make half their families' living, but that for the first time they have substantial control over their own income, along with the social freedom to remain single or to leave an unsatisfactory marriage. Also new is the declining proportion of their lives that people devote to rearing children, both because they have fewer kids and because they are living longer. Until about 1940, the typical marriage was broken by the death of one partner within a few years after the last child left home. Today, couples can look forward to spending more than two decades together after the children leave.

The growing length of time partners spend with only each other for company has made many individuals less willing to put up with an unhappy marriage, while women's economic independence makes it less essential for them to do so. It is no wonder that divorce has risen steadily since 1900. Disregarding a spurt in 1946, a dip in the 1950s, and another peak around 1980, the divorce rate is just where you'd expect to find it, based on the rate of increase from 1900 to 1950. Today, 40 percent of all marriages will end in divorce before a couple's 40th anniversary. Yet despite this high divorce rate, expanded life expectancies mean that more couples are reaching that anniversary than ever before.

Families and individuals in contemporary America have more life choices than in the past. That makes it easier for some to consider dangerous or unpopular options. But it also makes success easier for many families that never would have had a chance before—interracial, gay or lesbian, and single-mother families, for example. And it expands horizons for most families.

Women's new options are good not just for themselves but for their children. While some people say that women who choose to work are selfish, it turns out that maternal self-sacrifice is not good for children. Kids do better when their mothers are happy with their lives, whether their satisfaction comes from being a full-time homemaker or from having a job.

Largely because of women's new roles at work, men are doing more at home. Although most men still do less housework than their wives, the gap has been halved since the 1960s. Today, 49 percent of couples say they share childcare equally, compared with 25 percent in 1985.

Men's greater involvement at home is good for their relationships with their partners, and also good for their children. Hands-on fathers make better parents than men who let their wives do all the nurturing and childcare: They raise sons who are more expressive and daughters who are more likely to do well in school, especially in math and science.

In 1900, life expectancy was 47 years, and only 4 percent of the population was 65 or older. Today, life expectancy is 76 years, and by 2025, about 20 percent of Americans will be 65 or older. For the first time, a generation of adults must plan for the needs of both their parents and their children. Most Americans are responding with remarkable grace. One in four households gives the equivalent of a full day a week or more in unpaid care to an aging relative, and more than half say they expect to do so in the next 10 years. Older people are less likely to be impoverished or incapacitated by illness than in the past, and they have more opportunity to develop a relationship with their grandchildren.

Even some of the choices that worry us the most are turning out to be manageable. Divorce rates are likely to remain high, but more non-custodial parents are staying in touch with their children. Child-support receipts are up. A lower proportion of kids from divorced families are exhibiting problems than in earlier decades. Stepfamilies are learning to maximize children's access to supportive adults rather than cutting them off from one side of the family.

Out-of-wedlock births are also high, however, and this will probably continue because the age of first marriage for women has risen to an all-time high of 25, almost five years above what it was in the 1950s. Women who marry at an older age are less likely to divorce, but they have more years when they are at risk—or at choice—for a nonmarital birth.

Nevertheless, births to teenagers have fallen from 50 percent of all nonmarital births in the late 1970s to just 30 percent today. A growing proportion of women who have a nonmarital birth are in their twenties and thirties and usually have more economic and educational resources than unwed mothers of the past. While two involved parents are generally better than one, a mother's personal maturity, along with her educational and economic status, is a better predictor of how well her child will turn out than her marital status. We should no longer assume that children raised by single parents face debilitating disadvantages.

As we begin to understand the range of sizes, shapes, and colors that today's families come in, we find that the differences within family types are more important than the differences between them. No particular family form guarantees success, and no particular form is doomed to fail. How a family functions on the inside is more important than how it looks from the outside.

The biggest problem facing most families is not that our families have changed too much but that our institutions have changed too little. America's work policies are 50 years out of date, designed for a time when most moms weren't in the workforce and most dads didn't understand the joys of being involved in childcare. Our school schedules are 150 years out of date, designed for a time when kids needed to be home to help with the milking and haying. Many political leaders feel they have to decide whether to help parents stay home longer with their kids or invest in better childcare, preschool, and after school programs, when most industrialized nations have long since learned it's possible to do both. America's social institutions have some bugs to iron out. But for the most part, our families are ready for this millennium. ✦

Issue 19: Questions to Consider

1. Why do you think these two scholars have such different opinions about the status of the American family? Is it merely a matter of one person seeing the glass as half full and the other seeing the glass as half empty? Are they looking at different data to draw their conclusions or are they looking at the same data and drawing different conclusions?

2. Coontz is Co-Chair of the Council on Contemporary Families, and Popenoe is a member of the Institute for American Values. Find out what you can about these organizations. What are their purposes? What philosophies and values underlie what they do?

3. Do you agree with Popenoe that the causes of marital dissolution are affluence, women's economic pursuit, and state support of single parents? Can you think of other causes?

4. Coontz seemed to put major blame for marital dissolution on institutions and Popenoe puts the major blame on individuals within families. List everything you can think of that has some empirical backing that supports Coontz's position. Then list everything you can think of that has some empirical backing that supports Popenoe's position. Compare your lists. What conclusions do you draw after doing this exercise?

5. What are the value and the harm of focusing on negative findings regarding alternate family forms such as single parent families and stepfamilies? What is Popenoe trying to accomplish by focusing on negative findings?

6. What are the value and the harm of focusing on American families within a historical context? What is Coontz trying to accomplish by doing that? ✦

Issue 20: Introduction

How Harmful Is Divorce to Children?

According to demographer Andrew Cherlin of Johns Hopkins University, about half of recent first marriages will end in dissolution. Slightly more than half of all divorces involve minor children (i.e., under the age of 18), and it is estimated that about 40 percent of all U.S. children will experience parental divorce before reaching adulthood. Therefore, divorce is a common experience in our society. It does not seem to be an experience that people feel neutral about, however. In fact, the issue of divorce has evoked strong emotional responses from politicians, scholars, government officials, and hosts of others.

Paul Amato (2000), Penn State University sociologist, concluded from his review of the research on divorce during the 1990s,

> on one side are those who see divorce as an important contributor to many social problems. On the other side are those who see divorce as a largely benign force that provides adults with a second chance for happiness and rescues children from dysfunctional and aversive home environments. Based on the accumulated research of the 1990s—and of earlier decades—it is reasonable to conclude that both of these views represent one-sided accentuations of reality. . . . Divorce benefits some individuals, leads others to experience temporary decrements in well being that improve over time, and forces others on a downward cycle from which they might never fully recover. (p. 1282)

The following two articles give you a flavor of the sorts of arguments about divorce that are common. As you read look for *inflammatory language* (as a hint, the terms *"broken families"* and *"family values crusaders"* are used, both denoting stigma). Although there is certainly research indicating that, on average, children whose parents divorce do slightly less well on many outcomes (e.g., depression, learning difficulties), the differences are small. The problem comes when the meaning of these differences is misunderstood and generalized to all children who have experienced divorce.

Another problem with the conclusions people draw from the literature on divorce is that we tend to look for "one-variable solutions"—we want to find one cause for problems. For example, if a child has a reading problem and his parents are divorced, the divorce must be the cause of the reading problem. Unfortunately, one-variable explanations are almost never applicable in human behavior. Divorce is a complex process. It is obvious that there is still much that we need to know about divorce.

Reference

Amato, P. (2000). The consequences of divorce for adults and children. *The Journal of Marriage and the Family, 62,* 1269–1287. ✦

20a

Staying Together for the Sake of the Children

Walter Kirn

One afternoon when Joanne was 9 years old she came home from school and noticed something missing. Her father's jewelry box had disappeared from its usual spot on her parents' bureau. Worse, her mother was still in bed. "Daddy's moved out," her mother told her. Joanne panicked. She began to sob. And even though Joanne is 40 now, a married Los Angeles homemaker with children of her own, she clearly remembers what she did next that day. Her vision blurred by tears, she searched through the house that was suddenly not a home for the jewelry box that wasn't there.

Time heals all wounds, they say. For children of divorce like Joanne, though, time has a way of baring old wounds too. For Joanne, the fears that her parents' split unleashed feelings—of abandonment, of loss, of coming home one day and noticing something missing from the bedroom—deepened as the years went by. Bursts of bitterness, jealousy, and doubt sent her into psychotherapy. "Before I met my husband," she remembers,

> I sabotaged all my other relationships with men because I assumed they would fail. There was always something in the back of my head. The only way I can describe it is a void, unfinished business that I couldn't get to.

For America's children of divorce—a million new ones every year—unfinished business is a way of life. For adults, divorce is a conclusion, but for children it's the beginning of uncertainty. Where will I live? Will I see my friends again? Will my mom's new boyfriend leave her too? Going back to the early '70s—the years that demographers mark as the beginning of a divorce boom that has receded only slightly despite three decades of hand wringing and worry—society has debated these children's predicament in much the same way that angry parents do: By arguing over the little ones' heads or quarreling out of earshot, behind closed doors. Whenever concerned adults talk seriously about what's best for the children of divorce, they seem to hold the discussion in a setting—a courtroom or legislature or university where young folks aren't allowed.

That's changing. The children are grown now, and a number are speaking up, telling stories of pain that didn't go away the moment they turned 18 or even 40. A cluster of new books is fueling a backlash, not against divorce itself but against the notion that kids somehow coast through it. Stephanie Staal's *The Love They Lost* (Delacorte Press), written by a child of divorce, is part memoir and part generational survey, a melancholy volume about the search for love by kids who remember the loss of love too vividly. *The Case for Marriage* by Linda Waite and Maggie Gallagher (Doubleday) emphasizes the positive, arguing that even rocky marriages nourish children emotionally and practically.

The most controversial book comes from Judith Wallerstein, 78, a therapist and retired lecturer at the University of California, Berkeley. In *The Unexpected Legacy of Divorce* (Hyperion) she argues that the harm caused by divorce is graver and longer lasting than we suspected. Her work raises a question that some folks felt was settled back in the days of *Love American Style*: Should parents stay together for the kids?

Listening to children from broken families is Wallerstein's lifework. For nearly three decades, in her current book and two previous ones, she has compiled and reflected on the stories of 131 children of divorce. Based on lengthy, in-depth interviews, the stories are seldom happy. Some are tragic. Almost all of them are as moving as good fiction. There's the story of Paula, who as a girl told Wallerstein, "I'm going to find a new mommy," and as a young woman —too young, it turned out—impulsively married a man she hardly knew. There's Billy, born with a heart defect, whose parents parted coolly and amicably but failed to provide for his pressing medical needs.

It's the rare academic who can make a reader cry. Maybe that's why, with each new installment, Wallerstein's study has created shock waves, shaping public opinion and even the law. Her attention-getting style has proved divisive. For experts in the field of family studies (who tend to quarrel at least as bitterly as the dysfunctional clans they analyze), she's a polarizing figure. To her admirers, this mother of three and grandmother of five, who has been married to the same man for 53 years, is a brave, compassionate voice in the wilderness. To her detractors, she's a melodramatic doomsayer, a crank.

What drew someone from such a stable background to the study of marital distress? At the end of the 1960s, Wallerstein, whose Ph.D. is in clinical psychology, took a job consulting at a large community mental health center in Marin County just as the social dam began to crack. "We started to get complaints," she says, "from nursery school teachers and parents: 'Our children are having a very hard time. What should we do?'"

The prevailing view at the time, she says, was that divorce was no big deal for kids. So much for the power of positive thinking. "We began to get all these questions," Wallerstein remembers. "The children were sleepless. The children in the nursery school were aggressive. They were out of control." When Wallerstein hit the library for answers, she discovered there were none. The research hardly existed, so she decided to do her own. She had a hunch about what she would learn. "I saw a lot of children very upset," she says, "but I fully expected that it would be fleeting."

Her hunch was wrong. Paradise for kids from ruptured families wasn't easily regained. Once cast out of the domestic garden, kids dreamed of getting back in. The result more often than not was frustration and anxiety. Children of divorce suffer depression, learning difficulties and other psychological problems more frequently than those of intact families. Some of Wallerstein's colleagues, not to mention countless divorced parents, felt they were being guilt-tripped by a square. They didn't want to hear this somber news.

Now, decades later, some still don't want to hear her. For parents, her book's chief finding, to be sure, is hardly upbeat or very reassuring: children take a long time to get over divorce. Indeed, its most harmful and profound effects tend to show up as the children reach maturity and struggle to form their own adult relationships. They're gun shy. The slightest conflict sends them running. Expecting disaster, they create disaster. "They look for love in strange places," Wallerstein says. "They make terrible errors of judgment in whom they choose."

Marcie Schwalm, 26, a Bloomington, IL, legal secretary whose parents split when she was four, illustrates Wallerstein's thesis well. As a young woman she couldn't seem to stick with the same boyfriend. "I thought guys were for dating and for breaking up with a few weeks later," she says. "I would go into a relationship wondering how it was going to end." Finally, Marcie says, a college beau told her she had a problem. She's married now, and her feelings about divorce have a hardline, 1950s tone: "Divorce is not something I am going to go through. I would do whatever it takes to keep the marriage together."

Krishna Herrndobler, 17, isn't so sure that harmony can be willed. Now a high school student in Benton, IL, she too was 4 when her parents called it quits. She says she has no memories of the trauma, just an abiding skepticism about marriage and a resolve to settle for nothing less than the ideal man. "I don't want my kids to wind up in a single-parent situation," she says.

> And I don't want to have kids with a man I don't want to be married to forever. I don't believe in the fairy tale. I hope it exists, but I really don't believe it does.

And therein lies another problem, according to Wallerstein; the belief, quite common in children of divorce, that marriage is either a fairy tale or nothing. These jittery, idealistic children tend to hold out for the perfect mate—only to find they have a very long wait. Worse, once they're convinced they've found him, they're often let down. High romantic expectations tend to give way, Wallerstein reports, to bitter disillusionments. Children from broken families tend to marry later, yet divorce more often than those from intact homes.

So divorce often screws up kids. In itself, this isn't news, though many experts feel Wallerstein overstates the case. That divorce may screw them up for a long, long time and put them at risk for everything from drug abuse to a loveless, solitary old age is more disturbing—and even more debatable.

Besides her conclusions on children's long-term prospects following divorce, Wallerstein makes another major point in her book—one that may result in talk-show fistfights. Here it is: Children don't need their parents to like each other. They don't even need them to be especially civil. They need them to stay together, for better or worse. This imperative comes with asterisks, of course, but fewer than one might think. Physical abuse, substance addiction, and other severe pathologies cannot be tolerated in any home. Absent these, however, Wallerstein stands firm; a lousy marriage,

at least where the children's welfare is concerned, beats a great divorce.

The shouting has already started. Family historian Stephanie Coontz, author of *The Way We Never Were: American Families and the Nostalgia Trap* (Basic) questions the value of papering over conflicts for the kids' sake. "For many couples," Coontz says,

> things only get worse and fester, and eventually, five years down the road, they end up getting divorced anyway, after years of contempt for each other and outside affairs.

Coontz doesn't believe in social time travel. Unlike Wallerstein, whose investigation is deep but rather narrow (the families in her original study were all white, affluent residents of the same Northern California county, including non-working wives for whom divorce meant a huge upheaval), Coontz takes a long view of divorce. "In the 1940s the average marriage ended with the death of the spouse," Coontz says.

> But life expectancy is greater today, and there is more potential for trouble in a marriage. We have to become comfortable with the complexity and ambiguity of every family situation and its own unique needs.

That's just a lot of fancy, high-flown talk to Wallerstein and her followers. Ambiguity doesn't put dinner on the table or drive the kids to soccer practice or save for their college education. Parents do. And parents tend to have trouble doing these things after they get divorced. In observing what goes wrong for kids when their folks decide to split, Wallerstein is nothing if not practical. It's not just the absence of positive role models that bothers her; it's the depleted bank accounts, the disrupted play-group schedules, the frozen dinners. Parents simply parent better, she's found, when there are two of them. Do kids want peace and harmony at home? Of course. Still, they'll settle for hot meals.

David Blankenhorn, president of the Institute for American Values, says

> There was a sense in the '70s especially, and even into the '80s, that the impact of

divorce on children was like catching a cold: they would suffer for a while and then bounce back,

he says. "More than anyone else in the country, Judith Wallerstein has shown that that's not what happens." Fine, but does this oblige couples to muddle through misery so that Johnny won't fire up a joint someday or dump his girlfriend out of insecurity? Blankenhorn answers with the sort of certainty one expects from a man with his imposing title.

> If the question is, if unhappily married parents stay together for the sake of their kids, will that decision benefit their children?, the answer is yes.

We can guess how the moral stalwarts will answer such questions. What about ordinary earthlings? Virginia Gafford, 56, a pet product saleswoman in Pawleys Island, SC, first married when she was 19. The marriage lasted 3 years. She married again, had a second child, Denyse, and divorced again. Denyse was 14. She developed the classic symptoms. Boyfriends jilted her for being too needy. She longed for the perfect man, who was nowhere to be found. "I had really high expectations," says Denyse. "I wanted Superman, so they wouldn't do what Dad had done." Denyse is in college now and getting fine grades, but her mother still has certain regrets. "If I could go back and find any way to save that marriage, I'd do it," she says. "And I'd tell anyone else to do the same."

For Wallerstein and her supporters, personal growth is a poor excuse for dragging the little ones through a custody battle that just might divide their vulnerable souls into two neat, separate halves doomed to spend decades trying to reunite. Anne Watson is a family-law attorney in Bozeman, MT, and has served as an administrative judge in divorce cases. Restless couples who merely need their space, in her opinion, had better think twice and think hard. "If people are divorcing just because of choices they want to make, I think it's pretty tough on the kids," Watson says. "Just because you're going to feel better, will they?"

That, of course, is the million-dollar question. Wallerstein's answer is no, they'll feel worse. They'll feel worse for quite a while, in fact, and may not know why until they find themselves in court, deciding where their own kids will spend Christmas. It's no wonder Wallerstein's critics find her depressing.

Her chief message to married parents is clear: Suck it up if you possibly can, and stick it out. But even if you agree with Wallerstein, how realistic is such Spartan advice? The experts disagree. Then again, her advice is not for experts. It's directed at people bickering in their kitchen and staring up at the ceiling of their bedroom. It's directed at parents who have already divorced and are sitting alone in front of the TV, contemplating a second try. The truth and usefulness of Wallerstein's findings will be tested in houses and apartments, in parks and playgrounds, not in sterile think tanks. Someday, assuming we're in a mood to listen, millions of children will give us the results. ✦

20b

Divorcing Reality

Stephanie Coontz

Every time it seems America may finally be coming to terms with how much and how irreversibly our families have changed, a new wave of panic breaks over us. Most recently it's been a rediscovery of the "catastrophe" of divorce. This past summer a new law took effect in Louisiana, giving people the chance to choose a "covenant marriage" in which the state will enforce an agreement not to divorce except for adultery, physical or sexual abuse, alcoholism, or a year's abandonment. The sponsor of the bill says he has since received calls from lawmakers all over the country inquiring how to institute similar laws. At least 19 states already have legislation pending to "slow down" divorce.

Most of the ammunition for this campaign is drawn from Judith Wallerstein's longitudinal study of 131 children whose parents divorced in 1971. In 1989, Wallerstein published a study claiming that almost half had experienced serious long-term psychological problems that interfered with their love and work lives. This summer she released an update based on 26 of these young adults, all of whom had been 2 to 4 years old when their parents separated. They had been extremely vulnerable to drug and alcohol abuse as teens, she reported, and were still plagued in their 20s and 30s by unstable relationships with their fathers, low educational achievement and severe anxieties about commitment.

The media pounced. I found more than 200 newspaper articles and opinion pieces trumpeting the "new" finding that divorce was "worse than we thought," a "catastrophe" for kids. While Wallerstein herself opposes legal restrictions on divorce, she has done little to distance herself from those who cite her work in support of the new crusade. "I've been so misquoted in America," she told Mother Jones two years ago. "I cannot worry about it anymore."

But there is good reason to worry about the massive publicity accorded Wallerstein's work. Her estimates of the risks of divorce are more than twice as high as those of any other reputable researcher in the field. Her insistence that the problems she finds were caused by the divorce itself, rather than by pre-existing problems in the marriage, represents an oversimplified notion of cause and effect repudiated by most social scientists and contradicted by her own evidence.

Wallerstein studied 60 Marin County couples, mostly white and affluent, who divorced in 1971. Her sample was drawn from families referred to her clinic because they were already experiencing adjustment problems. Indeed, participants were recruited by the offer of counseling in exchange for commitment to a long-term study. This in itself casts serious doubt on the applicability of Wallerstein's findings. The people most likely to be attracted to an offer of long-term counseling and most likely to stick with it over many years are obviously those most likely to feel they need it. And after 25 years in a study about the effects of divorce, the children are unlikely to consider any alternative explanations of the difficulties they have had in their lives.

Wallerstein says she tried to weed out severely disturbed children, yet the appendix to her original study, published in 1980, admits that only one-third of the families she worked with were assessed as having "adequate psychological functioning" prior to the divorce. Half the parents had chronic depression, severe neurotic difficulties, or "long-standing problems in controlling their rage or sexual impulses." Nearly a quarter of the couples reported that there had been violence in their marriages. It is thus likely that many of the problems since experienced by their children stemmed from the parents' bad marriages rather than their divorces, and would not have been averted had the couples stayed together. Other researchers studying children who do poorly after divorce have found that behavior problems were often already evident eight to 12 years before the divorce took place, suggesting that both the maladjustment and the divorce were symptoms of more deep-rooted family and parenting issues.

This is not to say that all the problems Wallerstein found can be explained by pre-existing family dynamics. While children in intact families with high levels of conflict usually do worse than children in divorced or never-married families, children's well-being often does deteriorate when a marriage not marked by severe conflict comes to an end. Divorce can trigger new difficulties connected to loss of income, school relocation, constriction of extended family ties, or escalation of hostility over issues like custody and finances. (In Wallerstein's sample, many women had not been employed during the marriage; forced entry into the workplace increases the risk of depression and distraction, which can affect the quality of parenting.) Intense conflict after divorce can be even more damaging to children than intense conflict within marriage.

Still, more representative samples of kids from divorced parents yield much lower estimates of risk than Wallerstein's. Paul Amato and Bruce Keith, reviewing nearly every single quantitative study that has been done on divorce, found some clear associations with lower levels of child well-being. But these were, on average, "not large." And the more carefully controlled the studies under review, the smaller were the differences reported.

Interestingly, children whose parents divorced in more recent generations are experiencing less severe problems than those whose parents divorced when laws and social stigmas were stricter. Indeed, a just-published study of 160 Boston-area families conducted by psychologist Abigail Stewart found that while most youngsters had slightly poorer than average mental health a few months after the divorce, their overall mental health had rebounded to average levels after 18 months.

Wallerstein rejects these studies because they do not take account of what she terms a "sleeper effect," in which problems caused by divorce do not show up until years later. But larger long-term studies do not support this claim, though there may be a sleeper effect for children whose parents continue to battle after the separation. Mavis Hetherington, who has studied more than 1,500 children of divorced parents, reports that the large majority grow up socially and psychologically well-adjusted.

Some past studies have confirmed that children of divorced parents are more likely to get divorced themselves. But another new study shows that even this so-called inheritability of divorce is also on the decline. UCLA researcher Nicholas Wolfinger found that between 1974 and 1993 there was a 50 percent decrease in the tendency for people whose parents had divorced to get divorced themselves.

Family values crusaders often argue explicitly that a little bit of exaggeration, or at least a use of worst-case scenarios, is justified in discussing the effects of divorce because emphasis on children's resilience may lead couples to take divorce too lightly. It is probably true that some people are unwilling to do the hard work of trying to make a relationship succeed, or do not give sufficient thought to the difficulties they or their children may face after divorce. But rising rates of divorce and single parenthood come less from me-first individualism than from long-term historical forces that are not going to be reversed by trying to scare or guilt-trip people into staying married.

If you graph the divorce rate since the 1890s, the current rate is exactly where you'd expect it to be from the trends during the first half of the century. The age of marriage is at an all-time high for women; at the other end of the line, a person who reaches age 60 can expect to live, on average, another 20 years. The institution of marriage organizes a smaller portion of people's lives and social roles than ever before. The economic autonomy of women means that dependence no longer preserves marriages, and the number of people who exist comfortably and happily outside marriage creates an ever-present alternative for people who are unhappy with their mates. No amount of coercion is going to put the toothpaste back in the tube.

In these circumstances, coercion would only make things worse for the very people the anti-divorce crusaders say they want to protect. Contrary to conservative rhetoric, women have historically needed the legal protection of divorce more than men have. For centuries, men's greater social and economic power forced many wives to put up with a husband's affairs or his humiliating treatment. Men also had more resources to fight a divorce or penalize a woman for "fault" under older laws. The fact that two-thirds of all divorces today are initiated by women indicates that many women are grateful for the easing of divorce laws.

One group of women has been badly hurt by no-fault divorce in the absence of strong alimony laws: Women who played by the old female homemaker rules and whose husbands threw out the rulebook altogether. But making divorce harder and more acrimonious would not protect these women. Would a woman who doesn't want a divorce really be better off if the law says her husband can't divorce her except in case of adultery or violence? What would prevent him from deserting the family, engaging in abuse, provoking her into a compromising situation or even fabricating evidence of her adultery? Better to make sure that strong child-support laws are enforced,

and that husbands whose wives sacrificed income and education for the sake of the marriage pay spousal support.

Slowing down divorce is not necessarily in the best interests of children either. If a couple can repair their marriage and develop an effective parental alliance, their kids will certainly benefit. But getting people to "try harder and longer" can make things worse if the marriage does eventually fail. Most studies find that divorces are more damaging for kids when they occur between the ages of 11 and 16 than when they occur between 7 and 11. This doesn't mean parents should rush into divorce, but it does mean that we should beware of frightening or pressuring couples into prolonging a marriage that may well end up being intolerable to one or the other.

We may be able to save more potentially healthy marriages than we currently do, but only by modernizing marriage, not by shoring up a model based on women's self-sacrifice. Modernizing marriage means getting men and women to share child care and housework more equally, helping couples to manage conflict in less destructive ways and building family-friendly workplaces that make it possible to raise children with less stress. (Of course, such measures will also make it easier for divorcing couples, single parents, and unmarried partners to raise children.)

It may be true, as conservatives charge, that lessening the stigma and stress attached to single parenting will lead some people to turn to divorce before exploring other options, but it's also true that as divorce has gotten more acceptable it has also gotten less damaging. In 1978, a national sample found that only 50 percent of divorced couples were able to contain or control their anger in a way that allowed them to co-parent effectively. A more recent California study of divorcing couples found that three to four years after separation, only a quarter of divorced parents were engaged in conflict-ridden co-parenting.

Similar progress has occurred in post-divorce parental contact. Surveys at the beginning of the '80s found that more than 50 percent of children living with divorced mothers had not seen their fathers in the preceding year, while only 17 percent reported visiting their fathers weekly. But a 1988 survey found that 25 percent of previously married fathers saw their children at least once a week, and only 18 percent had not visited their children during the past year. As divorce has become more common, more fathers have begun to work out ways of remaining in touch with their children, while more mothers seem willing to encourage such involvement. Researchers can help promote these new trends by explaining what we know both about how to create better marriages and how to parent more effectively after a divorce.

Fortunately for the public, a national group of family researchers and clinicians has just formed a new organization to coordinate and disseminate the latest research on family relations and trends in the United States. The Council on Contemporary Families will counter politicized and oversimplified pronouncements such as those in the current anti-divorce crusade with a more nuanced account of the changing circumstances and challenges facing today's diverse families. In the meantime, parents and the general public should take a hard, critical look at the claims of the anti-divorce crusade. ✦

Coontz, S. (1997). "Divorcing Reality." *The Nation, 265 (16)*, 21–24. Reprinted with permission from the November 17, 1997, issue of *The Nation*.

Issue 20: Questions to Consider

1. People often say that "divorce is too easy," and "people need to work harder at their marriages and make them succeed." On the other hand, there is evidence that battered women often stay in their marriages because of family ideology—they don't believe in divorce. And have you ever talked to a real person who divorced and described the process as easy? Why do you think people offer these arguments?

2. Kirn said that for adults divorce is a conclusion. It brings a relationship to an end. Is that really true? Can you end a relationship if children were a part of the marriage?

3. Kirn's article was entitled, "Staying Together For the Sake of the Kids." What are the advantages and disadvantages of this stance?

4. Why do you think that the American media has been so taken with Wallerstein's work? List reasons why we should listen to Wallerstein and make another list of reasons why we should not pay attention to her.

5. Do you agree with Wallerstein that it is children whose parents have divorced who fear commitment, or is the fear of commitment more universal among young adults? What data did you use to determine your answer?

6. Interview approximately 10 students whose parents divorced when they were children. Ask them to list or tell you the major negative things they experienced as a result of the divorce. Also, ask them to tell you the major positive things they experienced as a result of the divorce. Compile your two lists and draw conclusions from your data. How do your conclusions fit with those of Coontz and Wallerstein? ✦

Issue 21: Introduction

Should Divorce Laws Be Reformed?

Although the rate of divorce has leveled off in the last few years, the rates of divorce in North America are among the highest in the world. This has concerned many people, and the last few years have seen several coordinated efforts by people who are interested in reducing divorce. Some individuals and groups have focused their efforts on improving communication and relationship-maintaining skills that people need in marriage, while others have centered their attention on reforming what they see as divorce laws that are too indulgent—that is, these individuals believe that divorce has become too easy to get. They think that lenient divorce laws have contributed to a tendency for married couples to seek divorce too readily, instead of trying to resolve marital problems. These divorce reformers want to change laws and social policy to make it more difficult to get a divorce. They also want to assist couples in working out problems if they can do so.

A number of policy initiatives have been proposed by those who want to reform divorce laws. One such initiative, covenant marriage, is described in the two papers that follow. In recent years Louisiana and Arizona have enacted covenant marriage laws, and several other states are considering similar laws. These laws represent attempts by state legislatures to develop public policies that will discourage divorce and encourage couples to stay married. Such public policy efforts are seen by advocates as well-meaning attempts to support the institution of marriage. Opponents see them as poorly conceived intrusions into the private lives of married couples that will result in harm to them while not helping to strengthen marriage at all. The issue of divorce reform is controversial for many reasons. Are there too many divorces? Do divorce laws need to be changed? Think about these questions as you read the following articles. ✦

21a

A Solution to America's Divorce Problem

Steven L. Nock, James D. Wright, and Laura Sanchez

Couples wishing to marry in Louisiana are now required to choose between the standard marriage with unrestricted access to no-fault divorce or a covenant marriage designed to be harder both to enter and to exit. The covenant option differs from conventional marriage in a number of additional ways: Covenant marriage requires premarital counseling. Counseling must include discussions of the seriousness of marriage, the lifelong commitment being made, the obligation to seek marital counseling if problems arise, and the grounds for divorce or legal separation in a covenant marriage. Couples must sign an affidavit acknowledging their commitment and prove they have received counseling. Divorce from a covenant marriage requires the couple to have marriage counseling and to have made a good-faith effort to resolve their differences.

Although a no-fault divorce is still possible for covenant marriages, the new law requires that the couple live apart for two years or be legally separated for 18 months. Dissolving a covenant marriage in less than two years requires one person to prove fault on the part of the other. Irreconcilable differences, incompatibility, irretrievable breakdown of the marriage, or "we just don't get along any more" are not acceptable grounds for divorce, so if these are the problem, then you have to wait the full two years. Marrying couples must choose either the covenant or the standard regime. The

law allows currently married couples to convert (or as proponents prefer, "upgrade") to covenants.

Since the 1970s, all states have had no-fault divorces available to any married person who wanted one. The only restriction in most cases is a waiting period that can be as short as a few months and is rarely more than a year. The no-fault revolution was motivated by a belief that the former marriage regime trapped many women and children in difficult, abusive, or otherwise unsatisfactory marriages.

Among pro-family advocates and other traditionalists and social conservatives, no-fault divorce is seen as having created a "divorce culture" where traditional values of love, fidelity, commitment, and obligation are no longer respected. By making divorce easy to obtain, the no-fault regime has ruined the lives of countless people, many of them children who are emotionally traumatized by divorce, and many others women whose financial well-being is ruined when their marriages fall apart.

The covenant marriage "movement" and the larger anti-divorce movement stem from widespread dissatisfaction with the current social and legal landscape of marriage and divorce and a concern that no-fault divorce laws threaten the institution of marriage. Many contend that the no-fault regime has fostered a model of marriage as a contract with the state acting as the neutral enforcer of the bargains struck by self-interested parties. This leaves women vulnerable, harms children, and undermines general social welfare; at the least, it is destructive of values of caring and commitment that produce stability in families. Others argue that no-fault divorce has transformed marriage into a contract that provides no remedy for the breach of marriage vows. In this view, no-fault divorce encourages opportunistic behavior by husbands and threatens the marital investments of wives.

Covenant marriage (CM) changes the terms of all marriages in a unique way. By forcing couples to decide between covenant or conventional marriage, the law introduces an element of contractual negotiation about the terms of the marriage relationship. This requires couples to contemplate and discuss their chances for a divorce and to express their understandings about marriage. In many respects, covenant marriage simply adds to the marriage vows a clause that affirms, ". . . and we really mean it!" What objection could possibly be mounted to anything that helps couples take their marriages more seriously if that is what they have freely chosen to do? Or that might assist them in keeping their marriages together some years in the future?

CM has been opposed by progressives, feminists, traditionalists, and religious leaders, although for different reasons in each case. Because of the religious origins and symbolism of covenant marriage, many were concerned that the new law violated the doctrine of the separation of church and state. The reality is that governments require people to obtain licenses and blood tests before they get married, grant authority to perform marriages, say who can marry and who cannot, establish minimum ages at which persons can marry without parental consent, set waiting periods for divorce, specify the terms of divorce, adjudicate disputes among divorcing couples about the distribution of property, award custody of children, place children in foster care, define appropriate sexual partners and sexual acts, and otherwise regulate practically every aspect of our intimate relations. Has government no right to do any of

this? Since the state must pay for much of the costs of welfare, diminished educational attainments, higher rates of out-of-wedlock births, and other problems that are among the consequences of divorce, the state has a legitimate interest in minimizing these costs.

To the extent that CM is an effort to make marriages stronger and not just harder to get out of, it [does this] through the mandatory counseling provisions. People on all sides of the debate express doubts about the likely efficacy of these provisions. Much of the concern was that religious-based counselors would simply tell women, "you should quit your job and serve your husband, like it says in the Bible." Or urge that all marriages, even profoundly destructive and abusive ones, should be preserved no matter the cost. One need not be an enthusiast for counseling to acknowledge that couples might profit from an extended discussion of marriage, commitment, and fidelity with a concerned adult sometime prior to the wedding. Granted, premarital counseling will not prevent all bad marriages from occurring and post-marital counseling will not solve every problem in a marriage, but the conclusion that there is no value to be derived from counseling seems harsh. Probably, the value lies less in the advice couples are given than in the process of confronting and discussing the possibility that the marriage will not last, the seriousness of each partner's commitment, the expectations each brings to the marriage.

Marriage can be a prison for women, and CM puts more guards in the towers. In some variants of the feminist world view, efforts to strengthen marriage or prevent divorce are looked upon with misgivings because women tend to suffer when marriages are "strong." Leaving women no way to escape from an abusive spouse is a particularly pressing concern. The Louisiana law allow[s] immediate dissolution of covenant marriages in the face of a felony conviction, adultery, abandonment, or abuse. The two-year waiting period does not apply in these cases. It is hard to see how no-fault divorce protects women any more than a fault regime would, or how a covenant marriage protects them less. Sooner or later in the process of terminating an abusive relationship, the wife has to "reveal her plans" and incur whatever risk the revelation entails.

Many women (and men!) actively seek a lifetime marital commitment and do all they can to achieve it. Covenant marriage provides people of this description with marginally stronger promises that are generally not available under the no-fault regime. It is now conceded by almost all experts that, on average, women suffer more from divorce than men. In the majority of cases, men are better off financially, and women worse off. In these cases, women will gain more than they lose if divorces are harder to get.

The Catholic Church has expressed reservations about covenant marriage, in part because in the eyes of the Church, all marriages are covenants between a man, a woman, and God. Creating a separate legal status for covenant marriages therefore implies that standard marriages are inferior—"marriage lite," a barely passable imitation of the real thing. (The Catholic Church also objects to the premarital counseling provision because it requires a discussion of divorce, which the Church also does not recognize.)

By defining one category of marriages as "better" than another the covenant marriage option opens up the possibility that couples will be coerced by parents, churches, and even one another into accepting the covenant option ("real" marriage) when, in fact, they would prefer not to. In one sense, this concern is pretty much the entire point of covenant marriage. Many people these days have a casual attitude towards marriage and divorce, and it was certainly in the minds of Louisiana state legislators that covenant marriage might cause people to take these things more seriously and, indeed, restore marriage to a privileged, not to say honored, status in society. It is also true that marriage itself is frequently used as "emotional blackmail" through which men and women are sometimes pressured into doing things they'd rather not. Just how is covenant marriage any different?

Progressive and feminist critics of CM are nearly unanimous in their belief that bad marriages are the real problem and that no-fault divorce is therefore the solution, since the no-fault regime makes bad marriages easier to dissolve. These critics correctly see the CM "movement" as part of a larger "anti-divorce movement," which in turn can be indifferent to the often-exorbitant costs of bad marriages. None of these critics allege that divorce is a positive or enjoyable experience for anyone. To the contrary, divorce is recognized as emotionally traumatic and often financially devastating. But bad marriages are also intensely traumatic, often more traumatic than the process of discontinuing them.

Nearly everyone concedes that divorce is, in the typical case, emotionally hurtful and often financially disastrous. No credible study shows otherwise, and no party to the dispute over CM disagrees. Likewise, no one in their right mind would assert that all marriages should be held at all costs, no matter what. We have already emphasized more than once that the law explicitly acknowledges that some marriages are destructive and require immediate termination; the law also provides the legal machinery by which to terminate them.

The pre-marital counseling provision, the post-marital counseling provision, the restricted grounds for fault divorces, and the extended waiting period for no-fault divorces are all meant to get couples to take their divorces more seriously as well. The symbolism of a covenant marriage is altogether too religious and traditional for the tastes of many, but it is hard to quarrel with the substance of what the law intends to accomplish.

It is not wrong to suggest that covenant marriage is a creation of the religious right and is motivated in most cases by deep, nearly fanatical desires to resurrect traditional family values, most certainly including the idea that men should be the heads of their households and women should be deferential and subservient towards them. Some therefore feel that covenant marriage is really little more than a misguided effort to put the force of law behind Biblical pronouncements about women's "proper role" in marriage. But one must guard against confusing the reasons why the covenant marriage law was passed with the effects it is likely to have, or mistaking the symbolism of the concept for its substance. The practical effect of covenant marriage ultimately has nothing to do with religion or traditional male and female roles. It has everything to do with giving people more choices. CM says in practical effect that no one other than couples themselves can decide which form of marriage is best for them. Thus, the law begins to change marriage from a status to a free contract between adults.

A great deal that is being said and written about covenant marriage is misguided. But that certainly does not mean that there are no interesting issues or questions raised by the emergence of covenant marriage regimes. What kinds of couples will choose covenant marriages? How does the covenant option affect pre-nuptial conversations and negotiations between the partners? What do people know about covenant marriage and how do they learn about it?

The big question is whether covenant marriages will prove to differ from standard marriages in their stability, duration, or overall health, net of the effects of selection factors. Do they produce fewer divorces? Happier marriages? More well-adjusted children? Are the spouses in covenant marriage less likely to cheat on one another? Is there less physical, verbal, and emotional abuse in covenant marriages than standard ones? Are family relations more functional? More democratic? Or do covenant marriages promote highly traditional patterns of familial interaction, where wives are subordinate to husbands and children are "seen but not heard?" What will become of the covenant when marriages start to fail and the adult partners are looking for a way out?

Right now, thousands of couples all over the country vow to "love and honor" one another "until death do us part." The wedding vow itself is intended to stress the permanence of the commitment being made. Many may think, but none utter, "or until something better comes along," and yet that seems to have become the tacit understanding, the unspoken rider in every marriage contract under the no-fault divorce regime. But some people actually mean what they say during their wedding ceremony, fully intending their marital commitment to be permanent, and two states (with more soon to follow) have now given their citizens a legal mechanism to affirm that intention, publicly and legally. It will be interesting to see what effects, if any, this has on marriage and divorce in the coming years. ✦

Nock, S. L., Wright, J. D., and Sanchez, L. (1999). "America's Divorce Problem." *Society, 36,* 43–52. Reprinted by permission of Transaction Publishers. Copyright © 1999.

21b

Divorce Reform Won't Lower the Divorce Rate

Ashton Applewhite

"Covenant marriage," now legally available in Louisiana and pending before numerous other state legislatures, is the first step in a nationwide movement led by "pro-family" activists to rewrite or repeal no-fault divorce laws. Under covenant marriage, divorce would be permitted only on narrow grounds such as adultery, abuse, abandonment, felony imprisonment, or a mutually agreed upon two-year separation. It seeks to "fortify" marriage by making divorce harder and thus less common. It won't work.

The prevalence of divorce in America is a result of sweeping social changes that cannot be wished away with a piece of sanctimonious and punitive legislation. Anticipating litigation, the covenant marriage contract is really a postnuptial agreement, guaranteeing that those who make mistakes will suffer exceedingly in their undoing. If anything, it should be harder to get married, not to end a union gone wrong.

There lies the sole benefit of this legislation: By forcing engaged couples to think a little harder about what they're getting into, covenant marriage should prevent a number of disastrous unions from occurring in the first place. Many more couples, however, pressured into feeling that "marriage lite" is a cop-out, will ignore their misgivings and live to regret it.

Covenant marriage won't affect the divorce rate. Covenant marriage will not suc-ceed in its primary objective because there never has been any correlation between the incidence of divorce and the laws on the books. The surge of divorces in the 1960s well preceded no-fault legislation, for example, and the American divorce rate has in fact declined slightly in recent years. As sociologist Andrew Cherlin of Johns Hopkins University in Baltimore, a noted scholar in the field, puts it, "The great misconception is that divorce laws change people's behavior. People's behavior changes divorce laws." That's why there is no indication that public attitudes support the current backlash.

Many conservatives maintain that if just one spouse can file for divorce, or if the legal hurdles are low, more couples will separate. It is a logical argument, but not an accurate one because restrictive laws simply are not an effective deterrent. Just as capital punishment does not lower the crime rate and restricting access to abortion only results in more back-alley operations, people who want out of their marriages will find a way—legally if they have the resources, illegally if not. The incidence of desertion and fraud which *does* correlate with stricter divorce laws would increase, as would marital homicides.

Covenant marriage will raise the human and economic cost of divorce. Because responsibility no longer had to be assigned, no-fault divorce eliminated the need

242

for one spouse to sue the other. This made the whole process more humane, simpler and much less expensive—and is precisely what covenant marriage legislation would undo. Assets would be spent on lawyers instead of building new lives or providing for children, a real irony given the pro-fault movement's "pro-family" stance. Energy would go into excruciating struggles about offspring and property, instead of into figuring out how to maintain decent relations with the person around whom life once centered and to moving on.

Described in a *New York Times* article, aptly subtitled "Blame Is Back," as "an emerging campaign to restore notions of guilt to divorce law," the repeal of no-fault would result in a tragic increase in the kind of hostilities that can turn divorce proceedings into scorched earth campaigns. As anyone who has been through a "fault" divorce knows, coming up with grounds is the most demoralizing and wounding part of the process. Ruling out mediation or civil compromise, this bitter exercise mires the couple in accusations and repudiations, making it all the harder to heal and move forward. Blame only damages, but the notion of retribution has endless appeal for the self-righteous. Perhaps the blame lobby would find no-fault divorce more palatable if it were renamed "bi-fault."

Covenant marriage will hurt children. Both sides in this debate can cite countless expert opinions as to the effect of divorce on children, whether devastating or benign. Clearly, divorce does not guarantee maladjustment any more than growing up in an intact home guarantees mental health. The real issue is how children of divorce who live in one, or two, calm and happy homes fare compared to those who grow up in intact homes filled with turmoil or icy silence.

One thing all the experts agree on, though, is that witnessing or being party to parental conflict is what harms children. By making their parents' divorce more difficult and more hostile, covenant marriage ensures the prolonged exposure of children to the most damaging possible circumstances: Parents who fight. Too often their deliver-

ance is left in the hands of strangers and overburdened courts. Fractured into warring camps, families often never fully recover. Significantly, even psychologist Judith Wallerstein, author of one of the most-cited studies about the negative effects of divorce on children, opposes legal efforts to make divorce harder.

Covenant marriage raises hurdles that already are high enough. The current outcry that divorce has gotten "too easy" is a periodic complaint, recalling Horace Greeley's displeasure in the late 19th century that too many people were getting "unmarried at pleasure." This charge is cheap to make but impossible to substantiate. Everyone believes divorce is a bad thing, yet everyone knows individuals who divorced for good reasons. By the same token, many think divorce is "too easy," but would be hard put to name a single person for whom the process was anything but painful and arduous—as it should be. Fault or no-fault, divorce is not lightly undertaken.

Neither is matrimony, the Donald Trumps of the world notwithstanding. To act as though the Louisiana Legislature had just invented a way to make marriage binding and meaningful demeans the vows which have joined men and women for millennia.

Covenant marriage is sexist. One of the principal rationales behind covenant marriage is that it will provide wives with legal recourse against errant husbands the way the old laws did. They linked property to "fault," forcing the divorcing wage-earner to continue to support his family and giving "innocent" wives considerable leverage in negotiating settlements. The loss of this bargaining power concerns women's-rights advocates as well, joining them in an unlikely alliance with "pro-family" forces.

But the automatic assumption that wives are victims does women no favors and is unfair to the many "innocent" husbands whose wives leave them. The underlying notion of innocence vs. guilt should be jettisoned. It reinforces the age-old link between goodness (innocence) and passivity, a big step backward for authentic women's rights. It also completely disregards the fact that divorce is twice as likely to be initiated by the wife as the husband, and that advancements in women's social and political status correlate with access to affordable divorce. Divorce indeed would become less accessible to women under covenant marriage because it would cost so much more.

Covenant marriage ignores social reality. Profoundly reactionary, the covenant-marriage movement invokes a return to a way of life that was rooted in postwar prosperity, only available to a privileged minority and never all that golden. Of course it would be wonderful if everyone lived happily ever after and all children were raised by loving parents who made it home by 3 o'clock. But, like it or not, most parents must work outside the home. Like it or not, the American family is changing shape. Like it or not, marriage is becoming less relevant: About 3.5 million unmarried opposite-sex couples now share living quarters, up from 2 million a decade ago; men and women now marry later, separate from one another more frequently, and, once separated, are less likely to remarry.

Because of these and other wide-ranging cultural forces, divorce is here to stay. As sociologist Arlie Hochschild puts it,

> Women have gone into the labor force, but . . . we have not rewired the notion of manhood so that it makes sense to participate at home. Marriage then becomes the shock absorber of those strains.

To cope, husbands and wives need help figuring out fairer ways to distribute responsibility and authority. Meanwhile, the question is not whether these changes are good or bad, but how Americans can adapt wisely and compassionately to a domestic landscape in profound transition.

Idealizing the traditional nuclear family excludes not just the divorced, but also widows and widowers, adopted and foster children, and all those who love and are loved outside of a legal contract. It sanctions job discrimination against working parents who need all the help they can get. It ignores the fact that divorce often brings terrible problems to light (problems that continue to seethe privately and damagingly in many intact families) and that divorce very often is the right decision for both the adults and the children involved. It denies the reality that many divorced parents continue to cooperate successfully in raising healthy children. And it perpetuates the myth that divorced people do not honor or value marriage. It is time for our religious and political leaders to stop looking back at outmoded models and reach ahead to innovative solutions.

Covenant marriage is morally problematic. Who really believes that physical abuse or abandonment must take place to render a marriage intolerable? Certainly no victim of mental cruelty, verbal abuse, confinement, financial or sexual withholding, threats against children, or dozens of other reprehensible behaviors against which covenant marriage will offer no recourse.

Even more troubling is the quality of married life implicitly sanctioned by this legislation. The threat of an ugly, protracted legal battle indeed will immobilize a number of deeply unhappy spouses. But the thought that someone would want to stay married against his or her partner's desires runs contrary to any humane notion of how people who once cared deeply about each other—and may still—should treat each other. What kind of marriage can it be when one spouse is present against his or her will? What kind of life can be lived in rooms full of rage and despair? Wedlock indeed, but no place for children, nor for responsible adults. ✦

Applewhite, A. (1997, October 6–13). "It Won't Lower the Divorce Rate and Will Raise the Human and Economic Cost of Divorce." *Insight on the News,* 13(37), 25, 27. Reprinted with permission to *Insight.* Copyright © (1997) by News World Communication, Inc. All rights reserved.

Issue 21: Questions to Consider

1. One premise of those who advocate covenant marriage laws and divorce reform is that divorces are too easy to get, leading to more people choosing divorce rather than working through problems. What evidence is there for or against this premise?

2. Legislators and public policymakers create laws and public policy to reduce social problems (the *intended consequences* of new laws and policies). All changes in social systems also have *unintended consequences*—unexpected outcomes that may be either good or bad. Sometimes, the *unintended consequences* that occur are worse than the original problems a new policy was designed to resolve. What are some potential unintended consequences of divorce reform?

3. Covenant marriage laws are examples of one approach to divorce reform. What are some other ways that the current divorce processes might be changed? Develop your own proposal for improving the present divorce system in the United States.

4. Some critics of covenant marriage argue that if divorce reformers want to improve the quality and stability of marriages, they should focus on laws related to getting married rather than on divorce laws. Think of ways in which laws and public policies could be developed that would focus on marriages rather than on divorces.

5. How will legislators, policymakers, and the general public know if covenant marriage laws are working? That is, what data (information) should be gathered to use as evidence of the effectiveness of this law?

6. Nock and his colleagues raise a number of arguments in favor of covenant marriage laws. Discuss these arguments—do they make a convincing case that such laws are good ideas? Are there other reasons to implement changes in divorce laws?

7. Applewhite presents a number of reasons why covenant marriage laws are not good ways to reduce the number of divorces. Discuss these reasons—do they make a convincing case that such laws are bad ideas? Are there other reasons *not* to implement changes in divorce laws?

8. Some conservative religious leaders support covenant marriage laws, while others oppose them. Why is the religious community split in their opinions?

9. Divorce reforms, such as covenant marriage laws, focus on marriages. However, some of the problems that reformers want to resolve are not limited to married couples and their families. As you know, many unmarried Americans are having children, and cohabitation in the United States is widespread. What policies could be developed that address these relationships and families? Should it be illegal to live together without being married? Should it be harder to have children? (See also Issue 11 on licensing parents and Issue 4 on cohabitation.) ✦

Issue 22: Introduction

Are Stepparents 'Bad' for Children?

Stepfamilies are among the fastest-growing family forms in North America. Approximately 30 percent of the children in the United States will live with a stepparent sometime before they reach adulthood (Bumpass, Raley, and Sweet, 1995). Based on current rates of cohabitation, divorce, and remarriage, as many as 40 percent of adults will have resided in a remarried or cohabiting stepparent household during their lifetime. Given these numbers, it is not surprising that more and more family researchers are examining stepfamilies (Coleman, Ganong, and Fine, 2000).

Scholars are divided in their views on whether stepfamilies are harmful, beneficial, or neutral environments for children and adults. In these essays, the authors focus on one aspect of living in stepfamilies for children—the risk of being abused or murdered by a stepparent. Although the authors have different views about the level of risk, the differences in perspectives are not limited only to debates over the accuracy or interpretation of the data being used to draw conclusions about stepparent abuse of stepchildren. It is true that Daly and Wilson vigorously dispute interpretations of data and the judgments of other scholars who disagree with them on the prevalence of stepchild abuse, and Mason argues for alternative explanations. However, Mason takes issue primarily with Daly and Wilson's theoretical position, claiming that evolutionary psychology serves as a thinly disguised attack on stepfamilies. To Mason, the evolutionary discourse on stepfamilies is motivated by politics and values, not by science. These essays thus center not only on the issue of stepfamilies, but also on the issue of how much of family life is due to evolutionary, biological "causes" and how much to environmental factors (e.g., poverty, stress, etc.).

As you read these essays, note the evidence for and against the proposition that stepchildren are at greater risk for abuse than other children. Note also the rationale offered to support these positions. What values underlie the positions presented in these two papers? What empirical support is used by the authors to solidify their arguments?

References

Bumpass, L., Raley, R. K., and Sweet, J. (1995). The changing character of stepfamilies: Implications of cohabitation and nonmarital childbearing. *Demography, 32,* 425–436.

Coleman, M., Ganong, L., and Fine, M. (2000). Reinvestigating remarriage: Another decade of progress. *Journal of Marriage and the Family, 62,* 1288–1307. ◆

22a

The Truth About Cinderella

Martin Daly and Margo Wilson

The abused stepchild is one of the stock characters of folklore. Cinderella, of which there are hundreds of variants, is probably the best-known example. In the usual version, the poor girl's mother has died and her father has remarried a dreadful woman who brings two daughters from a prior marriage to her new home. With Cinderella's wicked stepmother reigning in the domestic sphere, the girls are treated far from equitably. The heroine is unjustly relegated to the status of household slave, while her father is chronically off stage and apparently oblivious to her degradation. However, virtue eventually prevails, with a bit of supernatural assistance, and Cindy marries a prince. We needn't belabor the details, since almost everyone knows the story.

And what about stepfathers? Folk wisdom has it that they, too, are a menace. According to a 16th Century French proverb with many parallels elsewhere: *The mother of babes who elects to re-wed has taken their enemy into her bed*. Fairy tales about malevolent stepfathers are scarcer than those about stepmothers, but no cheerier. These maxims and tales cannot be arbitrary or chance inventions. The characters and their conflicts are too consistent.

Stereotypical Stepparents

Scholars have debated whether the uncannily similar Cinderella stories of Asia, Europe, and elsewhere represent numerous separate inventions or the spread of one or a few stories instead. But in a sense it doesn't matter. Cross-cultural Cinderella stories would not persist where their themes had no resonance. Those themes must have something to do with the human condition.

Is it truly the case that stepparents are relatively exploitative, neglectful, and cruel? Ordinary people think so. Several studies of perceptions and expectations of steprelationships have recently been conducted, mainly in the United States, and the results consistently indicate that such relationships are viewed at least somewhat pessimistically and pejoratively. People expect imaginary characters identified as stepparents to be more distant and less supportive of the children than otherwise identical characters identified as the "natural" parents, a presumption of difference that is reduced but not eliminated among raters who have actually lived in stepfamilies. But of course ordinary people also believe in horoscopes and saintly interventions and the immortality of Elvis, so the prevalence of these convictions can hardly be considered evidence for their validity.

In other words, stepparental wickedness *might* be just a popular fiction in spite of it all, and this is a possibility that clearly appeals to many writers. Those social scientists who have demonstrated negative perceptions of steprelationships usually refer to them as *stereotypes* and *myths*, rather than using more neutral descriptive terms such as *beliefs* or *expectations* or *generalizations*. Moreover, insofar as stepfamily life really does entail difficulties, researchers in this area have not hesitated to contend that the stereotypes and myths *cause* the problems.

But before we start arguing about the determinants of stepfamily dysfunction, it would be nice to have some notion of what we're trying to explain. Do children really incur risks of various sorts when one parent dies or departs and the remaining parent takes a new partner? And if so, to what degree: Are we talking about a slight elevation of risk, or something more dramatic? It turns out that the risk differentials are immense.

Children who reside with one genetic parent—the term we prefer to "natural" or "biological" parent, since there is nothing unnatural about substitute parenthood—and one stepparent—the term we shall use to refer to one who lives with an opposite-sex partner and is thereby *in loco parentis* to the partner's resident child or children of prior unions, regardless of marital registration—incur massive increases in the rates of the most severe forms of child maltreatment. Having a stepparent has turned out to be the most powerful risk factor for severe child maltreatment yet discovered.

Behaving Like Animals

One could hypothesize that stepparents will tend to nurture children less solicitously than genetic parents and will be more likely to misuse them. Contemporary theory and research concerning animal social behavior provide a rationale for expecting parents to be discriminative in their care and affection, and more specifically, to discriminate in favor of their own young. These expectations derive from consideration of how evolution works, and since the human animal has evolved by the same Darwinian processes as other animals, there is no apparent reason why the same principles should not apply.

Consider, for example, the social behavior of the African lion, the "king of beasts." A lion pride is a social group that hunts and defends a territory cooperatively. The pride is matrilineal: A typical female grows up and eventually breeds in the group into which she was born, whereas males disperse at maturity. One result is that the adult females in the pride are almost always

close kin: Sisters and cousins, mothers and daughters, aunts and nieces. The two or three or four adult males associated with the pride were born elsewhere, perhaps dispersing from a common natal pride together, perhaps teaming up as roving bachelors. They attained their current status by displacing another coalition of males, probably a coalition diminished in numbers or by age, and the new coalition's reign will last only a few years, at best, before they too are displaced.

After a pregnancy of about 110 days, a lioness nurses her cubs for about 18 months. The hormonal state induced by this nursing inhibits ovulation and hence delays the mother's next pregnancy, as it does in other mammals including Homo sapiens. The result is that almost two years will pass between one litter's birth and the next if the first litter survives until weaning. However, if some mishap befalls the cubs, then their mother's milk will dry up and her next pregnancy will occur sooner. Thus, when a coalition of young males succeeds in taking over a pride, one or more of the resident females is apt to be nursing dependent young, and it may be many months before such nursing females will be ready to mate again. So how do the new males respond to the cubs sired by their predecessors? The grisly answer is that they systematically search them out and kill them.

Killing a deposed predecessor's young is now known to occur in a wide variety of vertebrate and invertebrate animals. The perpetrators are usually males, but not always. Among the tropical marsh-dwelling birds called jacanas, for example, familiar sex roles are reversed. A large territorial female may have as many as four smaller males occupying sub-territories within hers. Each male builds his own nest and incubates four of her eggs in it, and he then guards the precociously mobile young without female assistance. But if one female jacana displaces a rival and thereby acquires a harem of dutiful fathers, she conscientiously goes about breaking the eggs of her predecessor.

As horrifying as such behavior may appear to the human observer, it is clearly not pathological. Indeed, its rationale is so compelling that the interesting questions are why it was not investigated and understood sooner, and why it is not even more widely distributed in the animal kingdom than it is. A mate's parental efforts may be considered a sort of "resource," and it should be no surprise to a Darwinian that when male lions or female jacanas gain control of that resource, they make sure that it is spent promoting their own reproductive success rather than that of their rivals.

Human Stepfamilies

It was in the context of this sociobiological zeitgeist that we were first led to inquire to what extent Cinderella stories might be based in reality. Hey, what about human stepparents? Everyone knows the stereotype: They're hostile and "wicked," right? Well, is there any truth behind this stereotype? Are stepchildren really disproportionately neglected and abused?

Our first attempt to measure the impact of steprelationships on the incidence of child abuse made use of a data archive maintained by the American Humane Association (AHA). This organization had assumed the role of central repository for legally mandated child abuse reports in most of the United States, and had a computer file containing thousands of case reports. For each victimized child, the data included basic facts about victim and (alleged) perpetrator, details of the nature of the abuse, the relationship between the victim and the persons *in loco parentis*, and whether the case had been "validated" in some sort of follow-up investigation beyond the initial report.

To compute the rates of abuse of stepchildren versus others, we needed data on the living arrangements of children in the population at large. This information was elusive; the U.S. Census did not distinguish among genetic, adoptive, and stepparenthood, and all we could find were estimates based on limited surveys. According to our calculations, a child under 3 years of age who lived with one genetic parent and one stepparent in the United States in 1976 was about seven times more likely a validated child abuse case in the AHA records than one who dwelt with two genetic parents [and of] the 279 fatal child-abuse cases, the estimated rates in stepparent plus genetic parent households had grown to approximately 100 *times* greater than in two-genetic parent households.

There could be no doubt that the excess risk in stepfamilies was both genuine and huge. But whether it really had anything to do with steprelationships *per se* was not necessarily resolved. Perhaps living with a stepparent was associated with some other factor of more direct relevance.

One obvious candidate for such a "confounding" factor is poverty. If stepparenthood is especially prevalent among the poor (which seemed plausible since marital stability was known to be correlated with income) and if the poor also have high rates of detected child abuse (which they do), then differentials of the sort we had observed might be expected even if stepparent and genetic parent homes were identically risky within any particular income level. But this hypothesis was rejected, for it turned out that the distribution of family incomes in stepparent homes in the United States was virtually identical to that in two-genetic-parent homes. Low income families were indeed over-represented in the AHA data set, but the association between abuse and poverty was independent of the association between abuse and steprelationship.

We later decided to conduct a better controlled smaller-scale study [in Canada]. Protection agencies provided us with information about all cases severe enough to have warranted filing a report with the provincial child abuse registry, and we surveyed the relevant population-at-large ourselves. About 1 in every 3,000 preschoolers residing with both genetic parents was reported to the Ontario child-abuse registry in 1983. The corresponding rate for those living with a stepparent plus a genetic parent was about 1 in 75, hence 40 times greater. This ratio was smaller than we had found for lethal abuse in the United States, but larger than that for all child abuse, perhaps because the case criterion in our Hamilton study was of intermediate severity.

The odds ratio of abuse risk in [Canadian] stepfamilies versus genetic-parent families was substantial for children of all ages, but it declined steadily from 40 for preschoolers to about 10 for teenaged victims. A similar trend had also been apparent in our U.S. study, and we saw an important implication. Most of those who had written on stepfamily conflicts apparently believed that the problems are primarily created by obstreperous adolescents rejecting their custodial parents' new mates; but this could hardly be correct if the elevation of risk from stepparents was maximal for infants. Our hypothesis that the more basic problem is the adult's resentment of pseudoparental obligation fits the facts much better.

Another consistent result from both studies was that excess risk in stepfamilies spanned the gamut of "abuse" from baby batterings to sexual molestation of older children. A paucity of concern for the welfare of a child in one's care would seem likely to raise the incidence of any sort of misuse. Still another consistent result was that stepparenthood's impact was statistically independent of poverty's additional effects. Family size, which we had not been able to assess in the U.S. study, proved to be another independent risk factor. Maternal youth was yet another.

All in all, although several additional risk factors were identified, stepparenthood held its place as the most important predictor, and its influence was scarcely diminished when the impacts of all the other risk factors were controlled. It warrants repeating that even severe child abuse is vulnerable to detection biases, but that these biases presumably shrink as the case becomes more extreme. We can be reasonably confident that child murders are usually detected and recorded.

So after completing our study of registered child abuse cases in [Canada], we undertook analyses of homicides, using an official government archive containing data on all homicides known to Canadian police departments. Once again, just as we had found in the United States, the over-representation of stepparents as perpetrators of

child murder in Canada proved to be even more extreme than their over-representation as perpetrators of non-lethal child abuse. The residing stepparent was approximately 70 times more likely to kill a child under 2 years of age than was a co-residing genetic parent, and this ratio was still about 15 for teenage victims.

It seemed likely, both from the evidence of these baby batterings and from our evolution-minded hypothesis about stepparental reluctance and resentment, that excess risk from stepparents might be especially severe with regard to angry outbursts. Little children are annoying, after all: They cry and soil themselves and sometimes refuse to be consoled. A caretaker with a heartfelt love for a squalling baby is motivated to tenderly alleviate its distress, but a caretaker who is simply playing the part without emotional commitment—and who might even prefer that the child had never been born—is apt to respond rather differently.

Filicides by genetic parents certainly occur. In absolute numbers, they exceed the cases perpetrated by stepparents, although the latter occur at much higher per capita rates. But the cases are not similar. About 80 percent of homicidal stepfathers are found to have battered, kicked, or bludgeoned their victims to death, whereas the majority of those who killed their genetic offspring did so by less assaultive means. Filicidal genetic parents of both sexes are often deeply depressed, are likely to kill the children while they sleep, and may even construe murder-suicide as a humane act of rescue from a cruel world, whereas homicidal stepparents are seldom suicidal and typically manifest their antipathy to their victims in the relative brutality of their lethal acts. In recent years, diverse strands of evidence from a variety of countries have shown that stepparental mistreatment of children is widespread.

A wealth of evidence, from a number of countries, [showed that] stepparents were massively over-represented as perpetrators of both sexual and physical abuse. Moreover, the data all showed that this excess was most extreme with respect to the most extreme sorts of child abuse, namely fatal batterings, refuting any suggestions that the abundance of stepparents might represent nothing more than biases in the labeling of marginal cases. Still another hypothesis, that the abuse differences might reflect an excess of violent personalities in remarriages, had been disposed of by demonstrations that mistreatment in stepfamilies was usually targeted at the stepchild, while the abuser's own children in the same household were well treated, just like Cinderella and her stepsisters.

Stepmothers as well as stepfathers are greatly over-represented in child maltreatment, and our best estimate is that the hazards are roughly comparable. In the large data archives of the American Humane Association, the odds by which homes with stepmothers exceed chance expectation is actually greater than the corresponding excess of homes with stepfathers, and the same is true of the families of homeless adolescents in New York.

But if stepmotherhood is as risky as stepfatherhood or even if it is riskier—the absolute quantity of violent and lethal abuse perpetrated by the more numerous stepfathers nonetheless exceeds that performed by their female counterparts. So why are wicked stepmothers so much more numerous in folklore than wicked stepfathers? A partial answer may be that stepmothers were not always so rare. Until this century, stepfamilies in Europe and America were more likely to be formed in the aftermath of a death than a divorce, and the mothers of young children incurred substantial mortality in childbirth and from other causes. Widowers often, though by no means always, kept the children and tried to import a replacement for their mother.

Cinderella Denied

In 1991, the excess risk in stepfamilies was called into question by the most prominent family violence researcher in America, Richard Gelles. One prong of his attack was a study co-authored with John Harrop, using data from a 1985 telephone survey. Respondents had been asked a series of questions such as whether they had "slapped" family members (considered one by one) within the last year, had "punched" them, had "used a knife or gun on" them, and so forth, when they "had a disagreement or were angry with them." It will probably come as no surprise that the 117 stepparents who completed the interview were no more likely to profess that they had assaulted the children under their care than were genetic parents. To Gelles and Harrop, this was the first test of the controversial hypothesis of differential abuse that "met the normal standards of social scientific evidence." They acknowledged the existence of evidence that steprelationships entail increased risk, but considered it to be tainted evidence, subject to "the confounds of using official child abuse report data." Their contrary result, on the other hand, was likely to be valid because the data were collected in a study of a "large nationally representative sample" that was "free" of such biases. (Incidentally, more recent evidence from the U.S. *National Survey of Families and Households* indicates that even in interviews, stepparents do report striking the children substantially more often than genetic parents if the question is framed in the more defensible language of "discipline" rather than with reference to "disagreement" and "anger").

In another paper, Gelles (1991) proposed that our analyses of American Humane Association (AHA) data might have been "flawed and biased" by virtue of our having compared abuse rates in stepparent versus genetic parent households without consideration of whether the stepparent was the identified abuser. This argument was supported by reference to an unpublished study in which Malkin and Lamb (1994) had analyzed a set of perpetrator-victim relationship data from the same source, and had, in Gelles' words, "failed to find that stepparents were more likely to abuse their offspring than biological parents." Anyone who troubled to check [Malkin and Lamb's study] against Gelles's citation must have been puzzled; the analysis merely compared the proportionate representation of stepparents in one category of abuse cases versus another, and contained no estimates of abuse rates at the hands of stepparents versus genetic parents at all. Malkin and Lamb did indeed seem to imagine that their analyses constituted some sort of failure to replicate our results, despite the fact that 39 percent of their victims living in "two-parent" homes dwelt with stepparents (the expected value for a population sample with the same age distribution would have been less than 5 percent), and despite the fact that stepparents were disproportionately the identified abusers. They did imply that analysis by perpetrator eliminated some unspecified artifact produced by our household analyses, despite the fact that analyzing by perpetrator actually produces greater stepparent/genetic parent ratios than our analysis. Ironically, the proportion of AHA abuse reports that involved stepparents had increased between 1976 and 1984, and so had the absolute and relative differences in abuse rates between stepparent families and genetic-parent families.

Gelles and Harrop's claim that confessions of child abuse to a telephone interviewer have greater validity than the injuries and deaths of battered babies has been endorsed by the American Medical Association (AMA). A report published in the *Journal of American Medical Association* in 1993 asserted that

> Families with stepparents have been reported to be at higher risk for both physical and sexual abuse of adolescents and younger children. However, several authors have argued that methodological flaws and the possibility of bias in official reports raise questions about these findings. Official reports are analyzed using households as units of comparison and do not identify the relationship of the perpetrator to the child. Therefore, it is unclear if stepparents are more likely to perpetrate abuse than are genetic parents. In addition, agencies may be more likely to classify cases as abusive if a stepparent is present due to assumptions about differences between a child's relationship with a genetic and nongenetic caretaker.

In accordance with this reasoning, the report's recommendations, which included a list of abuse risk factors that family physicians should screen for, do not mention stepparenthood at all.

Can We Help?

As we noted before, there is a substantial body of stepfamily research that has nothing to do with child abuse. But it has everything to do with the fact that conflicts are rampant. Study after study has shown that marital happiness is reduced in stepfamilies, and that stepparent and stepchild alike view their relationships as less loving and as less dependable sources of material and emotional support than genetic parent-child relationships. There is also a wealth of evidence that parental investment is withheld from stepchildren. Many studies have found that the parents in stepfamilies look forward to happier days once the children leave, and that children leave home at a relatively young age.

In a recent study of homeless adolescents aged 15 to 17 in New York, stepchildren were over-represented, and claimed to have been abused in the parental home or "pushed out" or both. In Britain, the *National Child Development Study* demonstrated that both the genetic and the stepparent express low aspirations for children's education in stepparent homes, lower even than the aspirations of single mothers, and that children's own aspirations follow suit. In the United States, it has been found that those stepchildren who do manage to enter college receive less parental help with tuition than those coming from genetic-parent homes with the same family income.

The picture is consistent and unsurprising. The man on the street might have guessed these things. But the researchers who have documented these facts generally try to steer wide of any implication that the stepfamily is an inferior vehicle for rearing children and finding marital bliss. Why? Perhaps the main reason is that the writers feel that stepfamily life is hard enough, without adding to the stigma. Duberman

(1975) set the tone: After reviewing evidence that the relationships between stepchildren and stepparents are "considerably less harmonious than between children and parents in primary homes," she added, "This author feels that many of the problems are generated by the Cinderella myth, and that the myth does not square with the facts" (p. 51). More recently, ostensibly scientific reviews of stepfamily dynamics evaluated the papers not with respect to the adequacy of their methods, but with respect to whether they adequately accentuate the positive by stressing such "stepfamily strengths" as the fact that stepchildren "have two sets of parents to whom they can turn for help" or that stepfamilies provide "valuable experience of complex social forms."

The prevalence of such vacuous pap is largely a result of well-intentioned efforts to help stepfamilies cope. But it is also a product of a naive psychology. Several researchers have proposed that the problem with being a stepparent is that the role is "incompletely institutionalized," and that stepparents therefore don't know what they are supposed to do. Some stepparents do indeed describe their anguish and inconsistent behavior as a sort of perplexity, but this is surely a sign of internal motivational conflicts rather than of the absence of a script. People are ambivalent when they feel that they must do what they don't really want to do.

Most of those professionally concerned with stepfamilies are practitioners first and scientists second. Fearing the insidious effects of "self-fulfilling prophecies," they have understandably made it their business to offer encouragement. Unfortunately, in attempting to counteract stepfamily "myths," they have created a counter-factual mythology of their own, in which relationships can be reordered by fiat and the facts about differential violence can be dismissed. We doubt that this flight from reality is helpful, and not just because distortions like those in the AMA's report are more likely to impede child-protection efforts than to facilitate them. Might it not be helpful if the stepparent's ambivalent and some-

times aggrieved feelings were acknowledged as normal, and if the genetic parent were encouraged to express appreciation for stepparental investment rather than to demand it?

Stepparental Investment in What?

By now, you may be thinking that the puzzle is not why step-relationships are *difficult*, but why they usually work out reasonably well. Why do they even exist? The evidence that we have reviewed can easily be read as implying that natural selection results largely support [the] prediction that replacement mates would not help rear their predecessors' young. However, this is by no means universal.

If a peregrine falcon of either sex loses its mate while young are still dependent, a replacement mate is likely to appear quickly, and it will routinely behave in a fashion that looks just like the efforts of a genetic parent. Many other bird species do likewise. However, there are other birds that ignore the young in the nest, and there are still others that kill them. What explains the differences? In certain contexts—such as in populations in which parents routinely divorce and disperse after nesting failures (as many do), or when re-nesting within the same season is impossible—infanticide will not help the killer re-nest sooner, and is therefore of little or no use; so ignoring or adopting young may then be favored. Where selection appears to favor adopting one's predecessor's young as one's own is where breeding territories or mates are scarce and are retained for a long time once acquired. In these circumstances, stepparental investment is evidently the price paid for future breeding opportunities with the genetic parent.

The human case seems analogous. Stepparents are primarily replacement mates, and only secondarily replacement parents. They assume pseudo-parental obligations with the genetic parent, who is likely to recognize that the new mate's tolerance and investment constitute benefits bestowed on the genetic parent and the child, entitling the stepparent to reciprocal considerations.

Having opted in to this situation, why shouldn't a reasonably well-appreciated stepparent be kindly, and even affectionate? People thrive by reciprocity and by establishing reputations that make them attractive partners, with the result that the desire to be generous and humane, and to be seen as generous and humane, is as human and as functional as more conflictual motives. There is no great conundrum in the fact that people treat their stepchildren for the most part tolerantly, even accepting some of the costs of raising those children. But such investment cannot be taken to imply that stepparents will often come to feel the same sort of love and commitment as is ordinarily felt by genetic parents.

Is the Darwinian worldview uglier in its implications? We think not. We reject the notion that a scientific, materialistic, Darwinian worldview is uglier than its anti-scientific alternatives. Instead, we suggest that more realistic worldviews invite more humane attitudes and practices than fantastic ones, because they entail better models of human nature and hence greater sensitivity to human needs and desires. How to allocate one's efforts after "remarriage" is a challenging problem that confronted hundreds of the ancestors of every person now living. No doubt indulgence towards a mate's children often had social uses. But it must rarely have been the case that a stepchild's welfare was as valuable to one's expected fitness as one's own child's welfare. A hypothetical psyche that treated stepchildren and genetic children exactly alike would be a psyche vulnerable to exploitation, and would be evolutionarily unstable in competition with more discriminating alternatives. There is, then, a strong theoretical rationale for expecting that the evolved human psyche contains safeguards against allowing a mere stepchild, however appealing, easy access to that special mental category occupied by genetic children, the appropriate objects for the most nearly selfless love we know. To the best of our knowledge, the research findings about stepfamily life are fully consistent with this Darwinian analysis.

References

Duberman, L. (1975). *The reconstituted family: A study of remarried couples and their children.* Chicago: Nelson-Hall.

Gelles, R. J., and Harrop, J. W. (1991). The risk of abusive violence among children with nongenetic caretakers. *Family Relations, 40,* 78–83.

Malkin, C.M., and Lamb, M.E. (1994). Child maltreatment: A test of sociobiological theory. *Journal of Comparative Family Studies, 25,* 121–133. ✦

Daly, M., and Wilson, M. (1999). *Darwinism Today: The Truth About Cinderella.* Published by Wiedenfeld & Nicolson. Reprinted with permission.

22b

Was Cinderella Right? The New Social Darwinism Targets Stepparents

Mary Ann Mason

Stepparents live in a twilight zone of acceptance. They receive little public acknowledgement and an awkward place at family gatherings. The law considers them legal strangers to the children they parent; stepparents can neither sign a field trip permission slip nor authorize teeth cleaning. And our popular culture offers few positive models for stepparent behavior. The old fairy tales depicting wicked stepmothers, like Cinderella's greedy stepmother, have not been replaced by modern myths of kind, loving stepparents. A recent film re-make of *Cinderella* updates the wicked stepmother as a cool, manipulative career woman, who, as always, plots to advance the fortunes of her vicious daughters at the expense of beautiful, virtuous Cinderella.

What is the nature of this reluctance to acknowledge an adult who increasingly shoulders a large share of American child-raising? Is it based on myth, on scientific fact, or half-forgotten historical realities? The trendy new wave of evolutionary psychology takes a decisive stand. Some of these social scientists elevate the negative cultural stereotypes of stepparents from historical myth to scientific findings. They find that stepparents are genetically programmed to kill or abuse their stepchildren.

Martin Daly and Margo Wilson argue that having a stepparent is the most powerful risk factor for severe child maltreatment yet discovered. They purport to represent the latest scientific findings on evolutionary theory applied to human behavior. According to this theory, the human male has evolved, through natural selection, a propensity to eliminate the non-related child of his mate so that his own children, who carry his genes, can replace them. By eliminate, the authors mean *murder*. Those stepfathers who are restrained from murder have a genetic propensity to inflict abuse on their unwanted wards.

Daly and Wilson present several types of evidence to support their bold claim. First, they briefly review the ubiquitous and seemingly timeless folk and fairy tales that depict a stepparent as wicked, evil, and sometimes murderous. These fairy tales, they assert, indicate that stepparents have always acted in a violent fashion, and the public had good reason to fear them. Then, relying on animal behaviorists, the psychologists present examples from the non-human world, most notably, male lions, who routinely kill the offspring of their new mates when they take over the pride. And finally, they offer their own studies on child abuse and infanticide by "stepfathers" in both the U.S. and Canada. It is from these studies that the authors claim that a child is "100 times more likely to be abused or killed by a stepparent than by a genetic parent." The authors conclude that

> this threat, although a recurring theme of folk-tales worldwide, has been scan-

dalously neglected by policy makers and opinion formers.

An Internet search of American newspapers confirmed this newly popular Darwinian interpretation of stepparents. Journalists, greatly enthusiastic about the new wave of evolutionary psychology, are rapidly picking up on this view of stepparents programmed to destroy the children of their mates. Jane Brody, the health columnist for the *New York Times*, begins her recent column thus:

> A woman's live-in boyfriend murders her child fathered by another man. A woman neglects her young stepsister and punishes her so viciously that she dies. A stepfather sexually abuses his wife's daughter by a former husband. As these examples drawn from news articles over the last year demonstrate, the Cinderella story is hardly a fairy tale. Researchers are finding that the incidence of violence and abuse is vastly greater in stepfamilies than in traditional families in which the children are biologically related to both parents and to one another.

Brody also observes that this new interpretation underrated traditional sociological explanation for abuse and conflict in stepfamilies that focus on economic stress, low socioeconomic status, and emotional instability. Evolutionary scientists, she explains, believe that these are only the proximate causes, that the underlying trigger are the "inherently selfish genes, which are biologically driven to perpetuate themselves."

This is not the first time that Darwin has been invoked to explain the negative characteristics of certain targeted groups. There appears to be an historical amnesia regarding the enormous popularity and the political clout evoked by late 19th century Social Darwinism, a theory most famously invoked by Darwin's contemporary, the influential social philosopher Herbert Spencer. Spencer claimed that the poor were poor because they were unfit for survival. And it was Spencer, not Darwin, who coined the phrase, "survival of the fittest." Not surprisingly, in his world-view the fittest were Victorian gentlemen. The conservative take on this pronouncement was to discourage aid to the poor on the grounds that it would interfere with natural selection.

Spencer also picked out women for evolutionary consideration. He believed that the demanding business of reproduction had retarded the evolution of women in their intellectual and emotional capacities. Although a few had the ability to perform abstract reasoning, this level of conceptualization was not a common feature of the sex. Higher education, therefore, would be wasted on women.

Nineteenth and then early 20th century evolutionary thinking spread quickly beyond the poor and women. Theories of biological racial inferiority targeting Jews, Slavs, Blacks, and others, bloomed, culminating most infamously in the Nazi regime. Hitler's social policy of exterminating inferior races to advance the survival of the superior Nordic race was firmly erected on a distorted view of evolutionary theory.

The horrors of the Nazi regime knocked the socks off evolutionary philosophy. Clearly, that line of thinking had taken the world to a place it did not want to return to. The kinder, gentler view of human beings as shaped by their culture, not their biology, was adopted and has predominated during most of the second half of the 20th century. In this optimistic framework, we are what our social environment determines we are, and we are capable of changing that environment. Even gender differences relating to sexual drive and parenting, the essence of species survival, were placed on the list of social constructions.

Meanwhile, in the 1950s, a couple of young scientists in England discovered the biological building block of life, DNA. The scientific revolution that discovery inspired ultimately revived an interest in the biological basis of behavior. After decades of research, it became possible to isolate genes, the material that presumably transmits human blueprints from generation to generation. Some scientists theorized that genes not only carry a map for replicating the prominent family nose, they provide important information on how to successfully reproduce in the mating and parenting game.

Admittedly, the new wave of evolutionary theorists is far more careful in their methodology and circumspect in their pronouncements than some of their predecessors. They almost never mention race and for the most part they have not yet chosen to tread into the treacherous waters of social policy. But through the wide dissemination of their ideas and books to mass audiences, ideas that previously had reached a fairly small circle of researchers are moving rapidly into the mainstream. The best-seller list is crowded with books with titles like: *The Selfish Gene; Born That Way: Genes, Behavior and Personality*, and the more daring, *Taboo: Why Black Athletes Dominate Sports and Why We Are Afraid to Talk About It.*

"Selfish genes" are at the heart of the new wave of evolutionary theory. Elaborated from Darwin's ground-breaking observations on natural selection, the new version maintains that humans, like all other animals, are programmed by their genes (in some manner not yet discovered), to maximize the success of their offspring. If they have no offspring, or if their offspring die before reproducing, their genes will not prevail and they are deemed failures in the grand evolutionary scheme. A second major pillar of modern evolutionary psychology is that most of human history, where presumably our basic human behaviors were laid down in the genes, occurred in hunter-gatherer cultures, which changed little over countless millennia. Therefore, many behaviors that do not seem adaptive in today's culture, which is a mere eye blink in human history, were formed to deal with the hunter-gatherer environment.

This theory is the new magnifying glass through which many social scientists now examine the minutiae of everyday human reproductive behavior, from the obvious target of what constitutes sexual attractiveness in women (big eyes, child-like features that suggest youth and, therefore, fertility) to why men rape (adaptive behavior to maximize fertility). After reproduction has been achieved, parenting takes over. All elaborate reproductive strategies fail if the offspring

do not survive. The differences between mothers and fathers as parents, recently dismissed as social constructions, have now returned as evolutionary science. Mothers and fathers in the larger animal world, we are told, do not always share the same interest in promoting their genes. Mothers will select certain offspring as worth raising and destroy others, while fathers will maximize their chances by spreading their genes among many females. Evidence of this behavior is sought in the human reproductive game as well.

Stepparents are only part of the large scheme of reproduction and parenting, but so far, they have been singled out for the greatest amount of negative attention. As with any "scientific" finding which has potential social impact, claims regarding stepparents deserve close critical attention. Is there truth in what evolutionary psychologists say about the dangerous propensities of stepparents? What is proven and what is not? Did Cinderella have it right?

Three types of evidence are offered by Daly and Wilson: Research on child murder and abuse; animal behavior studies; and the persistent negative images portrayed in fairy tales. Their strongest scientific claim is based on police records and national abuse statistics gathered in the 1970s. This line of investigation is unusual in modern evolutionary research since it focuses on contemporary, not hunter-gatherer culture. Most evolutionary scientists believe that modern behavior regarding reproductive activities has been seriously distorted by a culture that no longer represents the conditions of the Pleistocene age when our genetic propensities were firmly established. They prefer to focus on animal behavior or isolated "primitive tribes" where behavior has presumably not been tainted by modern conditions.

Daly and Wilson offer two sets of studies that identify stepparent abusers (almost always the stepfather): Those that focus on child murder and those that focus on child abuse. They are personally responsible for almost all of the research on infanticide and child murder, a relatively rare phenomenon in western industrialized countries, where penalties are severe. Their studies include police records in Detroit in the 1970s and in Canada from 1974–1983. According to their figures, 141 Canadian children between the ages of 1 and 4 were killed by parents, or parent figures, during the years studied. They claim 37 (25.5 percent) of those children were the victims of their stepfather (as they define stepfather).

This figure does not look good for stepfathers, but who is being called stepfather? The child murder studies are taken from police reports, where the identity of perpetrators is not clear. A male suspect who is not the father may be called stepfather, boyfriend, or more often simply listed as having the same residence as the mother. Since crime records are not likely to tell us if the suspect is married to the mother, or if the suspect has any parental relation at all to the child, it may be a stretch to call this person a stepparent. Mom's boyfriend does not a stepparent make. Nor does the fact that the man shares the same residence with mom. Men who have transitory relationships with mothers and have little real emotional involvement with her children are frequently categorized with remarried stepfathers in committed family relationships, even though remarried stepfathers have often made a serious and thoughtful commitment to the family which they are marrying into and are very different than the transitory man. The Oxford American Dictionary defines stepfather as "the husband of one's parent, by a later marriage." Yet the Daly and Wilson study simply requires coresidence to list the person as a stepfather.

And who are the parent figures who killed the great majority of the children? Overall, Daly and Wilson report that natural fathers kill children more often than stepfathers, and, in cases of infanticide, single mothers are the overwhelming culprits. They report that of 141 infant homicides in Canada, the natural mother was the accused killer in 88 cases. These accused mothers are likely to be teenagers and to be unmarried. The evolutionary explanation for this, they claim, is that older mothers would have fewer reproductive possibilities, and are therefore less likely to kill chil-

dren that will be difficult to raise on their own. Daly and Wilson do not deal at all with the touchy issue of abortion, which no matter how one views it, is always the choice of the mother and does affect the numbers of the reproductive game.

Humans have routinely practiced infanticide and continue to do so for reasons unrelated to stepfathers; usually to preserve scarce economic resources for other children. Among humans it is almost always the mother that makes that decision. According to primatologist Sara Hrdy, human mothers, unlike primate mothers, assess the qualities of their newborns before they decide to invest in raising them, while primates will raise every baby, no matter how frail. Until very recent history in the western world, a mother might assess the viability of a child by placing the infant in a situation that would kill it, if it were weak. Aristotle recommended that mothers employ "chilling," icy cold baths that would kill the most fragile infants. In Europe, sickly or persistently whiny babies were looked upon as "changelings," or "fairy children," imposters left by goblins. These babies would be left in the forest overnight, a version of "chilling." If they survived they were considered "cured" and brought home again.

But mothers in countries like Canada and the United States today do not receive cultural permission or guidance to commit infanticide. They will be punished severely, as will fathers or stepfathers who commit these acts. The killing of children, therefore, is highly maladaptive to bearing or caring for other children. This suggests that crime records are more likely to identify desperate aberrant behavior by poorly functioning adults than they are normative hunter-gatherer behavior. The traditional sociocultural explanations of child abuse that point to economic stress and emotional instability should not be abandoned by the rush to embrace the new social Darwinism.

This is also the message delivered by those who study severe child abuse. While infanticide is rare in modern western countries, physical abuse of children is not. There are many studies dealing with physical abuse of children; some of these, including several by Daly and Wilson, find a higher rate of child abuse by stepparents than by biological parents. But there are also studies that do not find a higher rate of physical abuse by stepparents. The Second National Family Violence Survey reported in 1991 by one of America's most pre-eminent family violence researchers, Richard Gelles, finds "no significant differences between genetic and nongenetic parents in the rates of severe and very severe violence towards children."

The Second National Family Violence Survey differs from most others because it questions the general population and does not rely only on police records and child abuse reports. Gelles suggests that studies that investigate only that part of the population which were reported to the police or to child protection may not reflect the whole society but just the more violent segment. Men who are violent, especially those with a history of violence, are far less likely to be married and to be the biological parent of all the children in the household. As psychologist Charles Lewis observes, "you bring a man who may have a weak or disturbed personality into a family like this and you have a lethal cocktail."

The Second National Violence Survey found that "the youngest, poorest, most socially isolated and economically frustrated caretakers are the most likely to act violently toward their children." This is the finding that the American Medical Association chose to adopt at its Annual Meeting in 1992.

What does this conflicting research mean? At a minimum, it is by no means firmly established by scientific findings that stepparents are "the most powerful risk factor for severe child maltreatment." This honor probably remains with mom. It also suggests that the legions of stepfathers who dutifully parent the children to whom they are not genetically attached should not be tarred with the same brush as violent men who share mom's bed, or at least mom's address, and the demographics of poverty and instability.

What about animal research? Darwin firmly placed human beings in the animal world and some of the strongest proponents of human evolutionary psychology have grounded their theories in animal behavior. Stephen T. Emlen, an evolutionary biologist at Cornell University, maintains that a dearth of shared genes is the unconscious force that underlies many of the difficulties encountered in stepfamilies. Emlen claims that this is as true of people as it is of lower animals that live in family groups, including wolves, mongooses, rodents, scrub jays, bee-eaters, wrens, ants, bees, wasps, and termites.

Still, there are many examples of caring stepparents among animals. If a peregrine falcon of either sex loses a mate a replacement soon fills the nest and acts in a genuine parental fashion toward chicks not his or her own. Similarly, there are examples of gorillas taking a kindly interest in offspring clearly not their own offspring.

Primates are the most interesting research subjects because they share human genes and the human problem of long dependent offspring. Some primates are among the animals that kill the offspring of other males. The langur monkey, for instance, when he invades new territory, stalks his infant prey. The male prowls for several hours emitting a strange vocalization, a "cackle bark." Then he kills the infants by biting their heads off with his dagger-like canine teeth. The females express no apparent anger. They readily mate with the male who just murdered their babies.

But most male primate behavior regarding infants who are not their own does not fit into a neat pattern which illuminates human behavior. Consider the two species closest to our own, chimpanzees and bonobos; both of which carry 98 percent of the same DNA as humans. Fatherhood is by no means clearly established among the chimpanzees. The females mate with what would be considered defiant promiscuity by human standards. Jane Goodall observed one female copulate with seven males 84 times in eight days. In the wild, baby chimps are born to mothers who, on average, have mated more than 100 times with a dozen or more different males. How does a male ensure the transmission of his genes in this highly competitive mating environment? Apparently, not by attempting to gain exclusive access by beating out the competition, but rather by producing more sperm than other males. Male chimpanzees have evolved large testicles, rendering them capable of ejaculating high sperm counts. Those with the highest sperm count, and presumably the largest testicles, have an evolutionary advantage.

Infant chimpanzees are raised in a multi-male, multi-female group where the males participate not at all in child-raising. For the most part they ignore the offspring. And the females do not depend on the males for food. Mothers do it all. It is believed that if a female strays into the territory of another group her infant may be killed by males in the other group. But a chimp mother has most to fear from other mothers in her own group. Chimp expert Jane Goodall observed over a period of years a pattern of infant murder by other "ambitious" mothers who, she speculated, wanted to assure their own maternal success by lessening the competition for their own offspring.

On the other hand, bonobo males, equally our genetic match, do not engage in infanticide. The females also have many mates, but they do not live in groups with males, they live largely with other females. Females seek out males for mating purposes, and there is a good deal of that. The bonobos are as noteworthy for their nearly constant sexual activity as they are for the lack of hostility and violence among them.

It is tempting to pick up discrete parenting behaviors among animals to prove a particular theory of human behavior, but the differences among primates and between humans and those primate species that are biologically very similar to humans are astounding. For instance, while human mothers routinely make judgments on whether a child is worthy of allowing to survive, mother monkeys and primates almost never abandon their infants, no matter how imperfect. Blind babies and those suffering from crippling diseases are tenderly cared for by their mothers. On the other hand,

male primates rarely ever engage in child rearing, while human fathers, to greater and lesser degrees, usually do.

Perhaps primatologist Sara Hrdy provides the most hopeful observations regarding fatherhood in both primates and humans. She notes that male primates, who normally ignore youngsters, may exhibit nurturing behavior if the circumstances are conducive. Darwin called it the "latent instincts" for nurturing that lurk "even in the male brain." Hrdy describes an event in a zoo where a male orangutan rescued an infant, not his own, who was in grave danger. Male orangutans are normally solitary,

> Shaggy hundred-kilo titans crash through the jungle oblivious to mothers and infants, passing females by like ships in the night meeting with them only to mate.

Almost all male primates, she observes, can develop a nurturing style and all youngsters will respond to that style. Human males, she believes, have the same capacity. Among humans, she cites the case of George Eliot's Silas Marner, the old bachelor who responded to the two-year-old orphan girl who found her way to his door in a snowstorm. The attachment grew as the child responded to Marner's ministrations. A kindly neighbor who offered to help was surprised by the bond the little girl already felt toward Marner. "See there, she's fondest of you. She wants to go to your lap, I'll be bound. Go then: Take her Master Marner."

If fatherhood is largely a learned behavior, developed as the need arises, it presumably can be learned by stepfathers or father substitutes, like Silas Marner, as well as by natural fathers. This fits with stepparent research that consistently emphasizes that parental involvement and attachment normally take a period of time to develop to their full extent. Our own studies and others have found that the more involved in the everyday activities a stepparent is, the more attached he or she will become to the child. Studies of fatherhood in general have consistently found this relationship. Across cultures, according to Hrdy, the amount of time men spend caring for kids is the best predictor of how connected they feel toward them.

Finally, the fairy tales. The evolutionary psychologists' point of view, expressed by Daly and Wilson, is that humans have always been aware of the danger of stepparents, which is why they have been depicted as evil and abusive in fairy tales. But do these tales really reflect the evolutionary march of the "selfish gene"? As a starter, virtually all the fairy tales in western culture, and similar tales identified in Asia, focus on stepmothers, not stepfathers. Yet it is the male "stepparent" in both the animal and human world who is accused of infanticide and abuse. It is the male co-habitor that appears in police reports, not the female cohabitor. And in the animal world there is no concept of stepmother since fathers rarely raise their children following the death of the mother.

One answer to the wicked stepmother puzzle is that fairy tales are not about selfish genes, they are about money and class. In this game males held all the cards and in order to win, women did not always play fair. Consider Cinderella. We all know that her own mother was good, her stepmother and stepsisters wicked, and that she was rescued by Prince Charming. This fairy tale, like most, reflects the basic collective fears and hopes of a shared culture over centuries and it presents a tale of something gone wrong in that culture's moral universe. We think of Cinderella as a tale of bad stepfamily relationships and of love prevailing over all, but it is also about family wealth and its wrongful distribution.

In this tale, Cinderella, following the death of her father, is robbed of her wealth and position and demoted several classes to the rank of servant girl, while her stepsisters, who are her father's stepdaughters, take what should be hers. Her dead father is not able to rectify this wrong, nor do the courts. It takes Prince Charming to set it right. One might note that Cinderella did not marry up from a servant girl into the highest class, Prince Charming restored her

to her proper class. Cinderella, in turn, understanding the nature of proper behavior in the moral universe, did not turn her back on her stepfamily, she arranged for them to live with her in the palace.

Money may not be at the root of all evil, but it plays a dominant role in family dramas. Anxiety about the preservation of family wealth is also reflected in western inheritance laws, which are recent in human history; about as recent as popular fairy tales. It is at least partly because of inheritance concerns that stepparents are given little legal recognition in western cultures. Although we do not know for sure, it is doubtful that hunter-gatherer cultures possessed a mode of preserving wealth over generations.

From a Darwinian perspective the Cinderella tale is a bust. Not only does Cinderella not kill her stepsisters, ensuring that they will not reproduce; her victory in regaining her father's wealth and status will not improve her reproductive chances over the long run. As critics of Herbert Spencer and the "survival of the fittest" school have pointed out, inherited family wealth does not lead to greater reproductive success in the long run. Overall, that honor remains with the poorer classes.

At the end of the day, does evolutionary science shed light on stepparent behavior? At the least, the investigations of animal behaviorists have emphasized the importance of future planning to the behavior of the human species, which sets them apart from all other animals. Human mothers make far-sighted choices about which children are important enough to warrant an investment of their time and energy, and which to let die, as primate mothers do not. Human fathers devise elaborate rules for the passage of resources to their children after they are dead, in a manner not even dimly perceived by their closest animal relatives. And human fathers and father figures, to a greater or lesser degree, participate in parenting as no primates do.

We can only guess what humans acted like in hunter-gatherer days, before the layer on layer of culture that we call home provided very different circumstances. Modern police records are not artifacts from the Pleistocene age. Since adults died at every age, there were probably rematings, if not remarriage. One can only speculate, but it seems unlikely that human mothers who have decided to invest in a child are likely to consider new males that murder or abuse their offspring as desirable mates. Far more attractive from a mother's point of view would be a male with resources who, at the very least, was not a threat to her offspring.

But at the end of the day it is only guesswork. There is no magic genetic map that clearly charts this behavioral territory, and recent history has taught us that extending evolutionary theory to contemporary human behavior can be an exciting, but dangerous, game.

Mason, M. A. (2000). *Was Cinderella Right? Evolutionary Psychology Targets Stepparents*. Unpublished manuscript. Reprinted by permission of M. A. Mason, University of California, Berkeley.

Issue 22: Questions to Consider

1. Do you agree with Daly and Wilson that because fairy tales about abused stepchildren are widespread throughout history and different cultures, they reflect the truth? Can you think of any examples of popular folk or fairy tales that do not reflect "the human condition" as Wilson and Daly label it?

2. Rutgers University sociologist David Popenoe has warned that people with children from previous relationships should not remarry because they are putting their children at risk for abuse. What would you tell a friend who had children and was considering remarriage?

3. Would Daly and Wilson's comments that a stepparent's investment in and commitment to stepchildren cannot be expected to be the same sort of love and commitment as is ordinarily felt by genetic parents apply to adoptive parents (who are also not biologically related to their children) as well?

4. Is parenting a behavior that must be learned (or taught), or is it an evolutionary instinct? Support your position with theoretical or empirical evidence.

5. Mason raises the specter of evolutionary theory (or any social or behavioral theory) being used to discriminate against a targeted group (in this case, stepparents). For what other groups of individuals, relationships, or families have social and behavioral theories been used to support discrimination against them? ◆

Issue 23: Introduction

Cultural Values and Caregiving

There are more people living into their seventh, eighth, and ninth decades than ever before. Although this longevity has been accompanied by improved health throughout the life course, eventually many older adults become frail and dependent on others. Consequently, families are increasingly facing the dilemma of how to help frail older family members. One of the many factors that influence what families do in such situations is ethnicity; cultural values held by ethnic groups affect how members of those groups think and behave. A family's ethnic background affects their beliefs about the importance of family, kinship obligations, and respect for elders. In addition, all ethnic groups have cultural traditions and norms that affect how family members relate to each other.

In the following essay, Radina reviews research on how the values and attitudes of four pan-ethnic groups (i.e., European Americans, African Americans, Asian Americans, and Latinos) may affect the caregiving to older kin. As you read, note differences and similarities between these ethnic groups. Think about your beliefs regarding caring for dependent older adults—which set of beliefs and behaviors fits best with yours? ✦

23a

Cultural Values and Caregiving

M. Elise Radina

Answer the following questions:

1. Think about your family. Which of the following best represents your definition of family?

a. My mother, father, siblings, grandparents, aunts/uncles, and cousins.

b. My mother, father, siblings, grandparents, aunts/uncles, cousins, in-laws, great-aunts/uncles, and second and third cousins.

c. My mother, father, and siblings.

d. My mother, father, siblings, grandparents, aunts/uncles, cousins, and important friends.

2. Think for a minute about the fact that your parents and grandparents are getting older. Which of the following best represents how you feel about them growing old?

a. "Old people give me the creeps. They are all sick and helpless."

b. "Growing old is a sign of maturity and an affirmation of life. As my parents and grandparents grow older, my respect for them grows."

c. "Older family members are an important source of wisdom and guidance for my generation. Therefore, honoring my parents and grandparents in old age is important to me."

d. "As people get older their behavior changes. That is ok because these changes are normal."

3. What if your parents and grandparents start having trouble taking care of their daily needs such as cooking, cleaning, bathing, or toileting? Which of the following best represents how you would feel about having to take care of them?

a. "Taking care of my parents and grandparents would mean that I would have to put aside some of my own goals."

b. "Taking care of my parents and grandparents would be a privilege and an honor."

c. "Taking care of my parents and grandparents would be my way of showing my respect for them."

d. "Taking care of my parents and grandparents would mean that I am fulfilling an important family role."

4. Think about the people in your family or community who are most likely to help your parents and grandparents take care of themselves when they are elderly. Which of the following best represents who these people would be?

a. "Most likely they would take care of each other. If that wasn't working, I am sure my siblings or I would offer to help out."

b. "My siblings and I would do it with the help of other family members."

c. "Since I am the oldest child, I have a responsibility to ensure that my parents are cared for. My spouse and I would take care of them in their old age."

d. "I think that they would take care of each other for the most part. Of course, my siblings and I would help too. Friends from the neighborhood and church would probably stop by to check on them a lot, too."

Your responses to these questions likely reflect the complex interrelationships of your personal, family, and cultural values. Personal values are often products of the cultural value systems in which individuals and their families live. In turn, these personal and cultural values influence the ways in which family members provide care to older members.

Much of what is known about the caregiving of aging family members is based on research done with European Americans, whose cultural value systems have strongly influenced the beliefs and practices of mainstream U.S. society. However, the U.S. is becoming increasingly multi-cultural, so attention should be paid to the values of all ethnic groups. In this paper, I focus on how the values of four pan-ethnic groups—European American, Hispanic/Latino, Asian American, and African American—affect how families provide care to older family members.

These four groups are considered pan-ethnic, in that they include many different ethnic communities that share some common characteristic such as a language or region of geographic origin. For example, Hispanic/Latinos may be from Cuba, Mex-ico, Central America, etc. Asian Americans represent Korea, Japan, and China, among others. Therefore, keep in mind that the comparisons made here are generalizations; the information may not apply to every member of these groups, nor to every subgroup. Indeed, we often find greater variability within groups than we find between the four groups.

How Is the Family Defined?

The definition of *family*, and what it means to be a family member, varies somewhat between pan-ethnic groups. Table 23a-1 compares the four groups in terms of how they define family and their values related to family life.

European American families tend to limit the definition of family to closely related nuclear and extended family members (e.g., grandparents). Although most Americans of European descent have relationships with cousins, aunts, uncles, and family members related by marriage, kinship obligations are generally limited to nuclear family members (i.e., parents, sibs, spouses, children), and possibly, to grandparents. Alone among these four pan-ethnic groups, European American families have what is called an *individualistic orientation*. This means they value independence, personal space and achievement, and the pursuit of individual interests. Although families may be very important to European Americans, often the needs of families take lower prior-

---

Table 23a-1
What Does It Mean to Be a Family?

	Who Is Family?	Values	Orientation
European American	Nuclear/Close extended	Independence/Autonomy	Individualist
Hispanic/Latino	Extended family	Familismo	Collectivist
African American	Extended family/ Fictive kin	Community	Collectivist/Community
Asian American	Emphasis on parent-child relationship	Filial piety	Collectivist

ity than the needs of individual family members.

In contrast, Latinos and African Americans define family more broadly, and they apply a different set of standards to understanding family responsibilities. Hispanics/Latinos' conceptualization of family includes extended kin networks that incorporates distant relatives. The value of *familismo* is the belief that family bonds should be strong and that one should be loyal to one's family. African Americans also place a high value on loyalty to broadly defined family ties. In fact, African Americans often consider non-related persons to be members of their families as well as individuals that are related to them genetically and legally. For example, their extended family may include as *fictive kin* friends and church members who pool their resources and provide mutual support for each other.

Asian Americans consider parent-child relationships to be more important than marital relationships. *Filial piety* governs the values of many Asian Americans. Filial piety means that elders are revered, and there is a moral duty to obey, honor, and assist parents. The relationships between fathers and sons are seen as particularly important.

Latinos, African Americans, and Asian Americans have *collectivistic orientations*. This means that the needs of the group take priority over the needs of individual family members, togetherness is emphasized, and there is a sense of responsibility to the family. Pan-ethnic groups with collectivist orientations think about caregiving responsibilities differently than families with individualist orientations.

What Is It Like to Be a Caregiver?

Table 23a-2 presents a comparison of pan-ethnic groups' views regarding providing care and aging. Caregiving has different meanings for different ethnic groups. Consequently, the degree to which caregiving is seen as a burden varies as well. High levels of caregiver burden often indicate high levels of perceived stress associated with caregiving, and low levels of caregiver burden indicate low levels of stress.

Many European Americans view caregiving as a loss of independence for both generations. Younger family members who provide caregiving assistance lose independence because they must reduce their social activities, their free time is limited, and their needs must have lower priority than the needs of the older person. Older European Americans prefer to remain independent and responsible for themselves as long as possible, so they may not willingly accept care from children, and may not appreciate it. Some European American elders react to

Table 23a-2

Views of Caregiving/Aging and Experiences of Caregiver Burden

	View of Caregiving/Care Receipt	View of Aging	Caregiving a Burden?
European American	Loss of independence	Illness, disability	Yes, often at high levels
Hispanic/Latino	Natural extension of commitment to family, privilege, honor	Affirmation of life	Usually at low levels
Asian American	Honor, respect for elders, moral duty	Wisdom	Yes, often at high levels
African American	Fulfilling important family role	Illness, disability; normalization of behavioral changes with aging	Usually at low levels

their unwanted state of dependency with anger or resentment towards their children, a reaction that makes family interactions difficult and emotionally painful for everyone. For example, consider the following:

> Thelma is an 83-year-old widow with a feisty personality. She lives alone in the home she and her husband purchased together shortly after their marriage some 50 years ago. Since the death of her husband about 10 years ago, Thelma has enjoyed the independence of living alone and has created an extensive rose garden in her yard. In recent years, Thelma has had increased difficulty with climbing stairs, cleaning, and bathing. Because none of her three children is willing to take her in, they have decided that it is in her best interests to move to a retirement community that they have picked out for her. When Thelma hears of this she is angry and refuses to leave her house. She argues that if she has to live with other people who can help her, then she wants to stay in her house and have one of her children move in with her. None of the children are willing to make this compromise. The result is several months of arguing between the two generations, angry, hurt feelings, and a stalemate.

In contrast, Hispanic/Latinos, African Americans, and Asian Americans share the view that caregiving is an expected family obligation. For example, Hispanics/Latinos perceive taking care of aging family members as a natural extension of a commitment to family as well as a privilege and an honor, and elderly parents expect their adult children to care for them.

> When Marta's 68-year-old mother grew seriously ill, there was no question in her mind about what to do. She says, 'I told mom that if it comes down to it, I will quit my job. Mom has taken care of us all of her life, and now it is our turn to take care of her. I just wouldn't feel right handling it any other way. Of course, we will take care of her. She knows we will do it and doesn't need to worry.' Marta enlisted the help of her husband and children as well as the family of a nearby sibling. Together they check on her frequently, and the grandchildren take

turns spending the night with her during school vacations.

Similarly, African Americans have deep devotion and respect for elders. Caregiving is considered rewarding because it fulfills an important role within the family. For care recipients, being taken care of by other family members is expected.

> Myia's grandmother died about two years ago. Since then Myia and her father have been taking care of her grandfather. Myia is pleased to be helping her father with some of the daily tasks that her grandfather needs to have done. Her grandfather makes her feel special about helping him and he shows deep gratitude for her help. Myia knows that she is making an important contribution to the family and fulfilling her family responsibilities. She is proud that she is able to do something so important for her grandfather and her family.

For Asian Americans, filial piety dictates reverence of elders: Children of any age are to respect and obey their elders. Thus, caregiving of elderly parents is viewed as a moral duty, and Asian American elders expect to be taken care of by their children.

> Lee is the oldest son in his family. He has just married and he and his wife expect to purchase a house. This house will include a room for Lee's parents. Lee and his wife know that being able to have Lee's parents move in with them when they need care is important to fulfilling their moral duty to Lee's parents. Preparing to care for his parents well before they need it is Lee's way of showing respect. He is demonstrating that he is willing to assume the obligations of the oldest son. For Lee, doing what is expected of him means bringing honor to his parents.

Views of Aging

European Americans often view aging as a negative experience, much like an illness or disability. Therefore, they avoid accepting care as long as possible. Seeing their parents age and become frail may be an anxiety-producing experience for European American children because it reminds them of their own mortality. European Americans annually spend billions of dollars on anti-aging products, cosmetic surgery, and other efforts designed to keep the signs of aging at bay.

Hispanics/Latinos and Asian Americans, on the other hand, see aging as a mostly positive experience. Hispanics/Latinos view aging as an affirmation of life more so than an illness. Similarly, Asian Americans' devotion to elders comes from the view that older family members are a source of wisdom and spiritual guidance.

African Americans have multiple views of aging. Some see aging as an illness subject to diagnosis and treatment by professionals. However, they also tend to accept the cognitive and behavioral problems that aging family members may experience as an integral part of the aging process. Therefore, problems of aging, such as forgetfulness or senility that some people may view as embarrassing are considered acceptable behaviors among African Americans.

Caregiving as Stressful

How do these various views of caregiving and aging relate to the experiences of caregivers in the four groups? Taking care of another person, and helping them meet their daily needs for eating, bathing, and dressing, is tiring, particularly when these demands must be met in addition to raising children, working outside of the home, and taking care of oneself. Every person who takes care of a dependent elderly individual experiences some degree of stress as part of fulfilling their responsibilities. However, at least some of the stress that caregivers experience may be attributed to the views they have about caregiving and aging.

European Americans often feel a great deal of stress related to caregiving because the circle of potential helpers is limited to immediate family and because their individualistic orientation may contribute to feelings of resentment and loss. Caregiving is seen as a great burden if the caregivers feel they have lost their independence by having to be on call to meet their parents' needs, or if their parents' needs infringe on their own needs. Caregiving can also be bur-densome if the recipient is not just unappreciative but resentful of needing care—and they express their resentment to the caregiver.

Hispanics/Latinos report considerably less caregiving stress than European American caregivers (John, Resendiz, and DeVargas, 1997). This is attributed to Hispanics/Latinos' positive perceptions of aging and their view that caregiving fulfills basic family responsibilities—attitudes that serve as buffers against stress.

Asian Americans' often experience relatively high degrees of caregiver burden. This may seem like a paradox, because the tenets of filial piety would suggest that they understand that elder care is expected, and they should see it as a duty that honors the elders. However, Asian Americans also have a cultural norm of avoiding any behaviors that would shame themselves and their families. Some Asian Americans experiencing stressful reactions to caring for an elderly family member may be hesitant to seek help from anyone else, lest this bring shame to the family. As a result, adult children, particularly daughters-in-law, may shoulder caregiving responsibilities without assistance from extended family members. Because of the burden of caregiving associated with marrying oldest sons, some Asian American women refuse to consider oldest sons as potential partners.

Researchers have attributed the lower levels of burden experienced among some African American caregivers to their positive view of aging (Guarnaccia, 1998). Also, African Americans may use more effective coping strategies than other groups, strategies developed over years of dealing with discrimination, that serve to reduce the stress of caregiving. Of the four groups mentioned in this paper, African Americans are the most likely to have a broad social support network to aid the family with caregiving tasks.

How Are Caregivers Selected?

Cultural value systems also play a part in determining who will take care of aging parents. Three factors are related to caregiver determination.

Hierarchy of Help

Each pan-ethnic group has a hierarchy of responsibility, a culturally appropriate order in which individuals are expected to take on caregiving based on family position (e.g., spouse, child, sibling). In European American families this begins with the spouse. If the spouse is deceased or too frail to provide care, the responsibility falls to adult children. Seldom are other family members expected to provide care. For Hispanic/Latino and Asian American families, the hierarchy begins with the adult children rather than the spouse. For Asian Americans, the oldest son is at the top of the hierarchy. If the oldest son is unable to uphold this obligation, the responsibility falls to the next oldest son and his family. In reality, it is the wife of the eldest son who provides the caregiving. In fact, many older Asian Americans resist care from anyone other than daughters-in-law. Therefore, the hierarchy of substitution of caregivers for Asian Americans begins with the wife of the eldest son, followed by the wives of other adult sons, and then adult daughters. The caregiving hierarchy for African American families starts with the spouse, if there is one. Caregiving responsibilities often fall to women in the next generations—daughters, followed by granddaughters, nieces, and other female relatives, family friends, and fellow churchgoers.

Proximity

In general, many aging adults need assistance in the completion of daily activities such as bathing, food preparation, and toileting. This level of support requires a readily available caregiver who lives near or with the older person. However, European American adult children often live long distances from their parents. This is particularly true for middle-class families and for adult children with higher levels of education. As a result, many European American children are not close enough geographically to assist elderly parents. Proximity is less of a problem for Latinos than for white

non-Hispanic families because Latino married children are expected to live nearby and have frequent contact with their parents and other family members. African American family members are also likely to live within a few miles of each other. In fact, African American elderly and their adult children may live together. Expectations about co-residence and family position in Asian American families dictate that the oldest son and his family should live with his parents and take care of them.

Gender Expectations

In all four groups, women are expected to provide care taking and nurturing for the family, including aging family members. Caregiving by men tends to occur only when no women are available to do it. The exceptions are husbands in European American and African American families, who are expected to care for their wives if they are able.

Culture and Caregiving

Culture is important in how family is defined, in expectations for caregiving, and in caregiver selection. The four pan-ethnic groups presented here are similar in many ways—a sense of responsibility to kin is present in all of them. There are distinct value differences, however, that subtly influence how caregiving is experienced.

Of course, the beliefs and values held by individuals are not necessarily identical to the values of the pan-ethnic group(s) to which they belong. Cultural values are taught to individuals in many ways throughout the life course, but among the members of any pan-ethnic group there exists a wide array of beliefs. Partly this is a result of living in multicultural communities where people are exposed to the traditions and beliefs of many other ethnicities besides their own. Also, as successive generations of immigrant families become acculturated to the dominant culture, family members adopt some of the values of that culture. Ethnic intermarriage also contributes to a blurring of pan-ethnic cultural beliefs. Nevertheless, many individuals continue to maintain the values taught to them as members of specific ethnic heritages. Cultural values do not *dictate* caregiving behaviors and attitudes, but they are *related* to how we think about and enact intergenerational assistance to older kin.

References

Guarnaccia, P. J. (1998). Multicultural experiences of family caregiving. In H. P. Lefley, et al. (Eds.), *Families coping with mental illness: The cultural context* (pp. 45–61). San Francisco, CA: Jossey-Bass.

John, R., Resendiz, R., and DeVargas, L. (1997). Beyond familism? Familism as explicit motive for eldercare among Mexican American caregivers. *Journal of Cross-Cultural Gerontology, 12,* 145–162. ✦

Radina, E. (2001). *Cultural Values and Care Giving.* Published by permission of Elise M. Radina.

Issue 23: Questions to Consider

1. Look back at the questions that began this chapter. How did you respond? Mostly A's means you have values similar to those of European American families, mostly B's reflects an orientation toward Hispanic/Latino values, mostly C's and your values are more in line with Asian American values, and mostly D's means your values are closer to those of African Americans. What do you think it means if you have a combination of responses? Compare your responses to those of classmates willing to share their answers and discuss your responses.

2. Consider this family:

Don and Patricia divorced when their son, Sam, was 10. After the divorce, Sam lived with his mother. Sam's mother, Patricia, died a few years ago. Sam rarely saw his dad after the divorce, and they have not been close to each other over the years. Don, now aged 70, never remarried. He is lonely and needs help with daily tasks like cooking, house cleaning, and doing laundry. Sam works at a drugstore, is married, and has two young children. Should Sam help his father?

Choose any one of the pan-ethnic groups described by Radina and predict what Sam would do if he was a member of that ethnic group. What do *you* think Sam should do? Why? What would you do in this situation? Would any of your answers to the preceding questions have been different if Don and Sam had remained close after the divorce? Explain why or why not.

3. Many families are not able to care for frail elderly members because of work commitments, distance, and financial problems. Generate a list of ideas for public policies that might help families meet obligations to elders in a way that respects ethnic cultural beliefs. ✦